In-action

In-

THE ABAKANOWICZ ARTS AND CULTURE COLLECTION

action

Viennese Actionism and the Passivities of Performance Art

Caroline Lillian Schopp

The University of Chicago Press   Chicago and London

The University of Chicago Press, Chicago 60637
The University of Chicago Press, Ltd., London

Published 2025
Printed in the United States of America

34 33 32 31 30 29 28 27 26 25 1 2 3 4 5

ISBN-13: 978-0-226-83919-6 (cloth)
ISBN-13: 978-0-226-83921-9 (paper)
ISBN-13: 978-0-226-83920-2 (e-book)
DOI: https://doi.org/10.7208/chicago/9780226839202.001.0001

The publication of this edition has been generously supported by the Abakanowicz Arts and Culture Charitable Foundation.

ABAKANOWICZ
ARTS AND CULTURE
CHARITABLE FOUNDATION

Published with support from the University of Chicago Department of Art History.

Library of Congress Cataloging-in-Publication Data

Names: Schopp, Caroline Lillian, author.
Title: In-action : Viennese Actionism and the passivities of performance art / Caroline Lillian Schopp.
Description: Chicago : The University of Chicago Press, [2025] | Series: The Abakanowicz arts and culture collection | Includes bibliographical references and index.
Identifiers: LCCN 2025004410 | ISBN 9780226839196 (cloth) | ISBN 9780226839219 (paperback) | ISBN 9780226839202 (ebook)
Subjects: LCSH: Wiener Aktionismus.
Classification: LCC NX548.V53 S36 2025 | DDC 702.8109436/1309046 – dc23/eng/20250208
LC record available at https://lccn.loc.gov/2025004410

∞ This paper meets the requirements of ANSI/NISO Z39.48-1992 (Permanence of Paper).

For my students in Vienna.

Contents

Introduction

Performance Art Histories: Mistaking Rudolf Schwarzkogler

In-action is easily mistaken: To the extent that it is seen, it is overlooked, and when it is registered at all, it is misconstrued or distorted. For more than fifty years, a perplexing case of such mistaking has accompanied the writing of performance art history. In both the international art history of performance art and the provincial art history of so-called Viennese Actionism, Rudolf Schwarzkogler has been mistaken as having documented his own death in a performance of suicide by self-castration. Yet Schwarzkogler fell to his death from a window. He did not announce the fall with a suicide note, nor did he have his fall photographed. If Schwarzkogler's death was a performance, it was of a very different kind from that for which he has become known. My aim in beginning this book here is not to correct the (long-since-corrected) mistake. Rather, I want to understand why the mistaking of Schwarzkogler retains such remarkable staying power in performance art history.

Consider *The Artist Is Present*, a blockbuster "performance retrospective" of work by Marina Abramović that opened at the Museum of Modern Art, New York, in 2010. In a catalog essay, Arthur Danto writes: "The Viennese Actionists poured blood over themselves or cut themselves to death."[1] Without even being named, Schwarzkogler provides the defining image of "Viennese Actionism," a phrase that typically refers to the work of Günter Brus, Otto Muehl, Hermann Nitsch, and Schwarzkogler, the latter of whom, despite the sensational fiction surrounding his art, remains the group's least-known affiliate.[2] Danto's summary statement does two things characteristic of its reception: It generalizes the distinct practices of each artist, and it hyperbolizes in order to scandalize.[3] To be clear, none of the artists cut himself to death, although Brus did cut himself in several of his best-known works, and Muehl and Nitsch did do quite a bit of blood pouring in their heydays.[4] The perceived extremity of Viennese Actionism has generated a reception that oscillates between awe and repulsion, celebrating it for its "radicality" while reproaching it as "sadistic," "misogynist," and "the most extreme form of violence in art."[5] I want to take another look at this difficult episode in art history and consider it without the overdetermination of its spectacularizing reception. *In-action* accounts for what has been mistaken, and recounts what has been overlooked, by attending to a wider field of practices and figures in this history.

Although I will still use the phrase Viennese Actionism throughout this book, I do so with invisible scare quotes. My discussion aims to contribute to an understanding of something more capacious than its sensationalist framing allows. For far from being actionist, much of Viennese Actionism explores conditions of passivity, vulnerability, and dependence in gestures of what I call in-action. On the one hand, in-action captures the provocative but often mistaken ways that certain performances fail to fulfill expectations of artistic and political action. On the other, it names an art historical approach that does not presuppose that performance art takes the form of action. In the art history of performance art, especially in the United States, Viennese Actionism represents an extreme case, often cited but little studied. My aim is to intervene in this historiography by telling a new story about Viennese performance art.

"If performance exists as an art form," Carrie Lambert-Beatty writes in her exhibition review of *The Artist Is Present*, "Abramović is at its center and has been for forty years."[6] Viennese Actionism, in contrast, has occupied its extremity. Given her polemical essay title, "Against Performance Art," the first part of Lambert-Beatty's statement strikes me as crucial. It indicates how the study and practice of performance art have been generatively accompanied by uncertainty about its reality as an art form. The existence of performance art is thus often necessarily connected with the question of the reality of what the artist does. Danto, reiterating a standard thesis around the most canonical examples, argues that performance art in the 1970s "brought the reality of extreme experience into being an artist." He inventories what performance artists "really" did to demonstrate such experience, including how Vito Acconci "really ejaculated" under the floor of Sonnabend Gallery in New York in *Seedbed* (1972), how Chris Burden really had himself shot in the arm with a gun in F-Space Gallery in Santa Ana in *Shoot* (1971), and how Abramović really included a loaded gun among the seventy-two objects laid out on a table in Studio Morra in Naples in *Rhythm O* (1974), inviting her audience to use them on her as they pleased. "The possibility of dying," Danto argues, substantiates performance art as an art form.[7] In his mistaking of Schwarzkogler, he is thus characteristically ambivalent: The Viennese Actionists supposedly took this possibility to its limit, but in so doing, they went far too far.

It is ironic that Schwarzkogler has been mistaken not only as the epitome of Viennese Actionism but also as the ultimate extremist in performance art history.[8] The scant art historical attention to his work has sought, in turn, to "redeem" him from his "unfortunate fate," to pathologize his work as "masochistic," or to diagnose the artist with "narcissism or solipsism."[9] This reception is all the more ironic because Schwarzkogler's performance art could not

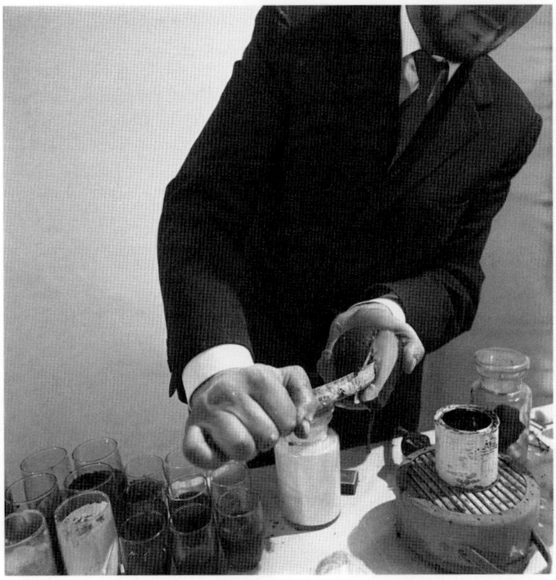

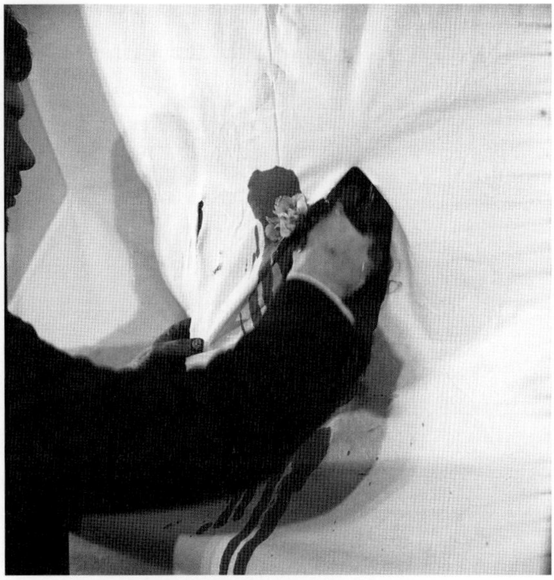

Figures I.1–I.2. Rudolf Schwarzkogler with Anna Brus and Heinz Cibulka, *Hochzeit* (Wedding), 1965. Photograph by Ludwig Hoffenreich. mumok – Museum moderner Kunst Stiftung Ludwig Wien, Leihgabe der Österreichischen Ludwig-Stiftung. © Rudolf Schwarzkogler; digital image © mumok – Museum moderner Kunst Stiftung Ludwig Wien.

be less self-centered (figs. I.1, I.2). Quite the contrary, it is self-effacing, understated, and withdrawn. Although parts of his body can be glimpsed throughout the archive, Schwarzkogler figures neither as a self-assertive person, nor as a familiar "concrete body," nor as "the explicit body" of the artist, "performing subjectivity."[10] Unlike Abramović, in the case of Schwarzkogler, the artist is not present. He declines to appear, retreats from view. One of his few planned public performances involved him crawling into a box and remaining there, in a corner of the room, while Brus and Muehl hosted an "action-concert."[11] What is going on in Schwarzkogler's work is difficult to discern and, disconcertingly, does not offer the consolation of emphatic action. Attempts to identify explicit action in his work mistake what I am calling its in-action. *In-action* describes a tendency toward intimacy, inarticulacy, and impotence. The term accounts for figures involved in a performance, yet disinclined to entirely take part, and inclined, rather, toward relations of dependency. *In-action* names a suspension, a hesitation, a reservation within the action. It affords, also within violent or upsetting scenes, space for figures that do not enact explicit violence but expose vulnerability and precariousness.

The tendency to mistake in-action owes to the dominance of what I call "the action paradigm." This is an entrenched expectation that performance art should model emancipatory action. Under the action paradigm, performance art is seen as activating audiences and individuals, freeing art of media constraints, liberating bodies and collectivities, and thus agitating politically. Understanding performance art with regard to this optimistic activist potential, art history, in turn, has sought out and venerated—and sometimes ridiculed—agents of action. To recall Lambert-Beatty's cautious formulation, "If performance exists as an art form," then art history has overcompensated with an assertion of its activism, often made by way of the confident or risky self-assertion of the artist. The action paradigm, I argue, imposes a too-restrictive framing on what performance art may be.

The term *in-action* attests to a more patient and troubling kind of looking that has not yet decided on the criteria that define performance art as an art form. The hyphen the term holds marks an art historiographical moment of pause. In performance art, *in-action* describes those gestures that invite a reconsidering of what is taken for action, of what counts as an action worth seeing, worth responding to. Neither inaction nor the opposite of action, in-action poses the question of action itself. In refusing the distinction between action and passivity, in-action does without the implicit normative standards of self-assertion, emancipation, and expressive action that have prevailed in performance art and in politics since the 1960s.

With this introduction, I propose that Schwarzkogler's work—like the Viennese performance art considered in each subsequent chapter—should be situated differently within performance art history: not as the dead end of a narrative of extreme actions, but as an instance in a long-mistaken story of in-action. To do so, I revisit the history of the mistaking of Schwarzkogler initiated at the *documenta 5* of 1972, delineating the institutional, historical, and theoretical development of the action paradigm. I then offer a brief history showing how the action paradigm came to be installed in performance art and historiography on both sides of the Atlantic. Prompted by feminist art history, I consider how the action paradigm has been troubled in artistically and politically consequential ways in sections devoted to Feminist Actionism, ordinary action, and, finally, in-action. Coming full circle, I return to Schwarzkogler by situating his work within an inverted archive that includes the contemporary artists Franko B and Aliza Shvarts, whose work shares its reservations about the norms implied in the action paradigm. Looking carefully at Schwarzkogler's performances reveals a painterly practice concerned not with depicting graphic violence, but with composing vulnerable relations in disconcerting still lifes.

"Individual Mythology"

The mistaking of Schwarzkogler can be traced back to the exhibition *documenta 5* of 1972, where photographs of Viennese Actionism were first integrated into a broad survey of contemporary art and shown to an international public. It was here, I propose, in the West German city of Kassel and in the writing prompted by *documenta 5*, that performance art history first began to take shape as a discernible field. In contrast to previous *documenta* exhibitions, *documenta 5* was unique in foregrounding performance art. As Lawrence Alloway wrote in his review, *documenta 5* developed the interest in "dealing lavishly with performance art" that its Swiss curator Harald Szeemann had shown two years earlier in his Cologne show *Happening & Fluxus*.[12] In Kassel, in the opening weeks of the hundred-day show, Joseph Beuys boxed "for direct democracy," challenging other artists and exhibition visitors to full-fledged boxing matches in a performance supposed to advocate for voting rights. Franz Erhard Walther "activated" (his term) the cloth objects of his *Erster Werksatz* (First work set), supervising visitors as they connected and constrained themselves in his participatory contraptions. James Lee Byars perched on the roof of the Fridericianum, shouting common German names through a megaphone, while the "living sculpture" duo Gilbert & George performed live in a gallery on the ground floor. Nearby, Vetter Pisani exhibited a naked woman chained to a dog-run cable and stood by to observe reactions. Ben Vautier exhibited himself, in a "thinking room," inviting visitors to ask him anything related to the question "what is art?"—a thought process that on one occasion involved the artist "banging his head into the wall until it bled."[13] Acconci, meanwhile, flown in by Szeemann, clambered blindfolded around a room dedicated to his performance *Cross Fronts*, which he presented as an examination of psychological and physical space. Alongside immersive installations in the exhibition, which were particularly critical of US political and cultural imperialism, these performances worked in two ways: through the presence of the artist whose live actions constituted the work and through the public's direct interaction with him.[14]

This marked a significant departure from the previous *documenta* exhibition of 1968, which was nicknamed "Americana" for its overwhelming focus on US artists and movements. Organized in the art historical categories that came to define the canonical account of 1960s art—including pop art, minimal art, op art, post-painterly abstraction—*documenta 4* had been criticized for its reticence toward contemporary global events in art and politics. Protesters were outraged that the exportation of US culture did not engage more critically with current workers protests, student protests, protests against the Vietnam War, the civil rights movement, and the surge of second-wave feminism that defined the year 1968 internationally.[15] No performance art was included, despite the prevalence of the happening and fluxus on the contemporary international artistic scene.[16] The German fluxus artist Wolf Vostell, along with the practitioners of Beuysian "social sculpture" Jörg Immendorff and Chris Reinecke, staged protest actions on-site in Kassel against the show, in which none of these artists was officially included. The *documenta 5*, in contrast, sought to welcome such alternative artistic forms without inhibiting their political dimensions.[17] It marked a significant dual shift in the unfolding narrative of contemporary art: from US back to European contexts, and from the object-based media of painting and sculpture to the unruliness of performance art as paradigm for contemporary art. The *documenta 5* nevertheless reproduced many of *documenta 4*'s oversights, in particular Szeemann's egregiously sexist exclusion of women artists.[18]

It is worth remembering that the *documenta* exhibition was originally founded after the Second World War to address the suppression of so much contemporary artistic practice under National Socialism in Germany and to

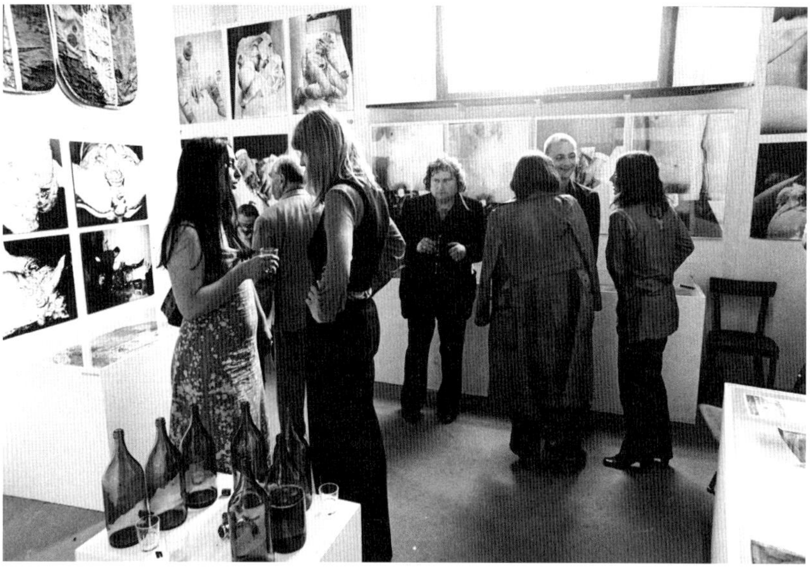

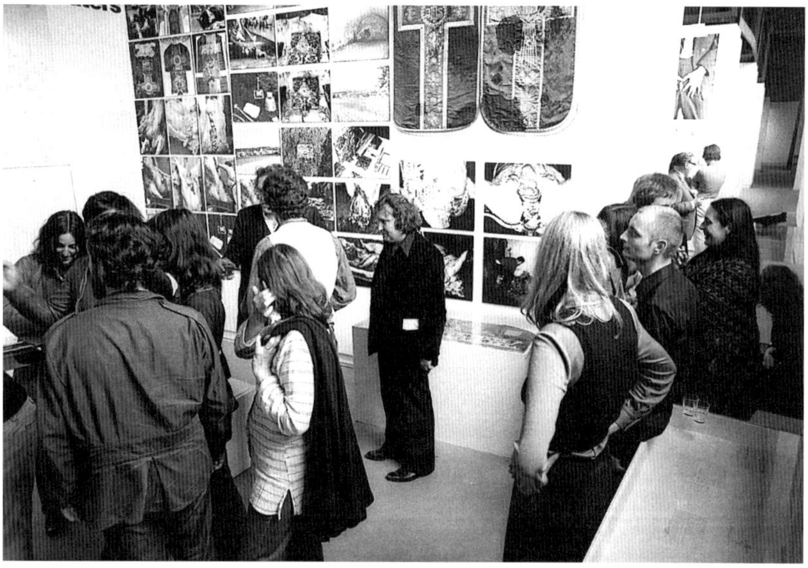

Figures I.3–I.4. Exhibition views of *documenta 5* with works by Rudolf Schwarzkogler (top image, back wall) and Hermann Nitsch (top image, left wall, and bottom image), 1972. © documenta archive / Photos: Brigitte Hellgoth.

showcase art—originally with a focus on painting and sculpture—that had been categorized by the Nazis as "degenerate" (*entartet*).[19] The exhibition was conceived to announce Germany's repudiation of National Socialist politics and proclivities and to celebrate the vanguard of contemporary art, however unsavory or unsettling. This is of particular interest in the art history of Viennese Actionism. On the one hand, *documenta 5* offered a forum for the first international exhibition of work by little-known figures—like Vautier and Pisani, Brus and Schwarzkogler. On the other hand, just as it established a lens through which to frame contemporary performance art as live art with a democratizing political message, *documenta 5* also spurred the idea of Viennese Actionism as an insidious deviant collective and an artistic "dead end."[20]

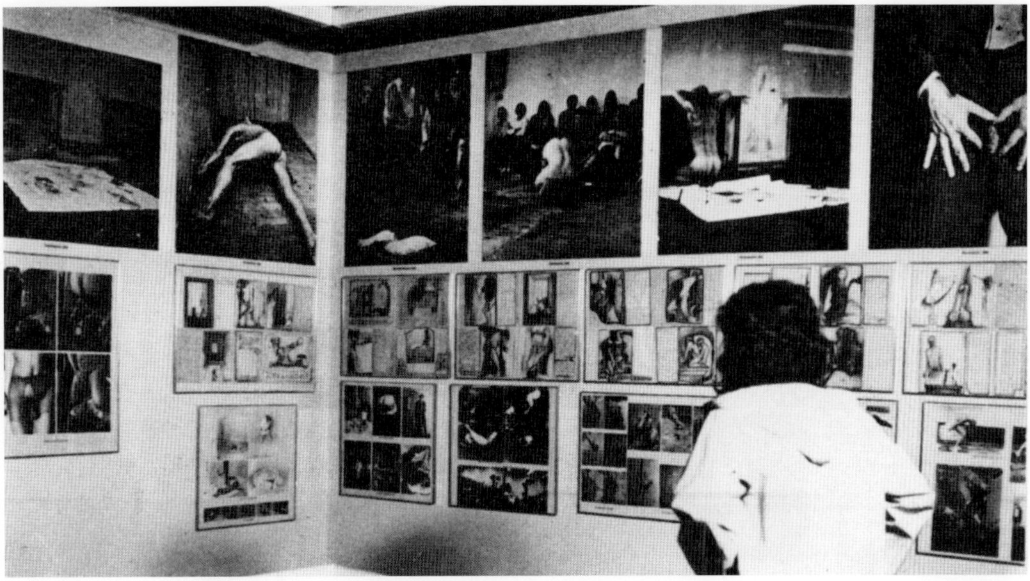

Figure I.5. Exhibition view of *documenta 5* with works by Günter Brus, 1972. Photograph by Lizzie Borden, published in *Artforum.*

While Brus and Nitsch attended the opening of *documenta 5*, none of the Austrian artists performed on-site (figs. I.3, I.4). In a section of the exhibition entitled "Individual Mythologies," documents of performances by Brus, Nitsch, and Schwarzkogler were clustered together in connected alcoves on the first floor of the Neue Galerie.[21] Color and black-and-white photographs, as well as writings and performance "relics" in vitrines, conveyed a sense of how Nitsch combined Christian and pagan iconographies in the participatory ritual performances of his *Orgien Mysterien Theater* (Orgies mysteries theater), parts of which he had staged across Europe and the United States in the late 1960s.[22] A generous selection of black-and-white photographic documents represented Brus's performances in Vienna throughout the 1960s and, more recently, in West Berlin, including *Wiener Spaziergang* (Viennese walk; 1965), *Aktion mit Diana* (Action with Diana; 1966), and *Zerreißprobe* (Stress test; 1970) (fig. I.5). Footage of *Zerreißprobe* included in the film program may be the work of this "Austrian anti-artist" that caused one self-proclaimed "hardened reporter" to "vomit on the spot."[23]

It was, however, the "individual mythology" constructed around Schwarzkogler that provoked the imagination of reporters and critics alike, ultimately displacing any careful consideration of his art. In the exhibition catalog, and in the Neue Galerie above vitrines containing a selection of his writings and drawings, photographs of Schwarzkogler's so-called *Aktionen* (actions) were aligned in stacked, sequence-like rows (figs. I.6, I.7).[24] Haphazardly, images of performances posthumously numbered by his friends as *2. Aktion*, *3. Aktion*, *4. Aktion*, and *6. Aktion* were intermingled.[25] These show hands holding a gutted fish; a slender supine body wrapped in gauze; a nude torso, seen from behind, leashed to a fish or tied with string bound to things beyond the frame; a nude torso facing the camera with a bandaged penis presented on a black square;

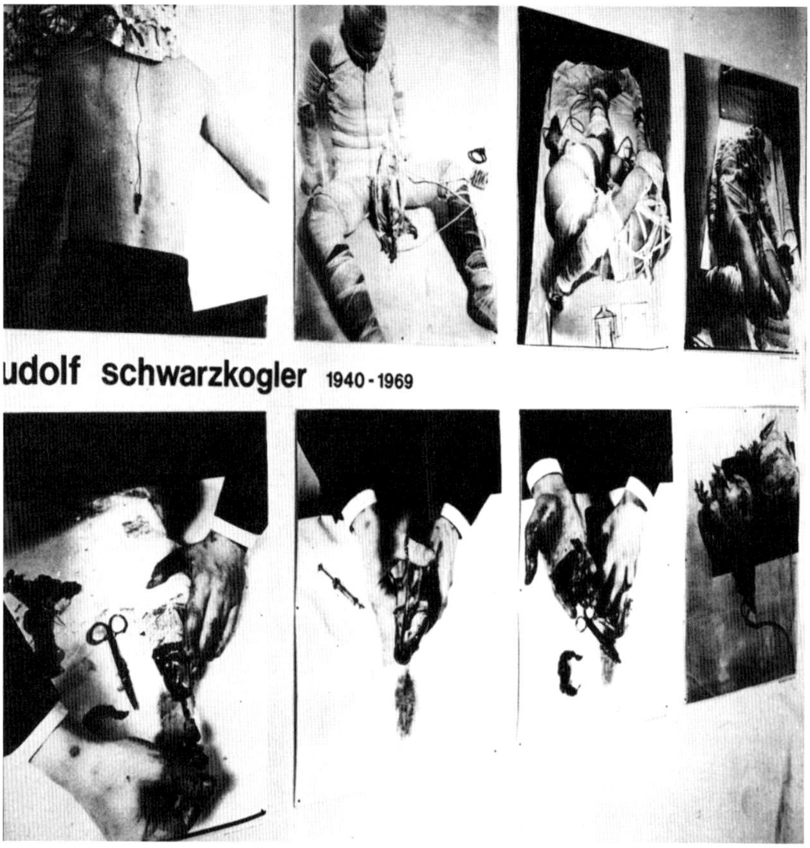

Figure I.6. Exhibition view of *documenta 5* with works by Rudolf Schwarzkogler. Photograph by Lizzie Borden, published in *Artforum*.

a bandaged face, wrapped in gauze. Though taken to be "the artist's," the body involved is almost always that of Heinz Cibulka, Schwarzkogler's frequent performance partner.[26] In the photograph seen in the upper-right corner of figure I.6, in which Cibulka's supine body is pressed up against the wall, Schwarzkogler's hands hold up a sheet to shield or blanket it.[27] These are, to be sure, disconcerting images.

Yet the negative responses they elicited are striking for their moralizing, accusatory tone. Horrified German critics recoiled at the "sadistic and masochistic actions of the Austrians."[28] One reserved "a special word" for Brus, Nitsch, and Schwarzkogler, condemning the Austrians' "sexual deviance" and offering his diagnosis of a collective "psychopathology of the highest level."[29] The German commentators anxiously read into the Austrian work a return of the repressed, situating it in a distinctively Viennese tradition of perversion, deviant sexuality, and cultural excess going back to writers like Leopold von Sacher-Masoch, Arthur Schnitzler, and the ever-present Sigmund Freud.[30] Across the Atlantic, Harold Rosenberg, champion of US action painting, also put on his psychiatrist's hat, distinguishing between the "genuine schizophrenia" represented at *documenta 5* in galleries dedicated to the art of medical patients and the "slasher photographs" of the Austrian artists. Their work he

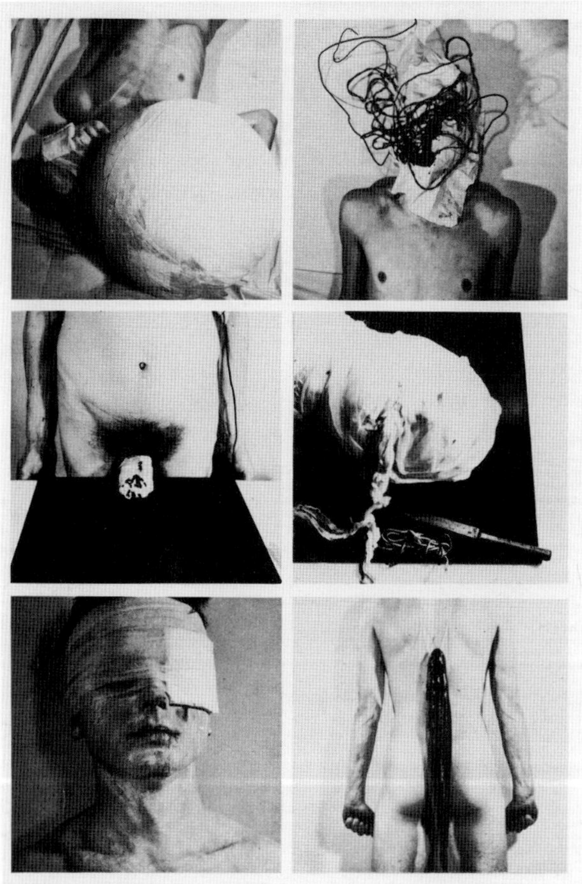

Figure I.7. Page opening in the catalog of *documenta 5* (1972, edited by Harald Szeemann) with works by Rudolf Schwarzkogler. © documenta archive.

describes as "'artistic' or drug-induced imitations" of mental illness and "photographic horrors involving fish heads, genitalia, evisceration, bloodstained religious vestments, and crude crucifixes." His conclusion: "It may be time for the avant-gardist reasoning to discover that if aesthetic standards are dissolved it becomes necessary to replace them with moral ones."[31]

In such ostensibly more distanced judgments of the English-language reception, the mistaking of Schwarzkogler gained traction. In July, Hilton Kramer, writing for the *New York Times*, named "an Austrian cartoonist—Rudolf Schwarzkogler"—as the artist "who carries the pornographic element to its most vicious sado-masochistic extremes."[32] Lizzie Borden's review for *Artforum* in October referred to "Schwarzkogler's chopped off penis" as an example of the "overly rhetorical work" at *documenta 5* intended to shock audiences.[33] Two months later, Robert Hughes, art critic for *Time* magazine, distinguished the ascendent artistic and moral value of painting from the "decline and fall of the avant-garde" in performance art, naming "a Viennese artist" as his paragon of failure: "Schwarzkogler seems to have deduced that what really counts is not the application of paint, but the removal of surplus flesh. So he proceeded, inch by inch, to amputate his own penis, while a photographer recorded the act as an art event." Hughes concludes: "Successive acts of self-amputation finally did Schwarzkogler in."[34]

Schwarzkogler's performance art features in this salacious fiction as the aesthetically and morally bad outcome of action painting. Hughes's entire derogatory take was reprinted in Gregory Battcock's anthology *Idea Art* in 1973, at which point the mistaking of Schwarzkogler became art history.[35] This narrative is an aberrant disarticulation of the thesis that New York stole the idea of modern art from Europe.[36] Instead, Vienna, capital of the Old World, figures as the "dead end" of the avant-garde's New World advances. After *documenta 5*, the mistaking of Schwarzkogler continued with surprising force to inform the art history of performance art, despite the fact that in 1987 Kristine Stiles made very clear that it was only a "myth" about Schwarzkogler's "self-mutilation" and "castration performance" that had been circulating for over a decade.[37] Two years later, Henry Sayre's monograph on American performance art would begin by repeating the Schwarzkogler fiction as fact, presenting it as the example of how the photographic record of performance art asserts itself "most horribly."[38] In English-language art history, the mistaking of Schwarzkogler persistently defines and exceeds the "real" extremism to which performance art is seen to tend.[39]

Even Amelia Jones reserves a special place—at once extreme and disparaged—for Schwarzkogler in *Body Art/Performing the Subject*, her indispensable and field-shaping book of performance art history from 1998. Considering how male body artists "have subjected themselves to the masochistic violence of others," she locates "the Viennese actionists (especially Rudolf Schwarzkogler)" anachronistically, between Chris Burden and "more recent S/M artists such as Bob Flanagan and Ron Athey."[40] And yet unlike (and well before) Burden, and in stark contrast to Flanagan and Athey, Schwarzkogler did not subject himself, or others, to the kind of violence Jones is talking about. Regarding the violence of performances like Burden's *Shoot* (1971), Jones remains circumspect.[41] But she ultimately justifies the "self-harm" in Athey's and Flanagan's work "as a mode of activism."[42] As if extending Rosenberg's thesis from his review of *documenta 5*, Jones sees performance art as the art form in which aesthetic categories give way to moral ones. The artist is "a kind of agent," and the violence of their actions—the "activation" and "enactment" of pain—thus "calls out to be acknowledged and demands that its political implications be grappled with."[43]

Viennese Actionism, in contrast, lacks what Jones calls "sincerity."[44] It is suspect because what its violence stands for is difficult, if not impossible, to distill. In contrast to a previous generation of critics, for Jones, the problem with Schwarzkogler is not that he killed himself in an act of self-castration, but that he didn't "really" do it. What she calls "sincere" art should not only have an identifiable cause but also be authentic as evidence of the seriousness of its cause. Lacking such authenticity as well as unequivocal political significance, Schwarzkogler's work thus comes across as frivolous. Confusing the date of his death with the date of a performance, Jones concludes, "Most notably, the violence of Rudolf Schwarzkogler's famous 1969 histrionic castration performance, documented by the seemingly incontrovertible evidence of the black and white photograph, was nonetheless faked, like most of the bloodshed in the Actionists' work."[45] Different though their interests and methodologies may be, all these viewers of Schwarzkogler's work in the aftermath of *documenta 5* mistake its disconcerting in-action. To mistake in this way involves seeking something documentary rather than artistic, real rather than reticent, explicit and deadly serious rather than tacitly playful, ironic, queer.

Aktionen/In-action

Careful looking at the so-called *Aktionen* exhibited at *documenta 5* reveals neither the artist "cutting himself to death" nor—to acknowledge the difficulty of affirmatively and consequentially describing this work—the artist *not* cutting himself to death, insofar as there is no real extreme action being either staged or faked (figs. I.8, I.9).[46] The absence of an obvious agent or cause of action is precisely the difficulty at stake. In cramped spaces—pressed against a wall, between a table and a wall, in a box, in a makeshift corner—touching, sometimes funny relations take shape between bodies. Odd objects—different kinds of cloth, bottles, cutting instruments both domestic and medical, string, lightbulbs, nets, balloons—are arranged in uncanny compositions. Conditions of containment often indicate positions out of view. One rarely sees a full face. More often it is bandaged, wrapped in gauze, turned away. There is no pregnant Laocoönian utterance of pain, but rather a furtive grin, delicately placed hands with painted fingernails, a chin propped tentatively on a balloon.

In *2. Aktion*, presumably the one that caused so much consternation in Kassel, a razor blade is balanced in the mouth of a large fish, which is positioned between a pair of legs, concealing the genital zone (fig. I.10).[47] This is not, to reiterate, Schwarzkogler's body, but rather that of his performance partner Cibulka. Schwarzkogler strokes the fish's head with a butter knife. He inscrutably applies a syringe as Cibulka's thighs grasp the ball (fig. I.11). As Schwarzkogler's careful cropping of the photographs makes clear, it is not so important who is who, whose body is whose, or who is doing what to whom.[48] In the relations that take place between these bodies, so gently placed on cloth mats or dark mirrors, there is more tenderness than "slasher" violence, as much humor as horror. The work is not about the body or the person of the artist. Rather, it performs a painstaking analysis of corporeal precarity that is unconcerned with affirming any expectation of agency, meaning, coherency, or intentionality.[49] The in-action of Schwarzkogler's performances divulges intense, if disconcerting, intimacy.

Instead of reproaching Schwarzkogler's performances for being "faked" or lacking "sincerity," I see them as in-sincere: as probing our expectations and disappointments with the serious matter of art and life. Looking again and

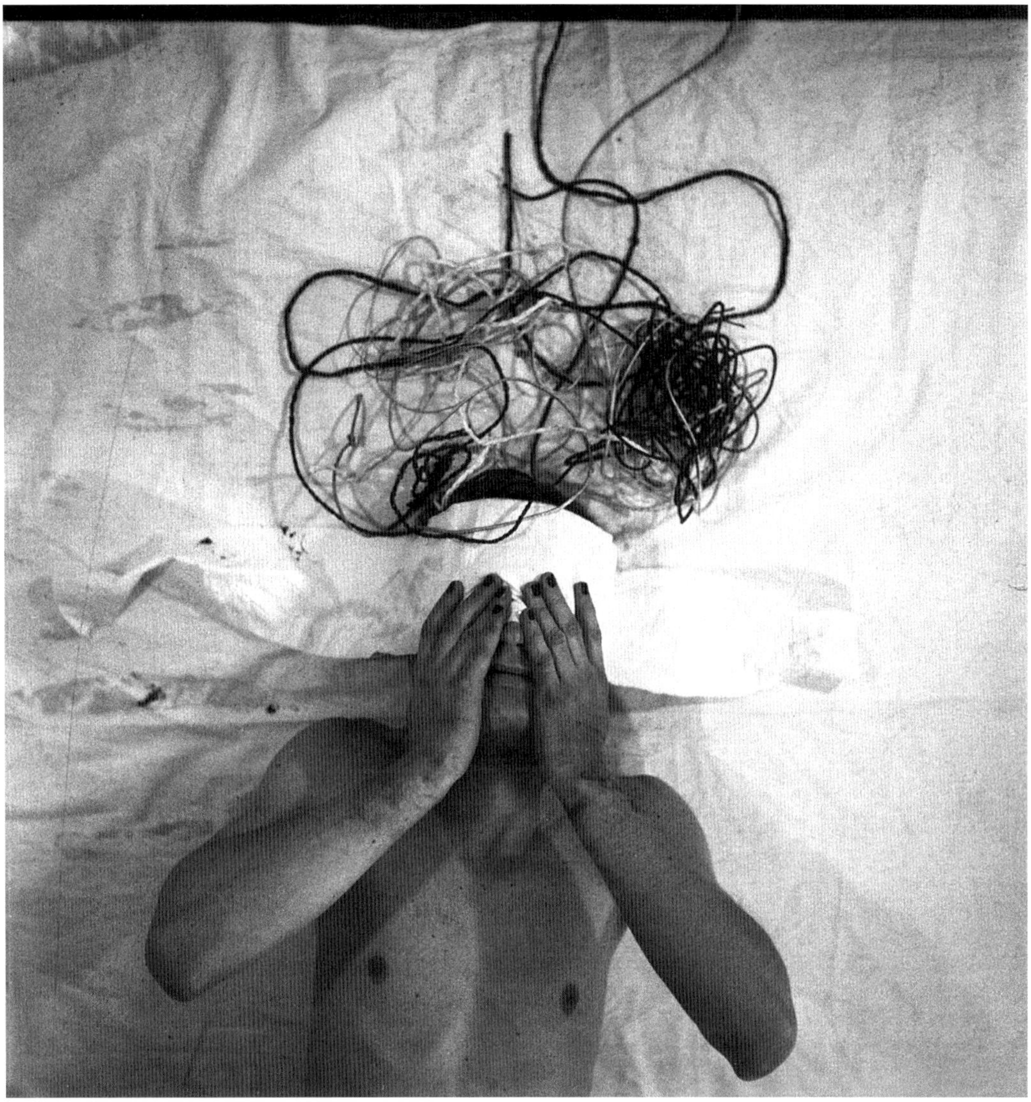

again at Schwarzkogler's work over many years, I see neither histrionics nor deceit, but rather the careful composition of very simple relationships in which bodies are exposed as vulnerable, positioned awkwardly, and attended to by others' hands. In their simplicity, these performances are remarkably affecting. Infused with desire, and not without a certain violence, the "actions" in Schwarzkogler's performances are gentle, slow-paced gestures; liquids seep, appendages are bound, openings are filled. Assurance and concern, quiet awe and anxiety, are equally conveyed.

To be sure, it is difficult to accept, let alone account for, the incapacitated figures and "difficult emotions" to which the in-action of Schwarzkogler's work gives rise.[50] I am aware of the intimate idiom I have adopted to share the

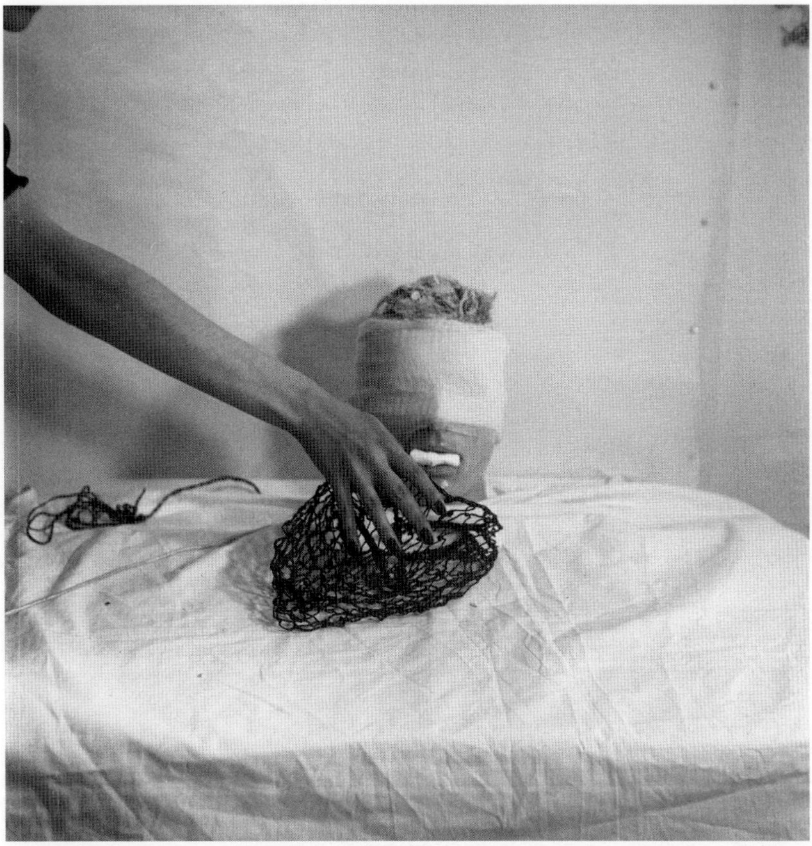

Figures I.8–I.9. Rudolf Schwarzkogler with Heinz Cibulka, *4. Aktion* (Action 4), 1965. Photograph by Franziska Wächtler. mumok - Museum moderner Kunst Stiftung Ludwig Wien, Leihgabe der Österreichischen Ludwig-Stiftung. © Rudolf Schwarzkogler; digital image © mumok - Museum moderner Kunst Stiftung Ludwig Wien.

way I see it: discerning in-action involves a kind of receptivity that itself is not unambiguously "active." As a viewer, one is not activated but rather sensitized by Schwarzkogler's performances, a condition that may help explain the virulent reactions his work has provoked. The tendency is to want to recover oneself by taking a stand and to pass judgment on, and thus rectify, the situation by doing away with the at times bewildering inexplicitness of in-action. Careful looking, in contrast, attends to performances for what they disclose rather than foreclosing what takes place in the name of "action."

Even Kristine Stiles, Schwarzkogler's most attentive interpreter, insists that Schwarzkogler's performances "were not performances" but rather "simulated events" that generated "images," "action images," and "tableaux."[51] In response to the mistaking of Schwarzkogler, she seeks to dispel the "myth" by proposing a "life-affirming" reading that redeems the artist from the spectacularizing narrative of his death.[52] She goes to great lengths to emphasize that the photographic record of Schwarzkogler's work shows "images of healing" that are but "an artificial construction, a series of fictional events." Stiles demands, in turn, that viewers of his work acknowledge a "true" fiction: "The truth of Schwarzkogler's images resides in their blatant black and white lies:

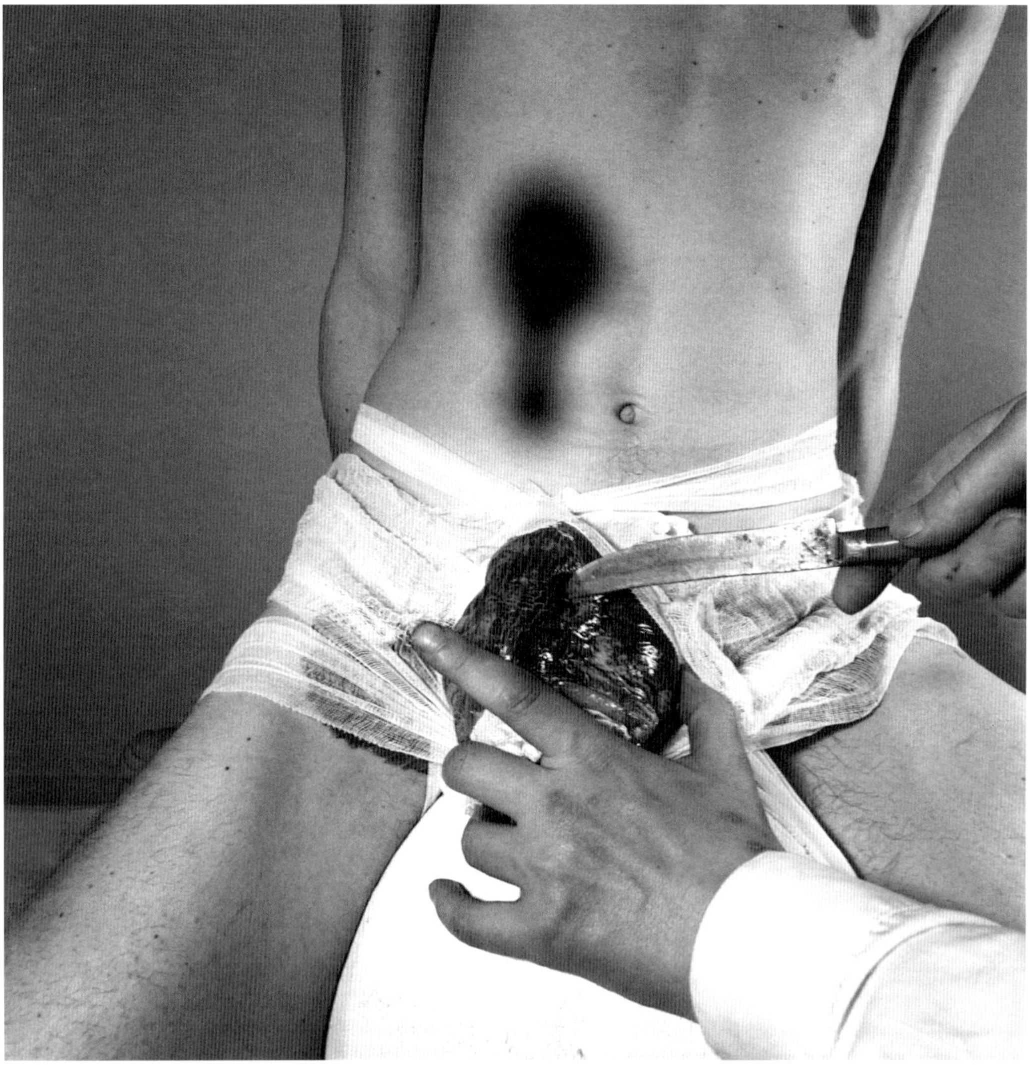

the simulation of a body in pain whose suffering is so exaggerated and theatrical that a truth . . . is grasped and believed." This "truth" she concludes, is the contingency of "the suffering body, the body in death, and resurrection."[53]

Stiles's redemption of Schwarzkogler's work seems to me to disavow the unsettling in-sincerity it occasions. I see neither exaggeration nor theatricality in his work—and I have reservations about any higher "truth" it might be said to be about. My attention is drawn instead to the bad forms, abject positions, and unwieldy tangles of materials and bodies (fig. I.12). And to the affective responses these solicit, which seem to oscillate so peculiarly between blind offense at or elaborate defense of the work, between exasperation and exultation. To not condemn Schwarzkogler as a perverted suicide does not require that he be resurrected as a Christlike figure or contemporary pagan god.[54] What if one did not feel obliged to redeem the artist, or make strong claims

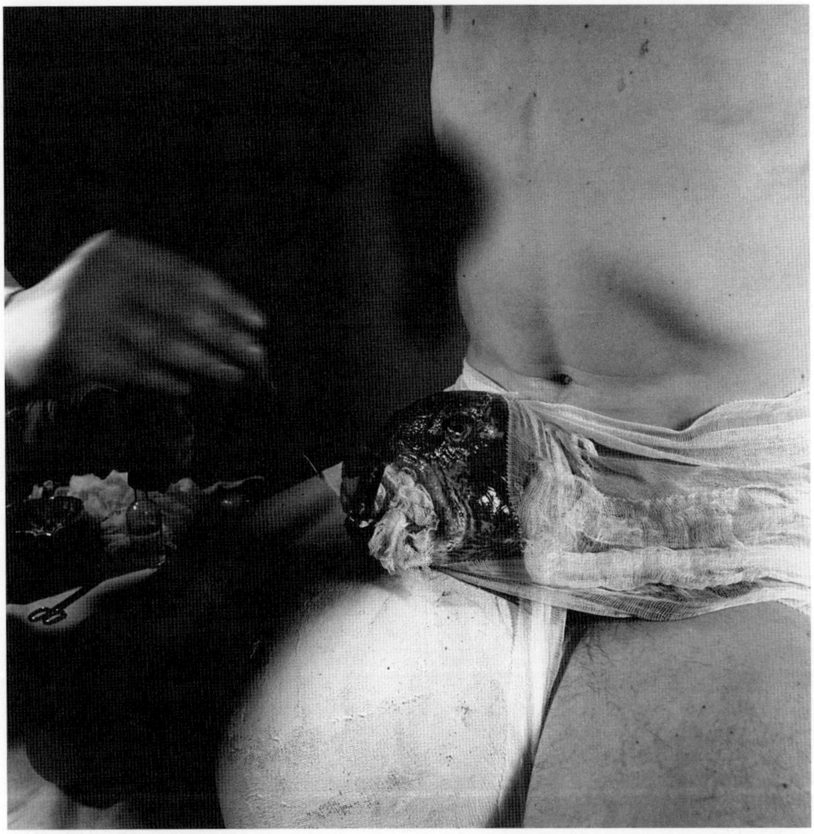

Figures I.10–I.11. Rudolf Schwarzkogler with Heinz Cibulka, 2. *Aktion* (Action 2), 1965. Photograph by Ludwig Hoffenreich. mumok – Museum moderner Kunst Stiftung Ludwig Wien, Leihgabe der Österreichischen Ludwig-Stiftung.

about the real, the extreme, or the truth to which the art attests—but instead just attended to its in-action?

The Action Paradigm

As I have been arguing, the endurance of the Schwarzkogler "myth" owes its force in the historiography of performance art to the action paradigm. Stemming from Western European and US rhetoric of liberation in the post–Second World War period, the action paradigm of performance art is part of a broader cultural narrative of emancipatory action. Stiles elaborated the action paradigm in 1998 when explaining why she preferred not to use the phrase "performance art," but rather "action art." "The term 'action,'" for Stiles, "keeps the pressure on the political reference inherent in the term activism," and it reflects "a highly determined strategy for artistic intervention in public life."[55] When contributing the much-needed term *performance* to the second edition of *Critical Terms for Art History* in 2003, Stiles emphasized: "Through its emphasis on action, performance recovers the social force of art. It remains one of the last and most effective modes of resistance to all forms of domination."[56] The notion that performance art be explicitly linked to, and thus

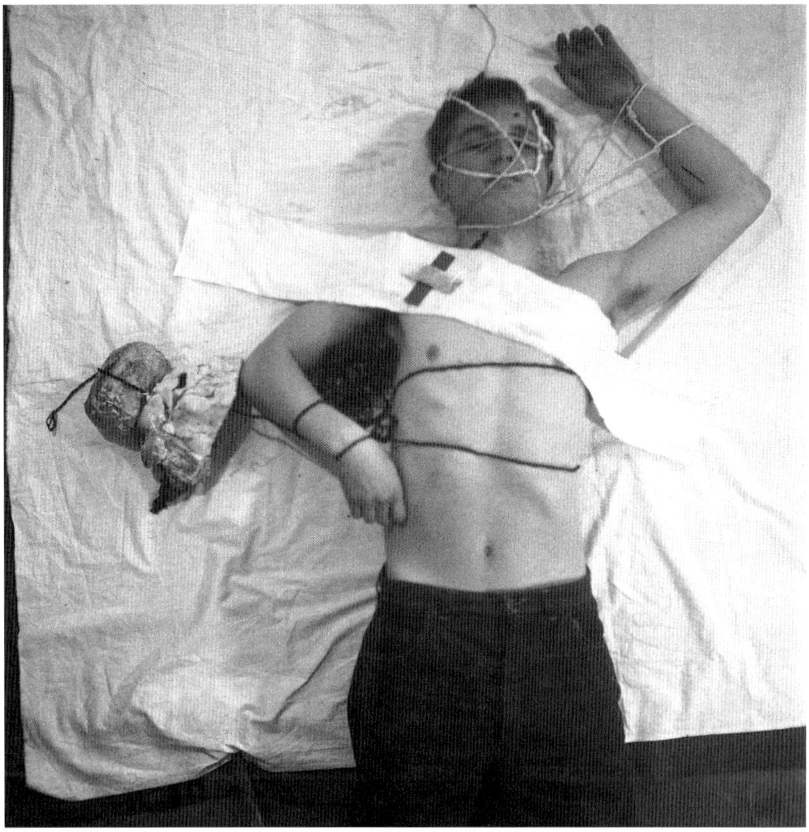

Figure I.12. Rudolf Schwarzkogler with Heinz Cibulka, *4. Aktion* (Action 4), 1965. Photograph by Franziska Wächtler. mumok – Museum moderner Kunst Stiftung Ludwig Wien, Leihgabe der Österreichischen Ludwig-Stiftung. © Rudolf Schwarzkogler; digital image © mumok – Museum moderner Kunst Stiftung Ludwig Wien.

accessible to interpretation via, a political referent propels the action paradigm, which is undergirded by the attitude that art can and should consequentially intervene in and transform life.

This alignment of artistic action with political activism, often optimistic and future-oriented if not programmatic, is connected in the action paradigm with the long-standing art historical association of performance art with liberation from artistic constraint. As RoseLee Goldberg writes in the concluding lines of her canonical study *Performance: Live Art, 1909 to the Present*, first published in 1979, performance art "will always be a means to break through any limits or conventions imposed on art activity."[57] This is part of what makes it difficult to pin down as an art form. Whether that of Acconci in New York or Vostell in West Berlin, Gilbert & George in London or Vautier in Nice, Burden in Los Angeles or Beuys in Düsseldorf, performance art seen through the lens of the action paradigm "breaks through" the medial and institutional conventions that constrain it. For Goldberg, whose book has been reprinted three times, "Rudolf Schwartzkogler [*sic*]" is another story, for "his wreckage-like self-mutilations ultimately led to his death in 1969."[58] Under the action paradigm, performance art is the ultimate avant-garde. Performance art should model, through the very "action" involved, emancipation from broader social and cultural constraints out in the wider world, thus reinforcing an understanding of politics as a sphere of action.

Since *documenta 5*, Viennese Actionism has been most often viewed within this narrative as an unfortunate apex—as the betrayal of the promise of the action paradigm. And yet nowhere is the problem of "action" in performance art history thrown into starker relief. Here, I need to address the irony of the phrase Viennese Actionism, which will come under further scrutiny in the ensuing chapters of this book. As I have mentioned, it tends to refer to the work of Brus, Muehl, Nitsch, and Schwarzkogler in the 1960s. Yet it is necessary to recall, as Mechtild Widrich does, that it was not the artists themselves, but rather their friends Peter Weibel and VALIE EXPORT, who retrospectively coined the phrase *Wiener Aktionismus* in 1970 for the title of their anthology, *wien: bildkompendium wiener aktionismus und film* (vienna: image compendium of viennese actionism and film).[59] This invaluable book archives the Viennese art scene of the 1950s and 1960s in over two hundred densely packed pages of images and provides a detailed timeline, synopses of groups and incidents, and affiliated artists' autobiographies. Even though few of the artists represented in it lived there by 1970, this image compendium served to place peripheral Vienna on the map of contemporary European art.

This context is important. The choice of phrase—Viennese Actionism—is arguably concerned less with the specific character of the various works the anthology documents than with situating Viennese performance art within current international discussions of art as "action."[60] As Günter Brus noted in 1970 in a review of books dedicated to this subject—in which he does not use the phrase Viennese Actionism to refer to his own art or that of his friends—Weibel and VALIE EXPORT's image compendium was strategic.[61] It was published at precisely the time that the action paradigm was establishing itself in artists' and critics' writings, art school pedagogy, and anthologies dedicated to the idea of art merging with, and having an impact on, life through the perceived force of political action. Calling it "Viennese Actionism" made Viennese performance art legible in the context of this emergent critical discourse, albeit at the expense of many of its most provocative facets being mistaken. Without comment, just a few photographs of Schwarzkogler's work, intermingling different *Aktionen*, are presented in the image compendium (fig. I.13). One page design would subsequently serve to represent Schwarzkogler in Szeemann's catalog for *documenta 5* (see fig. I.7). In a short synopsis, comparing Schwarzkogler's work to his own and that of Brus and Muehl, Nitsch does not write of actionism but rather states, "From the beginning he had a different position," and so "he created another type of action [*aktionstyp*]." For Nitsch, Schwarzkogler's different position is "apollonian" within a "dionysian" milieu, and his other type of action is that of the "aesthete."[62] What Nitsch is trying to indicate here is, I take it, Schwarzkogler's in-action, which is all but denied in his ensuing reception.

The action paradigm took shape in West Germany under the auspices of

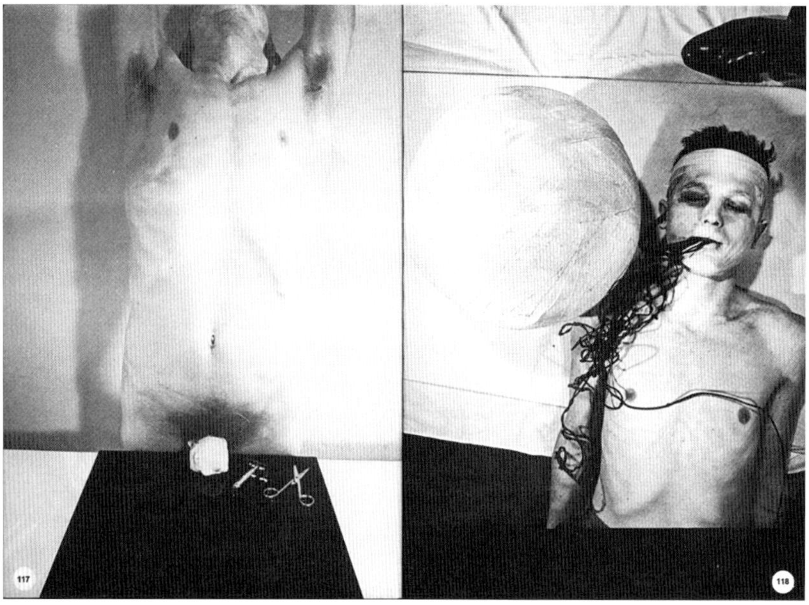

Figure I.13. Page opening in *wien: bildkompendium wiener aktionismus und film* (1970, edited by Peter Weibel and VALIE EXPORT) with works by Rudolf Schwarzkogler. The Sheridan Libraries, Johns Hopkins University; digital image: Digitization Services Unit, Johns Hopkins University.

Aktionskunst (action art). *Aktionskunst* was not painting or sculpture—or any given medium or genre. Heinz Ohff affiliated it with *Anti-Kunst* (anti-art), emphasizing the way it refused traditional artistic conventions much in the manner of the historical avant-garde.[63] Its unconventional form was solidified at venues like the Aktionsraum 1 in Munich, in exhibitions like *Happening & Fluxus* (1970), curated by Szeemann with Hanns Sohm in Cologne, and most influentially at *documenta 5*.[64] *Aktionskunst* was motivated, sometimes explicitly and sometimes obscurely, by current sociopolitical concerns, from the Vietnam War and students' rights to local environmental policy. Its practitioners understood the formal break with conventional artistic media to be connected to the political engagement of their work. This often required the artist to take a stand in unexpected spaces: out on the streets, in a university lecture hall, or in speeches for the radio. Joseph Beuys and Wolf Vostell most proactively contributed to the formation of *Aktionskunst* throughout the 1960s. In 1961, Beuys transformed his professorship of "monumental sculpture" at the Kunstakademie in Düsseldorf into a forum for what he called the practice of "social sculpture," a wide-ranging activism rooted in his belief in free education and in a pedagogy dedicated to creative encounter with the materials of everyday life. By 1970, he had set up his own *Aktionsbüro* in Düsseldorf to organize "direct democracy."[65] Although less well known than Beuys in the English-speaking world, Vostell was a key figure of transatlantic exchange. He formed the collective ADA (Aktionen der Avantgarde) in West Berlin in 1973, bringing together an international group of "action artists." Already in the early 1960s, he was coordinating "*décollage*-Happenings," participatory protest actions meant to call attention to everyday spaces and contemporary newsworthy events.[66] Beuys's motto for such *Aktionskunst* was "Jeder

Mensch ist ein Künstler" (any person is a [male] artist); Vostell's was "Kunst gleich Leben, Leben gleich Kunst" (art equals life, life equals art). The guiding assumption of each is a continuity between art and political life, the condition of which is action.

The extent to which *Aktionskunst* took shape in dialogue with international, but especially US, discussions around artistic action is striking. The word *Aktion*, after all, is an import. *Handlung* or *Tat* are the usual German words for "action." The noun *Aktion*, introduced through Latin and French usages related to the law and theater, came to refer increasingly throughout the twentieth century to military or political campaigns.[67] Already imbued with this philological internationalism, the word was taken up in 1911 by the editors of the left-wing arts and literary magazine *Die Aktion* in Berlin, which, together with many of the avant-garde artists for which it advocated, opposed the First World War.[68] Threatened by National Socialism, *Die Aktion* ended its run in 1934, and it would certainly have been condemned by the Nazis as a site of "degeneracy." Like the West German students in the 1960s, who organized political and "subversive" *Aktionen* in the antiwar and oppositional spirit of *Die Aktion*, West German *Aktionskunst* rehearses this inherited political valence of *Aktion* and extends its avant-garde legacy.[69] But however important this German antifascist legacy of the historical avant-garde was, and despite the misgivings West German students and artists had toward US culture and neo-imperialism, the renewed valence of the term *Aktion* in the period following the Second World War was a clear evocation of action in the US American style.

Aktionskunst was rapidly anthologized in books with indicative titular phrases, including Vostell's *Aktionen: Happenings und Demonstrationen* (1970), Udo Kultermann's *Leben und Kunst* the same year, and Jürgen Schilling's *Aktionskunst: Identität von Kunst und Leben? Eine Documentation* (1978).[70] The latter includes sections dedicated to Beuys, Vostell, and, for the first time in an art-historically-minded study, *Wiener Aktionismus*.[71] While offering an invaluable contextualization of *Aktionskunst*, Schilling's book operates—as his title indicates, and like so many of the anthologies of the period—first and foremost as a "documentation." So his mistaking of Schwarzkogler is significant. Writing of Schwarzkogler, he concludes: "The content of the documentation shows death as action."[72]

The history Schilling narrates turns on pivotal US terms like *action painting* and *happenings*. In all the books documenting *Aktionskunst* just referenced, a main conduit for the importation of these terms was Allan Kaprow, by way of Wolf Vostell. This was most impactfully formalized in 1965 in Vostell's publication with Jürgen Becker, *Happenings. Fluxus. Pop art. Nouveau réalisme. Eine Dokumentation*, and the following year in Kaprow's *Assemblage, Environments & Happenings*.[73] Kaprow and Vostell's exchanges institute the action paradigm. The year 1958 is its *Urszene*. Becker and Vostell's chronology begins with Vostell's own *Das Theater ist auf der Straße* (The theater is on the street), "intermedia" experiments by the Americans Dick Higgins and Al Hansen, and

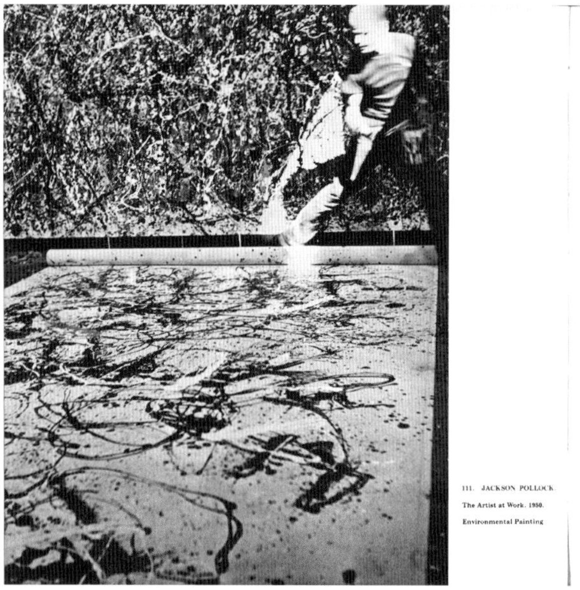

Figure I.14. Page opening in *Assemblage, Environments & Happenings* (1966, Allan Kaprow), with "Jackson Pollock, The Artist at Work, 1950." © 2025 The Pollock-Krasner Foundation / Artists Rights Society (ARS), New York. © 1991 Hans Namuth Estate, Courtesy Center for Creative Photography. Special Collections, The Sheridan Libraries, Johns Hopkins University; digital image: Digitization Services Unit, Johns Hopkins University.

unspecified examples of Kaprow's happenings, all dated to that year.[74] The year 1958 was also when Kaprow defined the happening as a consequence of Jackson Pollock's action painting in his now-canonical essay "The Legacy of Jackson Pollock."

Pollock, Kaprow claims, "*destroyed painting*," breaking through its conventions to discover everyday materials and public space.[75] With his characteristic masculine pronouns, he writes: "The young artist of today need no longer say 'I am a painter' or 'a poet' or 'a dancer.' He is simply an 'artist.'"[76] Kaprow is reiterating an influential insight of Harold Rosenberg from 1952, that action painting had "broken down every distinction between art and life."[77] In works of US abstract expressionist action painting, Rosenberg saw "a gesture of liberation," for the canvas was no longer an object of value or contemplation, but "an arena in which to act."[78] In Kaprow's account, Pollock opened this arena. He understood happenings as taking place on the site of the destruction of the conventions of painting, where the artist was liberated from media constraints, free to act. In 1965, Becker provided nothing other than the standard account when he introduced the documentation he prepared with Vostell by emphasizing how Pollock's "wild painting-actions" inaugurated a new awareness of "our contemporary reality" and the possibilities for a new art.[79] Over fifty years later, in *Radical Prototypes: Allan Kaprow and the Invention of the Happening*, Judith Rodenbeck summed it up again as follows: "Pollock was an action painter, and his legacy was not painting but action. Kaprow dubbed this new medium the 'happening.'"[80] This oft-rehearsed link, between action painting and the happening, undergirds the action paradigm, both in its artistic and in its art historiographical dimensions.

Coining a phrase that succinctly captures the impact of this legacy of Pollock on both sides of the Atlantic, Amelia Jones speaks of "the Pollockian performative."[81] For, as Serge Guilbaut and other scholars since have emphasized, Pollock's oversize influence in the period owed not only to his paintings but equally to widely disseminated photographic and filmic documents of him in the act of painting. These conveyed the characteristic masculinity, virility, independence, and heroism that came to be associated with US action painting.[82] These qualities indelibly shaped performance as an art form. There was the artist, as Jones writes, "standing above or within his huge canvases overtly and theatrically *performing* the act of painting."[83] The photograph of Pollock's performance included in Kultermann's *Leben und Kunst* of 1970 is the very same one Kaprow used for his own documentation of contemporary art in 1966 (fig. I.14).[84] Kaprow placed an image of himself, standing in his environment of tires called *Yard* (1961), on the facing page, to demonstrate all the more clearly the lineage from Pollock's action painting to his happenings. This artistic and art critical veneration of the Pollockian performative, canonized in 1958, has propelled the action paradigm into the present day, even as its vocabularies of "rebel genius" and "heroic American individualism" have affirmed masculinist tropes to the extent of excluding, as Andrew Perchuk convincingly concludes, all those "who could not or would not participate in it."[85] This is why Jones argues that "'performance art' proper" first in fact begins with the feminist "dislocation" of the Pollockian performative.[86]

I am inclined to agree. "If performance exists as an art form," then it expresses reservation about the action paradigm. This book is concerned with the reservations that defined so-called Viennese Actionism from the start. It therefore disputes narratives that claim to see throughout Viennese Actionism an "eminently political act of liberation."[87] Rather than amp up claims for its radical political efficacy, I want to carefully and critically revisit the history of Viennese performance art, without presupposing the optic of the action paradigm. I aim to recover the less extreme, more reserved, but all the more pressing artistic and political concerns disclosed in its ostensibly most passive moments.

In the next three sections, I sketch three different kinds of trouble in the action paradigm: Feminist Actionism, ordinary action, and in-action. Feminist Actionism "dislocates," to use Jones's term, and appropriates the position of the self-assertive artist in the arena of action, paradoxically reauthorizing the expectations of action on which this position is predicated. Ordinary actions, in contrast, de-escalate the powerful rhetoric of emancipatory action by attending to everyday life and sometimes transforming it—not so much by intervening in as by rehearsing its ordinariness. Feminist and queer methodologies have of course long contested the normative sensibilities underlying the action paradigm. Yet what is often maintained nonetheless is the idea of performance as emancipatory action corresponding to a political intention asserted by or imputed to the artist.[88] In contrast, in-action is what is mistaken for the extreme or assertive action it is not.[89]

Feminist Actionism

It is certainly no coincidence that, after coming up with the phrase *Wiener Aktionismus* with Peter Weibel in 1970, VALIE EXPORT went on to formulate her own related project, *Feministischer Aktionismus*, with an assertive and unruly capital *F*.[90] Feminist Actionism was VALIE EXPORT's riposte to what she saw as the masculinism of Viennese Actionism and its refusal to engage the project of feminist emancipation. Her Austrian affiliates "could not understand the emancipation of women," and, as she reflected with frustration: "There was no women's movement in the 1960s in Vienna and not a single woman artist working with feminist thought or new media. I drew all my information about feminist movements from magazines and books from the USA."[91] Carolee Schneemann was a particularly important source of inspiration for VALIE EXPORT, because Schneemann was not just a "woman artist" but also "taught feminist art history and fought against male culture as a theorist."[92] Both Schneemann and VALIE EXPORT were fighting, in short, against the action paradigm—and fighting for a place in it.

VALIE EXPORT first began to articulate the stakes of Feminist Actionism in the early 1970s in the pages of the progressive Austrian newspaper *Neues Forum*, and she formalized these in an art historical manifesto in 1980.[93] In 1989, as the first big exhibition of Viennese Actionism traveled without reference to her work, she translated it into English as "Aspects of Feminist Actionism."[94] In the meantime, in what can be understood as an example of Feminist Actionism in its own right, she had cocurated *Kunst mit Eigen-Sinn: Aktuelle Kunst von Frauen* (Art with own-sense: Current art by women) at mumok – Museum moderner Kunst in Vienna in 1985, the first large-scale exhibition in Austria dedicated entirely to women artists.[95] In her texts from this period, VALIE EXPORT is careful to note that Feminist Actionism is not simply a reaction to Viennese Actionism, but a response to how women artists have been excluded from the writing of the history of *Aktionskunst* and artistic actionism more broadly. While Feminist Actionism has, as VALIE EXPORT argues, a long history—she connects contemporary artists like Rebecca Horn, Gina Pane, Yvonne Rainer, and Schneemann back to European surrealism and such figures as Meret Oppenheim and Isabelle Waldberg—her point is that this history has been structurally obfuscated. "Human history," she contests, "is without dignity because it is solely male, a story of masculine activities."[96] This is nowhere in better evidence than in documentations of *Aktionskunst*, and most flagrantly, as noted already, in Szeemann's studious exclusion of women artists from *documenta 5* in 1972.[97]

Feminist Actionism sets out to make its own history and own sense. Writing the foreword to the catalog for *Kunst mit Eigen-Sinn*, VALIE EXPORT motivates the titular phrase (*Eigen-Sinn*, literally "own-sense") by insisting that artists who are women need to make work that is about the "appropriation of the right to one's own representation and expression, one's own world of experience, one's own history."[98] Without the dash, the word *Eigensinn* also means "obstinacy," which describes the mode of "escape from dependency" that VALIE EXPORT advocates, including techniques that are "self-affirming" and, invoking the suffragist Harriet Taylor Mill, about "self-will and self-assertion."[99]

In order to initiate a feminist history, attentive to acts of independent sense making in art by women, VALIE EXPORT takes a stand against the masculinism of the action paradigm. And yet, in the same gesture, Feminist Actionism affirms the action paradigm. In her manifesto, this is betrayed in VALIE EXPORT's frequent use of the phrase "just as." In a key passage, she writes: "Just as action aims at achieving the unity of actor and material, perception and action, subject and object, Feminist Actionism seeks to transform the object of male natural history, the material 'woman,' subjugated and enslaved by the male creator, into an independent actor and creator, subject of her own history."[100] If Feminist Actionism is supposed to articulate an alternative history to its masculinist counterpart, then history is still clearly understood as one defined by self-assertive willful emancipatory action. Feminist Actionism names the feminist appropriation of the action paradigm.

In art history, Jones has been the most influential proponent of this position. In her account, "'performance art' proper" begins with feminist performances that are "often explicitly activist" because they polemically foreground the feminist subject of the work of art.[101] In contrast with performance art by men in the 1960s—which Jones sees as "confirmatory" of the Pollockian performative, repeating the posturing of the "histrionically virile action painting body"—in performance art by women in the 1970s, Jones finds a response to this posturing that critically "dislocates" it.[102] An image of VALIE EXPORT's *Aktionshose: Genitalpanik* (Action pants: Genital panic; 1969; fig. I.15) illustrates Jones's argument in the major survey *The Artist's Body* of 2000. Hair excessively crimped and jeans cut out at the crotch to reveal her genital zone, VALIE EXPORT epitomizes the "hyper-sexualized feminist," staring defiantly into the camera, holding not a paintbrush but a machine gun.[103] Such "aggressive self-enactments" undergird Jones's interest in how feminist performance art dislocates "modernism's repression of the artist's body by proposing fully embedded and socially relevant feminist bodies that are also specific 'selves.'"[104] Seen from this perspective, performance art reveals the embeddedness, relevance, and specificity of the body of what Kaprow called the "'artist'"—with an important difference: The artist is a woman, and not only that, she is a feminist asserting her self and her position. To use Rebecca Schneider's term from her incisive study of 1997, *The Explicit Body in Performance*, feminist performance art "explicates" the feminist's body. Through "explosive literality," it makes that body explicit, in all senses of the term.[105]

The significance of feminist explication for the history of performance art cannot be overstated. But if in art history writing at the turn of the twenty-first century it was taken to articulate a strategy for forcefully occupying the action paradigm, then it also arguably contributed to the buttressing of the

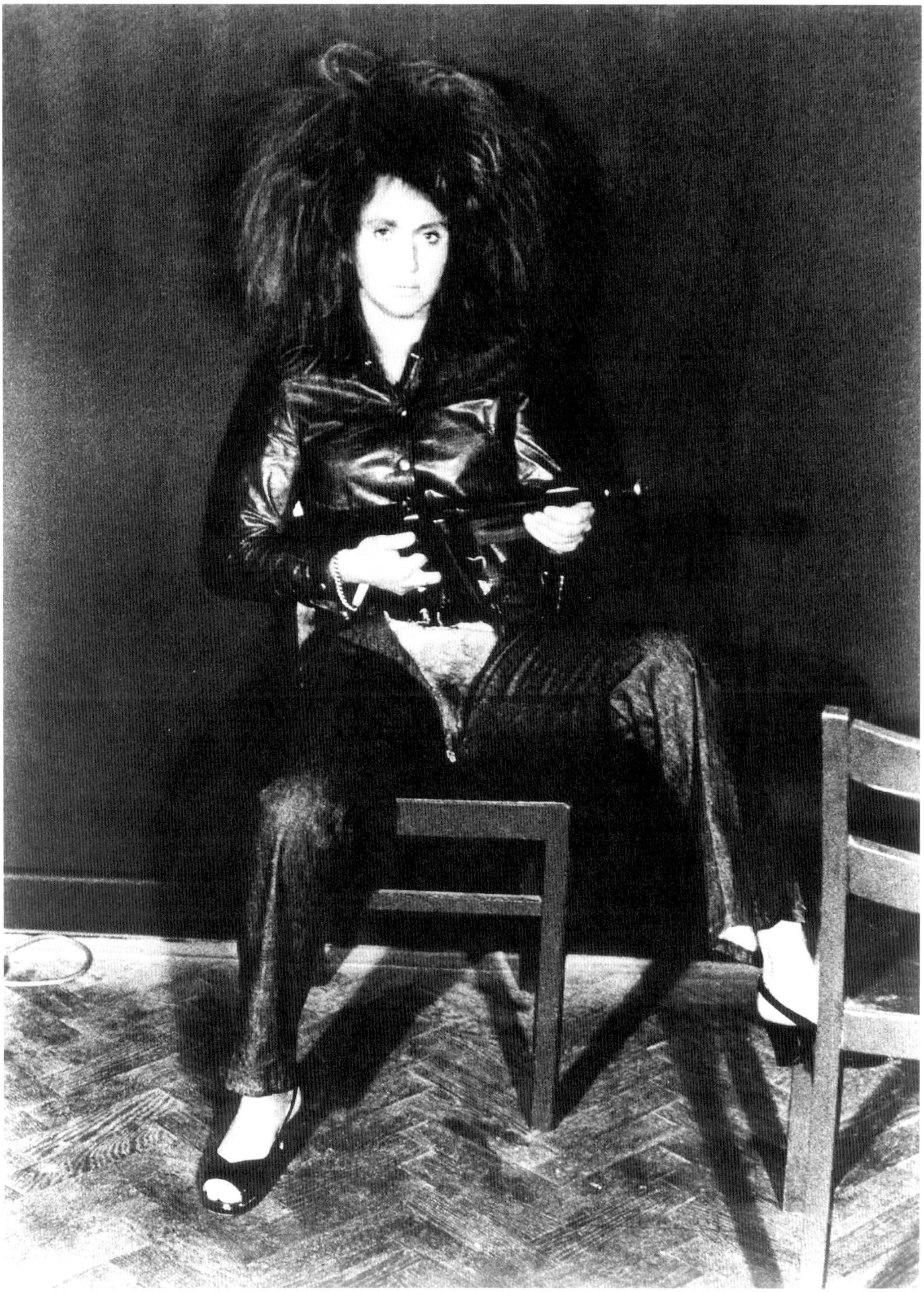

Figure I.15. VALIE EXPORT, *Aktionshose: Genitalpanik* (Action pants: Genital panic), 1969. Self-staging. Photograph by Peter Hassmann. © VALIE EXPORT, Bildrecht Wien, 2025.

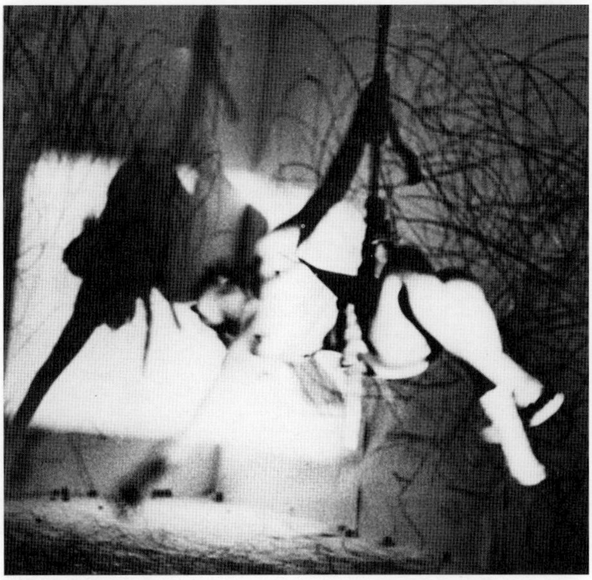

Figure I.16. Carolee Schneemann, *Up to and Including Her Limits*, 1976 (1973–1976). Photograph by Shelley Farkas. © 2025 Carolee Schneemann Foundation / Artists Rights Society (ARS), New York. Courtesy Lisson Gallery and P·P·O·W, New York. Courtesy the Carolee Schneemann Foundation.

action paradigm as definitive of both artistic and political sense making. In this regard, I want to look at a work by Schneemann, who for VALIE EXPORT is a pioneering Feminist Actionist and for Jones and Schneider is a leading example of feminist dislocation by means of explication. *Up to and Including Her Limits* (1971–1976; fig. I.16) is insistent in its dislocation of the Pollockian performative.[106] VALIE EXPORT saw Schneemann perform it in West Berlin in 1976.[107] Elevated off the floor in a harness, physically integrated into the space and process of painting, Schneemann swings her naked body between the paper-covered walls and floor, marking them with crayon. To follow Jones, Schneemann "deployed her sexualized body in and as her work within the language of abstract expressionism but against the grain of its masculinist assumptions."[108] By replacing the action painter with her explicit naked body, Schneemann outdoes him, outperforms him. In this interpretation of the performance, Schneemann is the quintessential Feminist Actionist, self-assertively inscribing herself into the arena of action and staking out a place of her own in the history of art. Yet, the very historiographical emphases that critique the action paradigm's masculinist dimensions make Schneemann exemplary of it.

To look at this performance without being so quick to insist on its liberatory ethos affords a different view. Schneemann does not independently deploy her body; she does not even take a stand. Rather, her body is suspended. *To suspend* is an interesting verb because it is not straightforwardly active. Schneemann's suspended body presents the inertia that accompanies movement, the weariness and constraints that attend action. Suspension destabilizes her relationship to verticality. The harness lifts but also restrains her, rendering her body exposed and precarious. As Schneemann swings, the straps of the harness press into her flesh and hold her back as she reaches to make marks.

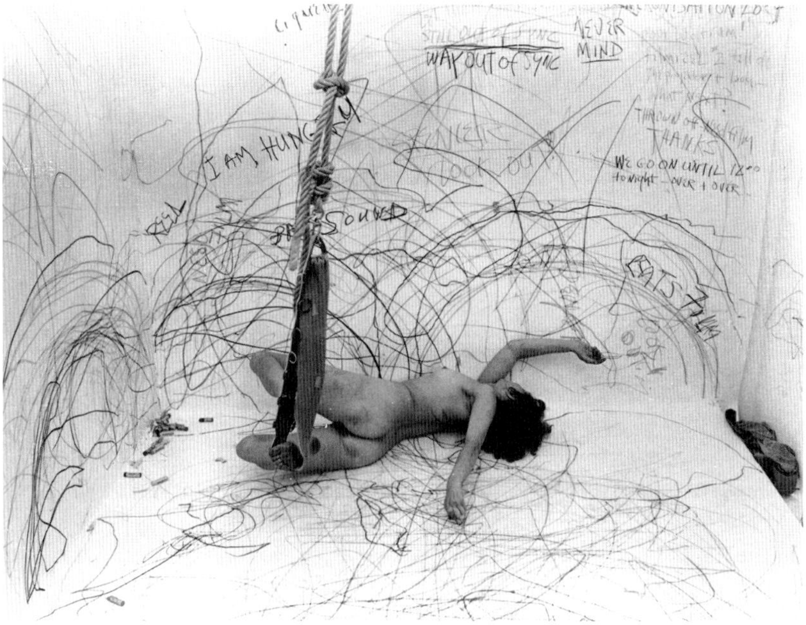

Figure I.17. Carolee Schneemann, *Up to and Including Her Limits*, 1976, Studiogalerie, Berlin (1973–1976). Photograph by Henrik Gaard. © 2025 Carolee Schneemann Foundation / Artists Rights Society (ARS), New York. Courtesy Lisson Gallery and P·P·O·W, New York. Courtesy the Carolee Schneemann Foundation.

Her body bumps into the walls and the floor, smudging her drawings, leaving its own traces, getting dirty and bruised. Of *Up to and Including Her Limits* Schneemann writes, "My entire body becomes the agency of visual traces."[109] Intriguingly, she does not present herself as assuming the position of the independent intentional agent, nor does she "enact" her body.[110] Rather, her body emerges as the site of disparate agencies exposed and implicated in the space and materiality of painting.

The performance is physically exhausting. In one iteration, she writes "I am hungry" on the wall, and some photographs show her sprawled out on the floor, just one leg looped in the harness, having fallen, barely managing to crawl (fig. I.17). These are not the postures or relations to which one habitually turns to model the emancipatory potential of artistic or political action. What I am suggesting is that *Up to and Including Her Limits* suspends the action paradigm. Schneemann is left hanging in, rather than escaping from, the arena of action. The performance explores articulations of art, and by extension politics, that emerge only when expectations about action are suspended. *Up to and Including Her Limits* is a performance, as I see it, of feminist in-action. As such, it solicits a different kind of viewing that is itself suspended in discomfort, delay, and difficulty. One is left to grapple with the feelings of uncertainty and vulnerability that accompany it.

Ordinary Action

If I have foregrounded the emancipatory action of the action paradigm, it is because Viennese Actionism has persistently been seen through this frame.[111]

There is of course a less heroic, less triumphalist iteration, the key term of which is more modest, namely, the ordinary. Rather than celebrating emancipatory Action with a capital *A*, in its self-assertive and activist forms, ordinary action attends to everyday actions, with a small *a*, in all their ordinariness. Instead of constituting an arena of action as a privileged site, ordinary actions emphasize the ordinariness of the sites in which they take place and the everydayness of the actions that they stage. "Embracing ordinary things, gestures, and sounds over virtuosic skill," as Elise Archias writes in *The Concrete Body*, a book dedicated to Acconci, Schneemann, and Yvonne Rainer, "promised a democratic shift for art, out of museums and studios and into the extra-artistic realm of everyday life."[112] Deflationary in orientation, the performance of ordinary action understands itself to be about doing justice to common and what Archias calls "matter-of-fact" aspects of life overlooked in art and politics.[113]

In the historiography of performance art, especially in the United States, the preoccupation with the ordinary can also be traced back to the "inventor" of the happening, Allan Kaprow.[114] In the very moment circa 1958 that produced the rhetoric of emancipatory action that drove the action paradigm in its triumphalist iteration, Kaprow was advocating for an art that revealed "the meaning of ordinariness." In a much-cited passage from "The Legacy of Jackson Pollock," Kaprow observes that for the artist liberated from formal, artistic, and medial conventions, "all of life will be open to *him*. *He* will discover out of ordinary things the meaning of ordinariness. *He* will not try to make them extraordinary."[115] If my emphasizing Kaprow's pronouns here seems presentist, then it underlines how the equation of art and life, on which not only the legacy of Pollock but also the celebration of the ordinary relies, is historically masculinist, to say the least.[116] Despite his democratizing political aspirations and commitment to participation, Kaprow too often conflated the ordinary with the normative. Catherine Spencer notes the "machismo" and "gender imbalances of Kaprow's 1960s Happenings," and even Judith Rodenbeck, who champions an antiheroic narrative of Kaprow in *Radical Prototypes*, concedes that "actions" like *Household* (1964)—in which men build a tower, "ambush women," "jack up a car," and "smoke cigarettes," while women build a nest, hang a clothesline, "screech," "call to men sweet-songy come-ons," and remove their blouses—rehearse "shockingly reactionary gender coding."[117]

In my view, ordinary actions become interesting as performance art only when they have reservations about, rather than rehearse, the normative assumptions of everyday life. They thus trouble, rather than affirm, the equation of art and life. Such work, the significant dimensions of which I can only indicate in this section, has been the subject of recent art history writing that carefully revisits period archives and often engages with feminist and queer thought to expand the vocabulary of what counts as an action worthy of attention in art, as in life, since the 1960s. While the artistic practices under discussion largely share Kaprow's commitment to bringing the ordinary to light, they demonstrate in contrast that the ordinary is by no means as "open" or accessible as it may seem. They reveal that the ordinary, in spite of its ostensible self-evidence and "matter-of-factness," is elusive, difficult to grasp, tendentiously overlooked, structurally demure—and this is both the political challenge and the artistic provocation it presents. Instead of simply reenacting the everyday, ordinary action acknowledges and engages this intractability.

One technique for this is what Catherine Spencer calls "acts of displacement."[118] In a book that in many ways gets "beyond the happening" in its US-centric, institutionalized, and masculinist dimensions, Spencer discusses Lea Lublin's *Mon fils* (My son; see figs. 1.36, 1.37).[119] In 1968, against the backdrop of student protest activism, the workers' movement, and demonstrations for civil rights in Paris, Lublin exhibited her baby in a crib at the annual Salon in May. In contrast to "dislocation," Jones's term for the feminist usurpation of the position of the artist in the arena of action, displacement involves staging an incongruity between action and site, between art and everyday life. Lublin does nothing more in *Mon fils* than care for her infant, but by doing so in a respected museum space, her work becomes a kind of demonstration. Her ordinary action—caring—presents the necessary supplement to the activism on the streets.

Ordinary actions contest the distinction between public and private space, as well as other openings and closures that define everyday life. Of the confluence of "house work and art work," Helen Molesworth writes that it "opens public space to the pressures of what it traditionally excludes, or renders invisible."[120] Molesworth has in mind such ordinary actions as Mierle Laderman Ukeles's *Hartford Wash: Washing Tracks, Maintenance Outside, Maintenance Inside* (1973). This work involved the artist performing custodial duties at the Wadsworth Atheneum in Hartford. She really, if not always efficiently, mopped, cleaned, and maintained the museum entrance and galleries. Similar to Lublin's *Mon fils*, Ukeles's *Hartford Wash* instigates an act of displacement. Exhibiting maintenance activities, usually discreetly carried out after hours and out of sight, she brings the conditions of the museum institution to light. There is no "pure individual creation," no avant-garde, no happening—indeed, nothing happens, as Ukeles wrote at the time, without care and maintenance work.[121] Her performance puts time-consuming, boring, poorly or un-remunerated, messy care work typically done by women front and center.

The demand in such performance art that ordinary actions denigrated as "women's work" be counted as work—and indeed, as art work—not only echoes the feminist slogan "Wages for Housework," but also anticipates the emergent discourse of feminist care ethics in the United States.[122] Feminist care ethics objects to the action paradigm in politics, just as performances of care object to the action paradigm in art. Contesting an ideology premised on the autonomous, sovereign individual, feminist care ethics proposes instead a prior condition of relationality and dependence upon which any self relies.[123] It provides a counterpoint to Feminist Actionism. In short, no action without care. Criticized for its perceived essentialism, feminist care ethics was reproached above all for the political passivity it was suspected of advocating.[124] Performances of ordinary actions like caring and cleaning make visible this very political conundrum: Can one oppose the action paradigm without entering into the arena of action and becoming an actionist? Can one advocate for care without taking a stand, and assuming an activist stance? The title of Ukeles's "Manifesto for Maintenance Art 1969! Proposal for an Exhibition 'CARE'" spells out this conflict.[125] For care is not exclamatory; its performance cannot be made emphatic in the equivalent of all caps.

Feminist histories of "women's work" in performance art are largely concerned with structures of looking and overlooking, of denigration and obfuscation in contemporary art as in everyday life.[126] This structural approach is complemented by art history writing attentive to performance art practices, notably by queer artists, that foreground personal eccentricities and explore deviance and subversion, often at the interstices and margins of the everyday. In grappling with the equation of art and life, it is what counts as life that is subject to artistic investigation. In *The Art of Living*, Dominic Johnson writes a "counterhistory" of performance art through the practice of oral history, tracing a genealogy of transgressive and otherwise queer practices since the 1960s. He defines this performance art as "the praxis of turning one's life—both body and subjectivity—into the stuff of art."[127] With attention to subcultures, alternatives spaces, and idiosyncratic and subversive practices, Johnson's "secret history" of the "art of living" is about expanding the field of performance art beyond the purview of today's mainstream art and politics.

David Getsy's *Queer Behavior: Scott Burton and Performance Art* offers a different kind of counterhistory, by questioning the privileging of the visibility of the artist and the insistence on the sincerity of their actions in performance art history. Getsy describes Burton's "imitation of ordinary life" in ordinary actions meant to camouflage, disguise, and mask his gay identity, and to "replay and restage the act of being otherwise but passing as normal."[128] Burton's performance art thus inheres in the reality of his lived experience but also in the moments of recognition, misrecognition, or nonresponse that it occasions. Rather than claiming for performance art the task of explicating everyday life in what is unambiguously intended as a kind of political activism, Getsy here describes a performance art that is deliberately, if I may suggest the term, in-explicit.[129] Indeed, it may be that much of the feminist and queer performance art that I have referred to briefly here under "Ordinary Action" could be described by the term *in-action*, especially insofar as it has often been mistaken—if not for a radical or extreme action, then for nothing really happening at all.

In-action (missing, in-sincere, wedding)

With the term *in-action*, I refer to performances that do not in the first instance dislocate or displace the idea of action that drives the action paradigm, but rather ones that are constitutively mistaken in it. What is going on in such performances is neither ordinary nor explicit but rather very difficult to discern. In-action indicates, as I suggested earlier, an uncertainty or reservation about action. It strictly corresponds to Lambert-Beatty's reticent phrase, "If performance exists as an art form." For in-action does not unambiguously exist as performance art; it inheres in its troubling status. The interest of in-action is that one cannot be sure that one is dealing with art or with life, with a determinate action or definable agent, with a performance or a failure—all these are cast into question.

As such, in-action resonates with but differs from contemporary discourses of "inoperativity" and "deworking" that have gained currency in recent years precisely in response to and disappointment with the dwindling scope and possibility of action in politics.[130] Bonnie Honig has referred to this minor tendency in radical political theory as "the Bartleby Left," evoking Herman Melville's character with the proclivity to "prefer not to."[131] These theorists oppose action insofar as it is conflated with the economic demand for productivity and the sociopolitical demand, especially in Western cultures, to be independent and, above all, "to perform." Barbara Gronau and Alice Lagaay have cultivated the compelling vocabulary of "performances of doing nothing" and "economies of constraint" to describe practices of refusal that demonstrate against imperatives to produce and to perform in modern capitalist societies.[132] In-action shares with the aesthetic embrace of political forms of resistance a frustration with the strictures of activism and the norms of social reproduction and upward mobility. But rather than undertaking the paradoxical work of outright opposition, or attempting to occupy and lay claim to a place altogether other to or outside of action, in-action unfolds within action. In-action is thus caught up, even complicit, in the action paradigm. It hesitates about the overcomings and breaking-throughs heralded in the action paradigm. Rather than presuming to destroy received forms, in-action remains within and is often occupied with artistic traditions and conventions like painting, and even—as the final chapter of this book shows—the tedious "women's work" of weaving.

Declining the assumptions that undergird the action paradigm—without its standards or metrics, without claiming good morals or rehearsing the norms of good politics—in-action names a specifically art historical remainder. It accounts for performances mistaken in art history as action taken to violent extremes, or as failed emancipation, when these performances have little to do with either. Of course, only so much can be said about in-action in the abstract. In what remains of this introduction, I return to Schwarzkogler to offer another take on his work by situating it in a different archive of performance art. Rather than placing it at the dead end of the action paradigm, or as the aberration in a genealogy that leads from Pollock to Kaprow to Burden and on to Abramović, I propose instead to consider it in the context of the distinctive feminist and queer practices of such contemporary performance artists as Franko B and Aliza Shvarts. Like Schwarzkogler's, their performances cannot without violence be situated in the tradition of the action paradigm. Each also evokes strategies to be found in the history of Viennese Actionism. With Schwarzkogler, Franko B and Shvarts share a reticence about the righteous posturing and progressive political imaginary to which the action paradigm contributes. All three of these artists undo the teleological expectations that continue, at great cost to many, to define models of the fulfilled life: sovereign selfhood, upward mobility, and heterosexual reproductive futurism. They explore ways not to oppose such norms outright but to be without them. Seen through the lens afforded by this inverted archive, certain long-mistaken aspects of Viennese Actionism come into view, in which performance art does not seek to rise to the call to action.

missing

Franko B's performance *Aktion 398* (1998–2002; fig. I.18) invokes the *Aktion* of *Wiener Aktionismus* precisely by inflecting its passivities.[133] It begins with waiting. It opens not in an arena of action but in one of administration. An entryway, typically in a gallery space, is converted into a bleak waiting room, as in a hospital or clinic, where visitors take a number from a paper-ticket dispenser and silently wait. There is no music or distraction. The artist is nowhere to be seen. When the ticket number is called, the holder is led by an assistant into an

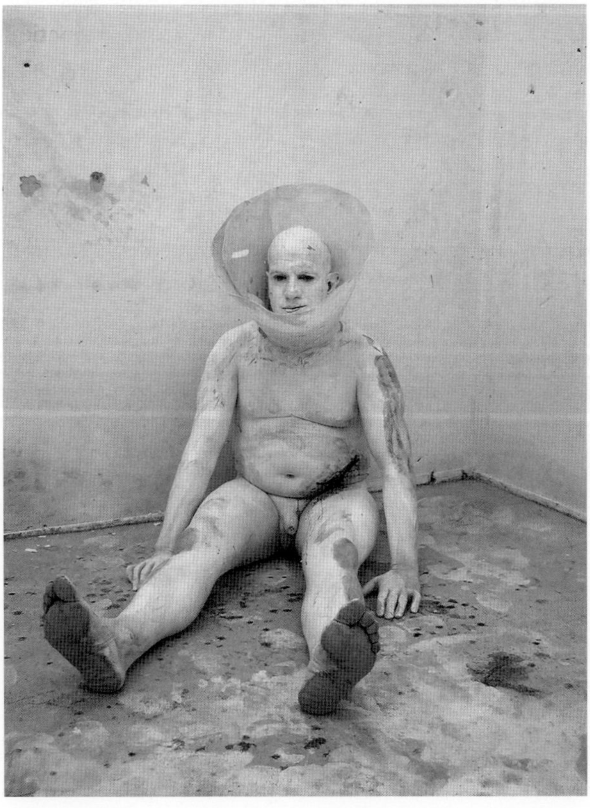

Figure I.18. Franko B, *Aktion 398*, 2001, Vienna (1998–2002). Photograph courtesy of the artist. © Franko B.

adjacent room. All furnishings have been removed. The bare light exposes the only occupant of the room. The artist is slumped against the wall or collapsed in a corner. His naked body is smeared with chalky white paint, and he is hurt. Blood spreads messily from a wound in his belly. Around his neck he wears a large plastic cone of the sort a dog would wear when injured to prevent it from licking its wounds. His blood marks the grimy walls and floors in a manner that seems to cite Schneemann's *Up to and Including Her Limits*, yet suspension has now given way to collapse. The artist is not active; he is incapacitated. His body does not express; it is just exposed.

Franko B's performance in *Aktion 398* produces a scenario that is aesthetically off-putting and ethically unnerving, for there is something not "right" about a work in which the artist is evidently not alright. In failing to assume the position of the artist in action—indeed, by appearing as an abject figure in need of care—Franko B suffuses his work with a sense of "missing." By missing, Franko B performs, as I see it, a distinctive kind of "queer art of failure." "Missing" could be added to the list of aesthetically, politically, and even ontologically "unbecoming" ways of being that, Jack Halberstam writes, do not speak in "the language of action and momentum" but are instead articulated "in terms of evacuation, refusal, passivity, unbecoming, unbeing."[134] Missing does not feel good—but that's OK. Jennifer Doyle has written about Franko B in her reflections on "hard feelings" in contemporary art, instances in which the art is not only about difficult feelings but also produces them.[135] Slowly, back and forth, back and forth, down the center of an illuminated white aisle as his blood drips from IVs inserted into each of his arms onto the white paper runway, Franko B performs *I Miss You* (2003–2007; fig. I.19). His blood leaves behind delicate patterns that become increasingly smudged as the performance continues. The constant clicking of cameras disquietingly stresses the glaring lack of glamour in this nude and silent fashion show. Each time he reaches an end of the aisle, Franko B pauses, taking time, gathering his depleted energy for another turn. *I Miss You* is an understated work of endurance: The artist walks back and forth until his body is so weak that he leaves the scene to receive medical attention.[136]

The "unnerving, depressing, or upsetting" experience of witnessing such art is all the more so, Doyle writes, because it does not offer "the positive message one associates with political art." It rejects "the basic geometries of identity and politics that normally ground discussions of art, identity, and politics."[137] To put this another way, in Franko B's work, these geometries are missing. To try to construct around his work an affirmative message or a political orientation would betray it, for the performance is nothing if not "the refusal of a redemptive gesture." Responding to this kind of work, Doyle suggests, means occupying "a different place, where emotion is a site of unraveling and dispossession."[138] It is about allowing oneself to be moved by a missing sense of self, taken to a place where neither sense nor self can be coherently asserted.

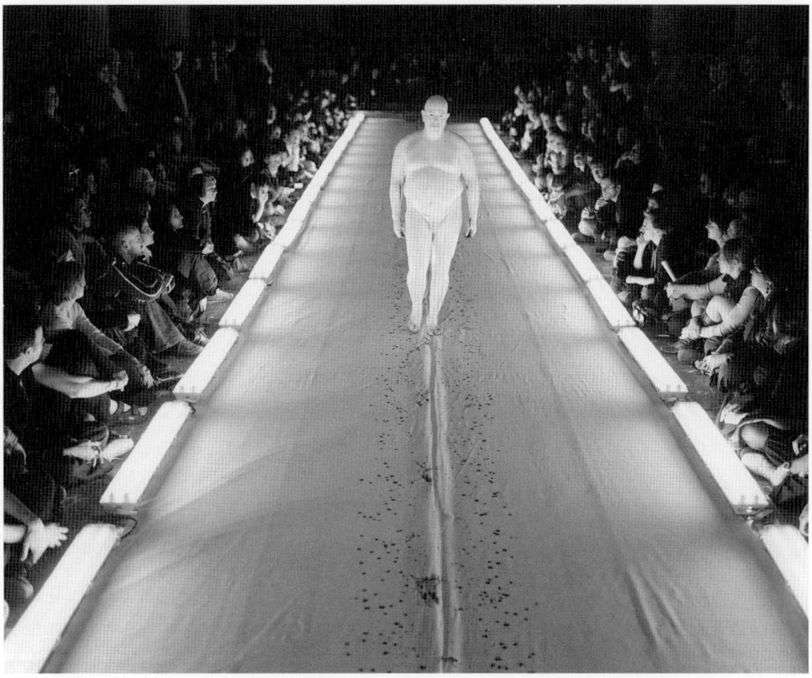

Figure I.19. Franko B, *I Miss You*, 2005, Brussels (1999–2005). Photograph by Hugo Glendinning. © Franko B.

Without trying to "right" it, I trace passages of dispossession and unraveling in Viennese performance art. This approach is about maintaining space in performance art history for what makes itself felt as missing, as opposed to merely absent. It involves, in the spirit of Halberstam and following Doyle's example, engaging art and writing art history in a manner that is ready to relinquish much of the repertoire of the author and the critic in order to be attentive to the failures and the hard feelings that, dishearteningly, pervade certain art and much of politics.[139]

in-sincere

There are few visual documents of Aliza Shvarts's *Untitled (Senior Thesis)* (2008), but there exists a vast compendium of what she calls "tellings"—rumors, stories, and fictions of the sort that surrounded Schwarzkogler's work in the wake of *documenta 5*. Shvarts decisively integrates such narratives into her performance, which, she contends, "exists only in its telling," which can take "textual, visual, spatial, temporal, and performative forms."[140] Having been at work for nine months on her senior thesis project at Yale University, Shvarts was ready to present it in the spring of 2008. The materials she submitted to the Art Department stated that she had been using donor sperm to artificially inseminate herself in each of the nine months of the academic year. She had then taken an herbal abortifacient to induce menstruation, ensuring that she did not get pregnant. The exhibition of the senior thesis would combine her writings on the project and what she described as "materials" related to it.[141]

Yet when news got out that Shvarts was going to "show" this piece, "tellings" proliferated. Under the censorious pressure of the public eye, Yale University officially denied the reality of the performance. Nothing Shvarts was saying she did, Yale insisted, had actually happened. "Ms. Shvarts is engaged in performance art," as a university spokeswoman put it: "The entire project is an art piece, a creative fiction designed to draw attention to the ambiguity surrounding the form and function of a woman's body."[142] When Yale officials told Shvarts that she could exhibit *Untitled (Senior Thesis)* solely on the condition that she signed a statement testifying that it was only "creative fiction," she refused. This gesture on the part of the artist was and is often taken as proof of the veracity of her performance. But *Untitled (Senior Thesis)*, as Carrie Lambert-Beatty puts it, is in fact about what "did or did not happen."[143]

Inevitably, Shvarts and her work were responded to with corrective measures, meant to insert the performance into the action paradigm and to translate the artist's untitled artistic thesis into an unequivocal thesis statement. In its tellings, *Untitled (Senior Thesis)* was a "scandal," "shock art," for it was seen as a controversial piece of artistic activism and an explicit feminist critique of reproductive rights.[144] Yet, as the artist underlines by her own refusal, there is no telling whether said action took place or not. In this feminist performance, the arena of action has shifted from the "woman artist" and her body to the no-less-invasive sphere of discourse. Shvarts's performance generates talk about action, agency, responsibility, control, "life," and "choice," as well as intense examination of the artist, her biography, and her body—and an almost frenzied speculation about what an artist who is also a woman may or may not do with it.

All this talk is produced, tellingly, by the very moral and political authorities—or supposed representatives of such authority—seeking to contain it. While Yale University insisted that Shvarts's performance was fiction, other vectors of the press condemned Shvarts for the reality of what she had done. The National Right to Life Committee condemned Shvarts and she received anti-Semitic hate mail that equated her performance with the Holocaust. Even pro-choice groups distanced themselves from Shvarts because her ambiguous performance art had so incensed their opponents that they worried it would work at cross-purposes with their sincere feminist activist aims.[145] This confusion of fiction and fact is at the heart of the "ethically risky" art of what Lambert-Beatty calls "parafiction." Parafiction is an art of "deception."[146] The artist is in on something that remains undisclosed to the public until, shockingly or disappointingly, the truth is revealed. Yet what makes Shvarts's *Untitled (Senior Thesis)* particularly effective as performance art is that it never discloses a truth.[147] Shvarts's performance is less parafictional, presenting fiction as fact so as to play with deceived expectations, than it is in-sincere, to use a term I suggested earlier in discussing Schwarzkogler's work. When treated as in-sincere, rather than mistaken as extremely earnest or just mere fiction, faked, *Untitled (Senior Thesis)* consists in the disturbing discourse it generates.

It asks, without offering an emphatic answer, discomfiting questions about the normative understanding of what constitutes good, proper, and authentic action, or art.

Shvarts's work is, of course, about reproduction and control—specifically, it is about the body of a woman as the site of reproductive processes often controlled by others. Her in-sincere performance thus presents a provocative response to what Lee Edelman has called "heteronormative reproductive futurism."[148] For whatever else may or may not have taken place, the work can be said to "miscarry" the promise of social futurity and economic progress coalesced in the figure of "the Child," around which so much of mainstream politics, and political action, is oriented.[149] Reflecting on a kind of action that could be added to the queer arts of failure, Shvarts remarks, "To miscarry, to carry wrongly—that is what I did."[150] Despite the many righteous tellings and rectifications it provoked, in the mood of in-sincerity and the practice of miscarrying, Shvarts exercises freedom.

wedding

Schwarzkogler's first performance, numbered *1. Aktion* by his friends but that he called *Hochzeit* (Wedding; 1964), was not included in *documenta 5*. The performance has never been discussed in any detail, very likely because it does not fit well within the historiographical framework in which the rest of his work has been situated as *Aktionen*.[151] When *Hochzeit* does appear, it is typically by way of a photograph showing Schwarzkogler, dressed as an ostensible "groom," throwing the contents of a bucket of paint onto the unveiled "bride" (the almost always unnamed Anna Brus), whose dress has been torn open to reveal her breasts (fig. I.20).[152] This moment in the performance serves, of course, to suggest a certain affinity with action painting. It also seems to rehearse a heteronormative expectation of the ceremony alluded to in its title. But when *Hochzeit* is presented in this way, distilled in this single scene, one misses the awkward stumbling and stooping that precede it, as the pair fall down and press themselves together in cramped proximity to the windows and walls of a domestic interior (figs. I.21, I.22). One also misses the many other figures involved in *Hochzeit*.[153] The limited selection of images reproduced from the archive of the performance tends to reinforce expectations of performance art that Schwarzkogler's work in fact undoes.

Consider Schwarzkogler's preparations. *Hochzeit* begins with the arrangement of objects on a large table, many of which are familiar from the long tradition of European still-life painting exhibited in Vienna's Kunsthistorisches Museum: fish, fruit, eggs, a plucked chicken, a kitchen knife, and scissors, but also, far less conventionally, gauze, glasses of brightly colored pigments, an electric hot plate, and a blowtorch. In stark contrast with the approach of both the action painter and the body artist, Schwarzkogler engages the tradition of still-life painting by painstakingly composing these materials (plate 1, fig. I.23).

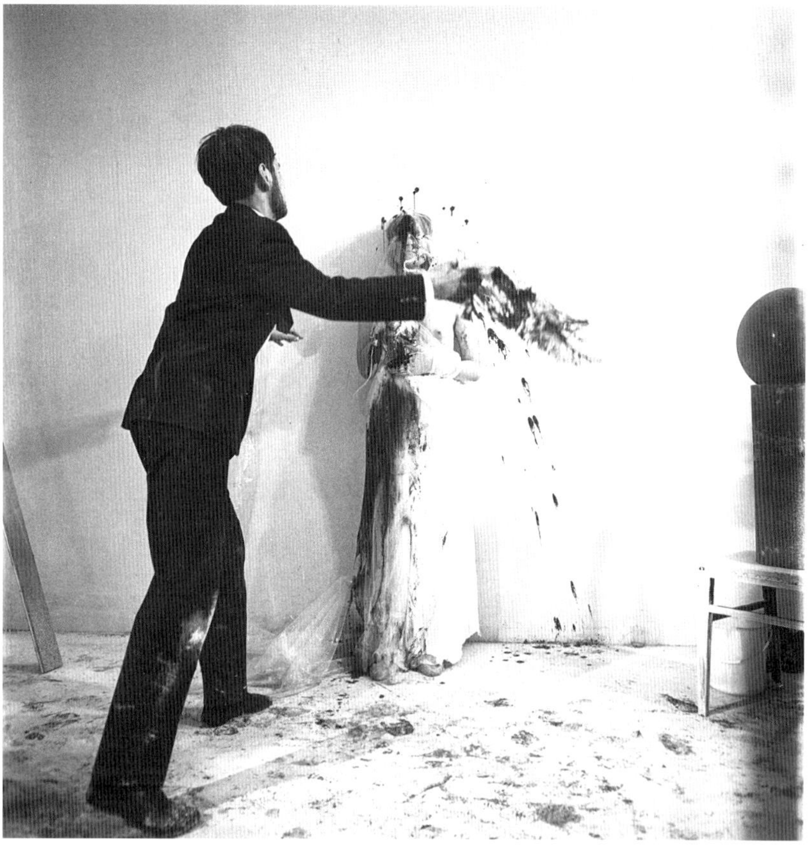

Figures I.20–I.21. Rudolf Schwarzkogler with Anna Brus and Heinz Cibulka, *Hochzeit* (Wedding), 1965. Photograph by Ludwig Hoffenreich. mumok – Museum moderner Kunst Stiftung Ludwig Wien, Leihgabe der Österreichischen Ludwig-Stiftung. © Rudolf Schwarzkogler; digital image © mumok – Museum moderner Kunst Stiftung Ludwig Wien.

His compositions, messy though they may be, evoke and transform the genre of *vanitas*. If there is indeed "death" in Schwarzkogler's work, then it is in the transience, fragility, and vulnerability disclosed in these still lifes. Perishable materials are combined in figurations that are as precise as they are formless. Dead fish are cut open, filled with flowers and granular pigments, tenderly wrapped in gauze, aligned with sheets of colored plastic, and nailed to a wall. A pear is sliced, its flesh prodded, and saturated with opaque liquid (see fig. I.1). The dead chicken is sprinkled with blue paint and wrapped in linen; an egg broken, penetrated with an enema syringe, and filled with paint. An animal brain is spread out on the table, covered in colorful powders, doused in lighter fluid and set on fire.

This series of material still lifes has a counterpart in the figural relations to which the performance turns. Anna Brus, who has been lingering around its edges with Günter Brus (her soon-to-be husband), is guided by Schwarzkogler to a spot within a window niche concealed by a hanging cloth, behind which she disappears. Using scissors awkwardly to cut out a flap, Schwarzkogler dribbles paint onto the opening in the cloth from the enema syringe and reveals Anna Brus's face (plate 2; see also fig. I.2). In her mouth, the "bride"

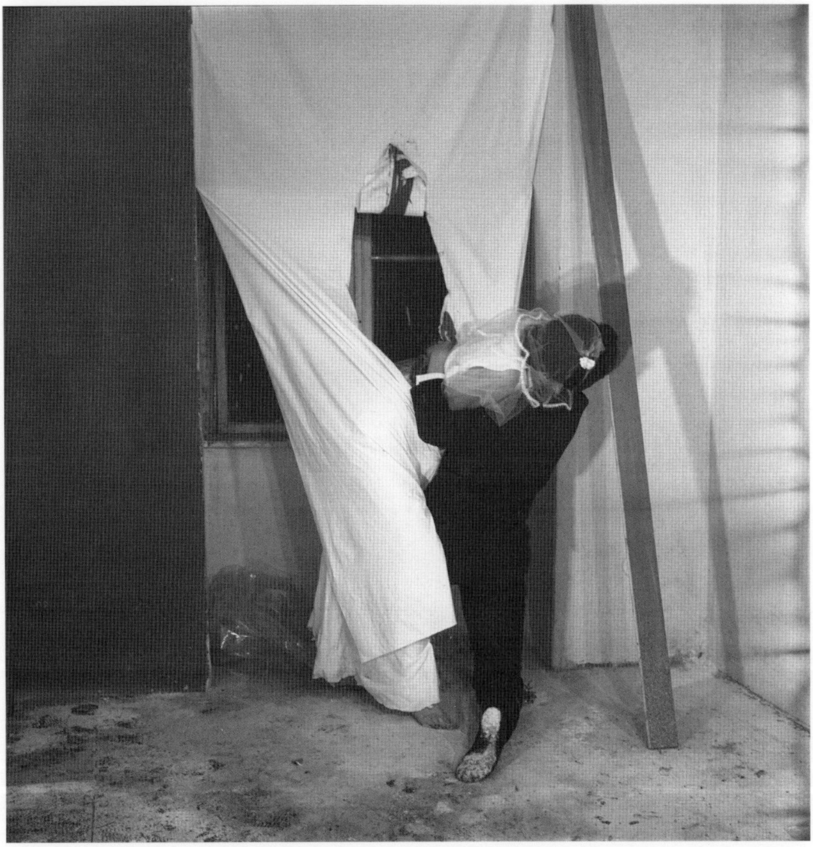

holds a sponge, which absorbs the paint as it seeps downward. She looks out deadpan (plate 3; see also fig. 1.17).

Anna Brus steps aside and Heinz Cibulka approaches Schwarzkogler. It is Cibulka's apartment in which the performance is taking place. Recall that Cibulka's body will later be mistaken for Schwarzkogler's in the *Aktionen* exhibited at *documenta 5*. In *Hochzeit*, he binds Schwarzkogler's head in gauze (plate 4). Schwarzkogler in turn binds Cibulka, douses him in paint, and proceeds to bind Cibulka and Anna Brus together with loose lengths of gauzy fabric, reciting his previous material compositions (figs. I.24, I.25). A paper crown placed on Cibulka's head is lit on fire. Instead of distinct individuals entering into a "lawful" relation, these figures are bound to one another in the sense that one binds a wound. Touchingly composed, the three figures begin something like a dance (fig. I.26). Throughout *Hochzeit*, it is easy to mistake who the "artist" is, who the "bride" or "groom," or even who is taking whom.

In contrast to the impression conveyed by the privileged image of Schwarzkogler as action painter (see fig. I.20), *Hochzeit* involves a different comportment to the formal and material conventions of painting. These conventions are connected in the performance to the queer inclination of Schwarzkogler's

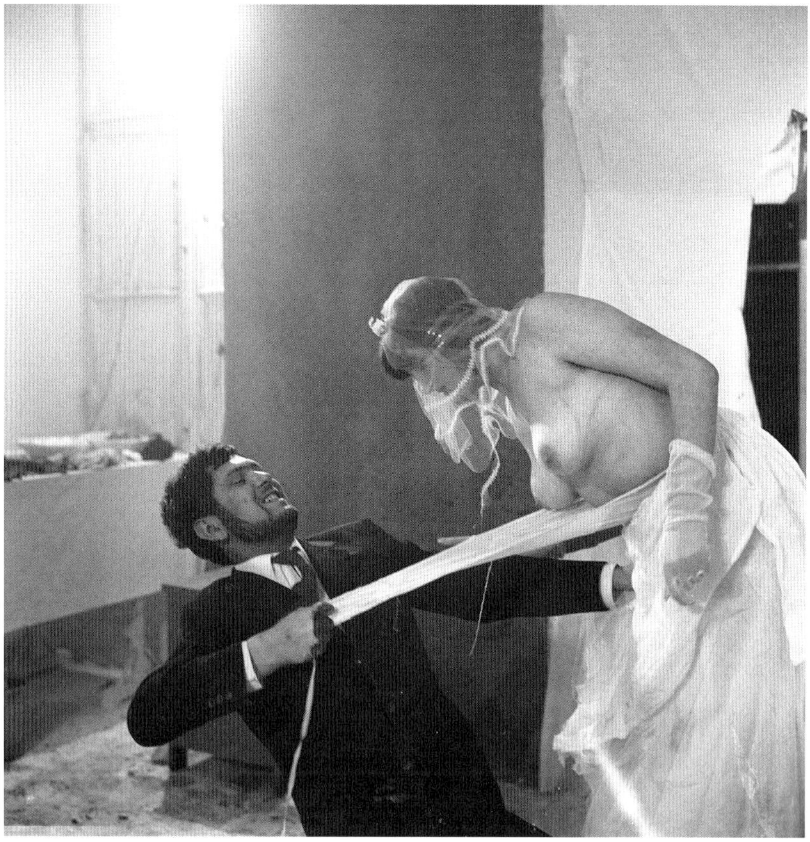

Figures I.22–I.23. Rudolf Schwarzkogler with Anna Brus and Heinz Cibulka, *Hochzeit* (Wedding), 1965. Photograph by Ludwig Hoffenreich. mumok – Museum moderner Kunst Stiftung Ludwig Wien, Leihgabe der Österreichischen Ludwig-Stiftung. © Rudolf Schwarzkogler; digital image © mumok – Museum moderner Kunst Stiftung Ludwig Wien.

work, which the favored photograph similarly covers over. I do not mean in the first instance to say that it is a matter of his work being "explicitly about queer themes" or about individuals who identify as queer, although Schwarzkogler's biography gives reasons to do so.[154] What is queer about Schwarzkogler's work is his formal practice of composition, which privileges—in an all-but-unrecognizable way—figuration rather than abstraction, and relation rather than independence.[155] His performances bring figures into relation in queer weddings, through the unsettling use of familiar materials drawn from the history of painting and from everyday life. His compositions operate within a tradition of social and artistic conventions that govern seemly relations between upstanding figures, epitomized in the normative ritual of the wedding (*Hochzeit*). These are then probed and prodded, with violence and with humor, in ways both tender and grotesque.

The queer inclination of Schwarzkogler's performance art may explain its persistent mistaking. The myth of his spectacular suicide registers anxieties generated by performances that fail to reproduce the heteronormative aspirations of art and life inscribed in the action paradigm.[156] A wedding, after all, is not just any ceremony; it is the ritual that culminates in the most paradigmatic of performatives: "I do." It is the celebration of felicitous action—action that,

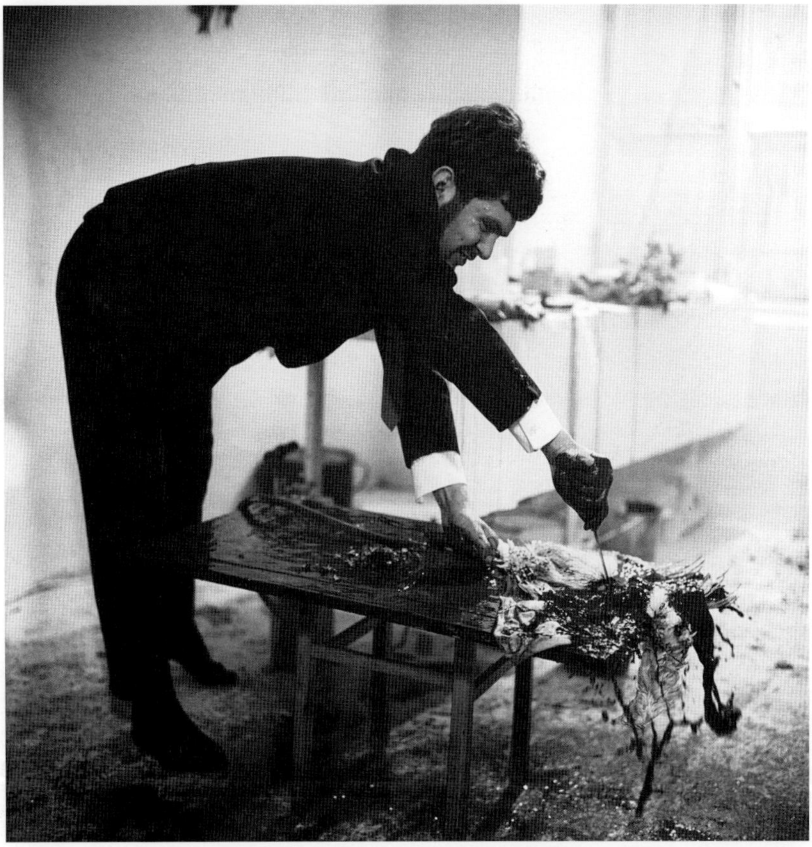

carried out in the right way and under the right circumstances, forcefully and happily formalizes a fundamental bond of ethical life.[157] *Hochzeit*, in contrast, unsettles the positive affect traditionally, or supposedly, associated with this most officiously cherished of ceremonies, especially in conservative Catholic Austria of the 1960s.[158] Evincing a melancholy humor, the performance elides the distinction between felicitous and infelicitous, failed and successful, performances. *Hochzeit* is in-felicitous. Instead of ceremoniously affirming the positions that construct a certain vision of "the good life," the various figures can be seen to undo them—and to be undone.

In-action is disposed to be taken for the explicit action it fails to be—and would perhaps prefer to have nothing to do with. This book is about assembling a vocabulary that better addresses, while acknowledging how difficult it remains to account for, work like Schwarzkogler's. In so doing, I am not trying to redeem an incidental chapter of art history from scandal or obscurity, or to claim that Viennese performance art is more significant or more radical than has been acknowledged. Rather, I am interested in carefully attending to what little is there. *In-action* traces my efforts to do justice to the uncomfortable, sometimes tedious, and often unsettling positions habitually mistaken and disparaged in accounts of artistic and political life.

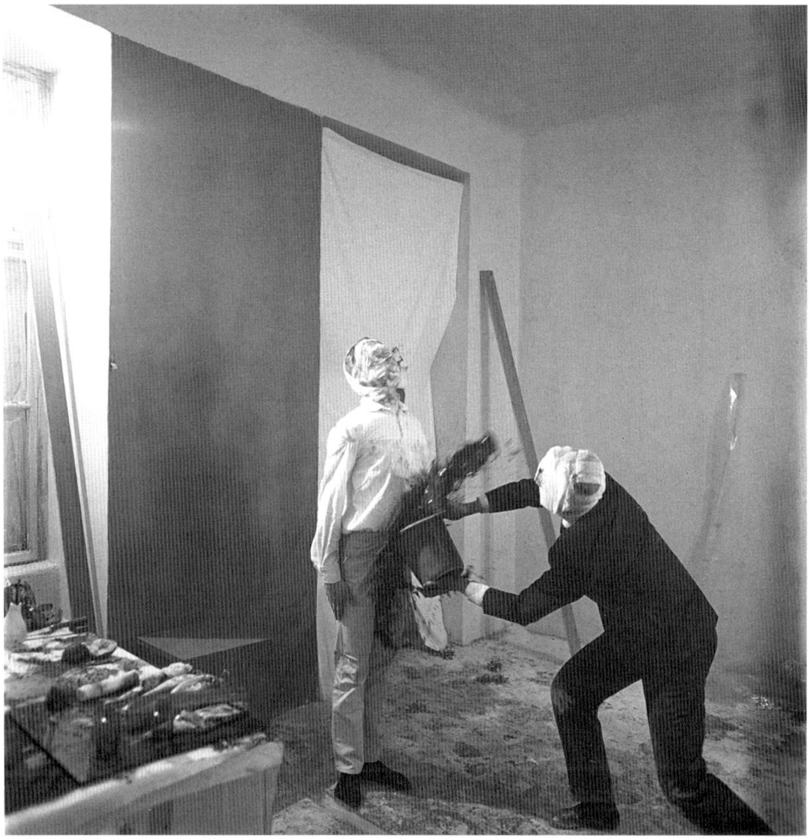

Figures I.24–I.25. Rudolf Schwarzkogler with Anna Brus and Heinz Cibulka, *Hochzeit* (Wedding), 1965. Photograph by Ludwig Hoffenreich. mumok – Museum moderner Kunst Stiftung Ludwig Wien, Leihgabe der Österreichischen Ludwig-Stiftung. © Rudolf Schwarzkogler; digital image © mumok – Museum moderner Kunst Stiftung Ludwig Wien.

Chapters of In-action

What would it look like to write performance art history with regard to figures involved in the action, yet who only ambivalently take part? Chapter 1 addresses this question of method by looking at two seldom-named figures, each of whom poses an objection to the action in which she participates. Anna Brus performs throughout the 1960s with each of the four main protagonists of Viennese Actionism. But she is disinclined to call herself an artist, or an actionist, or a Feminist Actionist. Anna Brus's disinclination to take center stage contrasts with the insulting figure of Hanel Koeck. While Anna Brus is involved, but refuses to be so entirely, Koeck takes part in the performance to a disconcerting extreme, embracing the gendered structures of action to the point of travesty. When acknowledged at all, both figures are considered, even in feminist art history, to be simply objectified. But the objections of Anna Brus and Hanel Koeck have provocative consequences for thinking about the misogyny of Viennese Actionism and its reception. From positions implicated within the action, they undo postural stereotypes that performance art inherits from the history of painting.

In both art historical and political accounts of postwar Austria, the infa-

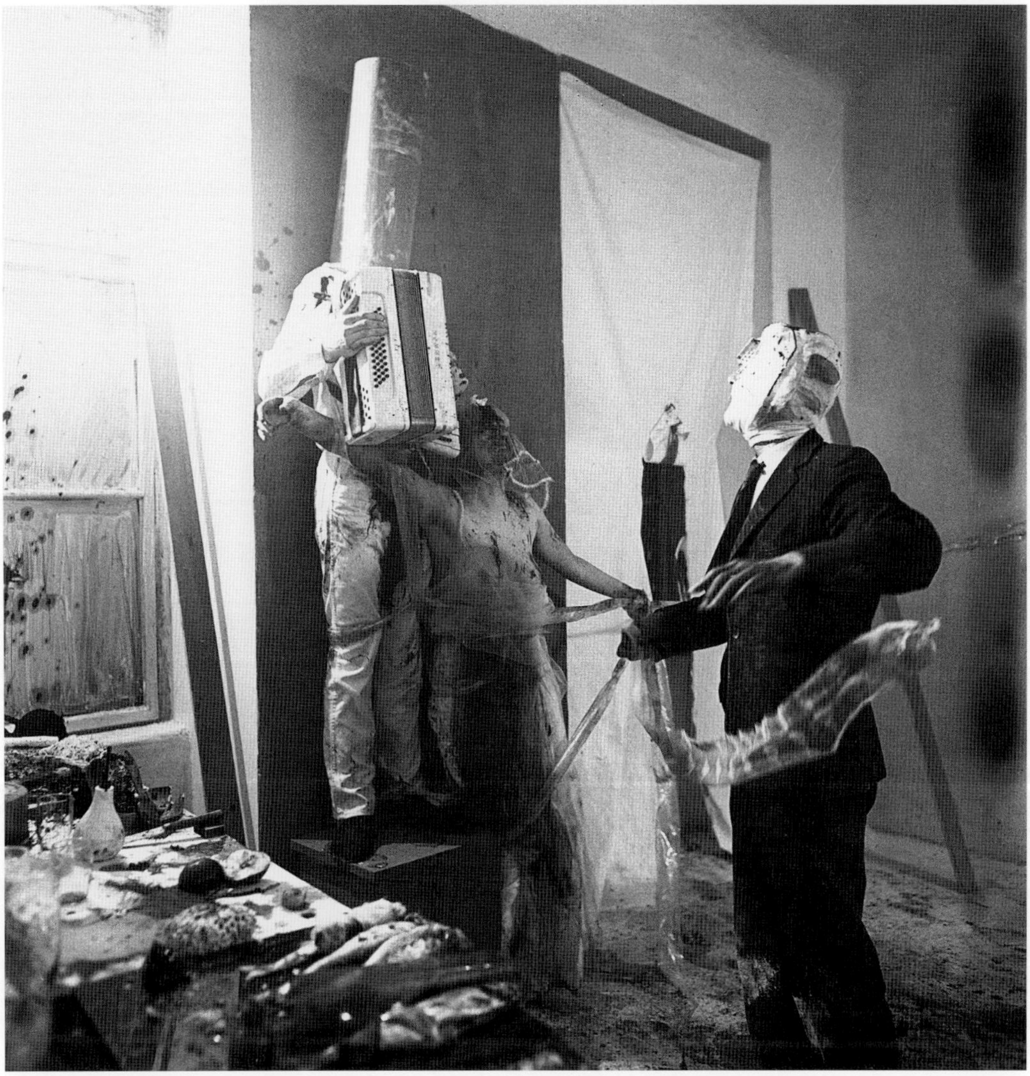

mous event *Kunst und Revolution* (Art and revolution) has come to stand for the failed and short-lived version of Vienna's 1968. This failure, I argue, was precisely the point: *Kunst und Revolution* produced a positive display of impotence in art, and in politics. Chapter 2 provides a deflationary assessment of the "incident," a term I draw from Günter Brus's depositions to the police. Instead of using documentary and archival material to trace *Kunst und Revolution* back to the "real" performance, its protagonists, and their intentions at a precise moment in time, I survey the media shitstorm it generated. The proliferation of anxious and censorious reactions by self-professed guardians of public morality presents a picture of the state of art and politics in Austria at the time that is at once ugly and hateful. Nowhere is this more evident than in the response to what I propose is the domestic continuation of *Kunst und Revolution*, staged for a Viennese newspaper by Anna Brus and Günter Brus with

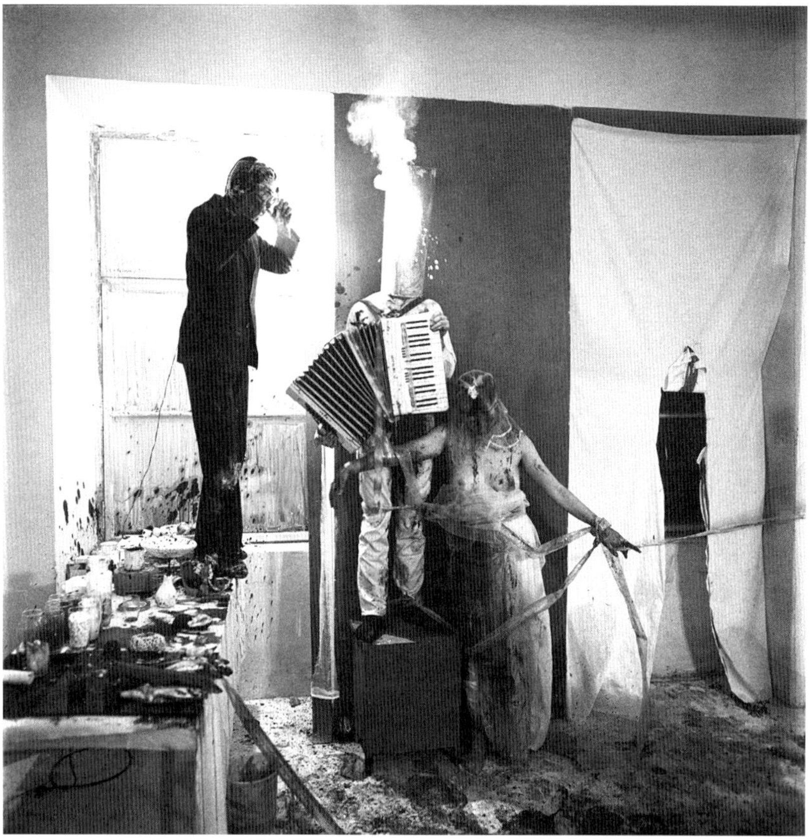

Figure I.26. Rudolf Schwarzkogler with Anna Brus and Heinz Cibulka, *Hochzeit* (Wedding), 1965. Photograph by Ludwig Hoffenreich. mumok – Museum moderner Kunst Stiftung Ludwig Wien, Leihgabe der Österreichischen Ludwig-Stiftung. © Rudolf Schwarzkogler; digital image © mumok – Museum moderner Kunst Stiftung Ludwig Wien.

their baby in their home. This chapter thus pairs a reading of the public performance and outcry with one of the politics of private space and family life, especially motherhood.

While chapter 2 addresses the social and institutional contexts that shaped performance art in Vienna, chapter 3 looks closely at the work of Günter Brus, situating it within wider art historical debates about painting and performance art. Whereas Brus has been duly celebrated as the inventor of body art for placing his body in the center of the action, I argue that his performance art involves an immanent exploration of the dispositive of painting, understood as a historical set of techniques for rendering the human figure in pictorial space. In contrast with the expressive and emancipatory aims of action painting embodied in the figure of Pollock, to whom he was explicitly responding, Brus's techniques of "self-painting" and "body-analysis" painstakingly explore positions of inarticulacy and constraint, often in the artist's home and in collaboration with Anna Brus. Relating his performances to the operations of the formless, I argue that Brus pursues the figuration of bad form. His performance art insists on precarious positions otherwise ignored in the dismissal of painterly figuration as a viable avant-garde strategy.

The final chapter claims the work of Ingrid Wiener for the history of performance art. Wiener began weaving in Vienna in the 1960s and shares her artistic training with her good friend VALIE EXPORT. In their distinctive comportments to the tradition of weaving, the two women present an impasse in feminist art history. VALIE EXPORT abandons weaving and repudiates its association with "women's work" to become a Feminist Actionist. Wiener, in contrast, immerses herself in the relation between weaving and care work in a practice she describes as "weaving on and on." Her tapestry collaborations with the Swiss German artist Dieter Roth, which took place over long distances and many years, provide occasion to rethink the temporality of performance art, the definition of artistic labor, and the character of collaboration. Drawing on feminist ethics of care, I argue that through weaving, Wiener tends to her fraught friendship with Roth in tapestries that archive the everyday life and labor that go into such relations. After all, weaving, like caring, is an activity that is not usually accorded the dignity of action and is easily mistaken for mere passivity.

1 Objections: Hanel Koeck's Insult, Anna Brus's Disinclination

Accounts of Viennese Actionism typically revolve around the performances of four main protagonists: Günter Brus, Otto Muehl, Hermann Nitsch, and Rudolf Schwarzkogler. Whether defending or condemning their art, Austrian and international art histories alike have sought to establish the extremity of these so-called actionists' work by narrating the "radical protest" and "upheaval" it caused.[1] Seen from this perspective, which aligns with a tendency in the study of performance art more generally, the actionists are positioned at the center of the action, as its agents and instigators. The significance of their work is defined, in turn, through an account of their actions. This chapter proposes a different methodology. What would it look like to write performance art history with attention to figures who are involved in the action, yet who only ambivalently take part? I am led to this question by observing the performances of two often unnamed figures who appear with each of the protagonists of Viennese Actionism throughout the 1960s: Anna Brus and Hanel Koeck.

This chapter reintroduces Viennese Actionism with an eye toward these two figures, for much of what is troubling and provocative about Viennese Actionism lies in the difficulty of their performances. In diametrically opposing ways, I argue, Anna Brus and Hanel Koeck object to the actions in which they are typically taken to be passively submitting. Which is to say, in performances of what is taken to be their objectification, Anna Brus and Hanel Koeck object.[2] If there is indeed "radical protest" or "upheaval" in so-called Viennese Actionism, then this owes in no small part to the objections within the action registered by their figures. Even as they are ignored or disparaged in the reception, it is, paradoxically, the irritation produced by the objections of Anna Brus and Hanel Koeck that first solicits attention to, and maintains the interest in, Viennese Actionism as performance art.

Although their contributions are rarely acknowledged, it is no exaggeration to say that there would be no Viennese Actionism without these two women.

For nearly a decade, with every one of the four protagonists, Anna Brus performed with characteristic impassivity. Hers is a recurring yet persistently unremarked-upon figure throughout the archive of Viennese Actionism. For her part, Hanel Koeck figured punctually in a culminating moment of its history. Her few performances with Nitsch and Muehl are taken as evidence of its most egregious and misogynist excesses, making hers the most overdetermined position in Viennese Actionism. In writing about Anna Brus and Hanel Koeck, in considering them in an art history of which they are already integral yet disregarded, my interest is not motivated by the conviction that either is a neglected Viennese Actionist. I am not making the case that, on the basis of their performances, they should be celebrated as actionists in their own right. On the contrary, I am interested in articulating their respective objections without forcing them to conform to the reductive idiom of the action paradigm.

In adopting this approach, I follow Anna Brus's reluctant lead. When asked recently if "she herself would count as an artist," Anna Brus demurred: "I would not want to make use of the word artist. Let's put it this way: I was a good assistant [*eine gute Mitarbeiterin*] to the actionists."[3] Anna Brus is disinclined to count herself as an artist—or as an actionist, or for that matter as a Feminist Actionist. I take her objection to be definitive of her involvement in Viennese Actionism. Within disparate performances, her unassuming presence and disarming look subtly unsettle the arena of action. Without drawing attention to her own person, she nevertheless disrupts the scene. She takes part and even "works with" (*mitarbeiten*) the actionists while at the same time registering her disinclination to do so. I want to respect Anna Brus's disinclination. This is challenging, for it means attending to Anna Brus while resisting the temptation to insist on a positive or affirmative position for her in the art history in which she so ambivalently figures.

In contrast with Anna Brus's disinclination, Hanel Koeck's performances present an altogether different objection—the insult. Koeck appears in just one performance with Muehl and two with Nitsch within the short period of October 1969 to January 1970. Anticipating her own erasure from the art history of Viennese Actionism, Koeck wanted to be named in her performances and articulates her assertive entrance into the action: "I went into it very deliberately" (*Ich bin ganz bewusst da hinein gegangen*). Her arrival in the arena of Viennese Actionism is abrupt, perverse, and utterly obscene. When asked about her role in these performances, Koeck claims *Mitverantwortlichkeit*—literally, "coresponsibility," or, as I would like to suggest, "complicity."[4] In altogether objectionable scenarios, she assumes stereotypical roles of objectification and objects by deliberately, shamelessly, and excessively engaging in the action—to the point that it becomes something else and, to judge from its reception, something altogether more disturbing. Rather than assaulting misogyny, Koeck insults it.

Why, despite Koeck's strenuous efforts to assert her role and her position in the history of Viennese Actionism, has her name been effaced even as images of her body continue to be disparaged? What kind of close looking is needed to do justice to her difficult and indeed demanding figure? And with regard to Anna Brus, how does performance art history take shape when it attends to gestures of reticence, to reluctance to take part in or even become a part of art history? Can performance art history account for such figures as Koeck and Anna Brus, who are ubiquitous in the action, yet persistently overlooked—or just mistaken on account of their provocative passivity? It is my wager that responding to these challenges, and responding to the objections of Hanel Koeck and Anna Brus, has consequences not only for Viennese Actionism but for performance art historiography tout court.[5]

Careful consideration of Anna Brus's disinclination and Hanel Koeck's insult provides a way to address the misogyny of Viennese Actionism in a manner that respects, rather than speaks for or disparages, the performances of women who actually took part. Viennese Actionism has long been criticized for its misogyny. Already in 1974, in an early feminist study of performance art, Lea Vergine diagnosed "the Austrians"—by which she means the four main protagonists of Viennese Actionism—with "true and proper gynophobia" and condemned their "ferocious misogyny."[6] The same year, in his anthology of "total art," Adrian Henri named Austria as "home of the most extreme forms of violence in art," noting of "Nitsch and the others" that "when women appear in their work, they are used as props, always debased and humiliated."[7] These international art critical perspectives tacitly reiterate earlier responses to Viennese Actionism in German-speaking spaces, including a book on the "phenomenology of religion" published in 1964 claiming that the work of Muehl and Nitsch revivified "satanic cult and black mass," evoking the ritualistic sacrifice of virgins, babies, and lambs.[8] A fascination with Viennese Actionism as a "dark" and criminally misogynistic art has persisted ever since.[9] If, however, the treatment of women by the protagonists of Viennese Actionism has rightly come under critical scrutiny, then the misogyny invested in the discourse of this reception must also be noted. For even feminist critics rarely take "the women" involved in Viennese Actionism to be more than "models" or "passive actresses" in the hands of the male artists who "use" them.[10] It is to this objective that Hanel Koeck and Anna Brus, in different ways, object.

Even more recent efforts focused on "the feminine in Viennese Actionism" or, with regard to Anna Brus, "her life with the Viennese Actionists," operate with the stark distinction between "the actions" of the four main so-called actionists and the adjacent passive role of "the women" who performed with them.[11] In the context of the exhibition *Amor, Psyche, Action—Vienna: The Feminine in Viennese Actionism* (2012–2013), a number of women who performed with the actionists were named but remained excluded from the index of artists in the catalog and occupied a strictly misprized position in the art historiographical discussion. "The women," as Pilar Parcerisas writes, present iterations of "the manipulated feminine nude"—"used" by the "Viennese Actionists."[12] Even after interviewing some of the "nameless nymphs and unappreciated assistants," including Hanel Koeck and Anna Brus, Almuth Spiegler emphasizes that "their role in the art was nevertheless primarily passive." She concludes, "There simply does not exist an art historically forgotten, consequent, and independent [*eigenständige*] woman artist from the Actionist-circle, like a Carolee Schneemann in the USA."[13]

This is not how I see it. To be sure, there is no forgotten "Carolee Schneemann" to recuperate from the archive of Viennese Actionism. But any art historical method that upholds the reductive dichotomy of action and passivity will recapitulate the objective of the action paradigm, along with its ingrained expectations of self-assertion, emancipatory action, and autonomy. Much might be gained for a feminist historiography of performance art by shifting the focus from "the artist"—specifically the artist as actionist—to other figures, especially to difficult insulting figures like Hanel Koeck, and to those who, like Anna Brus, only uncomfortably or reluctantly appear, disinclined to enter into this history.

My approach revisits the archive of Viennese Actionism to look at performances not in terms of actions carried out by its named protagonists but as composed of many differently comported figures. This approach attends to figures *in*—instead of the artists *of*—performance art, troubling the stereotypes that this work is seen as rehearsing. I try to look at Hanel Koeck and Anna Brus without ascribing either an explicit "feminist" stance, without claiming that either overtly resists her "use" (or today condemns it in retrospect), and without claiming that either ultimately emancipates herself as a woman, or an artist, through her own form of actionism or activism. Objectionable though this may be, neither can be hailed as an exemplary Feminist Actionist. But as I hope to show, this is not to say that their performances have nothing to contribute to our understanding of feminism and of art history.

The Insulting of Hanel Koeck

When the misogyny and "gynophobia" of Viennese Actionism are condemned, Hanel Koeck's body is taken as evidence. Close-up photographs of her performances with Nitsch, lens trained on her naked body, often cropped to show just her genital zone, have circulated widely since the early 1970s in documentations of *Aktionskunst* and anthologies of performance art (fig. 1.1).[14] The fascination with these images owes undoubtedly to how they rehearse a stereotype of the "woman's body" as that which is used and objectified. Alongside the mistaking of Schwarzkogler's castration-suicide, the fiction of Koeck's "wounded" body has ingrained itself in the reception of Viennese Actionism. But where many feminist critics see only violation, I see Koeck as inserting herself violently into Viennese Actionism. Koeck's conspicuous yet brief appearance around the end of 1969 marks the intensification of Viennese

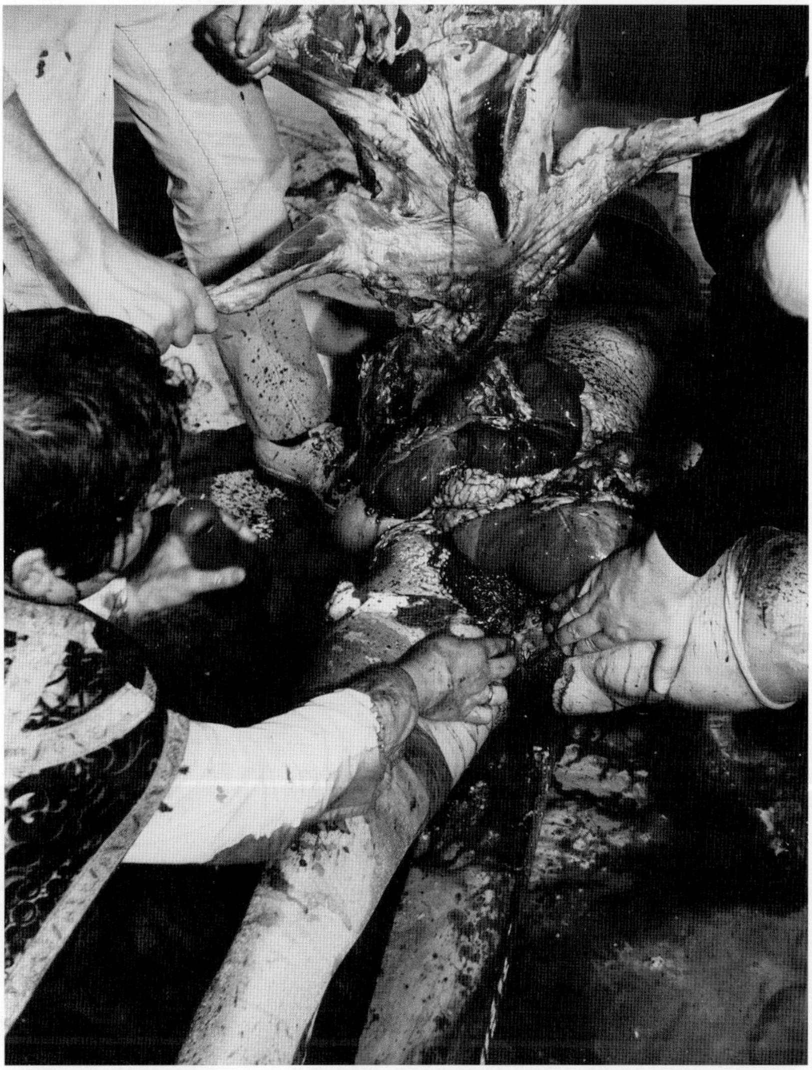

Figure 1.1. Hermann Nitsch with Hanel Koeck, *Maria Empfängnis - Aktion mit Hanel Koeck, 31. Aktion* (Immaculate Conception: Action with Hanel Koeck, Action 31), 1969. Photograph by Ludwig Hoffenreich printed in the artist's edition: Hermann Nitsch, *Das Orgien Mysterien Theater - Frühe Aktionen; 20. Aktion, 1965; 29. Aktion, 1968; 30. Aktion, 1969; 31. Aktion, 1969*, 1982. Silkscreen on cloth-bound case, photographs, blood on canvas on paper card, 84.5 × 66 × 3.5 cm. © Hanel Koeck © Hermann Nitsch; Courtesy of Archivio Conz, Berlin; digital image: Giorgia Palmisano and Giulia Baresi.

Actionism—and its undoing. In my view, after Koeck performs with Nitsch, his work becomes little more than spectacular yet boring ritual, and after she performs with Muehl, his work loses all artistic relevance. Recalling that it was only in 1970 that the movement earned its name, it is no overstatement to say that Viennese Actionism took shape around Koeck's body—and was, in turn, exhausted by her. Ironically, this has only left Koeck's role in performance art history all the more effaced.

Consider Hermann Nitsch's *31. Aktion* (Action 31), also referred to as *Maria Empfängnis* (Immaculate Conception; figs. 1.2, 1.3, 1.4). It was staged in Munich on December 8, 1969, the day celebrated in Catholicism as the Feast of the Immaculate Conception and still observed as a national holiday in Austria. Nitsch appears dressed in the embroidered tunic of a high priest. A woman, undressed, but for undergarments and hosiery, is bound to a cross on the floor.

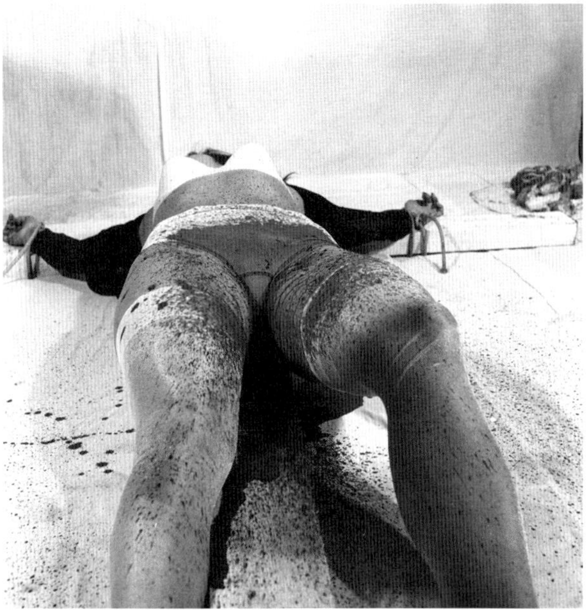

Figure 1.2. Hermann Nitsch with Hanel Koeck, *Maria Empfängnis – Aktion mit Hanel Koeck, 31. Aktion* (Immaculate Conception: Action with Hanel Koeck, Action 31), 1969. Photograph by Ludwig Hoffenreich. © Hanel Koeck © Hermann Nitsch; mumok – Museum moderner Kunst Stiftung Ludwig Wien, Gift of Hermann Nitsch, 2007; digital image © mumok – Museum moderner Kunst Stiftung Ludwig Wien.

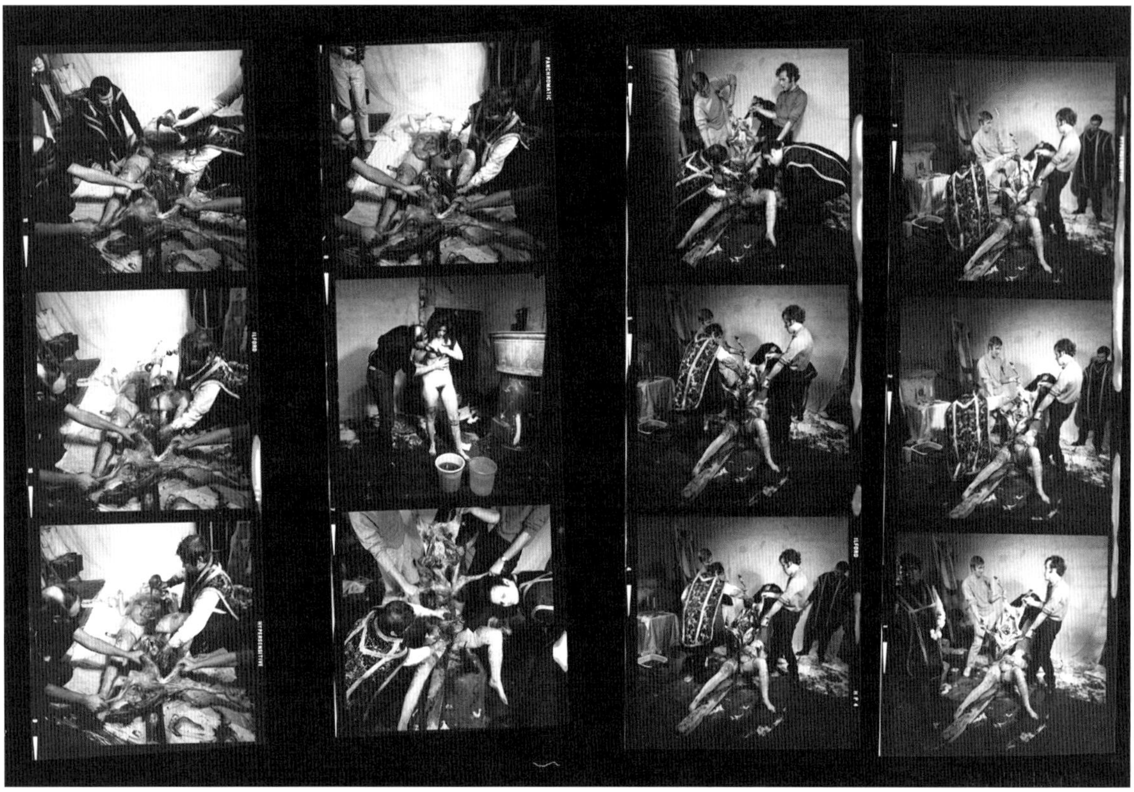

Figure 1.3. Hermann Nitsch with Hanel Koeck, *Maria Empfängnis – Aktion mit Hanel Koeck, 31. Aktion* (Immaculate Conception: Action with Hanel Koeck, Action 31), 1969. Photographic negatives by Ludwig Hoffenreich. © Hanel Koeck © Hermann Nitsch; mumok – Museum moderner Kunst Stiftung Ludwig Wien, Gift of Ph. Konzett, 2007; digital image © mumok – Museum moderner Kunst Stiftung Ludwig Wien.

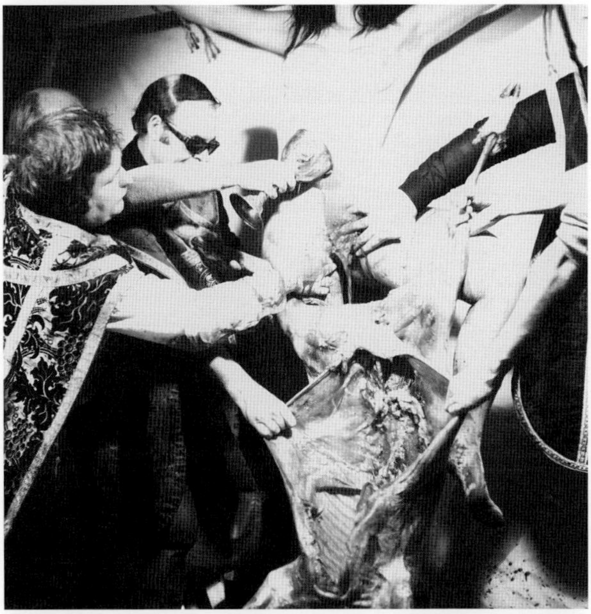

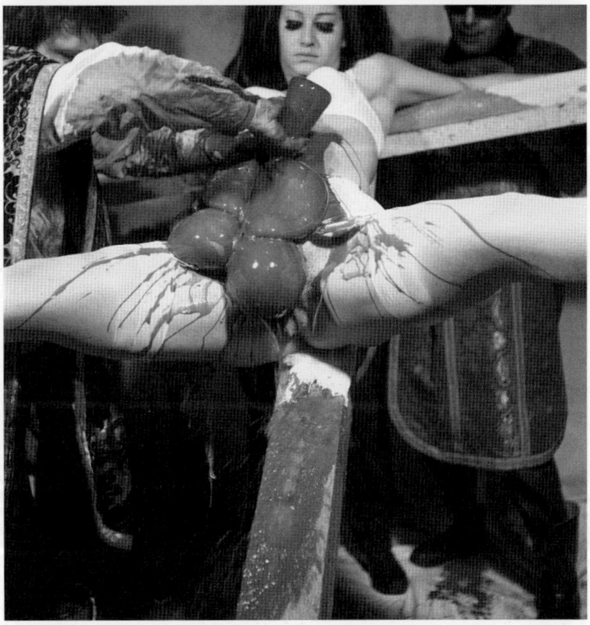

Figures 1.4–1.5. Hermann Nitsch with Hanel Koeck, *Maria Empfängnis - Aktion mit Hanel Koeck, 31. Aktion* (Immaculate Conception: Action with Hanel Koeck, Action 31), 1969. Photograph by Ludwig Hoffenreich. © Hanel Koeck © Hermann Nitsch; mumok - Museum moderner Kunst Stiftung Ludwig Wien, Gift of Hermann Nitsch, 2007; digital image © mumok - Museum moderner Kunst Stiftung Ludwig Wien.

Rarely named, this woman is Koeck. While the title of the performance cites the purity of the Virgin Mary and her preservation "free from all stain of original sin," the performance travesties this image and its tradition.[15] Blood is poured into Koeck's mouth; organs are removed from the nearby carcass of a lamb, manhandled, and piled on her body. Her remaining clothing is stripped away by Nitsch and his entourage of at least eight other men, who then hoist her around on the cross and leer at her body, several of them documenting the action with their cameras.[16] In some of the most disturbing images of the performance, one sees how they all press closely around her, holding down her arms, shoulders, and thighs, spreading open her legs to press the torn-up flesh of the lamb not only onto but into her. Her labia are indistinguishable from that flesh.

Now, try to consider this not simply as "a Nitsch performance." Other aspects invite attention. Koeck looks down her body at what is happening (figs. 1.5, 1.6). She opens her labia herself.[17] Nitsch reenters the scene wearing a crown of roses and a strap-on dildo and—the phrase suggests itself—fucks her as she is held splayed on the cross (fig. 1.7). Koeck is calm and still, her breathing amplified by a microphone, her expression vague—and I would venture to say, anticipating the indignation of some readers, a tiny bit amused.[18] She takes pleasure in it. At times she grimaces, at times she grins from ear to ear. The men, captured in their intense proximity to her body, concentrate their gazes and camera objectives intently on Koeck's vaginal zone.[19] Koeck presides, raised up against the wall on the cross. And toward the end, it is Koeck who wears the strap-on, and Nitsch who takes it in his mouth while a dark liquid is poured over him from above (fig. 1.8). Finally, deposed, in a tussle on the floor, Koeck holds down Nitsch's face in the carcass of the lamb (fig. 1.9). Koeck, with painted fingernails, presses him down forcefully.

However one looks at them, these are disconcerting images. For Amelia Jones, they are "horrifying." Jones needs to look at only one photograph in order to claim that Nitsch's performance "enacts misogyny." Describing in visceral terms what she takes the performance to stand for, Jones writes: "A woman's body is ripped open at the crotch, internal organs visible, a large shaft penetrates her vaginal canal, now a muscle stripped of its bodily surroundings."[20] From Jones's perspective, the performance thus participates in the long history of deadly violence against women, culminating in a shocking spectacle of rape and evisceration. In the face of the continuity of this violence and well-founded concerns about the relation between a misogynist tradition of graphic imagery and the expendability of women's bodies and lives, Jones's outrage is altogether understandable.[21]

Nonetheless, she fails to acknowledge how this performance of "immaculate conception" is explicitly set up to upset hallowed iconographies belonging to a long history that sanctifies unconsenting impregnation and motherhood. Nitsch, who had no qualms about playing God, is concerned in this performance with a ritualistic travesty of traditional religious forms. And Koeck is in on it. Indeed, it is Koeck who gives Nitsch's spectacle its unrelenting edge. Koeck's role would be clearer for many viewers if institutions like mumok – Museum moderner Kunst in Vienna did not truncate the full title of the performance.[22] As the two of them agreed, and as it is used by Nitsch in some of his own publications, the proper title is *Maria Empfängnis – Aktion mit Hanel Koeck*.[23] Koeck also holds artistic rights to the work, and I reproduce the images with her permission.

While the second half of the full title of the performance emphasizes that

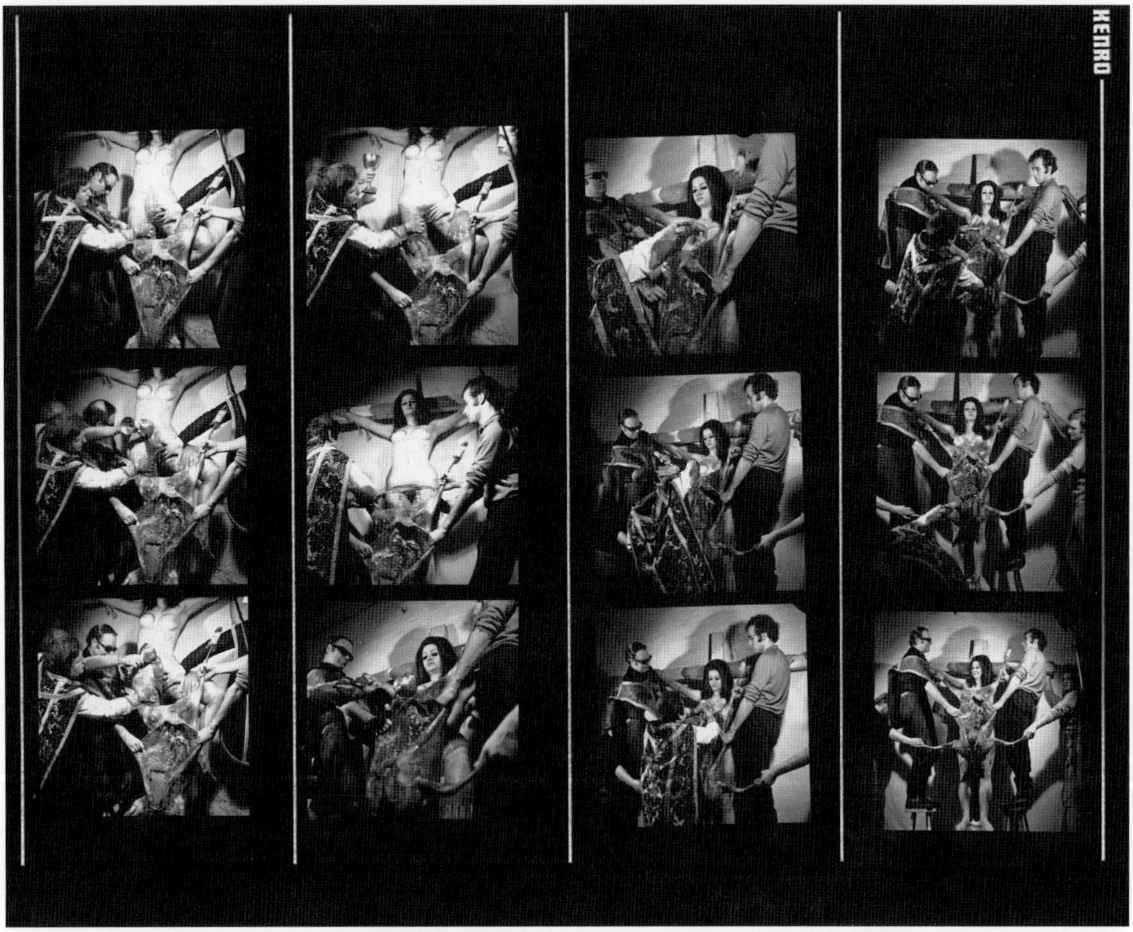

it is an "action with Hanel Koeck," the first half refers to the Catholic dogma that affirms the sinlessness of the "Son of God" by attesting not only to his own immaculate conception in Mary's womb but also to Mary's immaculate conception in her mother, Anne. When depicted in altarpieces like the one of the Roman Catholic parish church of the Immaculate Conception in Flachau, or in the large paintings of Rubens favored during the Hapsburg Empire, the iconography of the Immaculate Conception presents Mary's delicate figure balanced on a vaporous cloud, aloft a fragile orb or sickle moon, often threatened by a snake, with her hands supplicating or raised piously, her look serene, dispassionate, yet touched. An allegory in the Belvedere Collection in Vienna seems to show God himself, having orchestrated this impregnation with a little wand, being delivered the newborn Child from the arms of an angel (fig. 1.10). The phrase "immaculate conception" thus refers to Mary's "dual aspect" of "maidenly purity and motherly love," conveyed from on high.[24] The performance *Maria Empfängnis - Aktion mit Hanel Koeck* renders concrete the vulgar "truth" of immaculate conception, which is upheld in patriarchal heteronormative everyday life, especially in Catholic Austria.[25]

Figure 1.6. Hermann Nitsch with Hanel Koeck, *Maria Empfängnis - Aktion mit Hanel Koeck, 31. Aktion* (Immaculate Conception: Action with Hanel Koeck, Action 31), 1969. Photographic negatives by Ludwig Hoffenreich. © Hanel Koeck © Hermann Nitsch; mumok - Museum moderner Kunst Stiftung Ludwig Wien, Gift of Hermann Nitsch, 2007; digital image © mumok - Museum moderner Kunst Stiftung Ludwig Wien.

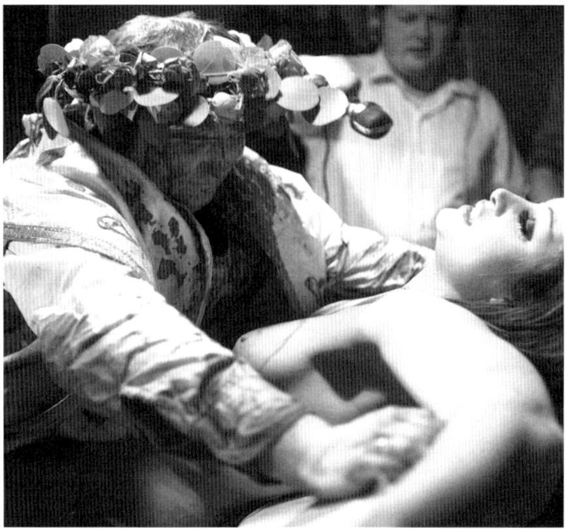

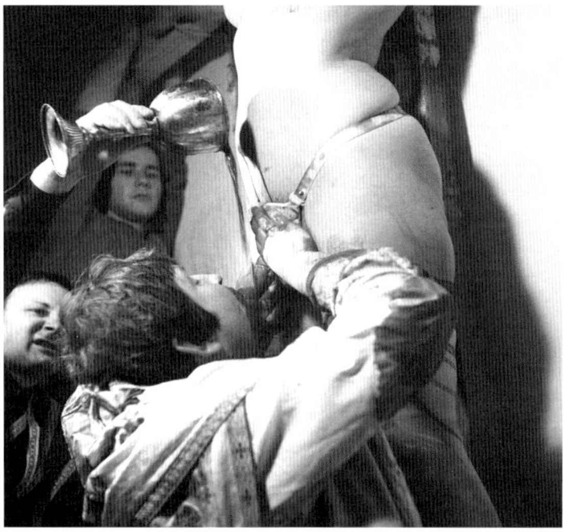

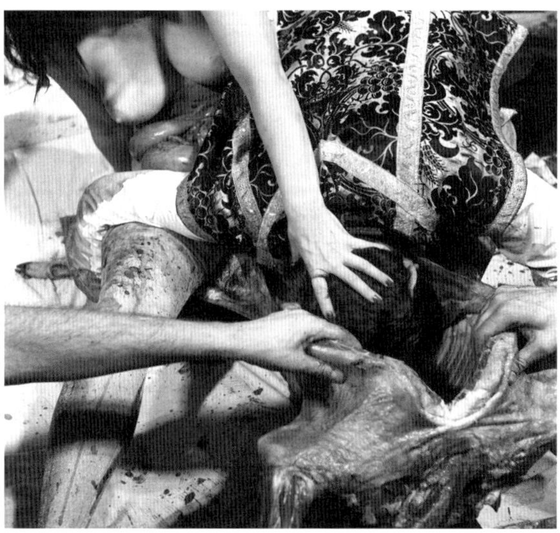

Figures 1.7–1.9. Hermann Nitsch with Hanel Koeck, *Maria Empfängnis – Aktion mit Hanel Koeck, 31. Aktion* (Immaculate Conception: Action with Hanel Koeck, Action 31), 1969. Photograph by Ludwig Hoffenreich. © Hanel Koeck © Hermann Nitsch; mumok – Museum moderner Kunst Stiftung Ludwig Wien, Gift of Hermann Nitsch, 2007; digital image © mumok – Museum moderner Kunst Stiftung Ludwig Wien.

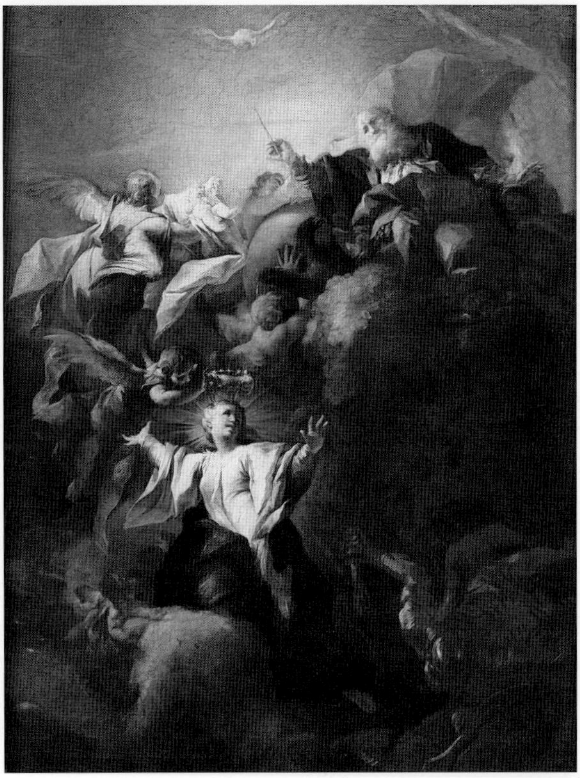

Figure 1.10. Paul Troger, *Allegorie auf die Unbefleckte Empfängnis Mariae* (Allegory of the Immaculate Conception of Mary), c. 1733. Oil on canvas, 109 × 85 cm. Courtesy of the Belvedere Museum, Vienna. Photo: Johannes Stoll / Belvedere, Vienna.

While Nitsch rather reverently travesties this tradition, Koeck's performance is a revolting insult—both to the iconography and to Nitsch's desecration of it.[26] Her irreligious performance exposes the violence it occludes: Mary as "virgin" and Mary as "whore" are, of course, two sides of the same stereotype—another iteration of her "dual aspect." Here, Koeck deliberately and passionately intervenes. If Nitsch critiques one form of misogyny by performing another, then Koeck neither denies nor defiles the stereotype; she aggressively occupies it. Doing so, she undoes the assumptions that inform and undergird it. She arrests the construction of the stereotype. Not content to be the mere object of attention, Koeck proactively provokes the attention she receives. Her performance does not just "enact misogyny," as Jones claims.[27] Rather, Koeck in-acts misogyny in upsetting scenes that take complicity in the rehearsal of misogynist stereotypes beyond travesty.

In *Maria Empfängnis - Aktion mit Hanel Koeck*, the dildo, it should be noted, is Koeck's. It might be called her signature piece. It features in a number of her performances and nowhere else in Nitsch's repertoire. It was made for her by the French photographer and painter Pierre Molinier.[28] Koeck, a French fashion designer and writer who studied at the École des Beaux-Arts in Paris and the Institut für Modeschaffen in Frankfurt, collaborated with Molinier throughout the 1960s.[29] They describe their performances as "fetishistic" acts of "transvestism."[30] Together, in the series *Pierre et Hanel—Les ambigus*

(Pierre and Hanel, the ambiguous ones; 1970–1971; fig. 1.11), the body of each caresses, mimics, and permeates the other. The title and concept for the performance were Koeck's, including the sheer mesh garments that "the ambiguous ones" wear.[31] The photomontage *Les trois Hanel* (The three Hanels; 1968; fig. 1.12) mirrors Koeck's face from three angles; fishnet-gloved hands and splayed legs extend in symmetries around a scrotum. An easy reading would be this: Koeck *is* the phallus. And yes, her name sounds like *cock* in English. But the cockiness of Hanel Koeck does not simply repeat the phallocentrism of the scenes in which she takes part. Instead, she perverts and insults it.

Early on in *Maria Empfängnis - Aktion mit Hanel Koeck*, Koeck "receives communion" from a man dressed like Nitsch in dark priestly garb. This is the Austrian art historian and cultural theorist Peter Gorsen. Koeck met Gorsen, her future husband, in Frankfurt in 1966. It is Gorsen who pours liquid on the dildo while Nitsch fellates Koeck in figure 1.8, and who looks on with some pleasure as Koeck holds Nitsch down in the final negative of figure 1.13. While Koeck was performing with Molinier, Gorsen wrote *Das Prinzip Obszön: Kunst, Pornographie und Gesellschaft* (The principle of the obscene: Art, pornography, and society), published in 1969, the same year *Maria Empfängnis - Aktion mit Hanel Koeck* was performed. *Das Prinzip Obszön* analyzes late-capitalist habits of consumption that disclose "Pygmalion-esque attitudes." The book is concerned with obscene cultural practices that break with bourgeois standards of aesthetic distance, "heretically" evoking the desire of the mythical Greek sculptor to enliven and possess his own beautiful marble female nude.[32] A central chapter is devoted to "travesty and hermaphroditism" in the work of Molinier and is dedicated to Koeck ("Für Hanel").[33] His subsequent book, *Sexualästhetik* (Sexual aesthetics), of 1972, theorizes the relationship between obscenity, pornography, and aesthetics, arguing for the emancipatory power of sexually explicit images in a post-Enlightenment culture of increasingly rigid bourgeois morality. Koeck again is at its center. She is arguably the "obscene" figure in which Gorsen discerns the moment of emancipation that motivates his "sexual aesthetics." Ten photographs of *Maria Empfängnis - Aktion mit Hanel Koeck* (giving the performance its full title) serve to conclude the book's argument.[34] Later, Gorsen dedicates a revised edition of *Sexualästhetik* to Koeck ("für Hanel").[35]

Gorsen's publications are testament to how difficult it is to positively account for Koeck's position. His provocatively feminist writings are ultimately weighed down by the Pygmalion myth to which he reverts. Even as he performs with her in *Maria Empfängnis - Aktion mit Hanel Koeck*, and recognizes her by name as an—if not *the*—impetus for his aesthetic and sexual theories, Gorsen fails to register a space in which she figures as anything other than the compliant object of Pygmalionesque proclivities. This incoherence when it comes to Koeck is even more pronounced in his subsequent writings on *Frauen in der Kunst* (Women in art). In the two-volume art historical study with this

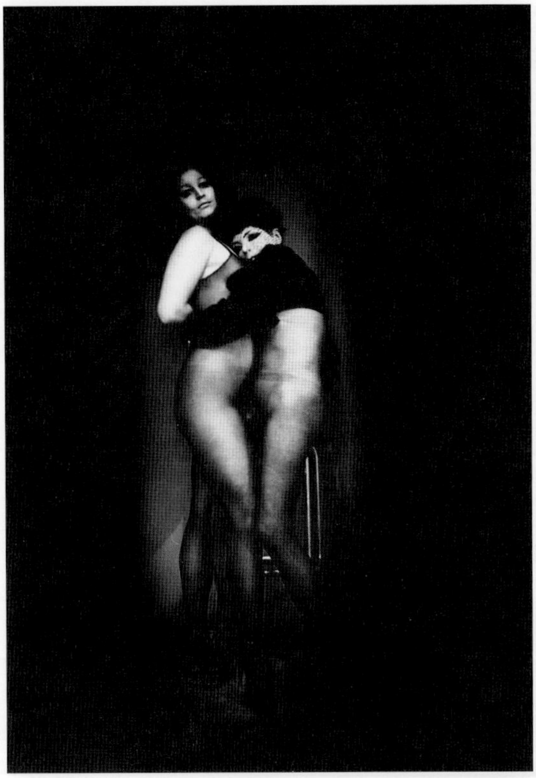

Figure 1.11. Pierre Molinier with Hanel Koeck, *Pierre et Hanel—Les ambigus* (Pierre and Hanel, the ambiguous ones), 1970–1971. Vintage silver print. © Pierre Molinier © 2025 Artists Rights Society (ARS), New York / ADAGP, Paris; image courtesy of Galerie Mennour, Paris.

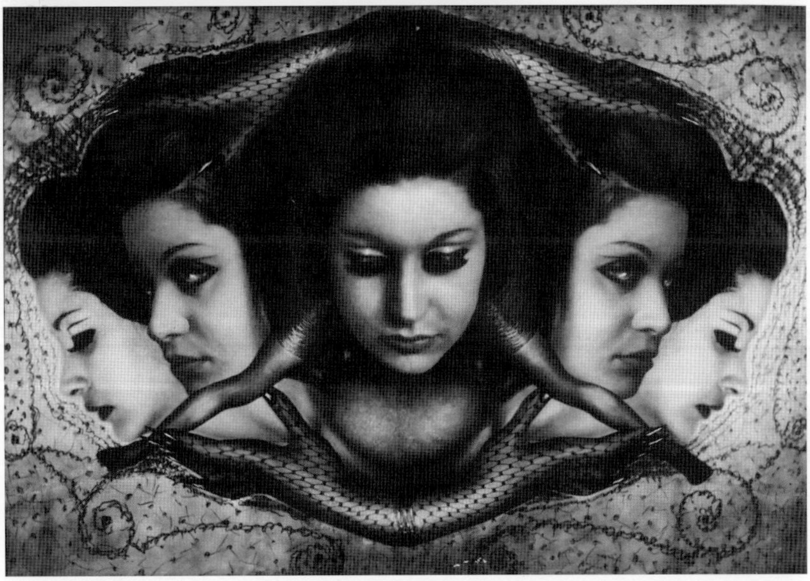

Figure 1.12. Pierre Molinier with Hanel Koeck, *Les Hanels 1 (Les trois Hanel)* (The Hanels 1 [The three Hanels]), 1968. Vintage silver print, 15 × 21 cm. © Pierre Molinier © 2025 Artists Rights Society (ARS), New York / ADAGP, Paris; image courtesy of Gallery Christophe Gaillard, Paris.

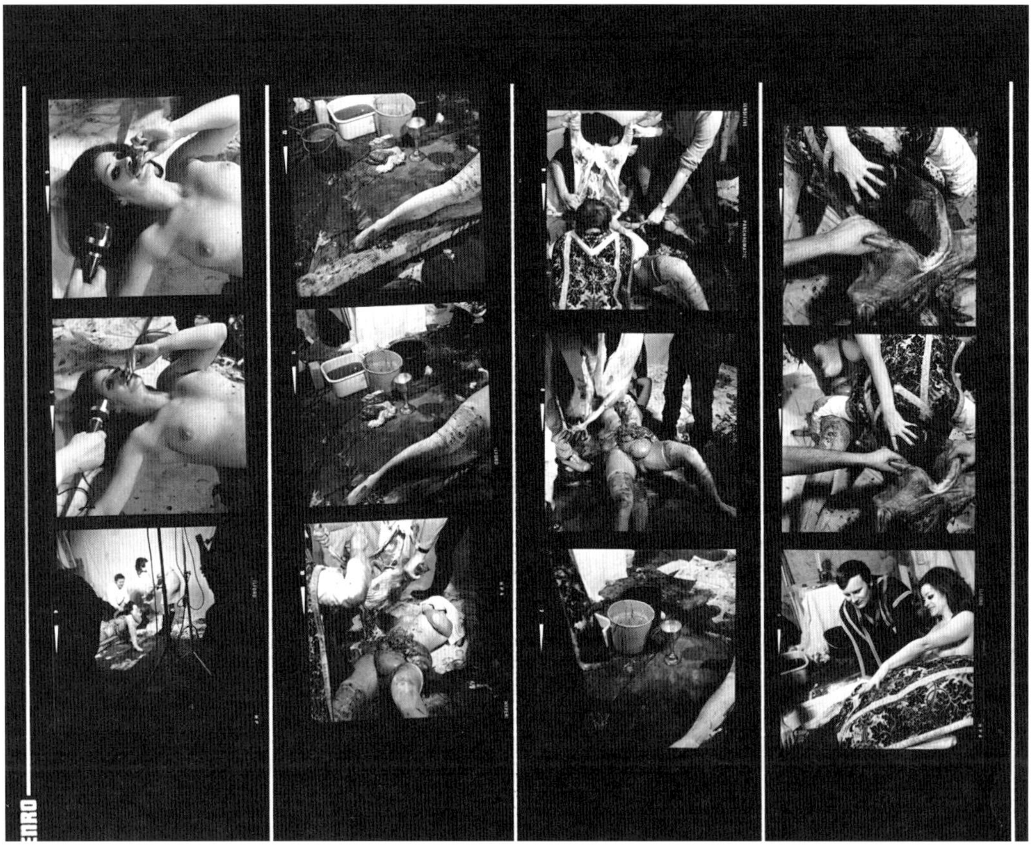

Figure 1.13. Hermann Nitsch with Hanel Koeck, *Maria Empfängnis - Aktion mit Hanel Koeck, 31. Aktion* (Immaculate Conception: Action with Hanel Koeck, Action 31), 1969. Photographic negatives by Ludwig Hoffenreich. © Hanel Koeck © Hermann Nitsch; mumok - Museum moderner Kunst Stiftung Ludwig Wien, Gift of Hermann Nitsch, 2007; digital image © mumok - Museum moderner Kunst Stiftung Ludwig Wien.

title, which Gorsen coedited in 1980, neither her image nor her name appears. Gorsen seems ultimately unable to conceive of a place for Koeck in art history.[36] The entire second volume of *Frauen in der Kunst* is dedicated to his own essay "Frauen und Frauenbilder in der Kunstgeschichte" (Women and images of women in art history), which opens with the illuminating analysis "Antifeminismus in der Kunsthistorik" (antifeminism in the history of art). The "subtlest version of sexism" in the art history writing of the nineteenth and twentieth centuries, Gorsen argues, "overemphasizes" the idea of "woman" as a "form and representational object in art, ornament, and aesthetics" while at the same time "downplaying" the contemporary "active role of women as artists and subjects of history."[37] Even in his efforts to offer a riposte to the antifeminist history of art, Koeck slips through the cracks of sexism's subtleties, for she is not *just* a "form and representational object"—her obscenity releases her from this stereotype—but she also does not, or so it seems in Gorsen's view, take on an "active role" as a "woman artist."

Yet with her deliberate entrance into the arena of Viennese Actionism, Koeck makes, in my view, a crucial contribution to Feminist Actionism. As I discussed in the introduction, Feminist Actionism names emancipatory practices of feminist self-assertion through the deliberate action of women artists. In fact, VALIE EXPORT coined the phrase in an essay first published in 1980—in the first volume of *Frauen in der Kunst*.[38] Koeck's intense self-assertion in her performances brings her into proximity with VALIE EXPORT's call for women to free themselves from their "thing-character" in acts of "self-affirmation." "As long as women have not escaped and been liberated from male history," VALIE EXPORT writes, in a passage that could well interpret Koeck's role in *Maria Empfängnis - Aktion mit Hanel Koeck*, "the history of humanity has not fulfilled its claim of humanity."[39] But Koeck is not counted among those contemporary artists whom VALIE EXPORT names. That Koeck is not taken as a leading "woman in art" by either Gorsen or VALIE EXPORT has doubtless to do with her refusal of the male-female, creator-object binaries that continue to inform ideas about "Frauen in der Kunst" to this day.[40] Her position is altogether too perverse. Today, she describes her collaborations with Molinier—whose life philosophy was *je suis ambigu* (I am ambiguous)—as "seelenverwandt," of kindred spirits, and calls herself simply "eine Perverse," a perverse.[41]

With regard to her involvement in Viennese Actionism, Koeck's perversity is tied to her complicity (*Mitverantwortlichkeit*), which jars the optic of Feminist Actionism and feminist art history writing alike. Koeck does not stage the emancipation of the "woman artist" as "an independent actor and creator"—an ideal of autonomy that may itself be the patriarchal fantasy par excellence.[42] Instead, her performances engage the contours of complicity within ingrained stereotypes. If the Feminist Actionist opposes misogynist stereotypes by appropriating masculinist positions, then Koeck, in contrast, unsettles the stereotype by demonstratively occupying it. Rather than assaulting one stereotype by means of another, she objects to the practices that reiterate such typologies—perversely, willfully, willingly—doubling down on the stereotype to the point of rupture. Ironically, the "objectification" she performs renders her illegible, and illegitimate, from the perspective of contemporary art and feminism.

The occlusion of Hanel Koeck from art history thus has to do with her being, in the double sense of the word, overseen. She is not seen because too much of her is seen. When Lucy Lippard writes her early feminist account of performance art in 1976, "The Pains and Pleasures of Rebirth: Women's Body Art," she oversees Koeck in precisely this way.[43] Significantly, Lippard's essay responds to the work of Hermann Nitsch in which Koeck figures. Her prompt is a Nitsch citation in an essay published the previous year by Max Kozloff, titled "Pygmalion Reversed."[44] Like Gorsen's work, Kozloff's essay indicates the actuality of the Pygmalion myth in responding to performance art in the 1960s and 1970s, and, like Gorsen, Kozloff obstinately persists in gendering the figure of the creative artist as male. Kozloff ends his essay with these lines from Nitsch: "Many of my theatre actions are like births. And a birth is like a crucifixion and resurrection together. There is blood, and meat, and pain, and then comes the newly born child, and he cries, and begins to live."[45] Kozloff uses this citation to cinch his ultimately stereotyped conclusion that contemporary body art radicalizes a Pygmalion tradition of "'birth envy' (of the female)."[46] In making himself into the material of his work, the male body artist achieves an auto-rebirth.

To this rather trite argument, Lippard responds with a contesting claim. With direct reference to Lea Vergine (cited at the beginning of this chapter), Lippard describes "the horror-show theatricality of the Viennese S & M school" and criticizes Nitsch for "using women" in performances she defines as "a destructive male imitation of the constructive female ability to give birth."[47] Lippard most certainly has *Maria Empfängnis – Aktion mit Hanel Koeck* in mind, for, among many other venues, photos of the performance had recently been included—without, however, naming Koeck—in the exhibition and catalog *Happening & Fluxus* (1970), in which Lippard's own writings appear.[48] In contrast with the "use" of women in Nitsch's work (and the masculinist lens of Kozloff's essay), Lippard proposes collecting an archive of women artists who affirmatively, if also critically, foreground their sex and sexuality in "body art with a feminist consciousness." Such work cannot be done in collaboration with male artists because "in fact," Lippard warns, "it is difficult to find any positive image whatsoever of women in male body art."[49] Such work is bound to be, to use Koeck's term, complicit.

Lippard's "positive image" of "body art with a feminist consciousness" is thus explicitly constructed against the "negative image" of an unnamed woman, namely, Hanel Koeck. But the figure Koeck provides is not without consequence for feminist consciousness. According to Lippard, a "positive image" requires "a new iconography." She somewhat ambivalently cites Carolee Schneemann talking about her performance *Up to and Including Her Limits*: "I didn't stand naked in front of 300 people because I wanted to be fucked, but because my sex and work were harmoniously experienced."[50] Lippard also revels at the "similarly defiant narcissism or 'vulgarity'" of the work of Lynda Benglis, who in the pages of *Artforum* in 1974 could be seen "greased nude in sunglasses, belligerently sporting a gigantic dildo." Glossing Benglis's performative self-staging as a "sexual transformation" of a very different sort from the one Nitsch describes in the citation from Kozloff's essay, Lippard quips: "The uproar that this last image created proved conclusively that there are still things women may not do." Lippard draws a line here: "A woman using her own face and body has a right to do what she will with them, but it is a subtle abyss that separates men's use of women for sexual titillation from women's use of women to expose that insult."[51]

In stark contrast to this reception, I take Koeck's work to be all about "exposing that insult"—including the insult she continues to receive at the hands of feminist art history. It may be hard to see any subtlety in Koeck's excessively obscene performances. Nonetheless, I would argue that they are altogether committed to traversing what Lippard calls, uncannily anticipating Gorsen, the "subtle abyss" of sexism, especially in its most abysmal guises. For Koeck's figure objects not only to the action of *Maria Empfängnis - Aktion mit Hanel Koeck* understood as a Nitsch orchestration but also to Lippard, who adds insult to injury by dismissing the agency of any woman who takes part in such an action. Koeck objects to the misogyny of the performance and its reception not by way of a new feminist iconography but by occupying traditional stereotypes in ways that are, indeed, positively insulting.

Koeck's performance in *Maria Empfängnis - Aktion mit Hanel Koeck* is about showing that one cannot just step outside the history of misogyny: One is always going to be tied to it, complicit in it. Rather than the understandable but ultimately questionable aspiration to abandon historical structures of violence and oppression, Koeck brings to the fore complicity as a—if not *the*—problem of feminist politics. In their writings on gender performativity, Judith Butler would theorize this problem at the end of the 1980s. To follow Butler, gender stereotypes are coercive iterative structures perpetuated and maintained by the individuals compelled to perform them. Insofar as one performs and has to perform within and with regard to established stereotypes, one is inevitably complicit in their tradition. The subversive rehearsal of these stereotypes can open up the possibility and political potential of alternative comportments, but gender cannot be freely chosen or reconceived from the ground up. Queer feminist practice, Butler has shown, cannot once and for all break with history, understood as a history of patriarchy. Instead, genuinely transformative practice takes the form of the interruption and travesty of tradition.[52]

The insulting of Hanel Koeck unfolds the problem with complicity so troubling to feminist performance art and art historiography. To Koeck's provocatively insulting participation is added the insult of the feminist reception of her figure, which objectifies Koeck by refusing to contemplate *her performance*. Performance art can offer insight into the broader problematic that Butler introduced with the concept of performativity. To do so, however, the reassuring but ultimately spurious approach of dismissing troubling scenes as rehearsals of subjection, and advocating naively for altogether new iconographies, needs to be complemented by an appreciation of differently inclined practices that explore, among other things, the intractability of complicity.

Anna Brus's Look, or, *St. Anna*

If the deliberate obscenity of Hanel Koeck has made her difficult to see, then Anna Brus has always occupied an unassuming position that is slightly off-scene. This contrast is set into relief in what mumok refers to as Nitsch's *32.*

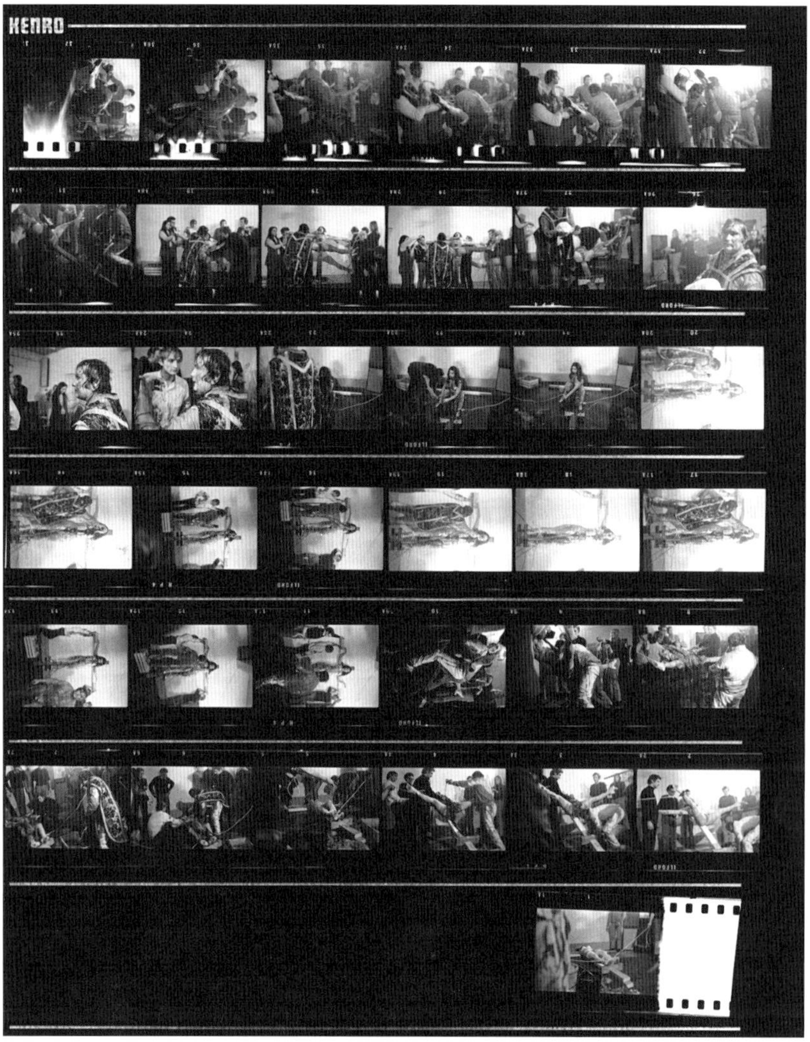

Figure 1.14. Hermann Nitsch with Hanel Koeck, *7. Abreaktionsspiel, 32. Aktion* (Abreaction play 7, Action 32), 1970. Photographic negatives. © Hanel Koeck © Hermann Nitsch; mumok – Museum moderner Kunst Stiftung Ludwig Wien, Gift of Hermann Nitsch, 2007; digital image © mumok – Museum moderner Kunst Stiftung Ludwig Wien.

Aktion (Action 32; 1970). Just two months after *Maria Empfängnis – Aktion mit Hanel Koeck*, Koeck steps into the arena of Viennese Actionism again, taking center stage in this so-called *7. Abreaktionsspiel* (Abreaction play 7; fig. 1.14).[53] The performance can be read as a series of scenes travestying christological iconographies and their prurient bourgeois counterparts. At its heart are crucifixion spectacles with many figures involved. A film by Ed Sommer and Irm Sommer captures some of the careful choreography of the action, a live orchestra present, and, very briefly, the public at the Aktionsraum 1, the space in which the performance was staged in Munich.[54] For most of its duration, the Sommers' film focuses excruciatingly on Koeck's bound body, strapped to a cross, scantily clad, held up and restrained by Nitsch's entourage as she is doused in animal innards and fucked by Nitsch with her dildo. Freed from the cross, the naked Koeck can be seen energetically shoving men's faces into

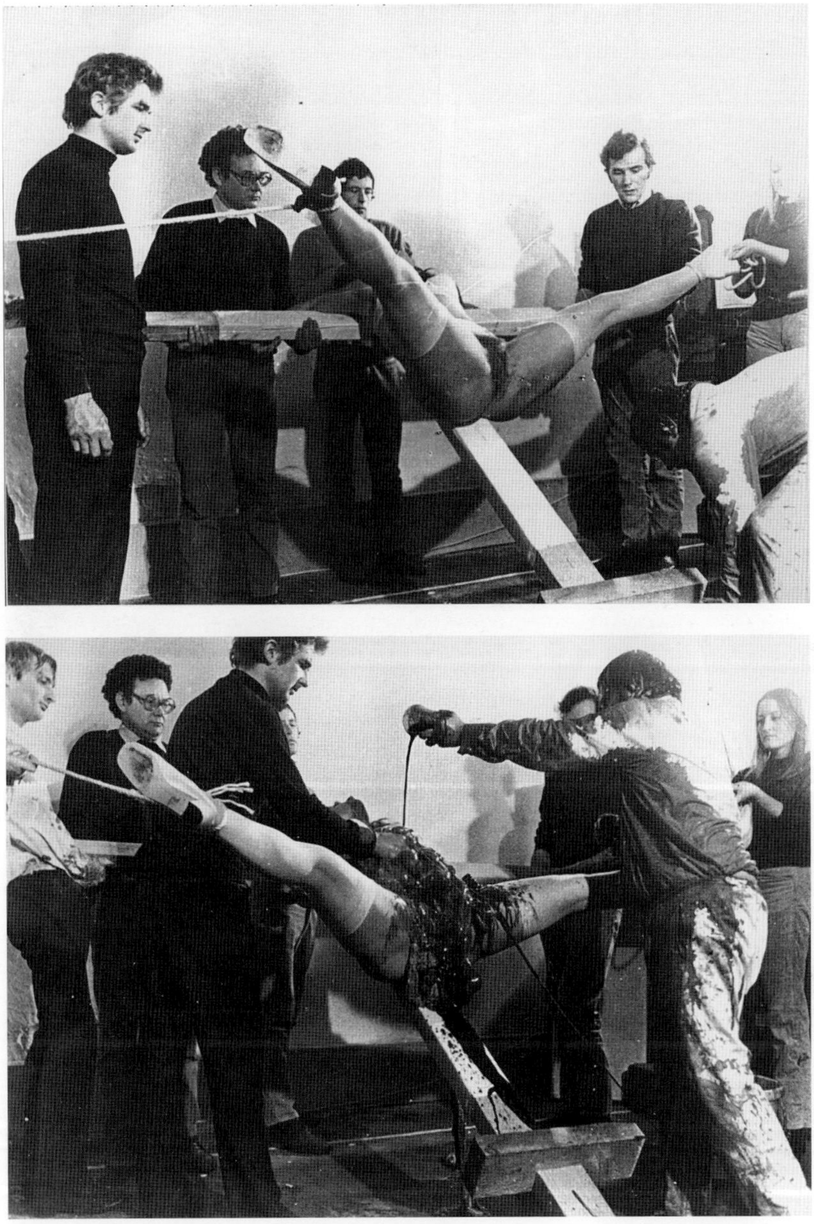

Figures 1.15–1.16. Hermann Nitsch with Hanel Koeck, *7. Abreaktionsspiel, 32. Aktion* (Abreaction play 7, Action 32), 1970, pictured in the anthology *Aktionsraum 1, oder, 57 Blindenhunde* (1971, edited by the A1 Informationen Verlagsgesellschaft). © Hanel Koeck © Hermann Nitsch; Special Collections, The Sheridan Libraries, Johns Hopkins University; digital image: Digitization Services Unit, Johns Hopkins University.

the strewn blood and guts, holding them down. The performance concludes with a bizarre act of cunnilingus: Nitsch crawls rapidly on the floor through the mess to Koeck and presses his face into her naked lap. Forcefully, Koeck embraces Nitsch as he seems to eat her out, finally releasing him gasping for air. The final scene evokes a stunningly insulting performance of the postural relation of Mother and Child.

I want to draw attention now to a figure who remains largely outside the frame: Anna Brus. Although she is cut entirely from the Sommers' filmic documentation, and from the frame of the vast majority of photographs of the performance, Anna Brus is there, not far from Koeck, close enough to touch her. With Koeck at its center, Anna Brus can only be glimpsed along the margins of the performance, occupying the photographic record at the moment it loses focus. Nonetheless, in the documents in which Anna Brus can be seen, her presence changes in a subtle way how one sees. Take for example figures 1.15 and 1.16, two photographs of the treatment of Koeck's body decried by feminist critics. In the second image, Anna Brus comes into view. Wearing a dark turtleneck and corduroy pants, she holds the rope looped around Koeck's left ankle, keeps it taut, lifts Koeck's leg—and looks on.

Although she barely features in it, Anna Brus irritates the scene. This irritation I attribute to what I want to call Anna Brus's look, which expresses a disconcerting combination of impassivity and concern. Cutting across the visual field from her position within it, Anna Brus's look introduces another angle on it. Neither altogether involved nor simply observing, she assists the action—yet at the same time her look conveys a reservation. If Koeck's provocative performance exposes Lippard's insult, then Anna Brus's look registers the insult by exposing her ambivalence. Her look is one of disinclination, a term that describes the posture of her detached involvement, how she submits to the "enacting of misogyny" while refusing to do so completely.

Consider figures 1.17–1.20, which show performances by each of the other three protagonists of Viennese Actionism. And now look at them again with attention to Anna Brus's look. Without drawing focus, her look has the effect of shifting the perspective on the scene, as if altering the angle of the objective. In *Hochzeit* (Wedding; 1965; fig. 1.17, see also figures I.1–I.2 and I.20–I.26 and plates 1–4), she is not simply doused in paint and stripped of her gown in Schwarzkogler's performance; she performs her look. In *Wiener Spaziergang* (Viennese walk; 1965; fig. 1.18, see also figs. 2.11–2.14), which Günter Brus performed on July 7, her birthday, like a gift, she can be seen looking on, deadpan, as he is removed from the street by the police. In *Silber* (Silver; 1965; fig. 1.19), Günter begins to undress Anna for one of their most intimate actions, which involves wrapping her in foil and tying her in cloth: It is her discrepant look that makes this an altogether moving performance. In *Nahrungsmitteltest* (Foodstuffs test; 1966; fig. 1.20), which she performed with Ziemi Schieb "for" Otto Muehl, Anna Brus is supine and partially concealed by a white sheet, reclining with Schieb as Muehl arranges foodstuffs over them both, her breast juxtaposed to a slice of deli meat. Hovering above them, Muehl adds more and more materials—foodstuffs and picnic paraphernalia but also colorful pigment and paint—until all bodies and objects are lost in a mess of indistinction (fig. 1.21). Anna Brus begrudgingly takes a pacifier into her mouth and an apple in her hand; on a finger is her wedding ring. Within this increasing frenzy, she looks on. Her look registers an implacable objection to this tendentious parody of the treatment of women's flesh as any other material for consumption.

Looking at the so-called Viennese Actionists' performances with regard

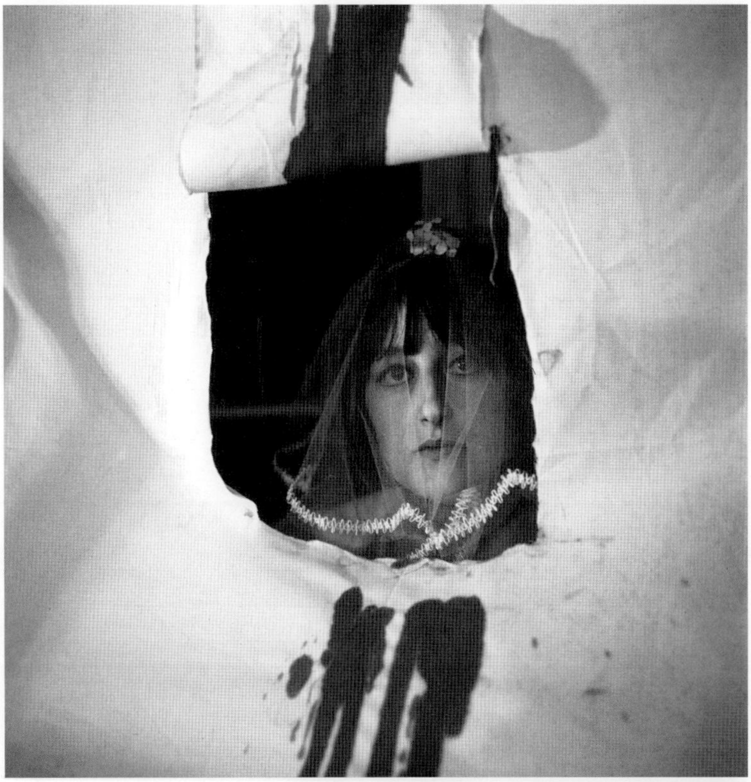

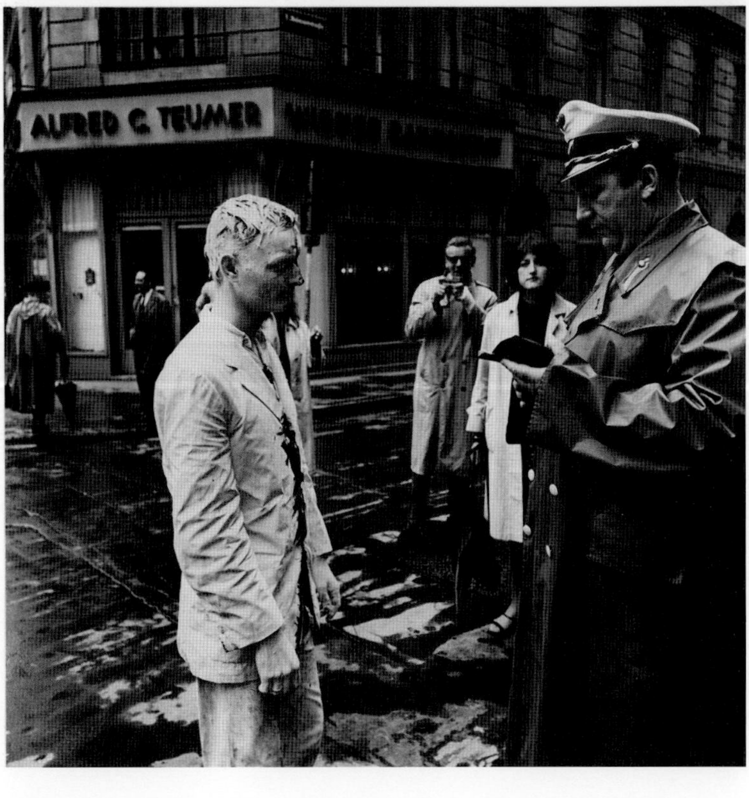

Figure 1.17. Rudolf Schwarzkogler with Anna Brus and Heinz Cibulka, *Hochzeit* (Wedding), 1965. Photograph by Walter Kindler. mumok – Museum moderner Kunst Stiftung Ludwig Wien, Leihgabe der Österreichischen Ludwig-Stiftung. © Rudolf Schwarzkogler; digital image © mumok – Museum moderner Kunst Stiftung Ludwig Wien.

Figure 1.18. Günter Brus, *Wiener Spaziergang* (Viennese walk), 1965. Photograph by Ludwig Hoffenreich. © Günter Brus. Courtesy of the BRUSEUM, Universalmuseum Joanneum.

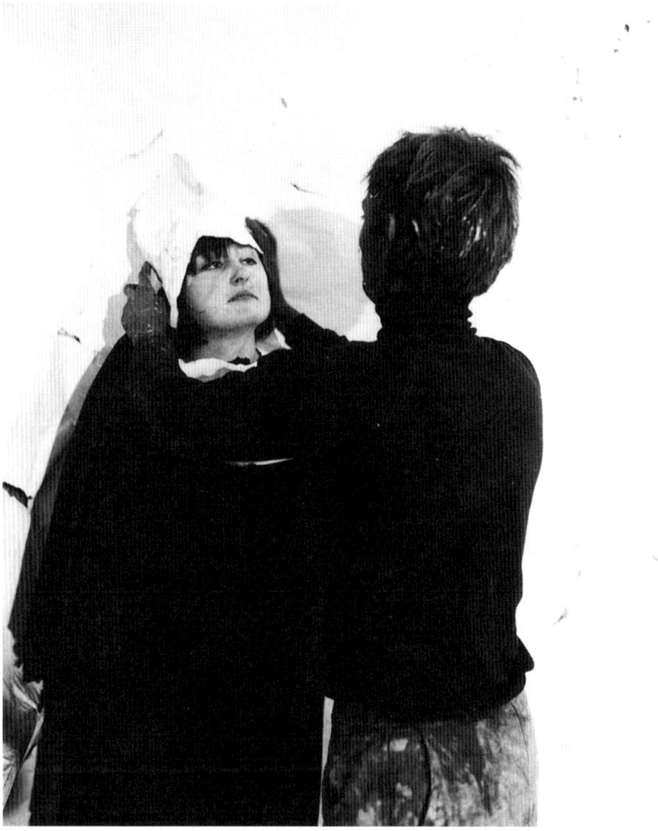

Figure 1.19. Günter Brus with Anna Brus, *Silber* (Silver), 1965. Photograph by Ludwig Hoffenreich. © Günter Brus. Courtesy of the BRUSEUM, Universalmuseum Joanneum.

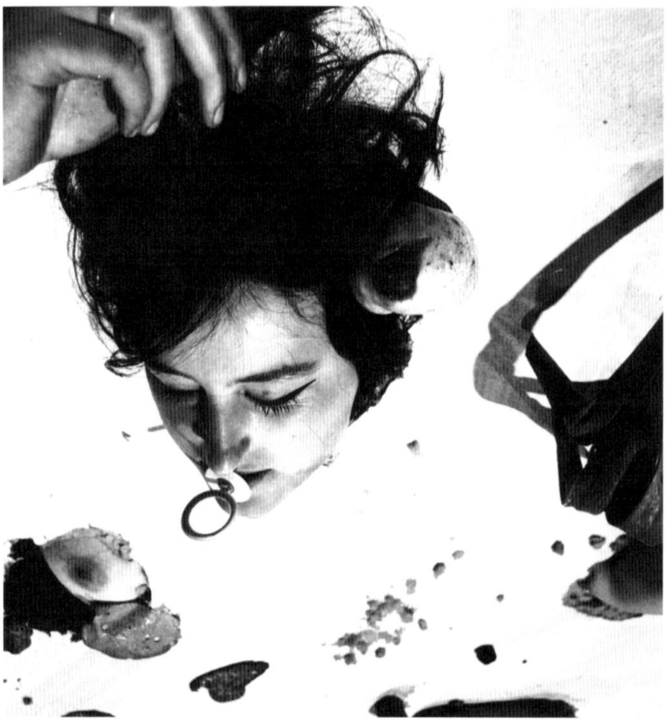

Figure 1.20. Otto Muehl with Anna Brus and Ziemi Schieb, *Nahrungsmitteltest, Materialaktion Nr. 26* (Foodstuffs test, Material Action 26), 1966. Photograph by Ludwig Hoffenreich. Getty Research Institute, Los Angeles (2011.M.38). © Otto Muehl, courtesy Archives Otto Muehl, Moncarapacho-Olhão Portugal; Hoffenreich photography © J. Paul Getty Trust; digital image © mumok – Museum moderner Kunst Stiftung Ludwig Wien.

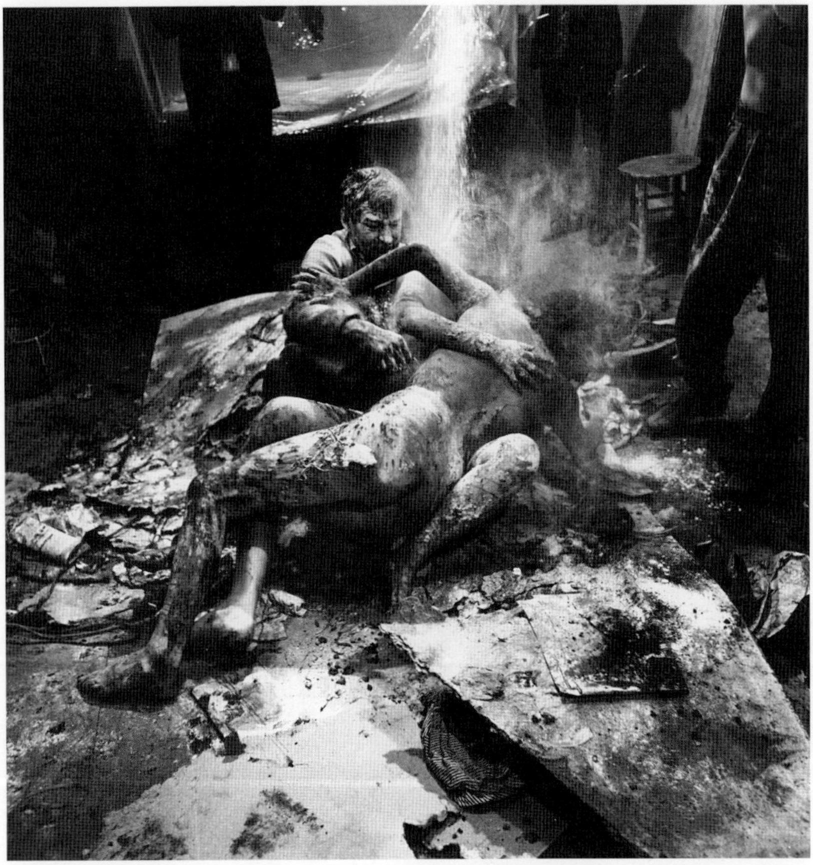

Figure 1.21. Otto Muehl with Anna Brus and Ziemi Schieb, *Nahrungsmitteltest, Materialaktion Nr. 26* (Foodstuffs test, Material Action 26), 1966. Photograph by Ludwig Hoffenreich. Getty Research Institute, Los Angeles (2011.M.38). © Otto Muehl, courtesy Archives Otto Muehl, Moncarapacho-Olhão Portugal; Hoffenreich photography © J. Paul Getty Trust; digital image © mumok – Museum moderner Kunst Stiftung Ludwig Wien.

to the figure of Anna Brus challenges any straightforward assumptions about action. In *St. Anna* (1966; fig. 1.22), Anna Brus reclines in a narrow enclosure, her eyes at first concealed with a strip of cloth, her hands piously, ridiculously, raised in prayer. Scattered with twigs, a white sheet covers her body; a slit is cut into it for her hands to extend from. Affixed to the interior of this coffin-like space are an ad for women's winter fashion, a braided loaf of bread, and, in large print on paper, the word *Geschlossen* (closed). The composition is simple, funereal, but also funny, replete with pathos-laden symbols and objects—until another woman, Ziemi Schieb, appears and gets into the long box as well. Both are naked and covered in white paint. They clamber together into the narrow space, mirroring their bodies in crouched, balled-up postures (fig. 1.23). If traditional portraits of St. Anne often employ a serene frontal posture, tending toward uprightness, then *St. Anna* is all about tumultuous inversions and behinds.

Standing over Schieb and Anna Brus, arms spanning the length of the container, Muehl scatters colored pigment and paint with both hands. He then tries rather comically to insert himself inside the box with them, landing with his back on their backs as they remain crouched over, bellies on thighs, faces

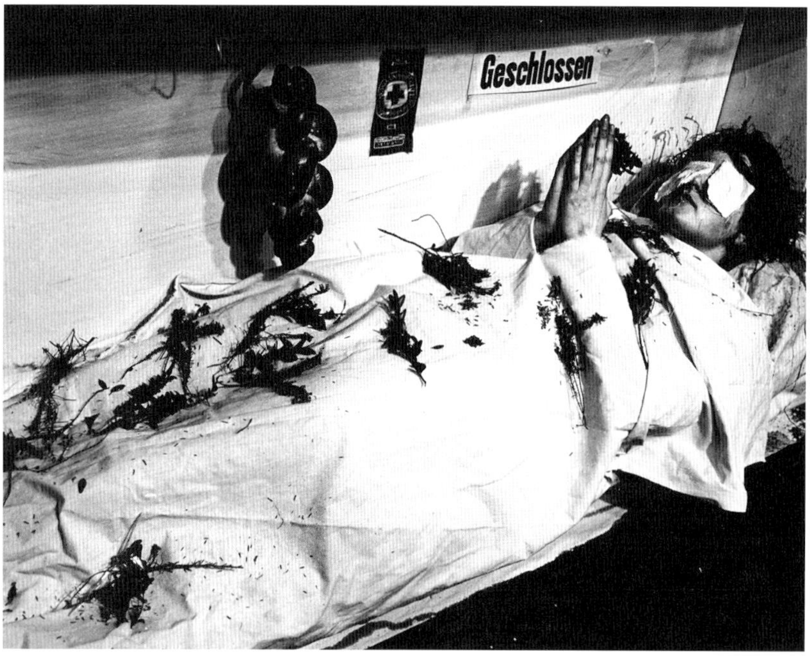

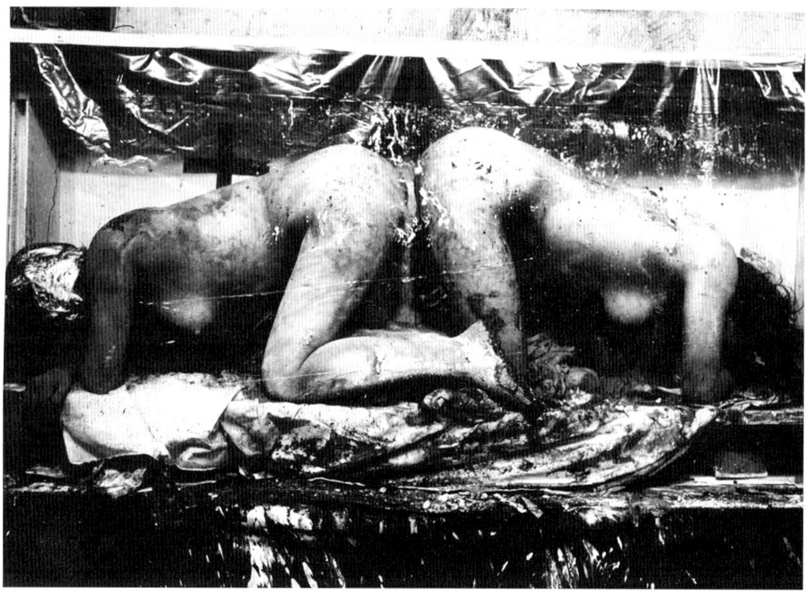

Figures 1.22–1.23. Otto Muehl with Anna Brus and Ziemi Schieb, *St. Anna, Material-aktion Nr. 27* (St. Anna, Material Action 27), 1966. Photograph by Ludwig Hoffenreich. Getty Research Institute, Los Angeles (2011.M.38). © Otto Muehl, courtesy Archives Otto Muehl, Moncarapacho-Olhão Portugal; Hoffenreich photography © J. Paul Getty Trust; digital image © mumok – Museum moderner Kunst Stiftung Ludwig Wien.

out of view, buttocks forward (fig. 1.24). Schieb scrambles over Anna Brus and Muehl hoists Schieb into a suspended harness, from which she hangs awkwardly, pedaling her legs and stretching her arms as Muehl flings more paint (plate 5). Schieb's is the most inelegant of ascensions. She flips over in the harness, hanging prone just from her knees. These activities are set into relief by the figure of Anna Brus, who remains reclined in the box, glancing at times askance, as if looking at how the performance is being seen. *St. Anna* ends with Anna Brus sprawled on the floor beneath Schieb's suspended body, still inverted in the harness. Grasping at her hands, Anna Brus tries, it seems, to support her, as Schieb dangles precariously from her knees and Muehl, standing upright again, tries to stick something between Schieb's thighs.

Of *St. Anna*, Anna Brus would later recall that the "sacred," pious gestures were her idea, to contrast with Muehl's chaotic material action. She remains pleased with her intervention: "When I look at it today I think to myself: 'Muehl really didn't want it like that—super." Her circumspection about being involved with Muehl expressed itself on occasion in a flat-out refusal. On *St. Anna*, she reflects: "I was meant to have been hung upside down by Muehl. That, I said, I would not do."[55] Yet it is the subtle refusal registered within the performance by Anna Brus's look that I find most compelling. In an abject scene of what could easily be dismissed as misogynist subjection, her look *objects* (fig. 1.25). It discerns her noncompliance in a performance in which she otherwise seems just "passive." Her look objects not to Muehl's vulgar intention to desecrate the iconography of a venerated (female) figure, St. Anne. Rather, it objects to the inadequacy of a practice that seeks to be critical of the tradition by simply inverting or degrading it. For this—inversion, desecration—she is disinclined to settle.

Anna Brus's disinclination can be compellingly cast into relief by juxtaposing the performance *St. Anna* to an icon of Renaissance painting, Leonardo's *The Virgin and Child with St. Anne* (1501–1519; fig. 1.26). In a curious composition, Mary perches on the lap of her mother, Anne, as she leans over, reaching out toward the Christ child. It is a tender yet precarious scene. In *Inclinations: A Critique of Rectitude*, Adriana Cavarero takes this painting as emblematic of what she calls "maternal inclination," drawing attention to the leaning posture of Mary. Off-balance, extended over the "'natural' axis" of verticality that otherwise lends the individual sovereign standing, Mary's inclination instead emphasizes "the movement of relationality."[56] Hers is a selfless gesture of care toward the vulnerable child, who wrestles with a lamb in the foreground. Although she does not mention it, implicit in Cavarero's discussion is a comparison with Leonardo's Vitruvian Man. This figure could serve as a prime example of the stereotype of "rectitude," around which, Cavarero argues, the "geometrical imaginary" of Western thought and philosophy is oriented. Rectitude names an "ethical posture" that equates uprightness, verticality, and equilibrium with all that is proper to good and respectable selfhood—autonomy, righteousness, correctness. At once highly gendered and supposedly generic, rectitude models the human as Man, erect and able-bodied. In drawing attention to the Virgin and Child in Leonardo's painting, Cavarero seeks to recover and advocate for an alternative feminine, specifically maternal, postural and affective ethics.

With reference to the two mother figures, Mary and Anne, Cavarero ob-

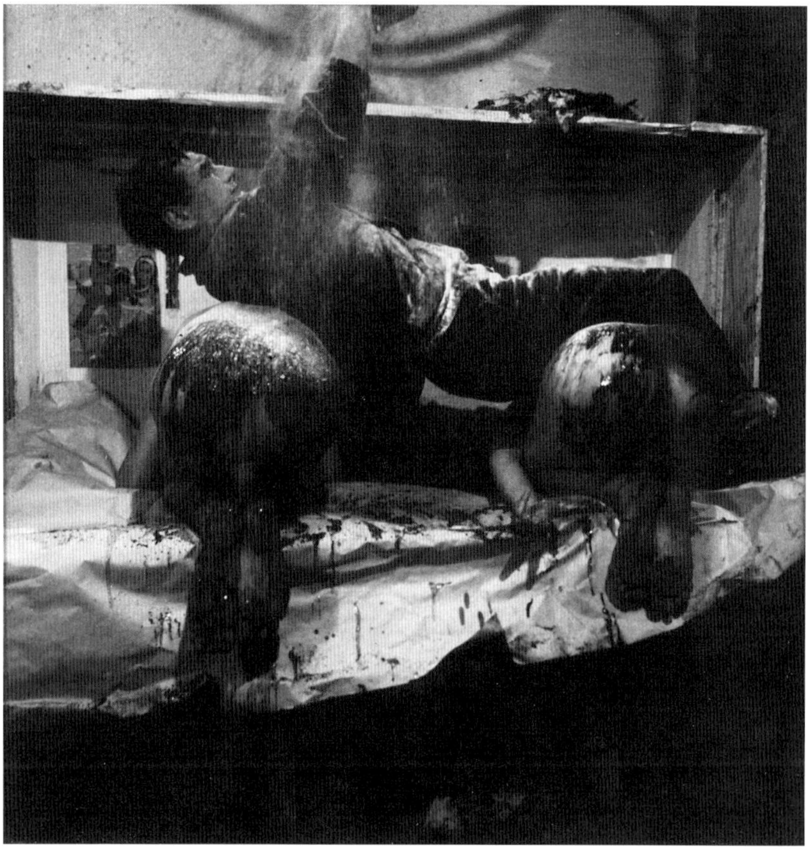

Figures 1.24–1.25. Otto Muehl with Anna Brus and Ziemi Schieb, *St. Anna, Materialaktion Nr. 27* (St. Anna, Material Action 27), 1966. Photograph by Ludwig Hoffenreich. Getty Research Institute, Los Angeles (2011.M.38). © Otto Muehl, courtesy Archives Otto Muehl, Moncarapacho-Olhão Portugal; Hoffenreich photography © J. Paul Getty Trust; digital image © mumok – Museum moderner Kunst Stiftung Ludwig Wien.

serves, "the oblique line that traverses the painting is a matrilineal line."[57] Looking at the painting with Cavarero's reading in mind, but with the eyes of an art historian rather than a philosopher, I am struck, in contrast, by its multiple lines of obliquity. St. Anne, her elbow perpendicularly bent, and hand (or fist) planted firmly on her left hip, leans back. The wry smile playing on her lips, of detachment that is not without concern, anticipates, it seems to me, something of Anna Brus's look. It subtly undermines the scene. What would it look like to revisit the long history of the implication of art and ethics through the history of painting and its representation of the human by attending to such subtle figural subversions as these? For if Leonardo's St. Anne indeed strikes a posture of inclination—with her toes inching over a not-so-subtle abyss—then it is not one that toes the matrilineal line. In Anna Brus's performance in *St. Anna* and the posture of St. Anne in Leonardo's painting, I see figures of disinclination. The two Annas tacitly upset the stereotypes they are seen to rehearse.

Cavarero seeks to restitute the stereotype of maternal inclination that has been historically undervalued and disparaged by the patriarchal privileging of rectitude. Yet her advocacy of inclination risks, like all ethics of care, valorizing real relations of oppression as the necessary conditions of social life. It

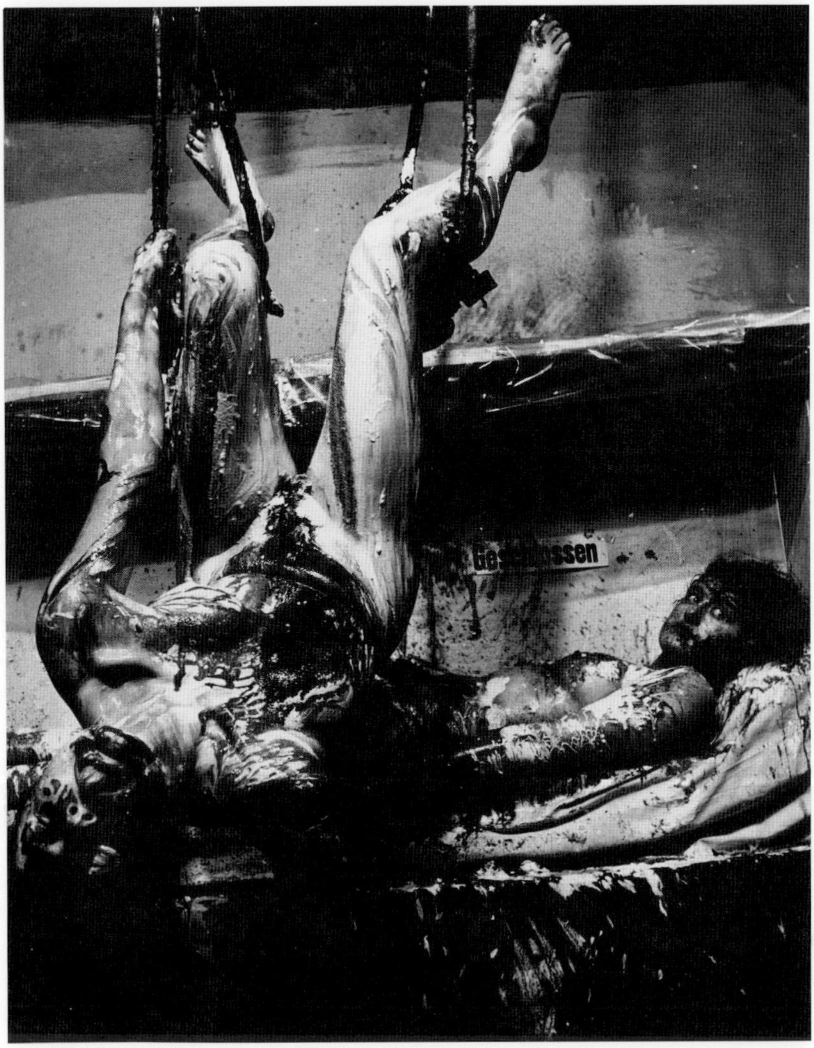

risks mistaking a historically feminine stereotype for one that is feminist. To recognize that relations of care are the unacknowledged condition for any "autonomous" vertical posturing is not the same as making the normative claim for the recuperation of such relations as they are stereotypically performed. Throughout Viennese Actionism, Anna Brus assumes unassuming postures of inclination and submission, even as her look conveys a disinclination to do so. Disinclination acknowledges the priority of relations that attend to vulnerability and dependence while at the same time refusing to exhibit any normative commitment to conventional postures and iconographies.

Anthropometries

Cavarero's critique of rectitude is compelling for thinking about Viennese Actionism more broadly, for she turns to the same Western iconographic tradi-

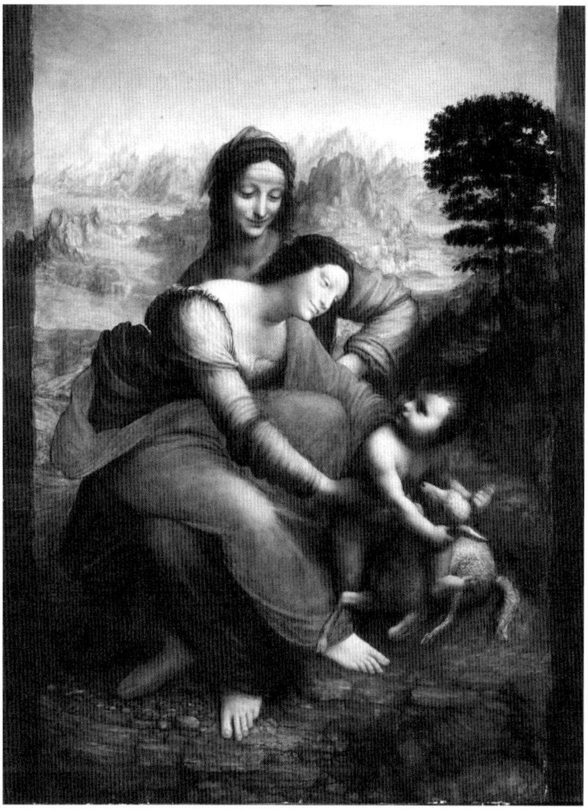

Figure 1.26. Leonardo da Vinci, *Virgin and Child with Saint Anne*, c. 1501–1519. Oil on wood, 168 × 130 cm. Musée du Louvre, Paris; Photograph: René-Gabriel Ojéda. © RMN-Grand Palais / Art Resource, NY.

tions and stereotypes with which it was preoccupied. Brus, Muehl, Nitsch, and Schwarzkogler were all concerned with intervening in different ways in what Cavarero calls the "*dispositifs* of verticalization the aim of which is the upright man" and with irreverently toppling forms of moral and political rectitude.[58] When I describe the in-action of Viennese performance art, I am referring to this common inclination within the four supposed actionists' otherwise disparate practices.

It is worth recalling that all four main protagonists of Viennese Actionism first described their interest in artistic action in relationship to the medium of painting. In 1965, in the pages of the appropriately titled student-run arts journal *Le Marais—The Marsh, Der Sumpf, La Palude*, Günter Brus collected all their artist's statements and works under the heading "Wiener Aktionsgruppe" (Vienna Action Group).[59] This is the one and only instance in their lifetimes in which all four Viennese Actionists contributed to a group publication. Each artist's statement links an ambivalent vocabulary of action with the space, temporality, and viewing dispositive of painting. Schwarzkogler describes a "panorama," a "total synesthetic act" in which painting is "freed from the aim of producing relics" through a unification of the time of the "act of painting" (*malakt*) and the time of viewing. Brus describes his interconnected techniques of "self-painting" (*Selbstbemalung*), "self-dismemberment" (*Selbstverstümmelung*), and "self-disembodiment" (*Selbstentleibung*) as a "further development of painting," emphasizing the continued resistant role of "pictorial surfaces." Nitsch describes what becomes his lifelong project, the "Orgies Mysteries Theater," as developing out of "*informel* action painting" (*der informellen aktionsmalerei*), transforming both painting and viewing in cathartic "theater events." And Muehl describes his process of material action (*materialaktion*) as "represented painting," a nondepictive process of painting that involves the excessive intermingling of unconventional materials: paint, foodstuffs, kitchen and household wares, and bodies.[60]

Yet the tendency in the reception of Viennese Actionism is either to insist on its extreme radicality—as a destructive break with the art of the recent and not-so-recent past—or to describe it as parasitic of developments in Western Europe and the United States, often in misleading manipulations of chronology.[61] Such a confusion is arguably already inscribed in *Le Marais*, in which the statements of the Austrian artists are preceded by an excerpt from an essay by the German art historian Udo Kultermann, who was pivotal in disseminating Allan Kaprow's "invention" of the happening in Europe. Like Kaprow, Kultermann emphasizes that, following Jackson Pollock's "destruction" of painting, the happening instantiates an "overcoming" (*Überwindung*) of its last conventions, "leaping over the boundaries between artist and public" and defying "the conventional tools of aesthetic judgment."[62] The affiliation of Viennese Actionism with the happening, and with the idea that performance art emerges from the "overcoming" of painting, which began with the idea of the destruction of figural painting in abstract expressionist action painting, has persisted ever since. One contemporary, however, sensitive to the way Viennese performance art objected in its techniques and aims to this very narrative, was Peter Gorsen, who for decades argued that the Viennese Actionists considered "the *Kunst=Leben* theory and the happening-philosophy to be an altogether imagined academic thought-experiment, which contradicted their own lives and work in Austria."[63] To put this another way and distill what Kultermann mistakes, the so-called Viennese Actionists remained committed—through inversion and degradation—to a long tradition of painterly figuration.

This commitment propels a claim that traverses each of the chapters of this book, namely, that overcoming by destroying is but one of the modalities through which performance art engaged the tradition of painting in the 1960s. As I argue in more detail in chapter 3 with regard to what I call the "bad form" of Günter Brus, performance art in Vienna can be seen instead to continue the history of painting, and even to intensify the project of figuration. In stark contrast with the US happening and its more international outcropping in fluxus, Viennese performance art persistently exhibits a preoccupation with one of painting's oldest conventions: the rendering of a spatial dispositive to "correctly" conjoin figure and ground and thus orient bodies in pictorial space in a manner pleasing to, and contiguous with, the beholder. Viennese Actionism exhibits an art historical understanding of painting as that art competent to take the measure of Man with a capital *M*, à la the Vitruvian model. The critical import of Viennese performance art lies in how it intensifies, rather than overcomes, this anthropometric project. My claim is that this intensification is brought most provocatively into view not around the self-posturing of the male protagonists themselves, but rather around figures like Hanel Koeck and Anna Brus.

Indicative on the European side of the Atlantic of this alternative genealogy of performance art, not *out of* but rather *in to* painting, is the work of the French artist Yves Klein. Klein became well known in the 1960s for theatrically orchestrated performances with the title *Anthropometries*, "human measurements" or, "measurements of Man" (figs. 1.27, 1.28).[64] These performances involved what can unambiguously be called the "use" of women's bodies in the production of paintings. Klein infamously referred to these women as his "living brushes."[65] Sometimes dressed in a tuxedo and preferring to remain clean, Klein would direct the performance from the sidelines of the action as they, naked, imprinted traces of their bodies on swaths of white canvas appended to the walls and floor: pleasantly plump torsos, thighs, buttocks, and breasts, brushy strokes of pubic hair, and, now and again, a hand. In this process, Klein's own patented color was used, IKB, or International Klein Blue, a vibrant, almost iridescent shade of blue—similar to the blue that Schwarzkogler, who was fascinated by Klein, used in *Hochzeit*.

While his Viennese contemporaries produced few objects, Klein sold these "measurements" as his own paintings. Even if they index a few unruly angles and undignified marks, Klein's anthropometries are ultimately about preserving the form, beauty, and propriety associated with the painterly tradition of depicting the female nude. In 1961, using plaster and IKB, Klein would even make a *Blue Venus*, an edition of three hundred life-size torsos replicating the harmonious proportions and delicate contrapposto of the nude in the likes of Botticelli's *The Birth of Venus* (1485–1486), yet cropping her head, arms, and legs, much as his *Anthropometries* do. Klein cites these figural conventions and commodifies them. His critical comportment is at best tongue-in-cheek, laughing (all the way to the bank) at the increasing affiliation of contemporary art with the market.

In contrast, Viennese performance art approaches the anthropometric tradition of painting with another objective that is altogether less edifying, and certainly less commercially remunerative. It rejects good measure and occupies itself instead with a withering analysis of bad form. Muehl's first *Versumpfung einer Venus* (1963), literally the "swamping," or more figuratively, the "degradation" of a Venus, involves Muehl in the center of the action making a huge mess. Like the unsurveyable zone of the swamp, the practice

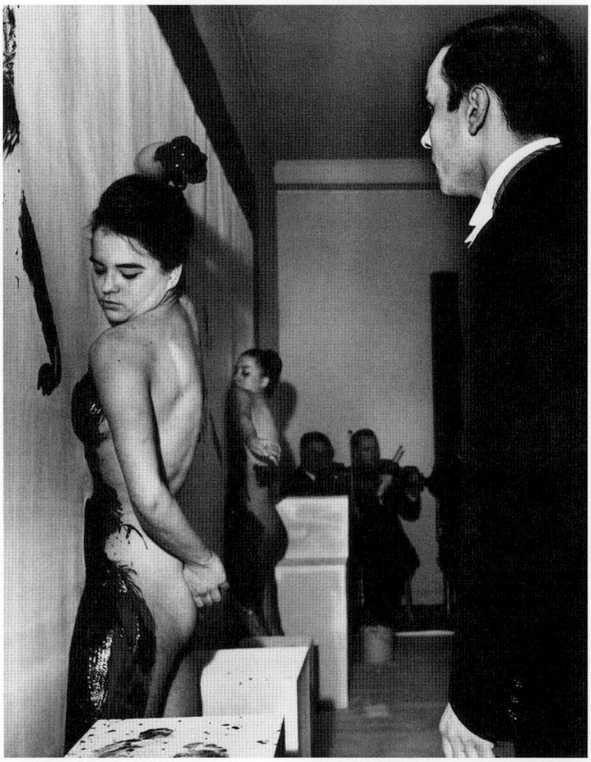

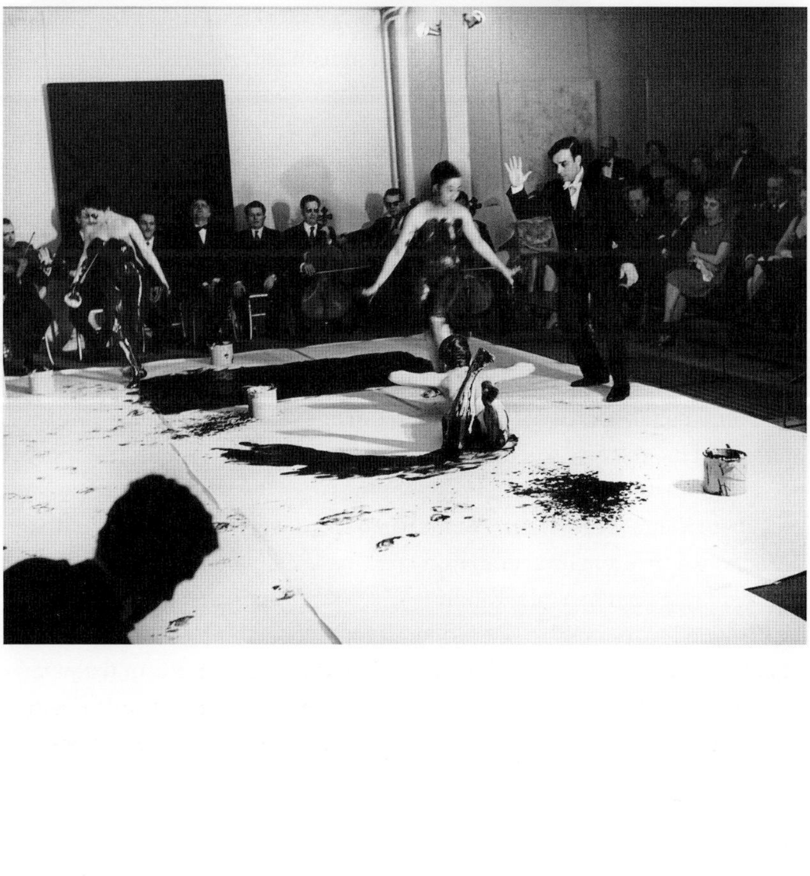

Figures 1.27–1.28.
Yves Klein, *Anthropométrie de l'époque bleue* (Anthropometries of the blue epoch), 1960. Photograph by Harry Shunk. © Succession Yves Klein c/o Artists Rights Society (ARS), New York / ADAGP, Paris 2025; Photograph: Shunk-Kender. © J. Paul Getty Trust; Getty Research Institute, Los Angeles (2014.R.20). Gift of the Roy Lichtenstein Foundation in memory of Harry Shunk and Janos Kender.

of swamping challenges any measure. In cleaner conceptual terms, Muehl's *Versumpfung* performances are not about degrading "the women" he "uses" (to recall earlier complaints about Viennese Actionism). Rather, they defy the stereotype of "Woman" enshrined in the iconography of Venus. Each *Versumpfung* begins with Muehl stripping naked the woman he performs with, after which he douses her with various materials—paint, milk, laundry detergent, tomato sauce—manhandles her in the slippery disorder, and restrains her with pieces of cloth, rope, and plastic that do little to veil or even unveil her body. The performance insists that the Venus cannot remain upright. The woman performing with Muehl inevitably falls or is wrestled to the floor, where he continues to manipulate her constrained figure. *Versumpfung einer Venus* debases and defiles the proportions, symmetries, and balance concentrated in the image of Venus. The iconography is abjected, and the figure of the woman is freed—this, in any case, is the idea—of the stereotype. In the 1963 iteration shown in figures 1.29 and 1.30, the performance concludes with Muehl grinning while dumping the contents of a rubbish can onto the woman sprawled out on the floor. This woman is known today only as "Babsi."

In their degradation of classical painterly conventions and measures, Muehl's performances in the 1960s tread a fine line between use and abuse. This is evidenced in the archive, where, like Babsi, the women who performed with him often remain unnamed despite featuring again and again in his work. In this regard, the recent effort by mumok to expand its archive to include the "models" in the account of Viennese Actionism is welcome but in practice disappointing. Of Schieb it reports only this: "Although she was a model in numerous Muehl-actions, nothing more is known about her."[66] Anna Brus recalls of Schieb: "No one knew where she went after each action. She literally disappeared from the scene."[67] In the art history of Viennese Actionism, Ziemi Schieb and Babsi are vanishing points. Can one register this tendency to disappear as part of the performance and its history? Rather than finding out more about their lives—although I believe this work should also be done, and with more care—I am interested in addressing a more strictly art historical deformation of these women's roles. To persist in writing of these figures, however sympathetically, as victims of the actions in which they were involved or even as "models for" so-called Muehl-actions only compounds their obscurity. In contrast, I am interested in attending to what such disappearances reveal about Viennese performance art when it is not conceived of as limited to the actions of a few male actionists.

This brings me to *Scheißkerl*, Koeck's first performance with a protagonist of Viennese Actionism in October of 1969, just months before she would appear in *Maria Empfängnis - Aktion mit Hanel Koeck*. The title of the performance, *Scheißkerl*, which translates more or less as "shithead," can also be read as naming Otto Muehl—and not only because his last name sounds like *Müll*, or "garbage." In *Scheißkerl*, Koeck performs what I take to be the insulting of

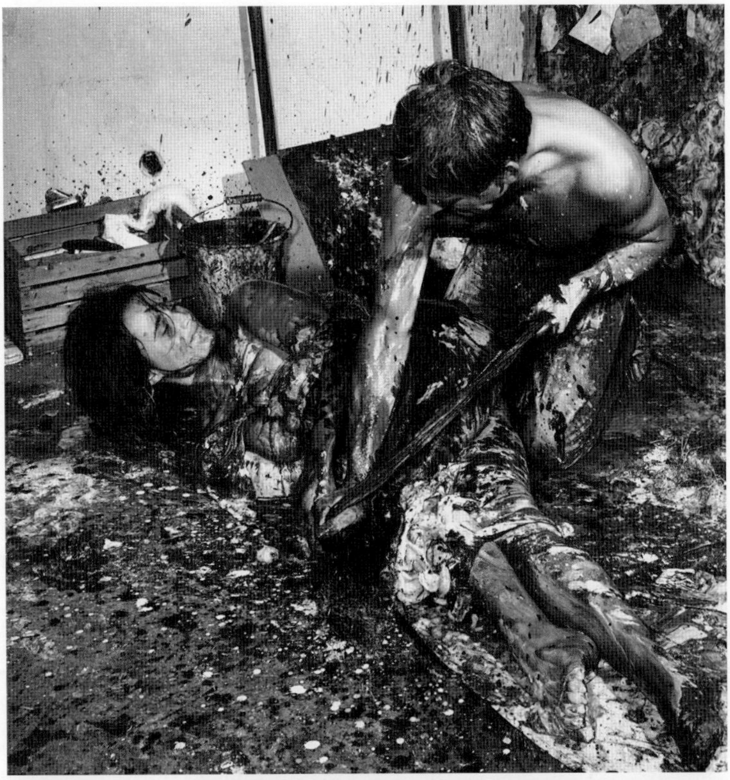

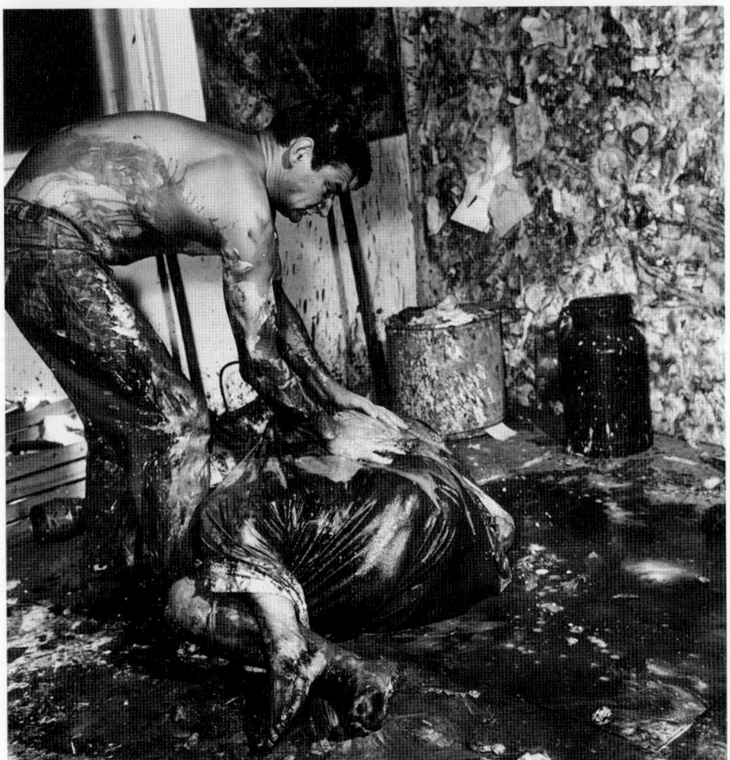

Figures 1.29–1.30. Otto Muehl with "Babsi," *Versumpfung einer Venus, Materialaktion Nr. 1* (Degradation of a Venus, Material Action 1), 1963. Photograph by Ludwig Hoffenreich. Getty Research Institute, Los Angeles (2011.M.38). © Otto Muehl, courtesy Archives Otto Muehl, Moncarapacho-Olhão Portugal; Hoffenreich photography © J. Paul Getty Trust; digital image © mumok – Museum moderner Kunst Stiftung Ludwig Wien.

his corpus. When discussed at all, *Scheißkerl* is one of the few works of Viennese Actionism consistently attributed to her.[68] Gorsen's "script" for the "perversion performance" suggests that *Scheißkerl* was conceived when Koeck met Muehl in Vienna a year earlier. Her idea was to illustrate Freud's writings on anality and sexuality through an act of coprophagia. How inconvenient that her friend in Paris with the coprophagia fetish was ultimately not able to take part. So Muehl stepped in, and Koeck took center stage.[69] Any viewer of the performance will immediately recognize her radical co-optation of Muehl's habitual position. *Scheißkerl* involves the violent "material action" of "swamping" Muehl—Man, Actionist, Trash, Shithead. After eating a scoop of ice cream served to her by Kurt Kren, who is dressed in the costume of a French maid, Koeck and her friend Waltraud Stieglitz (also Kren's partner) tie Muehl down naked to a table on his back. Everyone is "in" on the disturbing ensuing action. Koeck receives an enema from a figure Gorsen refers to in the script as a "transvestite" named Susanne. Susanne is also Gorsen, in a long blonde wig and nurse's apron. Enema administered, Koeck climbs up a ladder and shits on Muehl's face. She climbs down to help Stieglitz make sure he eats it, forcing her shit into his mouth. Struggling against the restraints, Muehl's body is roughly smeared by Koeck, Stieglitz, and Susanne. They focus their attention on his penis, which gets manhandled and fellated. In contrast with Susanne, who is masturbating nearby, it does not rise to the occasion. Koeck does not criticize rectitude, she ruins it. Her un-Venus-like performance violently outdoes Muehl's own efforts to travesty the anthropometries prized by and stereotypically presented in the history of painting. She devastates the measure of Man. And indeed, the man Muehl was affected by *Scheißkerl* for some time.[70] After this performance, the abjection of iconography that made his early work compelling would be abandoned. Muehl embarked in the direction of an ever more authoritarian self-aggrandizement that would culminate in his criminal activities as the leader of a "commune," for which he was sentenced to prison in 1991.[71]

Transfusion

Throughout the 1960s, Muehl and Nitsch engaged the anthropometric tradition of painting by inverting and defiling the iconography of Venus and the Virgin Mother, but their ostensibly subversive performances tend ultimately, in a kind of compulsive repetition, to anxiously reproduce rectitude in the figure of the artist himself. The performances of Günter Brus with Anna Brus, in contrast, in no way revolve around a lost or longed for ideal of rectitude. Instead, the painterly tradition of figuration is engaged from a different angle to explore uncanny anthropometries that are at once unsettling and intimate, arresting and everyday. In these performances, the Bruses unravel the conventions of painting to produce configurations of relations that fail to conform to any homogenizing spatial logic or to any recognizable iconographic idiom.

Ana (1964) is the first of a number of works that Günter Brus refers to as self-painting (*Selbstbemalung*). In a textbook account, Benjamin H. D. Buchloh sees *Ana* as marking Brus's "initial step into Actionism."[72] If *Ana* is indeed the inaugural work of Günter Brus's actionism, then it is crucial to observe the performance's painterly dimensions. In contrast with the figure of the artist in the cases of Muehl and Nitsch, each of whom emerges more or less unscathed—at least before the appearance of Hanel Koeck—the figure of the artist in Günter Brus's performance art is never authoritative or self-centered or self-contained but always leaning, off-balance, falling out or falling over, bleeding or leaking as if to expose the precarious relations on which his standing relies. In stark distinction to the grand posturing of Muehl and Nitsch, *Ana* begins with Günter Brus bound in ragged strips of cloth, balled up in the corner of an unfurnished room, inert. Huddled, bent over in a corner: This is Günter Brus's signature position (fig. 1.31, see also fig. 3.9). He awkwardly rolls around the edges of the room, disentangling himself until finally subsiding, sprawled out on his stomach on the floor. Regaining some composure, Günter covers himself and Anna, both naked, in white paint. Each of their figures loses distinction against the white-papered walls of the room. Pressed into the close proximity of the corner, the couple's performance renders, at once intimately and antagonistically, figure and ground together (fig. 1.32, see also fig. 3.10). Günter contours and grapples with Anna's body in black paint. This is no simple painting of a "female nude." Each smears their body against the other, crouching and twisting themselves into the corner, grasping and marking the walls as the whole space—room and bodies—becomes increasingly blotted with black paint, a vanishing point devouring the perspective that generates it.

Far from a "living brush" wielded, from a distance, by "the artist," Anna Brus participates in blotting her self and his self out. With just the bare coordinates of painting, figure and ground, the performance is a demonstration of its lack of iconographic precedent. In contrast with Carolee Schneemann's "kinetic painting" *Meat Joy* (1964), performed just a few months earlier in Paris at the Festival de la Libre Expression, *Ana* foregrounds proximity and constraint. It dwells unexcitingly on compositions without movement; its erotic dimension is subdued rather than festive or ebullient. Not without pleasure, *Ana* does without the sexual norms that, in the 1960s, would drive second-wave feminist critiques of sexual subjugation. This is just one reason searching the archive of Viennese Actionism for an "independent" woman artist "like a Carolee Schneemann in the USA" leads, indeed, to an impasse.

In contrast with Klein's *Anthropometries* and Muehl's *Versumpfungen*, the Bruses' *Ana* is, in its engagement with the tradition of painting, less interested in stereotypes than in formless figures and unstable grounds. In the postures they assume as they fall and fold and bend over each other, Anna and Günter fail to cohere into distinct figures of the sort that one would associate with the anthropometric imaginary of the coherent self. In this "self-painting," their

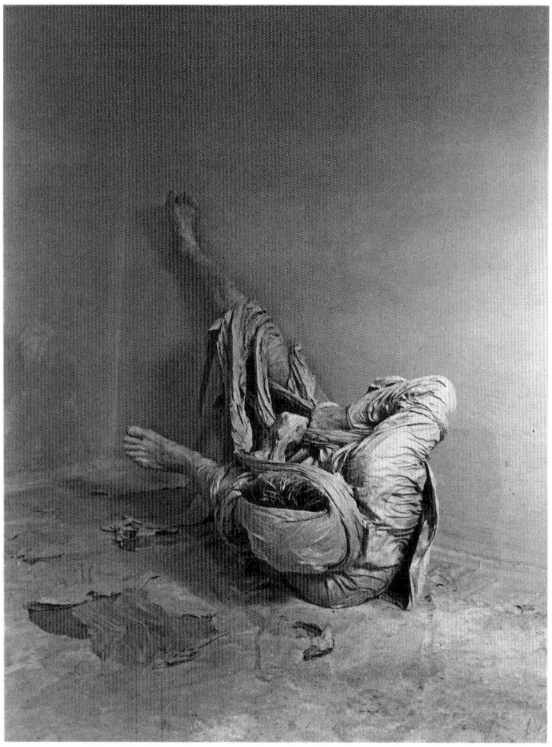

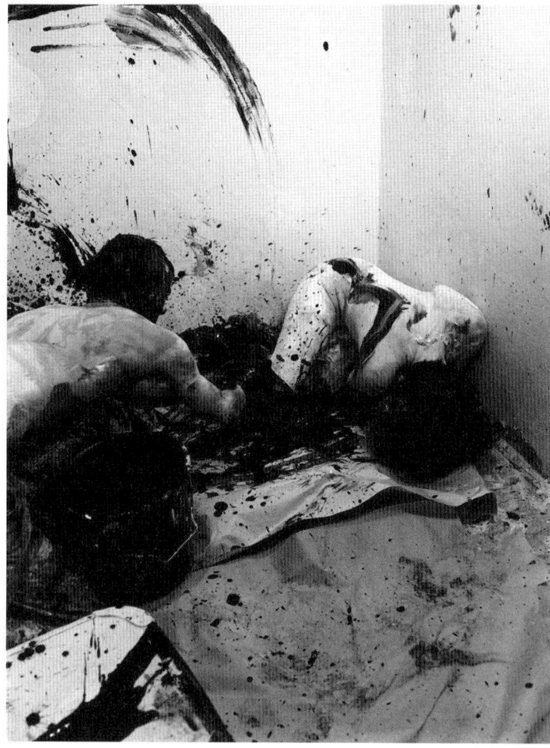

Figures 1.31–1.33. Günter Brus with Anna Brus, *Ana*, 1964. Photograph by Siegfried Klein (Khasaq). © Günter Brus. Courtesy of the BRUSEUM, Universalmuseum Joanneum; Photography of Siegfried Klein courtesy of Julius Hummel.

figures seem to permeate and interpenetrate one another. Reciting neither rectitudinous pretensions nor wholesome inclinations, *Ana* foregrounds instead tender relations of dependence that are always also on the verge of violence and injury. The performance ends with the figures entangled, collapsed together in the corner, exhausted in an abject smear of paint (fig. 1.33). If this is anthropometry, it does not contour an autonomous self. Rather, *Ana* affords a measure of the human that is transfused across bodies, relations, and spaces.

Even the palindrome, *Ana*, seems to perform this transfusion. It also names Anna, spelling her name in Croatian, recalling her immigration from the former Yugoslavia to Austria, where she and Günter met at a play in 1962. She left early; he followed her out. She told him she thought it was "Scheißtheater" (shit theater); he agreed. This encounter, in more ways than one, may be the *Urszene* of Viennese Actionism. Anna married Günter four years later, changed her name, and soon became pregnant with their daughter, all the while supporting them with her work as a seamstress for a lingerie designer.[73] Thinking back on their collaborations in the 1960s, Günter would much later muse, "It remains today a mystery to me where she found the strength to persevere in the miserable conditions of life in Vienna and, on top of this, to participate in the most intensive way [*intensivst*] in the actions."[74]

Although they present on paper the most ordinary of heterosexual married couples, there is nothing "romantic" or "conventional" about the Bruses' performances. They are engaged not with the dubious formation of relation-

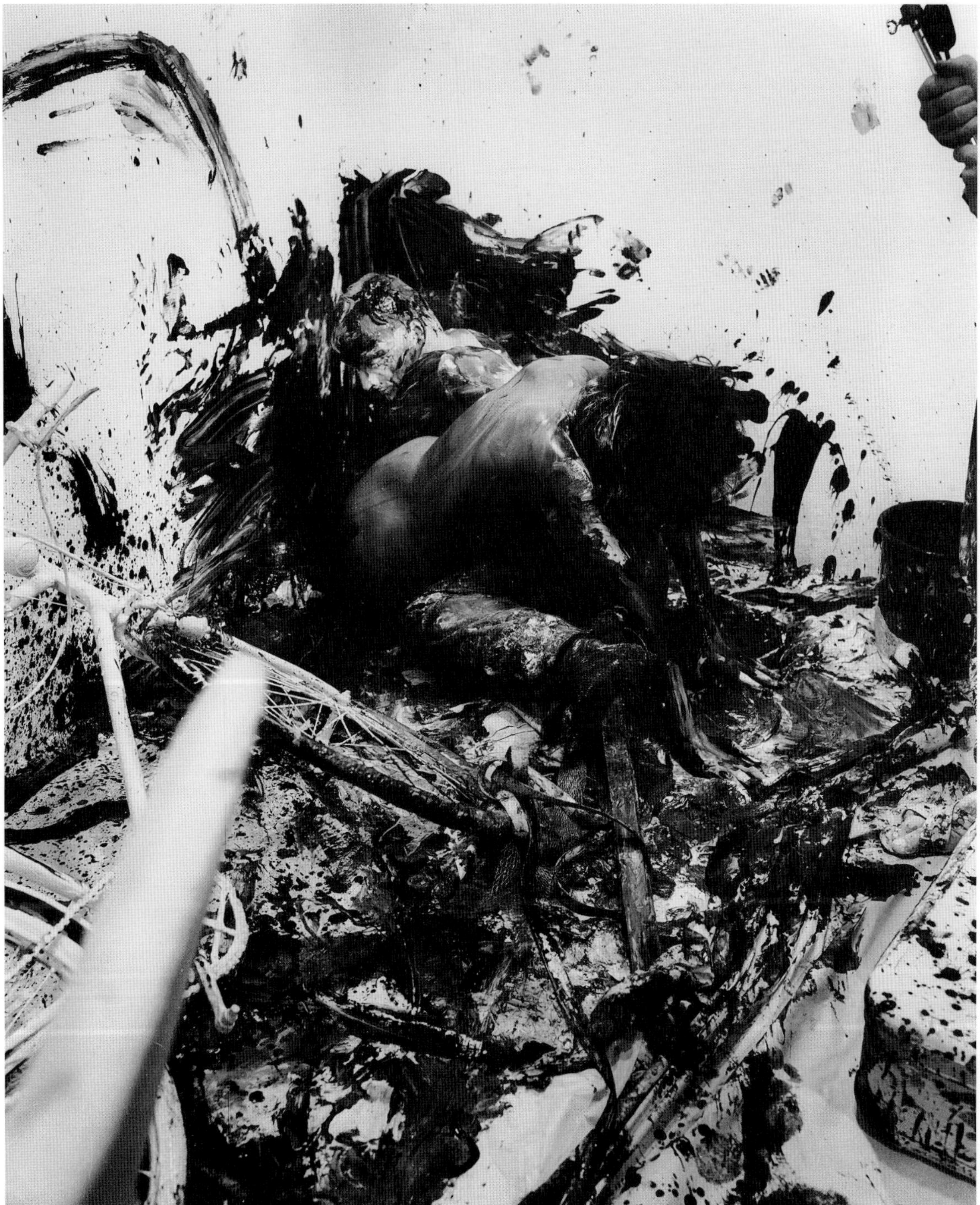

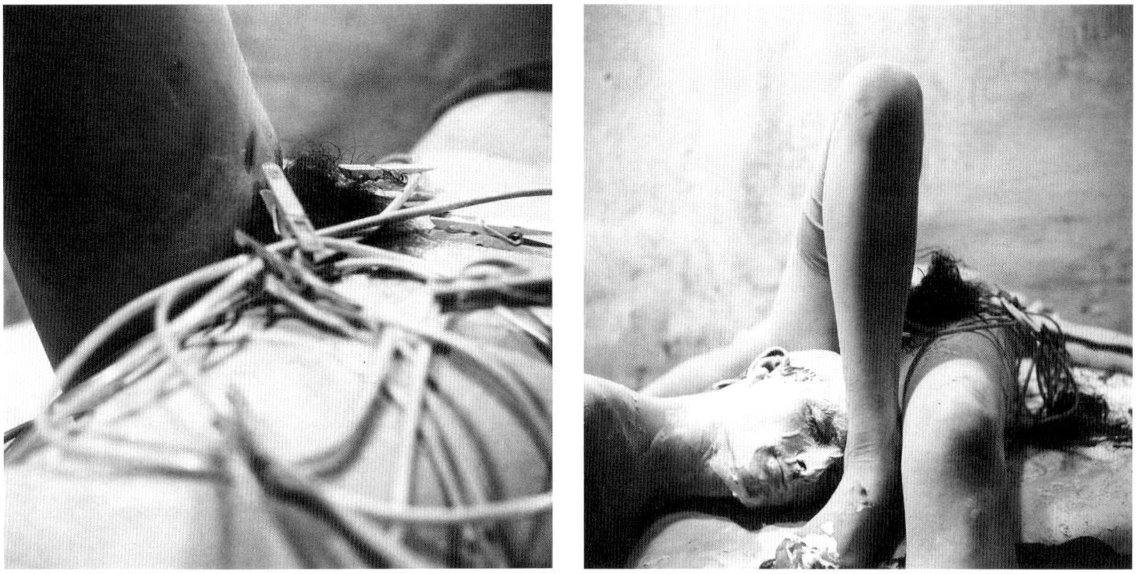

Figures 1.34–1.35. Günter Brus with Anna Brus, *Transfusion*, 1965. Photograph by Ludwig Hoffenreich. © Günter Brus. Courtesy of the BRUSEUM, Universalmuseum Joanneum.

ships between discrete human figures, but rather in exploring human bodies as sites of perviousness. In their couplings, the consolation of anything like a heteronormative reconciliation is refused.[75] *Transfusion* (1965) intensifies the painterly dimensions of *Ana* in a proliferation of color: The basic black-and-white contours that belonged to the graphic articulation of pictorial space in *Ana* are supplemented here with primary colors—crimson, cadmium yellow, bright blue. Staged within the confined space of a table, which serves as a horizontal frame, *Transfusion* explicitly inclines the rectitudinous logic of painting's perspectival apparatus, which is cited within the performance by a disorderly assortment of grids and lines (figs 1.34, 1.35). Even as it focuses on the figures of the Bruses, *Transfusion* declines to offer in this frame the reassuring form of a unified human figure. Instead, the constrained visual space becomes the site of intimate corporeal exchange and material transfer, foregrounding penetrability and responsiveness.

Lying on the table, Anna has Günter's head nestled between her legs (plate 6). Catheter tubing connects his mouth and nostril to her vagina. Broken chalk pieces of red, yellow, and blue are strewn across Anna's belly. Razor blades rest on her chest; strokes of blue paint brush down the underside of her left arm and across her hip. Numerous photographs of the performance detail the colorful topography of Anna's torso and the rich red pigment scattered in her pubic zone. Clothespins clipped unpleasantly to her pubic hair fasten rubber bands over her stockinged thigh, holding her ineptly, drawing little lines in space (plate 7). The bottle caps and corks and many nails hammered into the tabletop on which she reclines indicate openings, but they also enforce a sense of connection, of conjoining, of holding in place. Scissors inserted into the stockings she wears suggest cutting, release, division. At certain angles,

Anna's wedding ring glints, an uncanny mooring of this relationship in the world governed by more conventional signs and ritual performances.

Painted entirely in white, Günter moves slowly around Anna as she shifts in various supine positions. He leans on her, rests against her, his eyes often closed. The pigment on her body transfers to his as he leaves behind smears of wet white paint. Their intercourse is not sexual but formal: slow and painstaking, a process of permitting and resisting touch. If, as I find, the performance is very moving, the motion—like the emotion—takes the form of transfusion. The anthropometric figure of the independent self, and the sacrosanct interiority it is supposed to enclose, is here undone by a formless figuration, which conveys a much more vulnerable intimacy and respects no clear boundary demarcating inside and out. Neither rectitude nor inclination is modeled here. Sometimes repulsive, sometimes curiously appealing, disconcerting and yet all too familiar, *Transfusion* explores relations of disinclination. At one moment, Anna can be seen slouched against the wall, nudging Günter's head away from between her thighs (plate 8). She barely smiles. This moment, intimate yet distant, tender and with a touch of humor, captures the disinclination of Anna Brus, which transfuses the Bruses' performance art.

Maternal Disinclination

The critique of rectitude invites consideration of figures who incline differently, whose agency is not authoritative, whose position does not dominate center stage, and whose posture is neither vertical nor righteous. In the archive of Viennese performance art, Anna Brus presents such a figure. Yet she is certainly not a paragon of what Cavarero calls inclination, for she does not embody the maternal stereotype. Anna Brus does not "lean in" to the postures of inclination that she assumes, but rather, as I have argued with attention to the unsettling effect of her figure and her look, she in distinctive ways leans out.[76] When responded to, her disinclination can be seen as infusing the space of performance art with a certain hesitation, opening up the possibility for an array of inclinations that, without presuming to step outside the historically determined field of stereotypes, are nonetheless without them.

When she calls herself just "a good assistant" (*eine gute Mitarbeiterin*), one cannot hear this self-deprecation without a hint of *Schmäh*—that mischievous Viennese irony well translated as "sarcasm" but perhaps better as "irreverent humor." For if she indeed lends a helping hand, inclines to the directions of her male collaborators, largely submits to being subjected to their disparate "actions"—and in no small measure makes them happen—she at the same time insinuates a reservation into the performance, which she never looks to be taking altogether seriously. Alongside Koeck's deliberate complicity, the figure of Anna Brus affords another insight into how performance art grapples with the persistence of misogynist structures. This is most clear not in performances that rehearse sexualized violence but in ones that cite iconographies supposed to define the relationship of mother and child.

Concluding the 1976 essay on "women's body art" that I cited earlier in this chapter, Lucy Lippard reflects on how "no women dealing with their own bodies or biographies have introduced pregnancy or childbirth as a major image." And yet "sex itself," she muses, "is a focal point." With regard to this "curious void," she speculates, "Perhaps procreativity is the next taboo to be tackled."[77] Lippard's essay is exemplary of a watershed in feminist debates of the late 1970s about the role of motherhood, marked by a revaluation of the creative as well as the social political significance of pregnancy, domestic labor, care work, and "women's time."[78] It nuances the valuations of a previous generation of feminist ideals of independence and autonomy that seemed to be irremediably patriarchal. In Lippard's historical context, it was necessary to assert the significance of motherhood: not only to understand the labor and care involved in motherhood as work but also to recognize postures of dependence and precarity as worthy of political, and artistic, attention. Although *Inclinations* was first published in 2014, in her unwavering affirmation of "maternal inclination," Cavarero shows herself to be very much a product of this generation.

Had she known of it at the time, Lippard might well have been interested in the work of Lea Lublin. As I discuss in the introduction, Lublin had already tackled the taboo of procreativity in May 1968, in a feminist performance set against the backdrop of student and worker protests in Paris. For *Mon fils* (My son; figs. 1.36, 1.37), Lublin brought her baby son and his crib into the prestigious exhibition of contemporary art in Paris, the annual May Salon. Invited to exhibit paintings, she instead performed maternal inclination. In the first instance, what Catherine Spencer has called Lublin's "act of displacement," her "performance of motherhood" in an art institutional space, makes a critical claim about the labor of motherhood and the work of art.[79] The performance draws attention to the ways in which cultural institutions perpetuate an asymmetrical appreciation and mutual exclusion of maternal labor and artistic practice. By occupying the gallery space with *Mon fils*, Lublin resituates the labor of creating and maintaining a life as an explicitly creative practice commensurate with producing a work of art. The performance also presented a contentious feminist contribution to Paris's 1968. In the midst of militant demonstrations with workers and students, who were taking an assertive stand out on the city streets, *Mon fils* made the case for the less righteous but arguably no less politically consequential posture of maternal inclination. As long as it has no patience for such laborious and time-consuming practices as childcare, the project of social justice is bound to be frustrated. For it remains beholden to a geometric imaginary that disparages, overlooks, or seeks to rectify postures of inclination.[80]

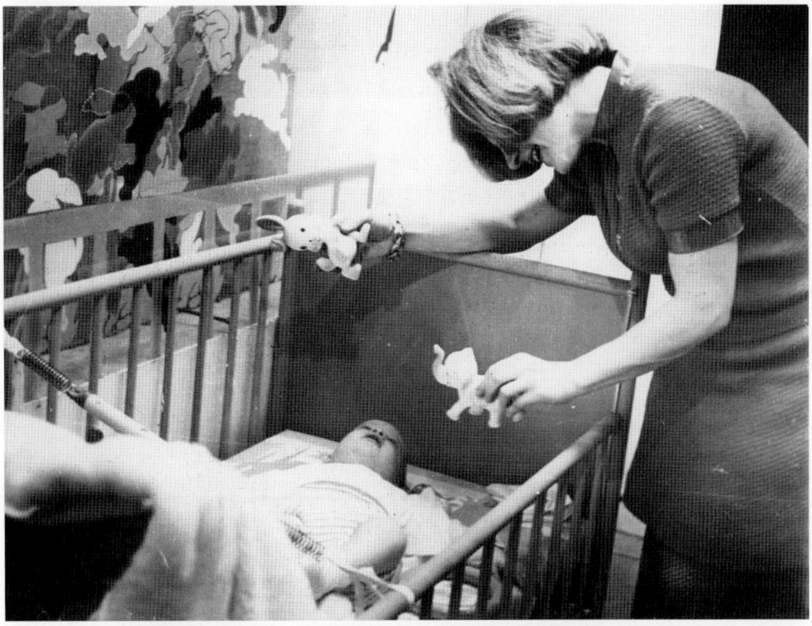

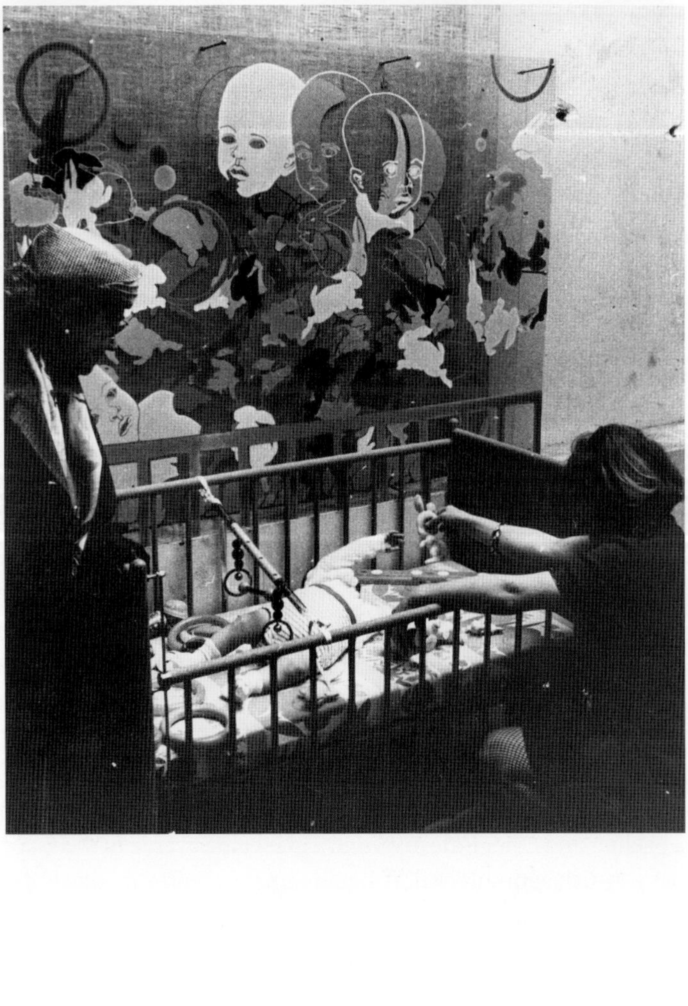

Figures 1.36–1.37. Lea Lublin with Nicolás Lublin, *Mon fils* (My son), 1968. Courtesy of Nicolás Lublin & 1 Mira Madrid.

In 1968, Lublin walked a fine line, for the danger of advocating for maternal inclination is to uncritically reproduce "the maternal stereotype." Over fifty years later, Cavarero, curiously, walks this line again—and trips over it.[81] As queer critiques of her theory have noted, she sometimes appears to be unreflexively invested in heteronormative stereotypes, and most notably in the imperatives of reproductive futurism.[82] Given her altogether affirmative reading of Leonardo's *The Virgin and Child with St. Anne*, Cavarero can quite justifiably be seen as a proponent of the figure that Lee Edelman calls "the Child," with a capital C, the structure around which so much of the politics and mores that define everyday life remain organized.[83]

In this regard, Anna Brus's performances as a mother are striking. In a trilogy of films they made together in 1967, which could well be exhibited as a triptych, Anna and Günter, together yet isolated within each part, partial yet connected across each frame, perform visual and embodied forms of intimate permeability. In *Pullover* (Sweater; fig. 1.38), Anna Brus knits, naked and heavily pregnant. The Bruses have the camera framed to cut unnervingly through her eyes, distorting the lower half of her face. Slowly, the performance of knitting conceals Anna's pregnant body from view. The mood is slightly tense, anticipatory. In triptych format, *Pullover* could be flanked by *Osmose* (Osmosis; fig. 1.39) and *Einatmen und Ausatmen* (Breathing in and breathing out; fig. 1.40), each of which shows Günter. In *Osmose*, he is curled up naked in a fetal posture in the empty corner of a room; a balloon inflates and deflates slowly between his knees, never popping. In *Einatmen und Ausatmen*, his bare torso fills the screen, a piece of clear tape pulling taut against his skin as he breathes steadily, in and out. Together, these performances present an ambivalence toward maternity. They draw out the uncertainty and temporality of waiting, knit together the parental positions as vulnerable and exposed, earnest yet anxious about what is to come, and suggest an unconforming portrait of conception and gestation.

Once Diana was born, and one year before Lublin's institutional intervention with *Mon fils*, Anna and Günter composed a performance with their six-month-old child in their apartment in Vienna, *Aktion mit Diana* (Action with Diana; 1967; figs. 1.41, 1.42, 1.43). Anna Brus recalls fondly: "*Diana* for me really is one of the most beautiful and poetic actions," for at its center, "the baby is the dominant figure. A new human being has arrived!"[84] Bemused, Diana—whose permission I obtained, along with Anna's and Günter's, to reproduce these images—lies naked on a cushion on the floor. She is surrounded by a curious selection of household objects gradually supplemented throughout the performance by Anna: First, a ball of yarn unravels into the room, connecting the performance to *Pullover*. A baby rattle, surge protectors and two eggs, as well as paper clips, tacks, loose lightbulbs, a plate of food, a corkscrew, a pacifier and other little toys, and a glass pipe accrue in the space around the baby. A dish with a thick dark liquid remains, quite ominously despite the apparent good humor, in the foreground. As the baby squirms to see him, Günter

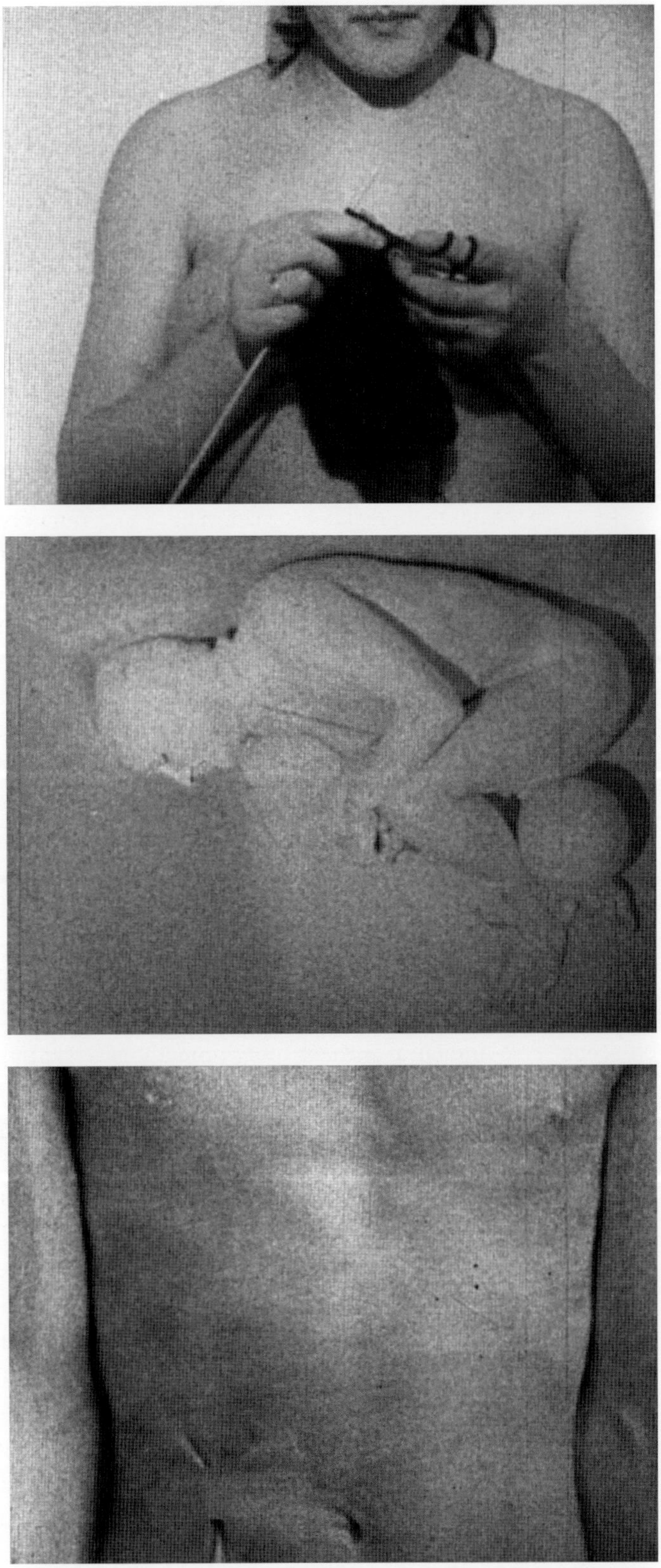

Figures 1.38–1.40. Günter Brus with Anna Brus, *Pullover* (Sweater), *Osmose* (Osmosis), and *Einatmen und Ausatmen* (Breathing in and breathing out), all 1967. Film by Helmut Kronberger. © Günter Brus. Courtesy of the BRUSEUM, Universalmuseum Joanneum.

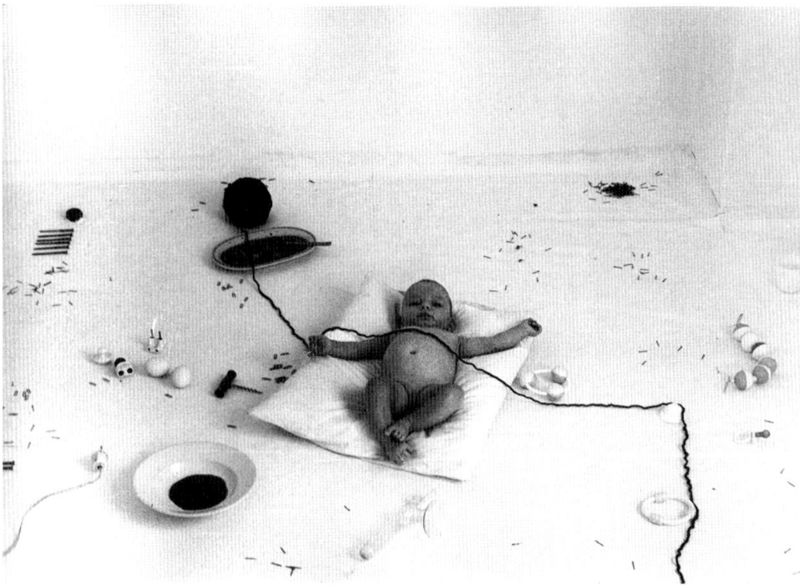

Figures 1.41–1.42. Günter Brus with Anna Brus and Diana Brus, *Aktion mit Diana* (Action with Diana), 1967. Photograph by Kurt Kren. © Günter Brus. Courtesy of the BRUSEUM, Universalmuseum Joanneum.

enters the scene and paints himself white, standing on one leg and then the other, cropped from the frame, which centers on Diana. In the overexposed photographic documentation, one can just make out Günter's white-painted figure against the wall as he shuffles along it, resting his forehead against it, his back to the baby in the center of the room. Assuming postures of inclination gradually approaching the horizontal, he crouches, balls himself up, sprawls out flat on the floor until he is supine next to the baby, yet without touching her.

Aktion mit Diana is the most extreme instance of the inconspicuous ubiquity of Anna Brus in Viennese Actionism. For in this performance she does not appear at all—and yet her presence is most definitely felt. Her involvement is evidenced most immediately in her child's face, which responds to her look, off-scene. This liminal or perhaps more properly parergal position is epitomized in the one and only photograph in the archive of this performance that shows Anna, in everyday dress, holding the bewildered Diana, comforting her for a moment in the midst of the strange goings-on (fig. 1.44). Having figured along its margins, Anna appears suddenly within the archive but still outside of the "action," performing motherhood.

As with other works where Anna figures as a mother, her performance in *Aktion mit Diana* is disinclined to affirm the maternal stereotype. I see this as an important form of feminist refusal, one that complements the contrasting gesture Lublin would make the following year.[85] What Anna Brus works through in her performances with her child is captured in her phrase "a new human being has arrived." The human being celebrated here is by no means "the Child" but simply a child. And as performances with Anna Brus show, the arrival of a child is no less a source of wonder and of care, of labor and of joy, when one refuses to submit to social impositions to venerate the infant or,

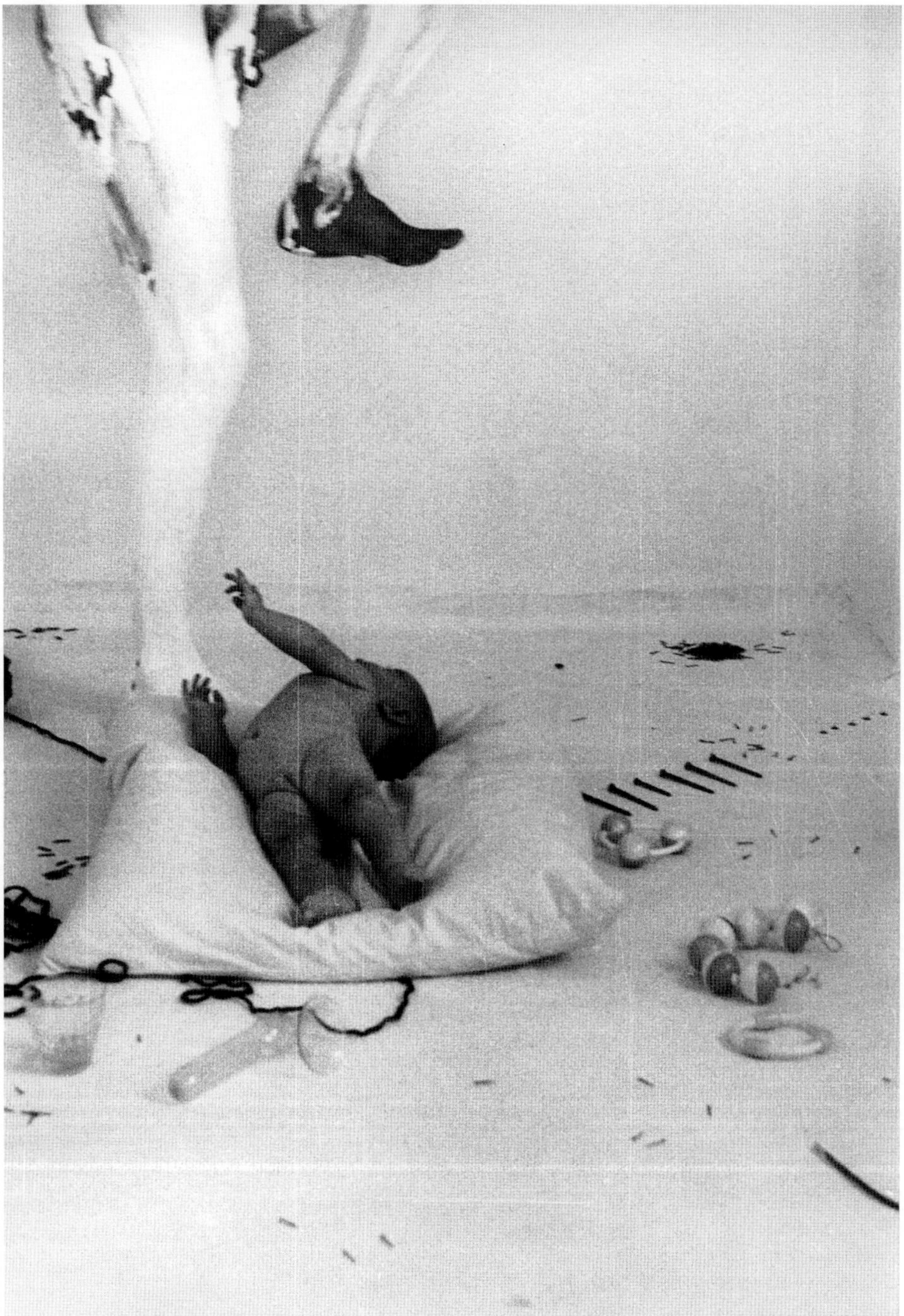

for that matter, the maternal relation. In contrast to Cavarero's reading of the Virgin and Child in Leonardo's painting, Anna's figure articulates a range of postures that emphasize the ambivalent cares of motherhood in ways that are perhaps less pure, less wholesome, less pleasing to the eye, but by no means less attentive.

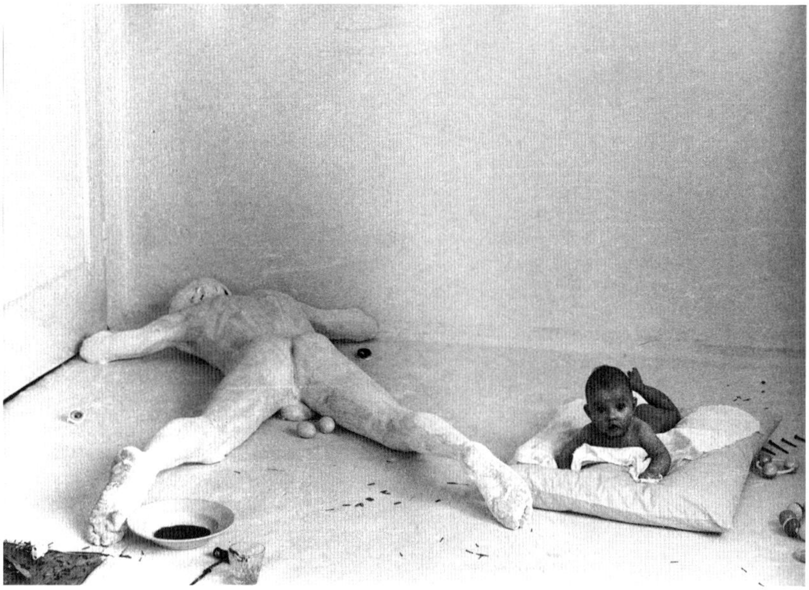

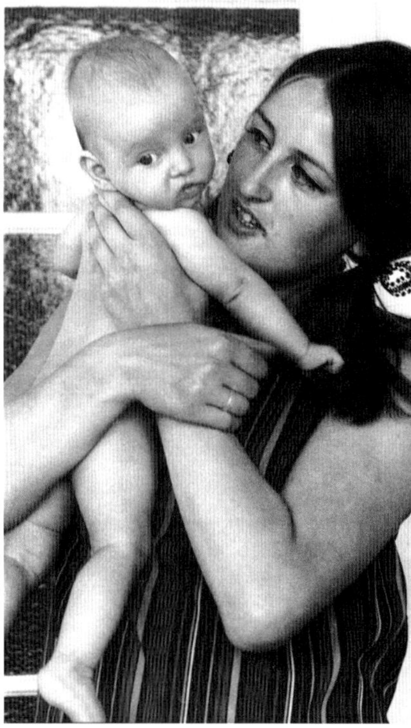

Figures 1.43–1.44. Günter Brus with Anna Brus and Diana Brus, *Aktion mit Diana* (Action with Diana), 1967. Photograph by Kurt Kren. © Günter Brus. Courtesy of the BRUSEUM, Universalmuseum Joanneum.

Anna Brus's disinclination pursues a deflationary anthropometric that is everyday rather than stereotypical. Performances with her child decline to rehearse the stereotype of the Virgin Mother and explore, rather than idealize, the awkward conditions of vulnerability that are disclosed by the arrival of a new human being. These conditions are the delightful and disgusting focus of a performance with Nitsch, referred to as *24.b Aktion* (Action 24b; fig. 1.45), in the Bruses' home in January 1968.[86] Their naked baby is placed alone, prostrate on a white sheet. She cries. Animal innards, gauze, bandages, and blood are carefully arranged around her. Anna removes Diana from the mess and comforts her, as Nitsch then reclines naked on the same sheet, with the guts of a lamb spread across his groin. The performance scandalously travesties tired analogies between the Savior and the Lamb of God, each an iteration of the Child. The gruesome juxtaposition suggests instead a relentlessly immanent schema of biological life. Although this is not the performance Lippard has in mind when she disparages Nitsch's "destructive male imitation of the constructive female ability to give birth," it could easily be read in this vein.[87] But this would be, once again, to overlook the figure of Anna. She does not offer what Lippard seeks: neither an affirmative "positive image" of women in male body art nor a clear assertion of "feminist consciousness." And yet if *24.b Aktion* is considered in view of her peripheral presence, Anna Brus's disinclination shifts the scene. From one consumed by Nitsch's preoccupation with received iconographies, we are led to a scenario concerned, not without humor, with unassuming relations that matter.

In several performances on the second Sunday of May 1968, Mother's Day—and thus just at the time of Lublin's performance in Paris—Anna Brus engages in some of her most troubling performances of motherhood. *Alles Gute zum Muttertag wünscht Ihr Otto Mühl* (Happy Mother's Day from Otto Muehl) places mother and child front and center.[88] The formality of offering "good wishes" for Mother's Day, with all its heteronormative and paternalistic overtones, is subject to withering ridicule that leaves no one looking good. Günter Brus remains outside the camera's frame. Anna Brus, fully dressed, is seated at a simple table. Muehl stands to her left; Schwarzkogler kneels, already completely naked, to her right. Anna holds Diana in her lap, who looks about curiously while playing with a rubber catheter. This is the least disturbing component of the scene. In what follows, Muehl undoes his pants and Anna starts to jerk him off. A cat wanders in and out. Muehl can't get it up so Schwarzkogler lends a helping hand. In short, there is no climax. Schwarzkogler smiles wryly; Muehl pours a thin opaque liquid—it looks like baby formula or breast milk—from a bottle onto the floor. Anna looks on impassively; Diana remains unperturbed.

With the figure of Anna Brus with her child at its center, at once engaged and looking on at the impotent male figures posturing disconsolately around and for her, this is a most abysmal performance of in-action. Little happens

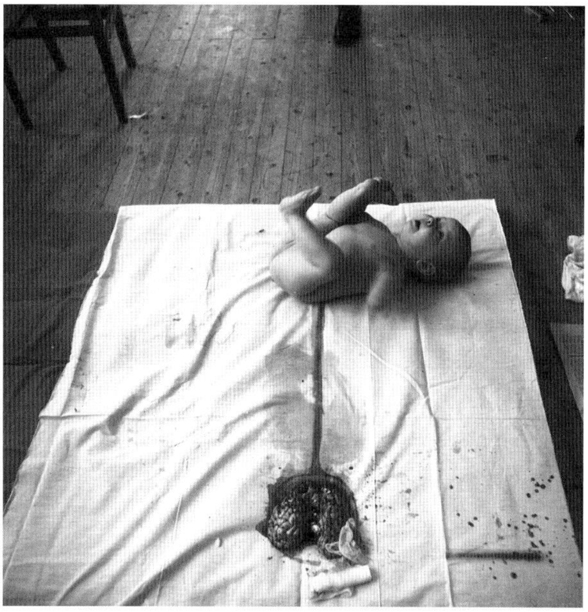

Figure 1.45. Hermann Nitsch with Diana Brus, *24.b Aktion (Action 24b)*, 1968. Photograph by Ludwig Hoffenreich. © Hermann Nitsch; digital image © mumok – Museum moderner Kunst Stiftung Ludwig Wien.

even as stereotypes of maternity and masculinity are upset. It is easily mistaken. For insofar as it presses on deeply held affective and ideological sore points in Viennese society of the 1960s (and not only then and there), it provokes a certain consternation, even outrage. The impassivity of disinclination, especially when it comes to such cultural flash points as motherhood, proves capable of igniting incendiary passions, especially among those invested in the stereotypes that are here subversively exposed. Less than one month later, in the context of the infamous event *Kunst und Revolution* (Art and revolution), the Bruses staged another performance of parenting and motherhood in their home for the local newspaper, *Das Wiener Wochenblatt*. As I discuss in chapter 2, this incident, which I see as a domestic continuation of *Kunst und Revolution*, leads to a public outcry focused on Anna's failure to perform maternal stereotypes and to the demand to remove their child from their care.

Inclined obliquely in scenes that solicit care, the figure of Anna Brus complicates the "alternative ontological root for action" that Cavarero sees exemplified in maternal inclination.[89] If this "root for action" is to be found, as Cavarero argues, not in rectitude and autonomy, but in inclination and relations of dependency, then Anna Brus's disinclination is devoted to the ambivalence of these relations. Her figure gives rise to a tension that traverses Viennese Actionism, unsettling the expectations that it otherwise awakens. In refusing to wholeheartedly engage in the action, refusing to unambiguously inhabit stereotypes or to outright oppose them, which may come across to some as simply abstruse and to others as obscene, she withholds affirmation. In the history of Viennese performance art, Anna Brus's disinclination opens a barely discernible angle in the geometric imaginary, it registers a *dis-* in the position she inhabits, just as it registers an *in-* in the action. As a form of feminist refusal, Anna Brus's disinclination reticently discloses an unassuming space for the cultivation of nonstereotypical positions, practices, and relations *within* historical and traditional structures. Anna Brus's disinclination is the complement to Koeck's insult. Like many other unnamed or overlooked figures, Anna Brus and Hanel Koeck make space in performance art history for the otherwise inclined.

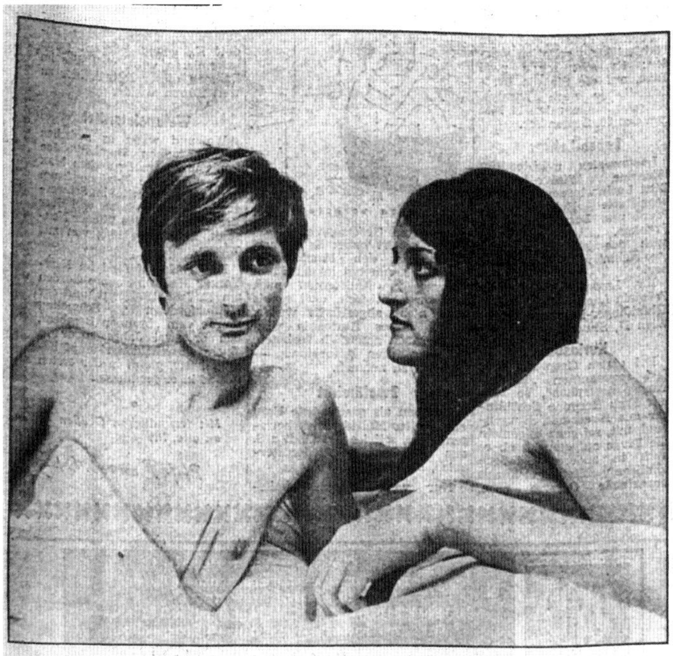

Rädelsführer Brus privat: Mit seiner Ehefrau Anna

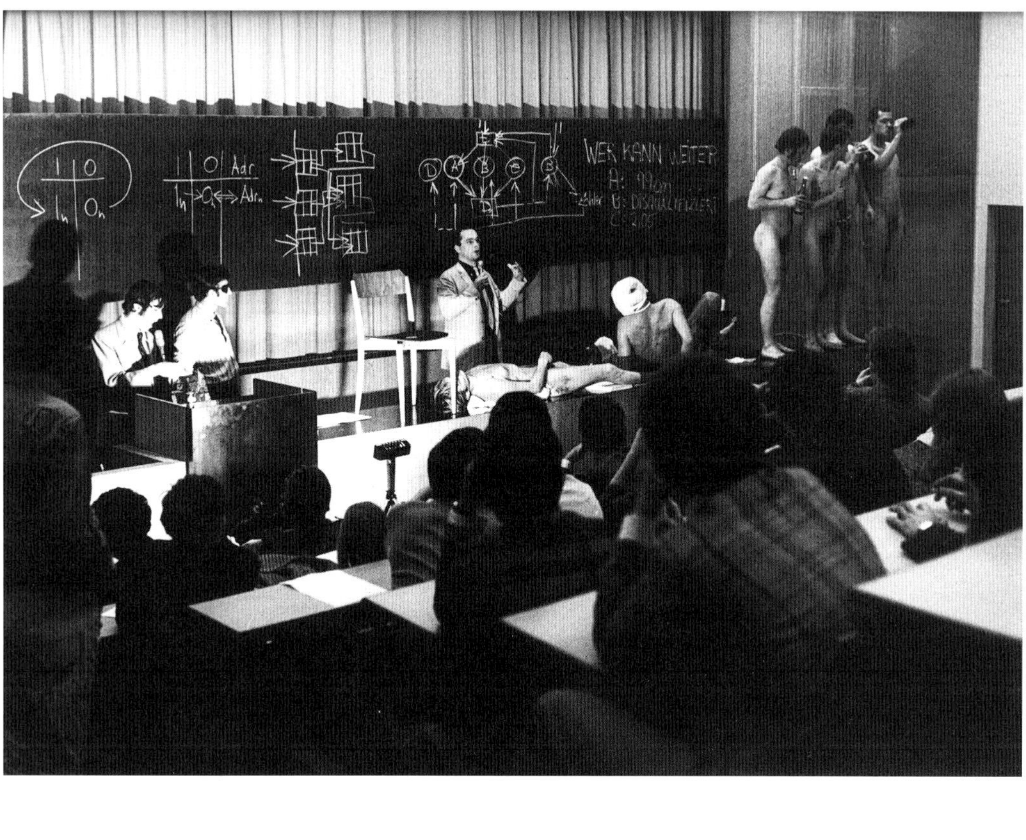

Incident: On Failing to Perform, Vienna 1968

2

June 22, 1968 (fig. 2.1): Anna Brus and Günter Brus pose together in bed in their apartment in Vienna, partially unclothed. Their hands touch gently in the foreground, and each looks away from the camera, a smile playing on their lips. "Ringleader Brus in private: with his wife Anna" reads the image caption. The photograph was taken while Günter was out of prison on remand, charged with "debasing national symbols" following his involvement in the infamous event *Kunst und Revolution* (Art and revolution) two weeks earlier at a lecture hall of the University of Vienna. This "private" look at the Bruses complements the public image of Günter, who is referred to in the accompanying newspaper article as the "the most hated human being in Austria."

Figure 2.1. Front page of the newspaper *Wiener Wochenblatt*, June 22, 1968, detail. Scanned by the author in the Austrian National Library, Vienna.

Figure 2.2. Günter Brus with Otmar Bauer, Peter Jirak, Otto Muehl, Herbert Stumpfl, Christof Subik, Peter Weibel, Oswald Wiener, and "Laurids," *Kunst und Revolution* (Art and revolution), 1968. Photograph by Siegfried Klein (Khasaq). © Günter Brus. Courtesy of the BRUSEUM, Universalmuseum Joanneum.

June 7, 1968 (fig. 2.2): an image more recognizable as a document of performance art. A group of men, in various stages of undress, occupies an auditorium lectern in front of a long chalkboard, where the seemingly systematic presentation of information offers a perplexing backdrop for their disorderly activities. Two men hold microphones and both appear to speak at once. Four others drink from beer bottles while standing naked on the lectern. A note on the chalkboard behind them reads: "Who can further" (*Wer kann weiter*). Next to them, two barely clothed figures recline awkwardly; one holds a crumpled sheet of paper, his head wrapped in gauze; the other wears only socks. In the audience, one person appears to take notes, while several others hold their heads in their hands, amused or appalled, perhaps covering their eyes or noses. This is one of the few photographs taken of *Kunst und Revolution*, accounts of which in the coming days would generate scandalizing rumors, reports, and investigations of ever more outrageous and obscene behavior. Known colloquially as Vienna's 1968, *Kunst und Revolution* has come to be referred to as "a hot quarter-hour."[1] The disparaging turn of phrase conveys the sexual anxieties that incited the excessive interest of the press and the police. Attention to the mediatization of the event, however, shows that it was neither as "hot" nor as brief as one might be led to believe.

Kunst und Revolution was a failure both artistically and politically.[2] It marked the dismemberment of the fragile student left in Vienna and the beginning of the end of the tenuous artistic movement that would, in 1970, be retrospectively called Viennese Actionism.[3] Especially for advocates of a postwar Austrian avant-garde, *Kunst und Revolution* is a source of considerable embarrassment.[4] But its failures are precisely the point of the performance. *Kunst und Revolution* produces a perspicuous display of the impotence of art and the impotence of politics in Vienna circa 1968. Rather than discredit it for being ineffective as a form of either artistic actionism or political activism, *Kunst und Revolution* is better seen as an incident of in-action. It was never entirely clear, neither for the artists nor for the administrators, press, and police who responded so vociferously to their work, whether what was happening was artistic or political.

In his first of many depositions to the police, Günter Brus stated: "It is my art to produce such incidents" (*Es ist meine Kunst, solche Vorfälle zu produzieren*).[5] I translate *Vorfälle* as "incidents" to emphasize the aspect of occurrence, danger, occasionality, and passivity that Brus insists on, and that traverses Viennese performance art. Not the staging of actions, but the production of incidents. *Kunst und Revolution* demonstrates that what is called Viennese Actionism responded in the 1960s to an anxiety about "action" in the broadest sense: about the possibility of concrete political action on the one hand, and, on the other, of artistic production as an aesthetic and critical social practice. Unsettling such esteemed Austrian institutions as the university, the courts of law, the traditions of the fine arts, and the Viennese family home, the incident drew out the conditions that explain why Vienna's 1968 could be nothing other than a "tame revolution," if one can speak of a revolution at all.[6]

The study of an incident as opposed to an action involves an approach to performance documents that is art historical rather than forensic. Instead of using such documents to trace back to protagonists' singular graphic acts in order to establish what they really did, I consider the performance as consisting in its mediatization, in its recording and retelling. This method offers insight into the institutions that structured the scope, possibility, and impact of artistic and revolutionary action in Austrian society in the 1960s. And it evinces a different temporality: Far from occurring at a punctual moment in time and at a particular place, *Kunst und Revolution* reverberates around the dates of June 7 and June 22 within the various institutions and discourses it provoked. In this regard, figures 2.1 and 2.2—of the Bruses together at home and of the unruly university lecture hall—present two aspects of the same incident: *Kunst und Revolution*.

Rumors, Records, Mediatizations

Kunst und Revolution was scheduled to take place on the evening of Friday, June 7, 1968, in the main auditorium of the New Institute Building of the Uni-

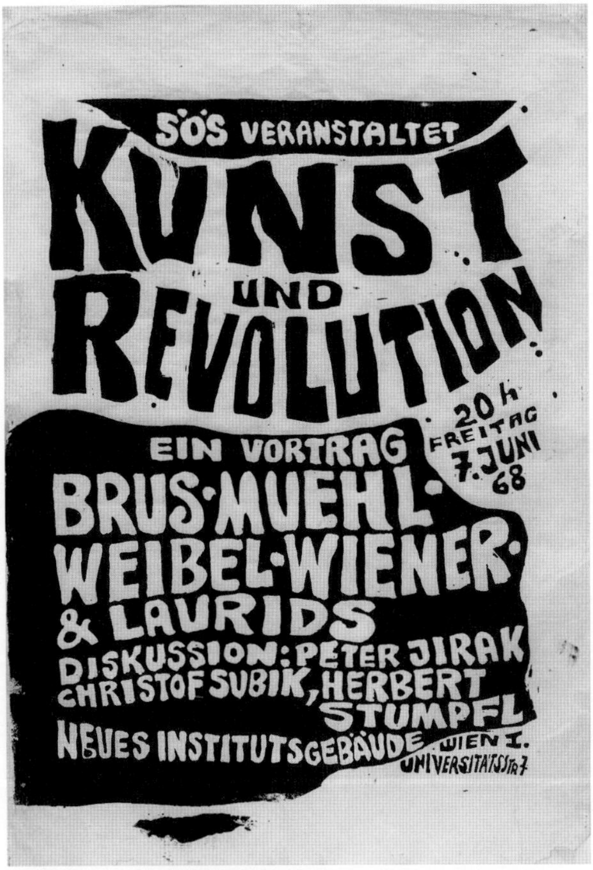

Figure 2.3. Günter Brus, *Kunst und Revolution* (Art and revolution), 1968. Poster, screen print. © Günter Brus. Courtesy of the BRUSEUM, Universalmuseum Joanneum.

versity of Vienna. In the days leading up to the event, screen-printed posters (fig. 2.3), made by Günter Brus, announced that the Austrian Socialist Students' Union (SÖS) had organized "a lecture" (*ein Vortrag*) by several local artists, including Brus, Otto Muehl, Peter Weibel, Oswald Wiener, and an enigmatic figure simply called "Laurids." The lecture was to be followed by a discussion with the university students Peter Jirak, Christof Subik, and Herbert Stumpfl. Yet before *Kunst und Revolution* began that night, rumors of something not quite so academic in format were circulating: "I can only explain the rumor that spread on Friday afternoon announcing excesses at the event insofar as the propagators of the rumors had already experienced events by Brus and Muehl and expected something similar that evening."[7] This is how Jirak, a graduate of the painting program at the Academy of Fine Arts in Vienna, a doctoral candidate in philosophy at the University of Vienna, and president of the SÖS, concluded a protocol he recorded under the supervision of a senior official from the rectorate of the university three days later. Until the event, Jirak stated, he had "never seen an action [*eine Aktion*] by Mr. Muehl or Mr. Brus."[8]

In contrast with Jirak's equanimity, several other students were motivated to attend *Kunst und Revolution* by the association of the very names Brus and

Muehl with "excessive" actions. Their explicit intention was to inhibit what they were already certain would be a "provocative event." The University of Vienna student Herwig Friesinger, in a statement made to the police on Monday June 10, explained, "I had heard over the course of the afternoon . . . that the Austrian Socialist Students' Union was planning a provocative event in the Institute Building the same evening. I arranged with numerous colleagues to attend the event and to remain in the Institute Building in order to prevent any conspicuous excesses."[9] It was, however, the university porter who would first take action once *Kunst und Revolution* was underway, calling the rector, Fritz Schwind, back to the building to witness the scene in the auditorium. In his statement to the police on Sunday, June 9, the porter related what compelled his call: "I saw a completely naked man, whose upper body was smeared in blood, lying on the lectern. He was moving his hands in such a way, as though he were masturbating. At the same time, someone was reading in my opinion something pornographic out loud, because I heard words like '*Penies*' and '*Fallus*.'"[10]

Upon arriving at the university, Rector Schwind was too late to witness the events on the lectern. He was met, however, by Friesinger and his "colleagues," all of whom straight away set about writing a *Gedächtnisprotokoll* (report written from memory), which they would submit to the authorities along with official witness statements two days later at the State Court of Criminal Affairs. While they prevented none of the so-called excesses that unfolded that evening, they certainly contributed to the excessive discourse that would come to define *Kunst und Revolution* by initiating the proliferation of protocols and records supposedly meant to document it. These provided a specific tone, timeline, and vocabulary that was subsequently put to use in the legal investigation of, and media attacks on, a number of participants. It is no exaggeration to say that *Kunst und Revolution* was and continues to be produced by the mediated perspectives it generated.[11]

In a strenuously bureaucratic style, the *Gedächtnisprotokoll* sought to record the facts of the event—the "facts" insofar as they were recalled by those willing to take part in such a formal administrative process. The earnestness of such an official approach to documentation takes on a comical, if not ridiculous, tone:

> This organizer [Peter Jirak] gave an introductory lecture on the topic of Art and Revolution at the beginning. . . . Next . . . [Peter Weibel] demanded that the tech team raise and lower the volume of the microphone and at the same time brighten and dim the lighting. . . . After this, speaker Mr. Otto Muehl, former middle school teacher, stepped up to the lectern and began his lecture with the words *gailer Robert* [horny Robert] (meaning Robert Kennedy). . . . During Mr. Muehl's performances, Mr. Brus undressed completely, mounted the auditorium stage with his chair, stepped up onto the lectern desk, placed his chair on it, and cut himself with a razorblade on the left side of his chest, so

> that the blood ran down to his sex organ. At the same time, the Viennese writer Oswald Wiener began with theoretical explanations of society, which . . . were barely audible. The students jeered, and shouts of *Schweine* [pigs] could be heard. Brus began to urinate into the audience and took urine into his hand and swallowed it. While urinating, he sang the song "Gaudeamus igitur." Muehl then came back into the lecture hall with a man with a bandaged head and whipped him with a leather belt, so that blood poured out of his body from multiple places. The bandaged guy read throughout something about lesbian love. . . . In the meantime, Brus had turned around and began to shit and sing the Austrian national anthem. The feces that came out he smeared then and there over his entire body. Under the direction of Otmar Bauer, a student at the Technical Academy, three more naked men stepped up to the podium, as Bauer commanded them in lockstep with a whistle. Brus was at this point in a supine position on the auditorium desk and masturbated for about twenty minutes. The group of naked men was to the right of the table. Additionally, one of these naked men urinated while groaning. Brus also made groaning sounds.[12]

Numerous typos and "mis-takes"—not to mention Freudian-slips—pepper the recording of such statements, providing an indication at the paralegal and linguistic level of the disturbance the event seemed to cause. The very attempt in the *Gedächtnisprotokoll* to follow a standard bureaucratic form in order to produce a reliable and accurate recounting of events brings into focus the challenge to this manner of accounting that made *Kunst und Revolution* into such an inflammatory issue—not least for the administrators and administrations tasked with establishing what had really happened. These curious documents betray the anxieties that the performance occasioned, reproducing the ambivalence, incoherence, and confusion that seemed to define it.

While it was reported that six film cameras and numerous other cameras were in use that evening, including by representatives from Austrian television, few visual documents of the event have emerged. A handful of black-and-white photographs by Siegfried Klein, as well as film footage taken by Ernst Schmidt Jr., none of which particularly confirms or contradicts the written reports, have since circulated widely (figs. 2.4, 2.5, 2.6).[13] That June, however, the photographs printed alongside the press coverage of *Kunst und Revolution* were almost exclusively images of so-called happenings and actions that had taken place previously in Vienna, leading to further confusion about what had or had not happened on June 7.[14] Then, on August 1, photographs of Brus, Muehl, and Wiener in their first court appearance were published. *Kunst und Revolution* took place in this escalatory tension generated between rumor and written record in the press. For this reason, the event is best understood in terms of both the effects of its mediatization and the negative affects it occasioned. Neither a one-off political demonstration nor a live performance that happened at a particular place and time, *Kunst und Revolution* is defined by the

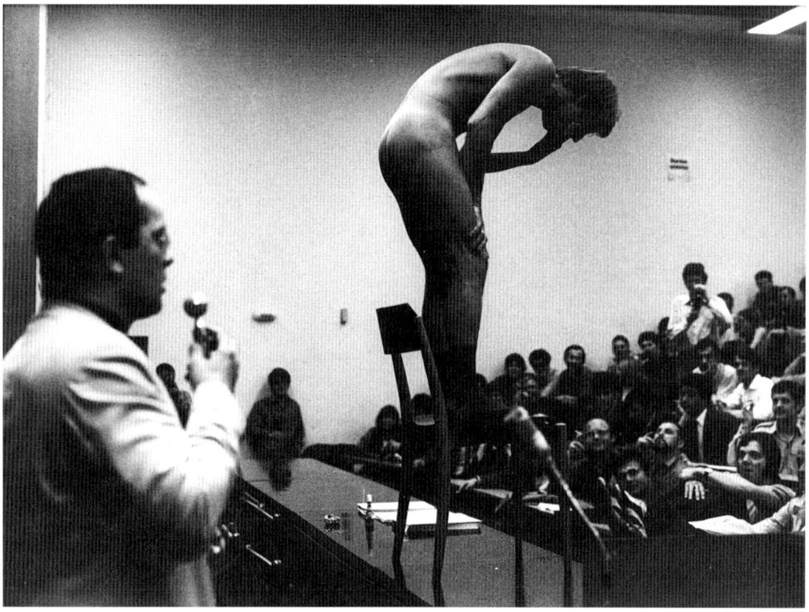

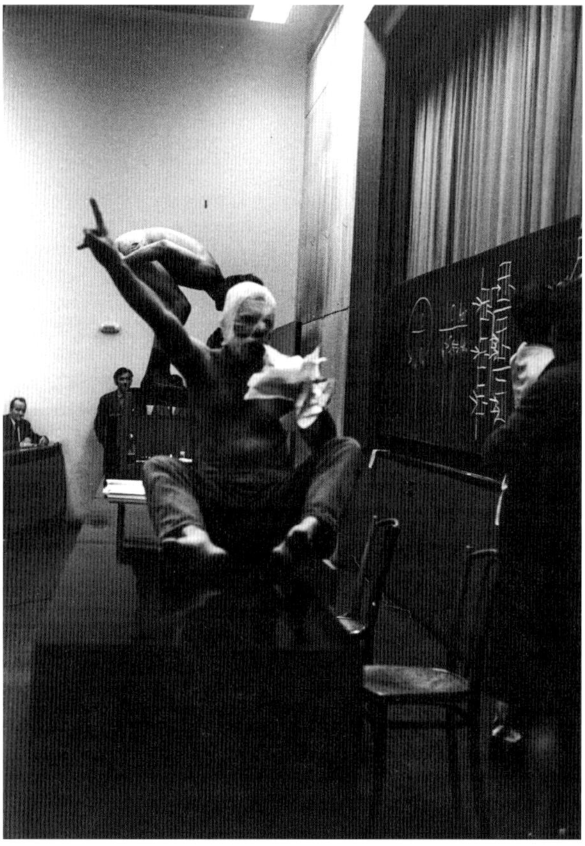

Figures 2.4–2.6. Günter Brus with Otmar Bauer, Peter Jirak, Otto Muehl, Herbert Stumpfl, Christof Subik, Peter Weibel, Oswald Wiener, and "Laurids," *Kunst und Revolution* (Art and revolution), 1968. Photograph by Siegfried Klein (Khasaq). © Günter Brus. Courtesy of the BRUSEUM, Universalmuseum Joanneum.

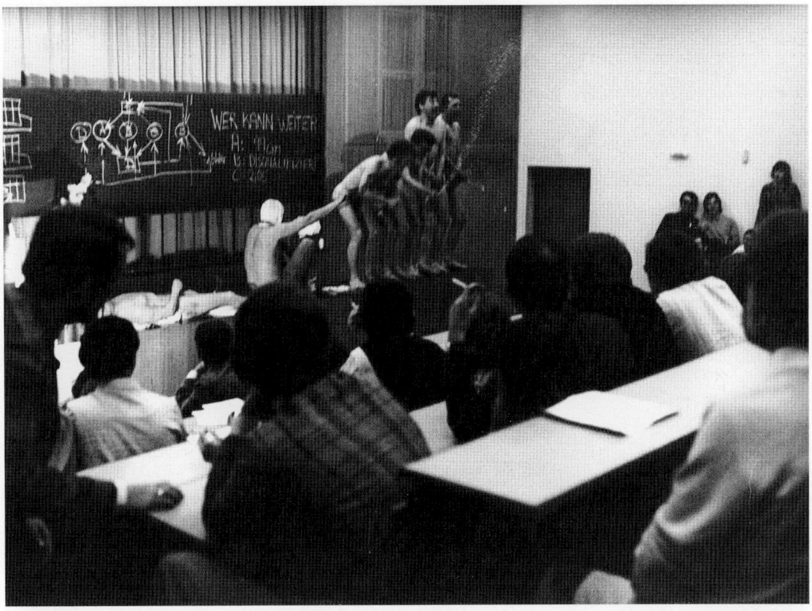

conflagration of documents, processes, images, and imaginings it produced within the Austrian establishment, represented by the university, the media, and the police.

On Sunday, June 9, 1968, from the pages of the conservative *Kronen Zeitung* to those of the socialist *Arbeiter Zeitung*, the first headlines referring to the "excesses" and "scandalous scenes" at the university appeared in the press.[15] On Monday, June 10, the participants were called to the State Court of Criminal Affairs to make statements. The judgment was swift. By Wednesday, June 12, everyone named in the *Gedächtnisprotokoll*, as well as Stumpfl, who was named on the poster, had been arrested. Brus, Jirak, Muehl, and Wiener were initially sentenced to twenty-eight days, Bauer and Stumpfl to twenty days, and Weibel to fourteen days in prison.[16] Brus, Muehl, and Wiener, who came to be seen as the main exponents of the "excesses," were taken into investigative custody and scheduled to be further prosecuted in court the following month. On July 31, 1968, accused of "the public debasement of the institutions of marriage, family, and property, or the approval of unlawful or immoral actions," Wiener was exonerated.[17] He promptly moved to West Berlin with his life-partner, Ingrid Wiener, where they opened a café. Accused of "the debasement of Austrian symbols" and "causing willful bodily injury," Muehl was cleared of the former charge and given four weeks in prison for the latter, which he had already served by the time of the sentencing.[18] Together in a shared apartment with Bauer and Stumpfl, he would soon realize the first phase of what became the Commune Friedrichshof, where he would engage in genuinely criminal behavior.[19]

Brus alone pleaded guilty from the start. He stood accused of "the debasement of Austrian symbols" and "the transgression of causing gross public

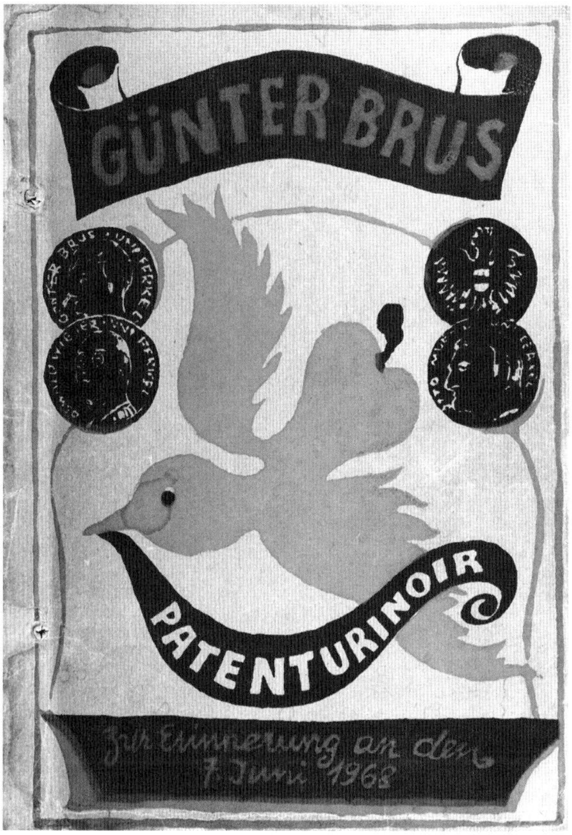

Figure 2.7. Günter Brus, *Patent Urinoir - Zur Erinnerung an den 7. Juni 1968* (Patent *urinoir*: In memory of June 7, 1968), 1968. Artist's book, cover. © Günter Brus. Courtesy of the BRUSEUM, Universalmuseum Joanneum.

unrest thus bringing about the violation of morality and decency."[20] He was ultimately sentenced, after a failed appeal, in February 1969 to five months of "harsh imprisonment" (reduced from six), with hard labor and fasting days.[21] At this time it was further noted that, in addition to those material damages Brus had caused—referred to as "cleaning and repairs"—he was responsible for "unforeseeable immaterial damage," for having marred, domestically and internationally, the reputation of the University of Vienna and indeed the Republic of Austria.[22] To avoid his impending imprisonment, and thanks to an administrative glitch, Günter Brus and Anna Brus fled to West Berlin. Without the legal option of registering as a resident of Germany, Günter's activities were limited.[23]

In October 1968 in Vienna, he had self-published *Patent Urinoir - Zur Erinnerung an den 7. Juni 1968* (Patent *urinoir*: In memory of June 7, 1968; fig. 2.7), a pamphlet collecting news coverage, student protocols, police protocols, psychiatric evaluations, and hate mail related to *Kunst und Revolution*, all of which he interspersed with his own writings and drawings. In West Berlin, Brus continued to make artist's books and graphic works (fig. 2.8), and to explore the intimate private performances of what he called *Körperanalyse* (body-analysis).[24] Anna Brus found work as a seamstress, supporting him

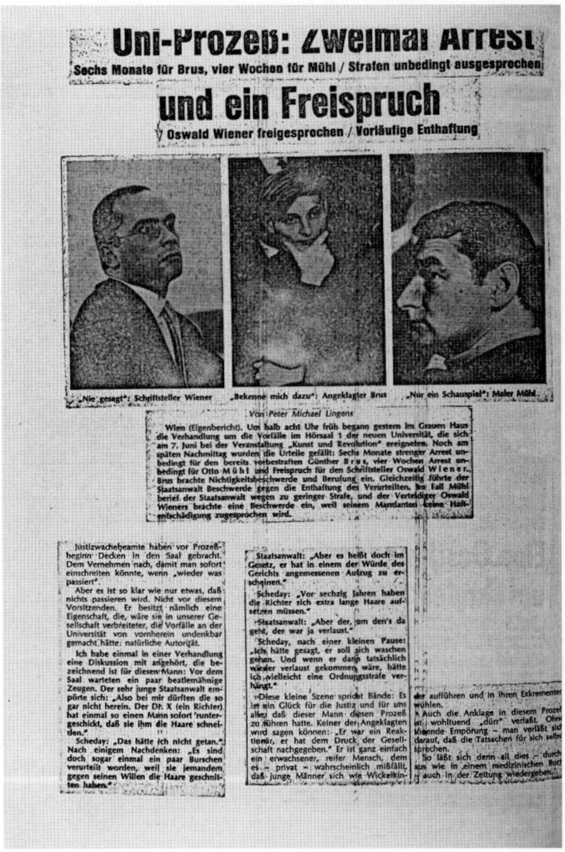

Uni-Prozeß: Zweimal Arrest

Sechs Monate für Brus, vier Wochen für Mühl / Strafen unbedingt ausgesprochen

und ein Freispruch

Oswald Wiener freigesprochen / Vorläufige Enthaftung

„Nie gesagt": Schriftsteller Wiener — „Bekenne mich dazu": Angeklagter Brus — „Nur ein Schauspiel": Maler Mühl

Von Peter Michael Lingens

Wien (Eigenbericht). Um halb acht Uhr früh begann gestern im Grauen Haus die Verhandlung um die Vorfälle im Hörsaal 1 der neuen Universität, die sich am 7. Juni bei der Veranstaltung „Kunst und Revolution" ereigneten. Noch am späten Nachmittag wurden die Urteile gefällt: Sechs Monate strenger Arrest unbedingt für den bereits vorbestraften Günther Brus, vier Wochen Arrest unbedingt für Otto Mühl und Freispruch für den Schriftsteller Oswald Wiener. Brus brachte Nichtigkeitsbeschwerde und Berufung ein. Gleichzeitig führte der Staatsanwalt Beschwerde gegen die Enthaftung des Verurteilten. Im Fall Mühl berief der Staatsanwalt wegen zu geringer Strafe, und der Verteidiger Oswald Wieners brachte eine Beschwerde ein, weil seinem Mandanten keine Haftentschädigung zugesprochen wird.

Justizwachebeamte haben vor Prozeßbeginn Decken in den Saal gebracht. Dem Vernehmen nach, damit man sofort einschreiten könnte, wenn „wieder was passiert".

Aber es ist so klar wie nur etwas, daß nichts passieren wird. Nicht vor diesem Vorsitzenden. Er besitzt nämlich eine Eigenschaft, die, wäre sie in unserer Gesellschaft verbreiteter, die Vorfälle an der Universität von vornherein undenkbar gemacht hätte: natürliche Autorität.

Ich habe einmal in einer Verhandlung eine Diskussion mit angehört, die bezeichnend ist für diesen Mann: Vor dem Saal warteten ein paar beatlemähnige Zeugen. Der sehr junge Staatsanwalt empörte sich: „Also bei mir dürften die so gar nicht herein. Der Dr. X (ein Richter) hat einmal so einen Mann sofort 'runtergeschickt, daß sie ihm die Haare schneiden."

Scheday: „Das hätte ich nicht getan." Nach einigem Nachdenken: „Es sind doch sogar einmal ein paar Burschen verurteilt worden, weil sie jemandem gegen seinen Willen die Haare geschnitten haben."

Staatsanwalt: „Aber es heißt doch im Gesetz, er hat in einem der Würde des Gerichts angemessenen Aufzug zu erscheinen."

Scheday: „Vor sechzig Jahren haben die Richter sich extra lange Haare aufsetzen müssen."

Staatsanwalt: „Aber der, um den's da geht, der war ja verlaust."

Scheday, nach einer kleinen Pause: „Ich hätte gesagt, er soll sich waschen gehen. Und wenn er dann tatsächlich wieder verlaust gekommen wäre, hätte ich vielleicht eine Ordnungsstrafe verhängt."

Diese kleine Szene spricht Bände: Es ist ein Glück für die Justiz und für uns alle, daß dieser Mann diesen Prozeß zu führen hatte. Keiner der Angeklagten wird sagen können: „Er war ein Reaktionär, er hat dem Druck der Gesellschaft nachgegeben." Er ist ganz einfach ein erwachsener, reifer Mensch, dem es – privat – wahrscheinlich mißfällt, daß junge Männer sich wie Wickelkin-

der aufführen und in ihren Exkrementen wühlen.

Auch die Anklage in diesem Prozeß ist wohltuend „dürr" verfaßt. Ohne lodernde Empörung – man verläßt sich darauf, daß die Tatsachen für sich selbst sprechen.

So läßt sich denn all dies – durch aus wie in einem medizinischen Buch – auch in der Zeitung wiedergeben.

Figure 2.8. Günter Brus, *Unter dem Ladentisch* (Under the table), 1969. Artist's book, page opening with newspaper clippings related to the trial of Günter Brus, Otto Muehl, and Oswald Wiener. © Günter Brus. Courtesy of the BRUSEUM, Universalmuseum Joanneum.

as she had already in Vienna. In May 1969, in a lighthearted continuation of their artistic and "revolutionary" activities, Günter founded with several fellow Viennese expatriates the "Austrian Exile Government" and its "organ," a journal of art, literature, and cultural criticism, *Die Schastrommel* (The farting drum).[25]

Media Shitstorm

Preparations for *Kunst und Revolution* had indeed been made very quickly. On May 30, 1968, Jirak had met Wiener by chance in a Viennese coffeehouse and, recognizing Wiener as the author of the serially released installments of *Die Verbesserung von Mitteleuropa, Roman* (The improvement of Central Europe, novel; 1965–1969), approached him to talk.[26] In the light of their shared interest to "improve" the sociopolitical and artistic conditions shaping Central Europe in general, and Vienna in particular, the two decided to plan an event, and Wiener—who was not a student at the university—joined the SÖS.[27] On Wednesday, June 5, Jirak met with Rector Schwind and received the necessary written and stamped approval for the use of the main auditorium in the New Institute Building, having assured Schwind that the planned event would just be a lecture and not turn into a "sit-in" (*Hörsaalbesetzung*). Jirak also borrowed loudspeakers, tape recorders, and a sound amplifier from the Academy of Music.[28] Little regarding the content of the so-called lecture had at this point been established. Only on Thursday, June 6, the eve of the event, did Jirak and fellow members of the SÖS meet with Brus, Muehl, Weibel, and Wiener for the first time. Fearing a performance that would be harmful for their own cause, some members of the SÖS sought to cancel the event. Muehl purportedly assured them, however, that although "the actions [*Handlungen*] of the artists would be spontaneous," there was no need to be concerned.[29] Collectively, those present decided to proceed, printing an informal invitation with the statement: "'art' is not art. 'art' is politics that creates new styles of communication."[30] As it turned out, the media shitstorm provoked within established styles of communication proved most decisive. The discourses of representative Viennese institutions inadvertently realized the aim of the instigators of *Kunst und Revolution*, presenting the incident as art that is not art—and therefore a political matter.

In the meantime, Michael Jeannée, a journalist for the *Express*, had received "a tip-off" about the event.[31] His pivotal article appeared on Sunday, June 9. Alongside international news of the arrest of Martin Luther King Jr.'s assassin James Earl Ray and the burial of Robert Kennedy the previous day, and of the increasingly militarized response to student activism on the streets of Paris, the cover page announced "Unprecedented Scandal in front of 500 People Friday Evening at the University of Vienna." The article headline, "Sex Orgies of Radical Students," introduced what Jeannée referred to as the "facts" of the event.[32] Perhaps most significantly, he mistook all those participating in *Kunst und Revolution* for students. The rest of the Austrian press quickly followed suit. Across the board—from the national liberal newspaper *Die Presse* to the regional Catholic *Volksblatt*—*Kunst und Revolution* was defined in the first days of press coverage in terms of "bad students." Unanimous in its incendiary vocabulary and moralizing tone, the press focused on alleged "unprecedented provocations," "indescribable orgies," "perverse activities," and "sexual excesses" of students, cultivating an image of "radical" student sexuality to condemn what was repeatedly referred to and denigrated as the "so-called student left."[33]

Under the headline "Scenes of Scandal at the University—At SÖS Event: Lecture Hall Becomes Pig Sty," also on June 9, the *Volksblatt* mulled over the "sexual excesses" that had supposedly been the climax of the evening. Throughout the "academic proclamations," it reported, numerous participants had stripped naked, and "it then came to the previously mentioned un-repeatable scenes."[34] The interplay of casting aspersions and self-censoriousness, of mentioning and then insisting on the unrepeatability of what has been mentioned, served only, of course, to heighten the sense of scandal. On Monday, June 10, Jirak received his first death threat. The same day in the *Express*, Jeannée pub-

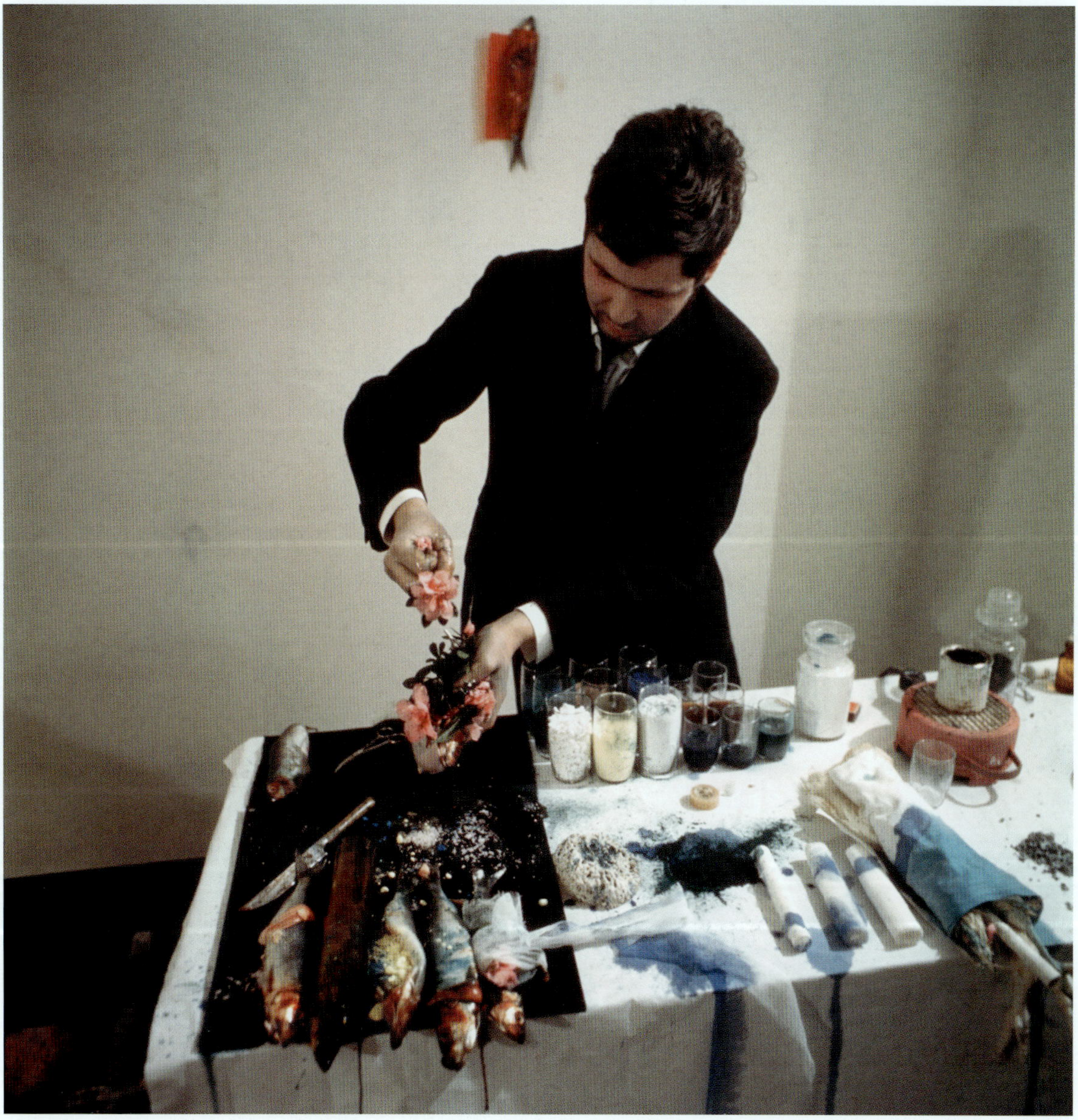

Plate 1. Rudolf Schwarzkogler with Anna Brus and Heinz Cibulka, *Hochzeit* (Wedding), 1965. Photograph by Walter Kindler. mumok – Museum moderner Kunst Stiftung Ludwig Wien, Leihgabe der Österreichischen Ludwig-Stiftung. © Rudolf Schwarzkogler; digital image © mumok – Museum moderner Kunst Stiftung Ludwig Wien.

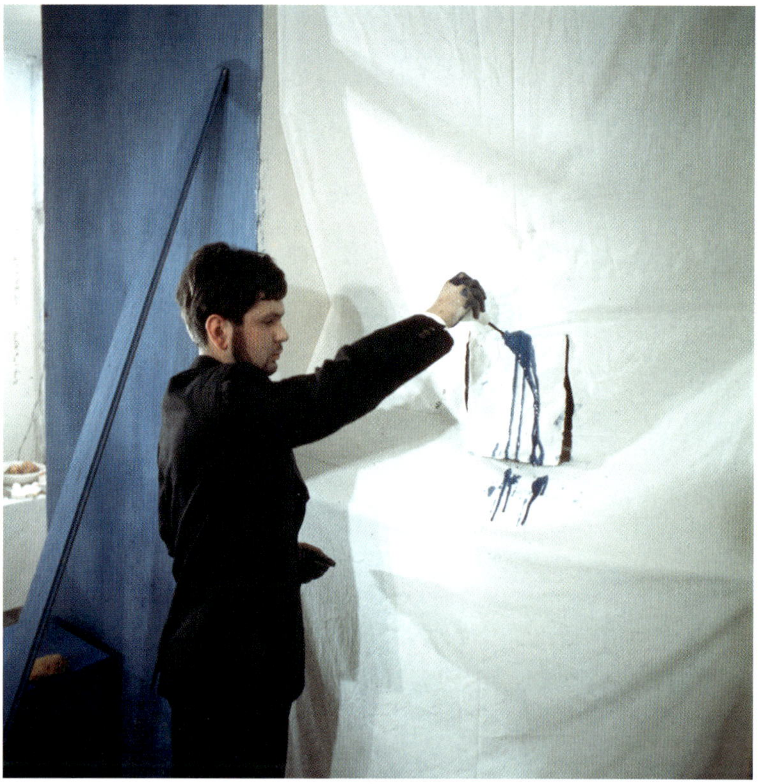

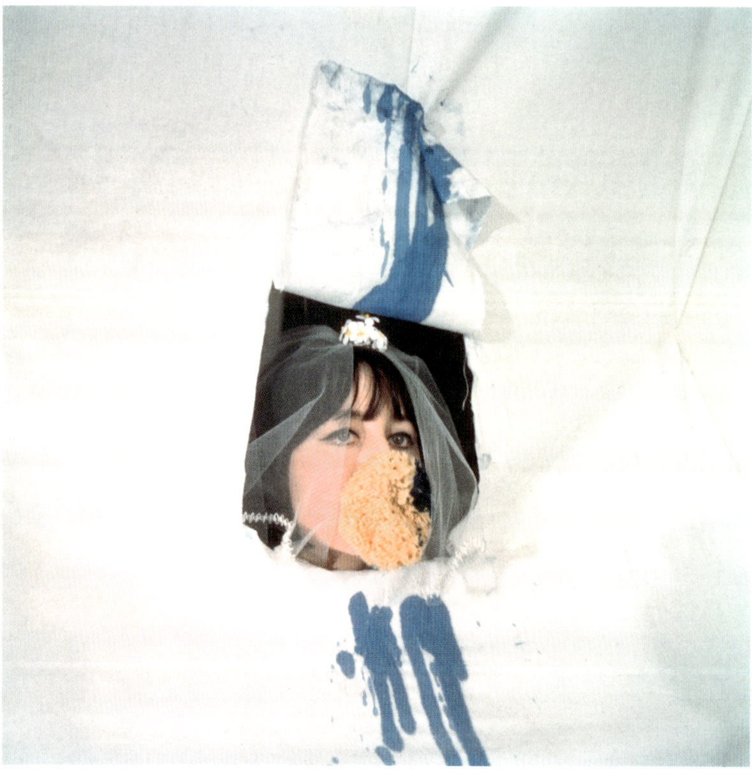

Plates 2–4. Rudolf Schwarzkogler with Anna Brus and Heinz Cibulka, *Hochzeit* (Wedding), 1965. Photograph by Walter Kindler. mumok – Museum moderner Kunst Stiftung Ludwig Wien, Leihgabe der Österreichischen Ludwig-Stiftung. © Rudolf Schwarzkogler; digital image © mumok – Museum moderner Kunst Stiftung Ludwig Wien.

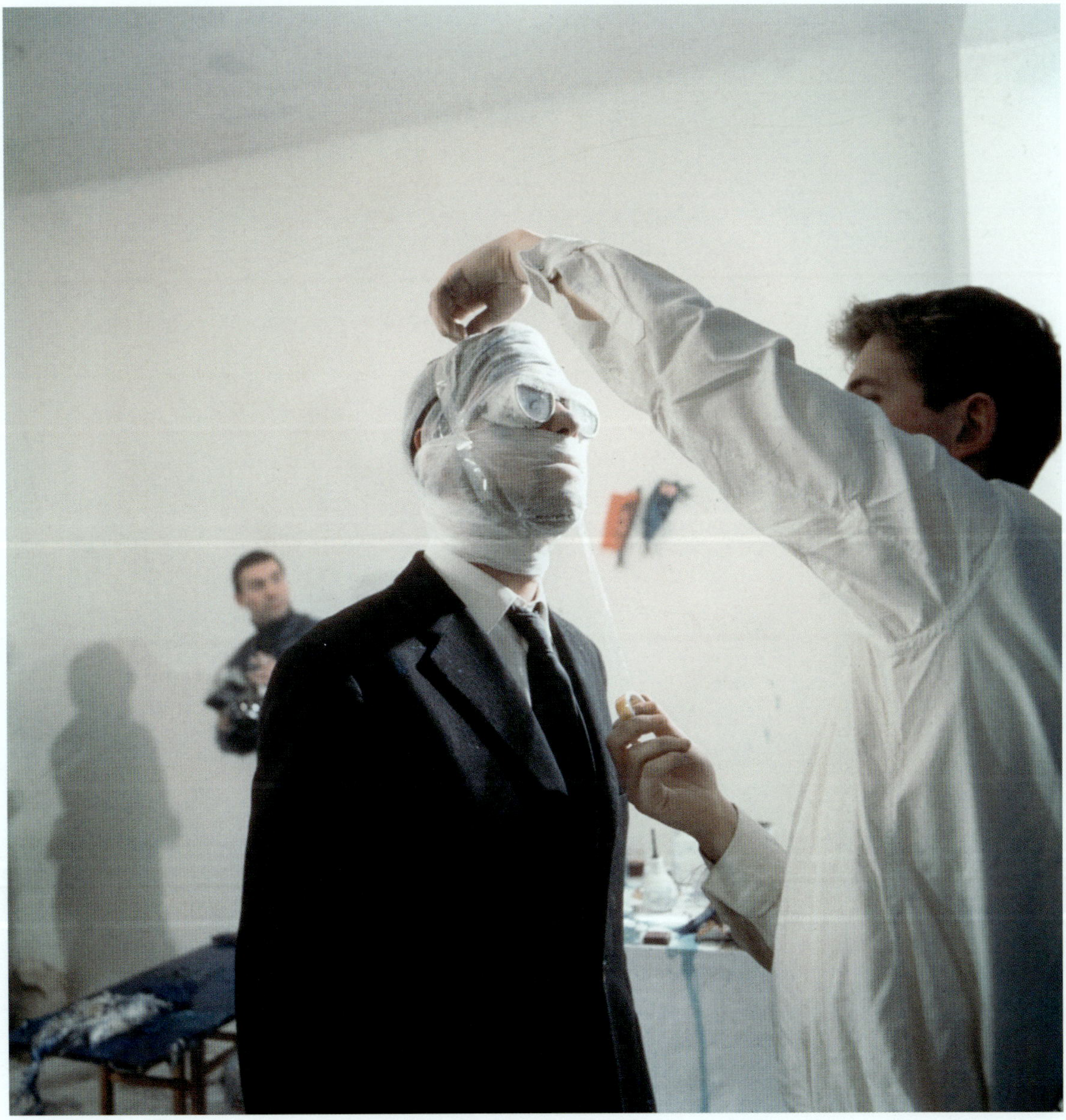

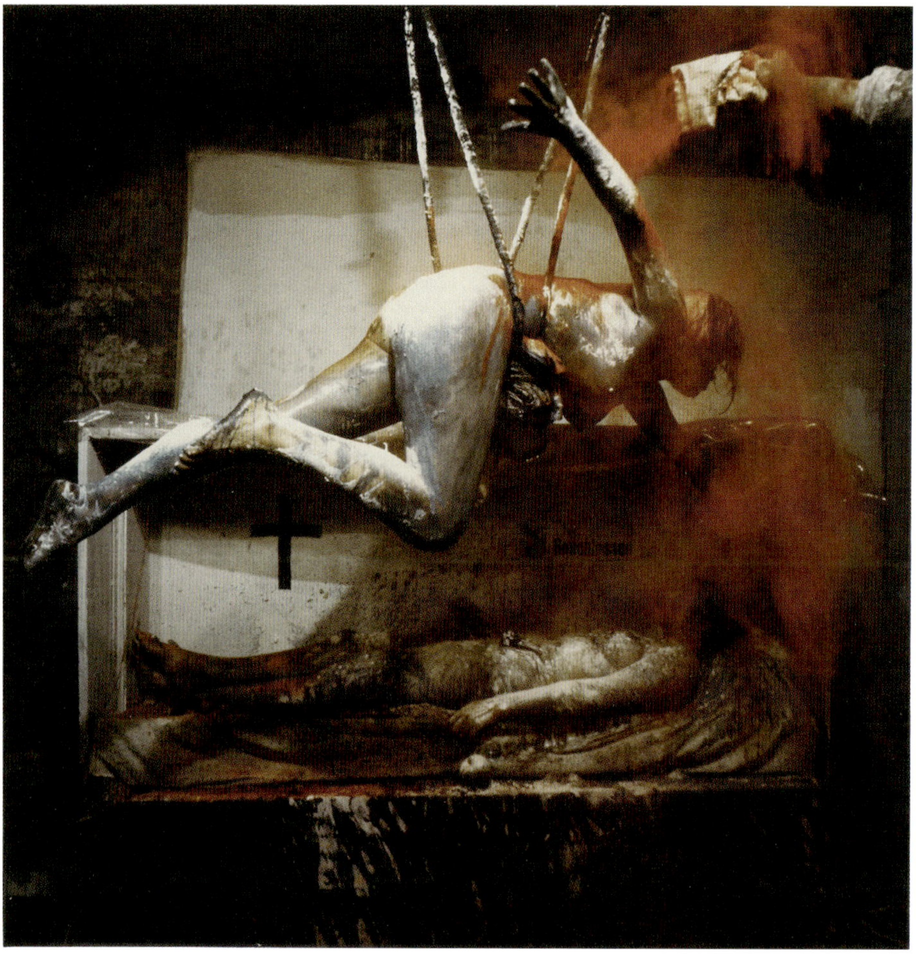

Plate 5. Otto Muehl with Anna Brus and Ziemi Schieb, *St. Anna, Materialaktion Nr. 27* (St. Anna, Material Action 27), 1966. Photograph by Ludwig Hoffenreich. Getty Research Institute, Los Angeles (2011.M.38). © Otto Muehl, courtesy Archives Otto Muehl, Moncarapacho-Olhão Portugal; Hoffenreich photography © J. Paul Getty Trust; digital image © mumok – Museum moderner Kunst Stiftung Ludwig Wien.

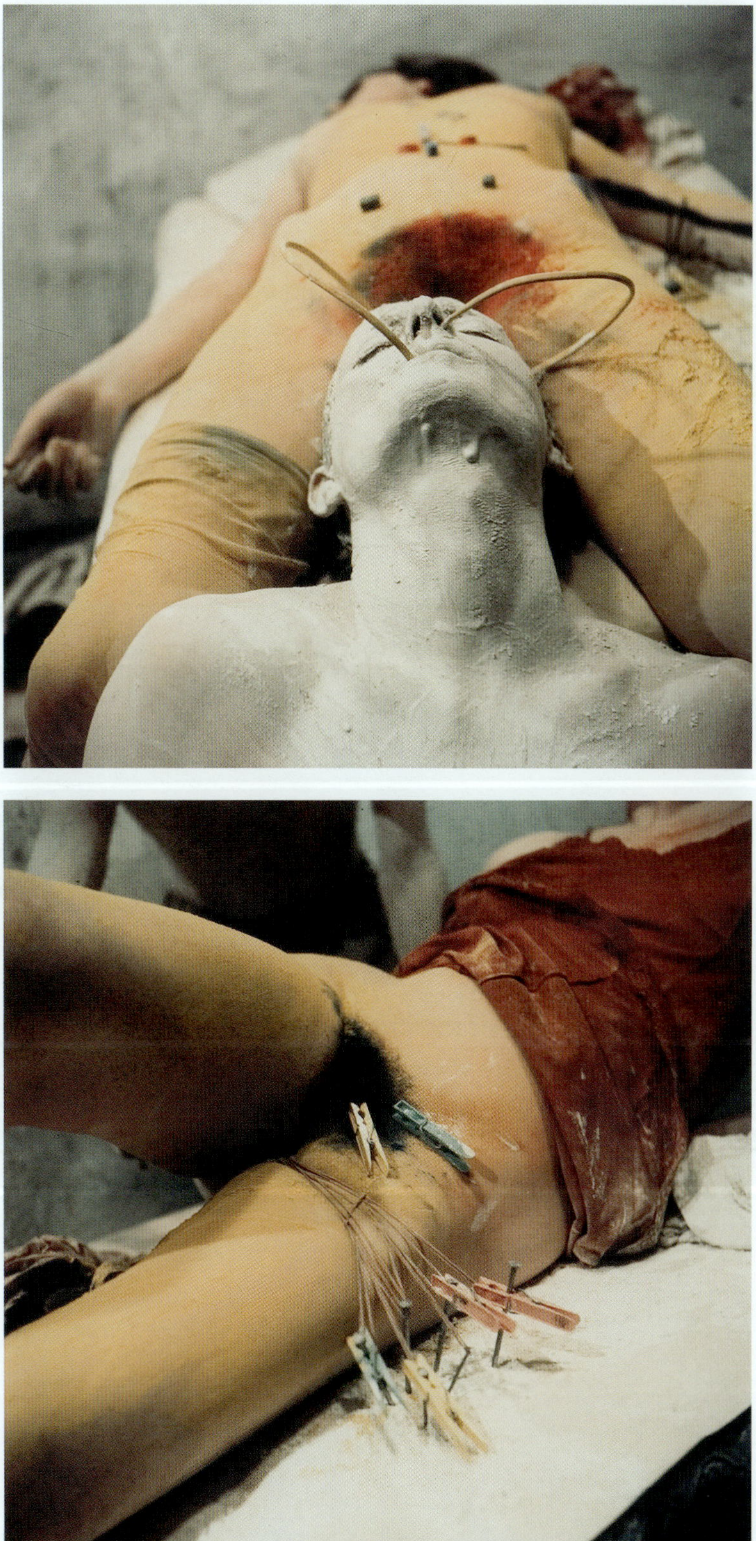

Plates 6–7. Günter Brus with Anna Brus, *Transfusion*, 1965. Photograph by Ludwig Hoffenreich. © Günter Brus. Courtesy of the BRUSEUM, Universalmuseum Joanneum.

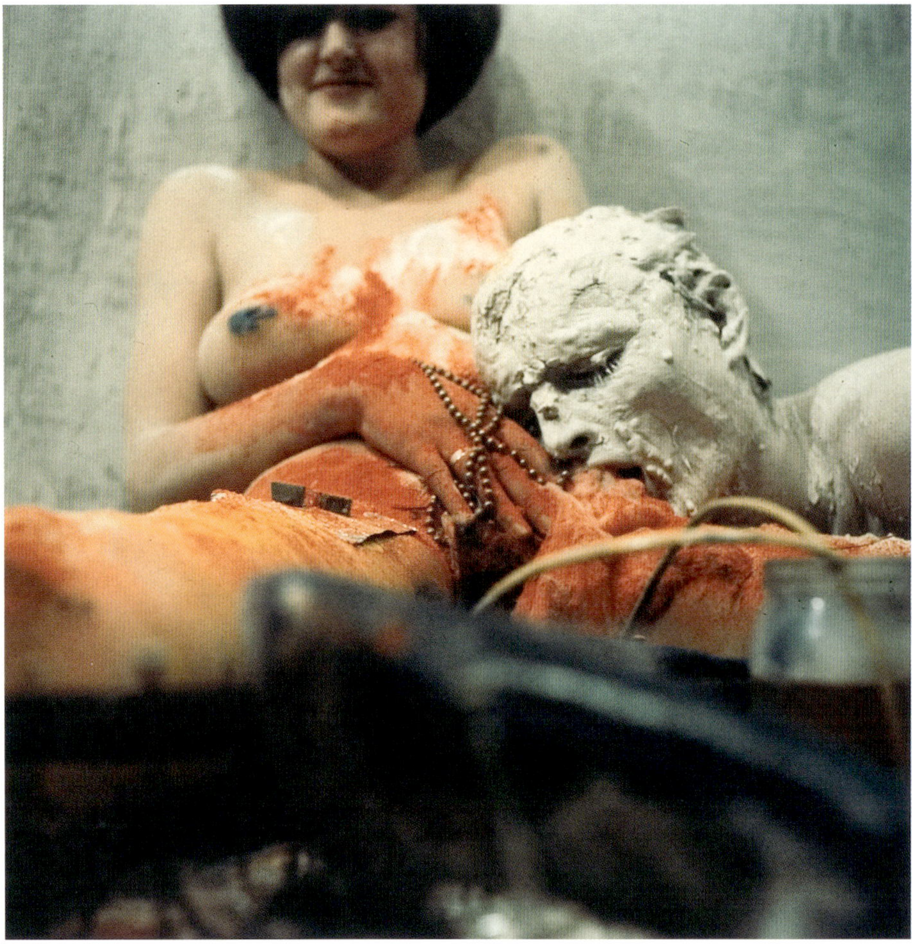

Plate 8. Günter Brus with Anna Brus, *Transfusion*, 1965. Photograph by Ludwig Hoffenreich. © Günter Brus. Courtesy of the BRUSEUM, Universalmuseum Joanneum.

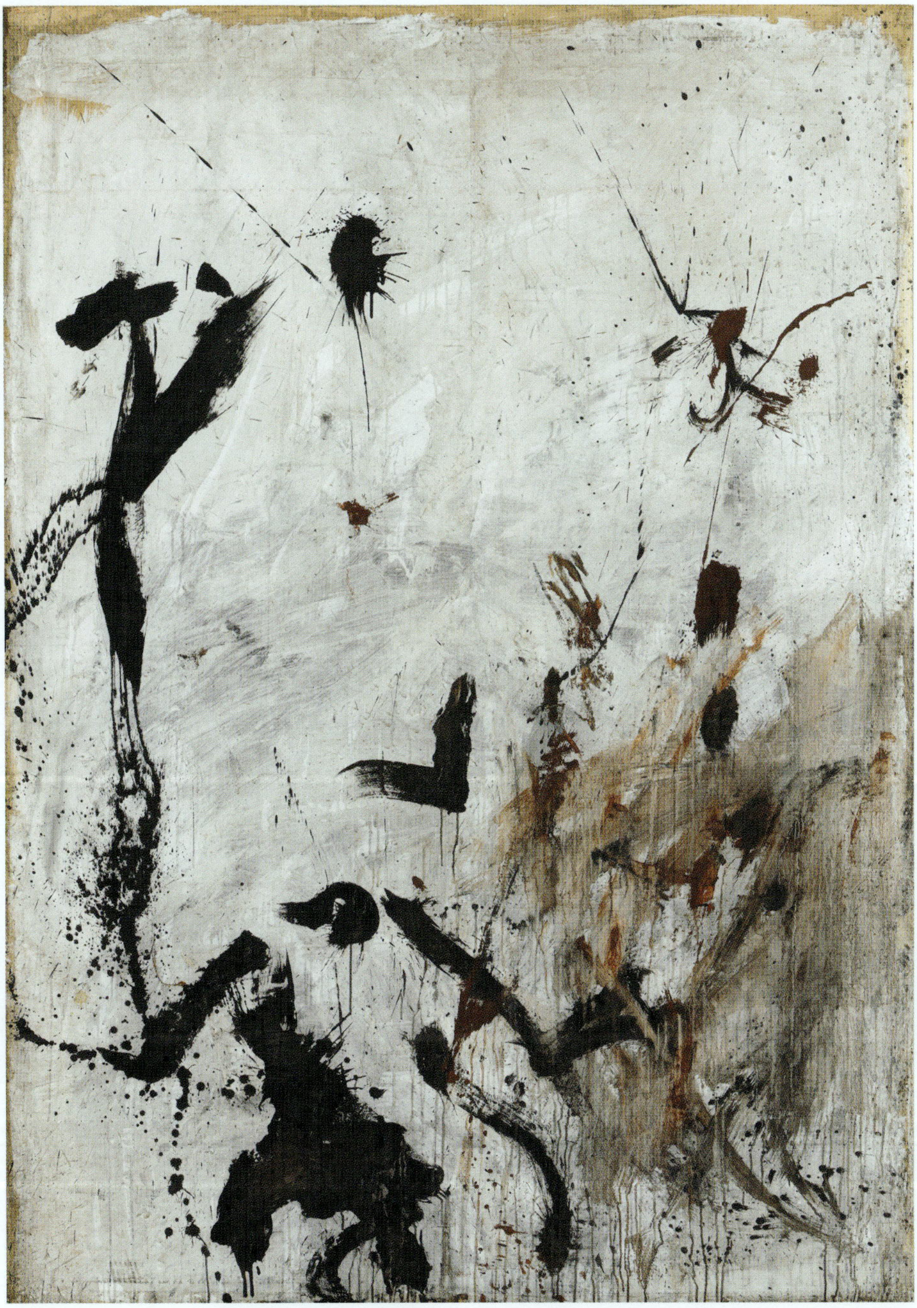

Plate 9. Günter Brus, *Aktionsmalerei (Ohne Titel)* (Action painting [Untitled]), 1960. Dispersion on white-primed packing paper, 243 × 175 cm. © Günter Brus. Courtesy of the BRUSEUM, Universalmuseum Joanneum; ALBERTINA, Vienna—The ESSL Collection; photo: Mischa Nawrata.

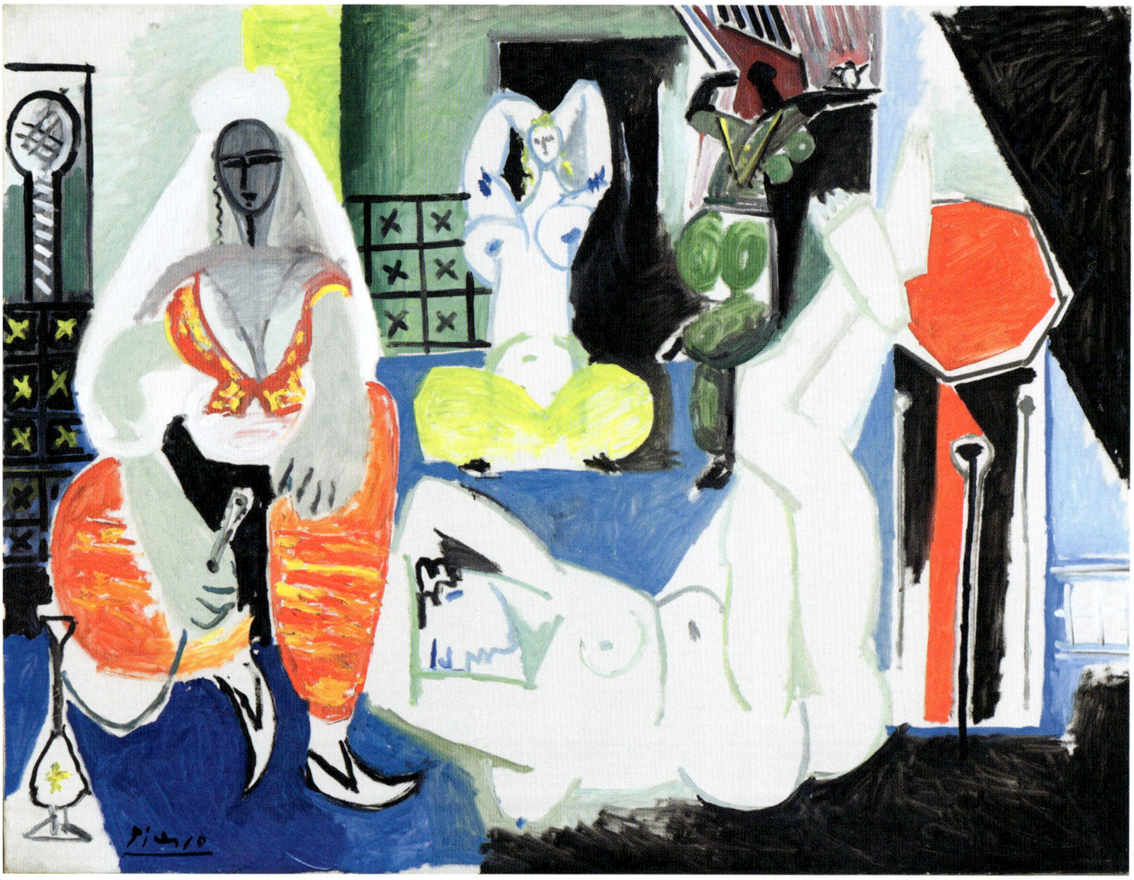

Plate 10. Pablo Picasso, *Femmes d'Alger I* (Women of Algiers, version "I"; January 25, 1955), 1955. Oil on canvas, 96.8 × 129.9 cm. © 2025 Estate of Pablo Picasso / Artists Rights Society (ARS), New York; Norton Simon Art Foundation.

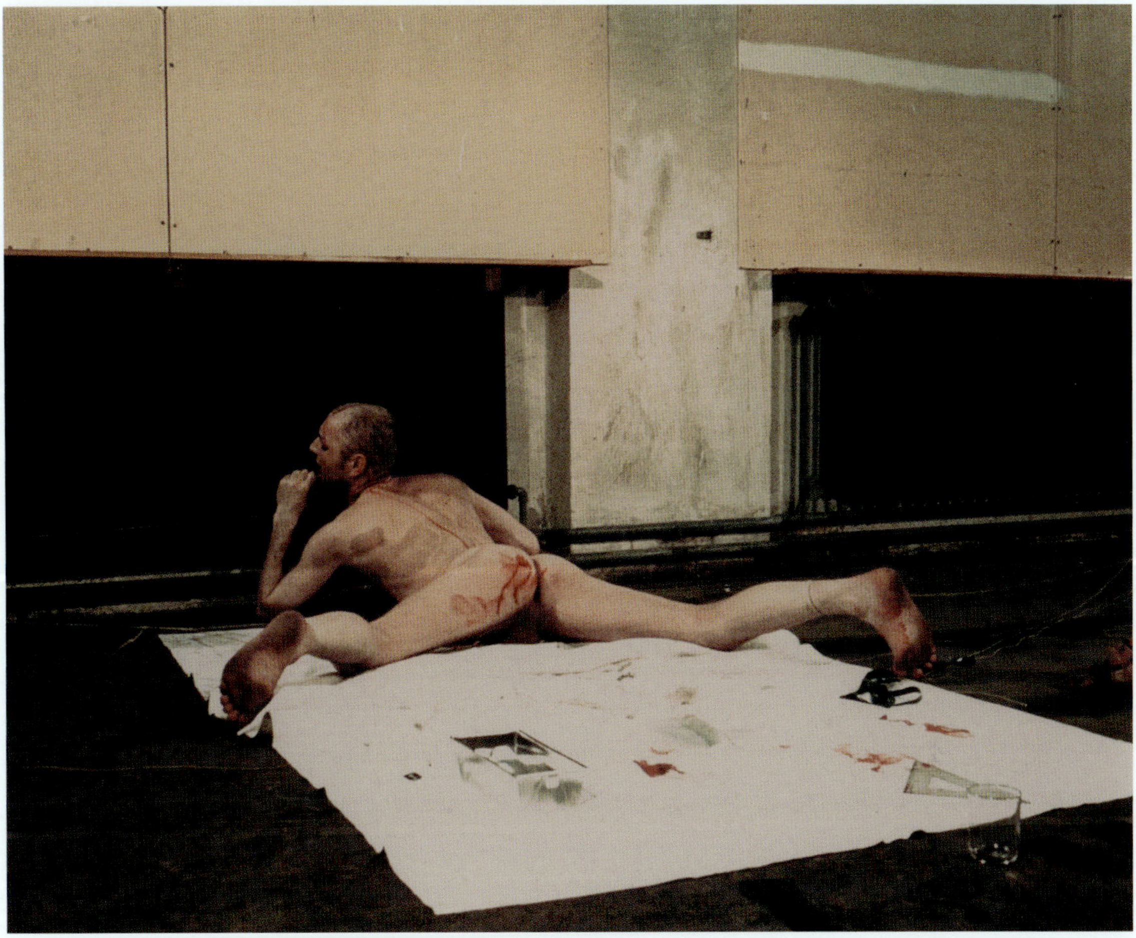

Plate 11. Günter Brus, *Zerreißprobe* (Stress test), 1970. Photograph by Klaus Eschen. © Günter Brus. Courtesy of the BRUSEUM, Universalmuseum Joanneum.

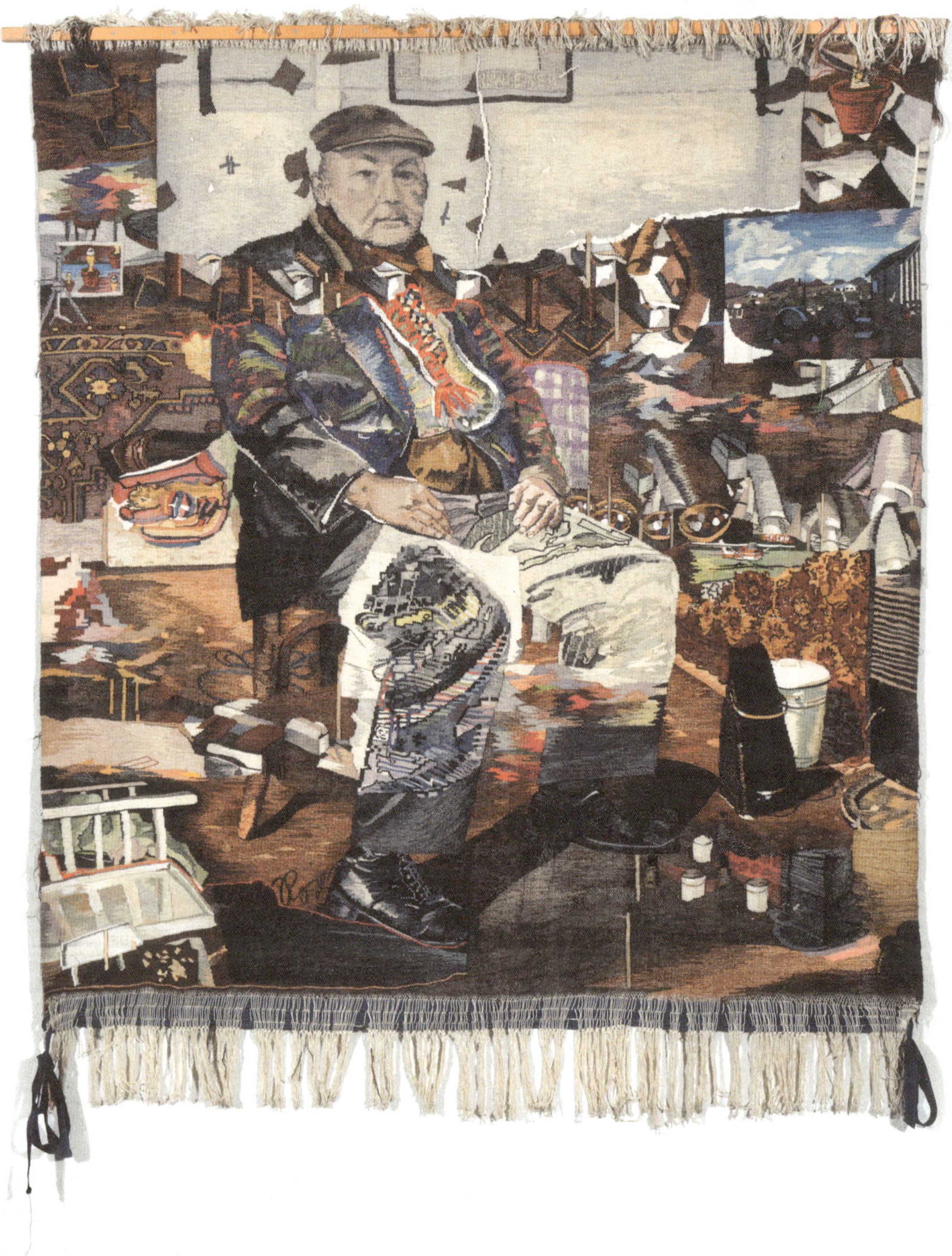

Plate 12. Ingrid Wiener and Dieter Roth with VALIE EXPORT, *Großer Teppich (Porträt Dieter Roth)* (Large Tapestry [Portrait of Dieter Roth]), 1981–1986. Woven wool and wood, 220 × 182 cm. Museum of Modern Art, New York. © Dieter Roth Estate, Courtesy Hauser & Wirth © Ingrid Wiener, Courtesy of Ingrid Wiener; photo: Ingrid Wiener.

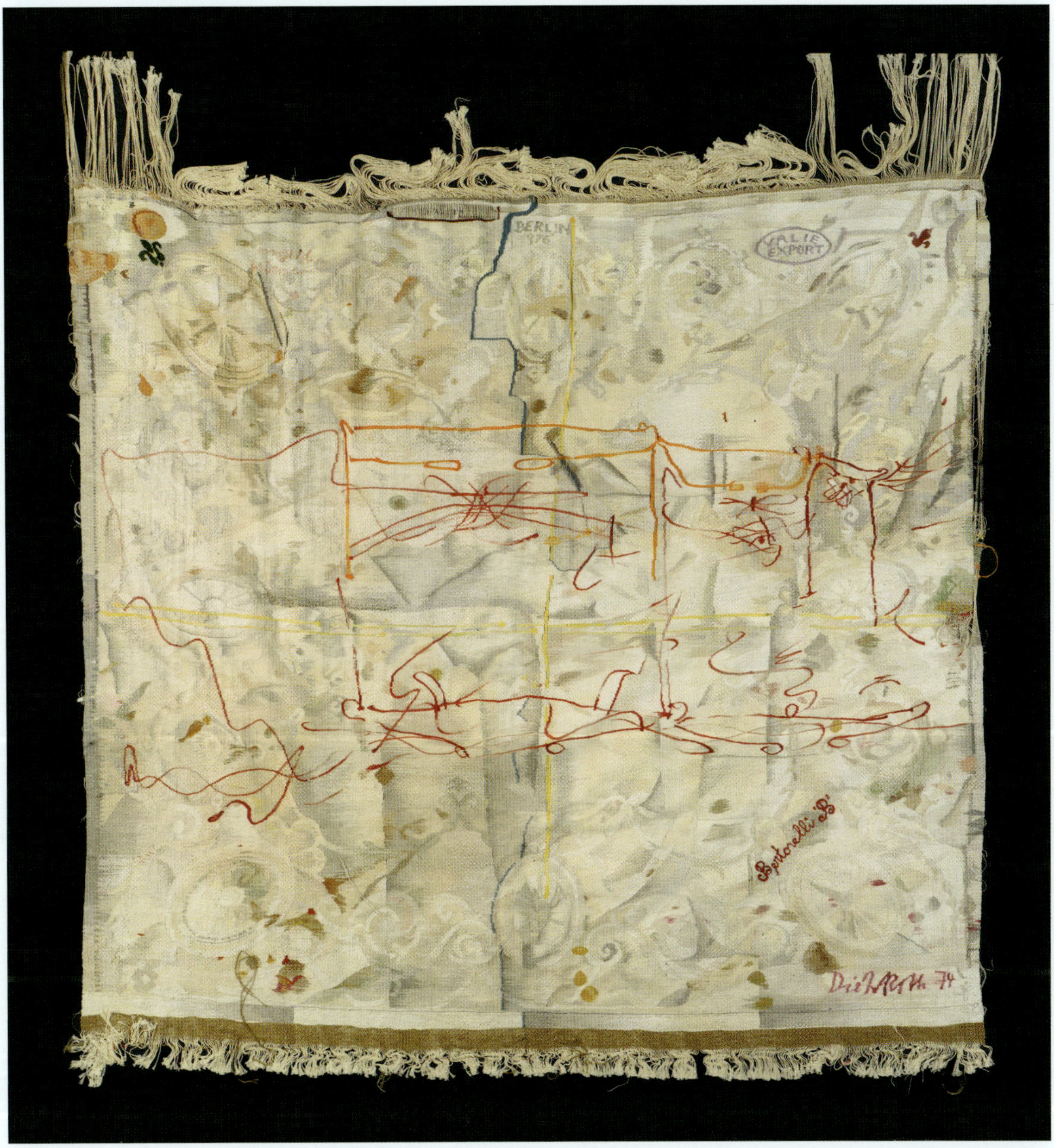

Plate 13. Ingrid Wiener, Dieter Roth, and VALIE EXPORT, *Gobelin (Bertorelli 'B')*, 1974–1976. Gobelin (woven wool), 210 × 189 cm. © Dieter Roth Estate, Courtesy Hauser & Wirth © Ingrid Wiener, Courtesy of Ingrid Wiener; Kunsthaus Zürich, 1981.

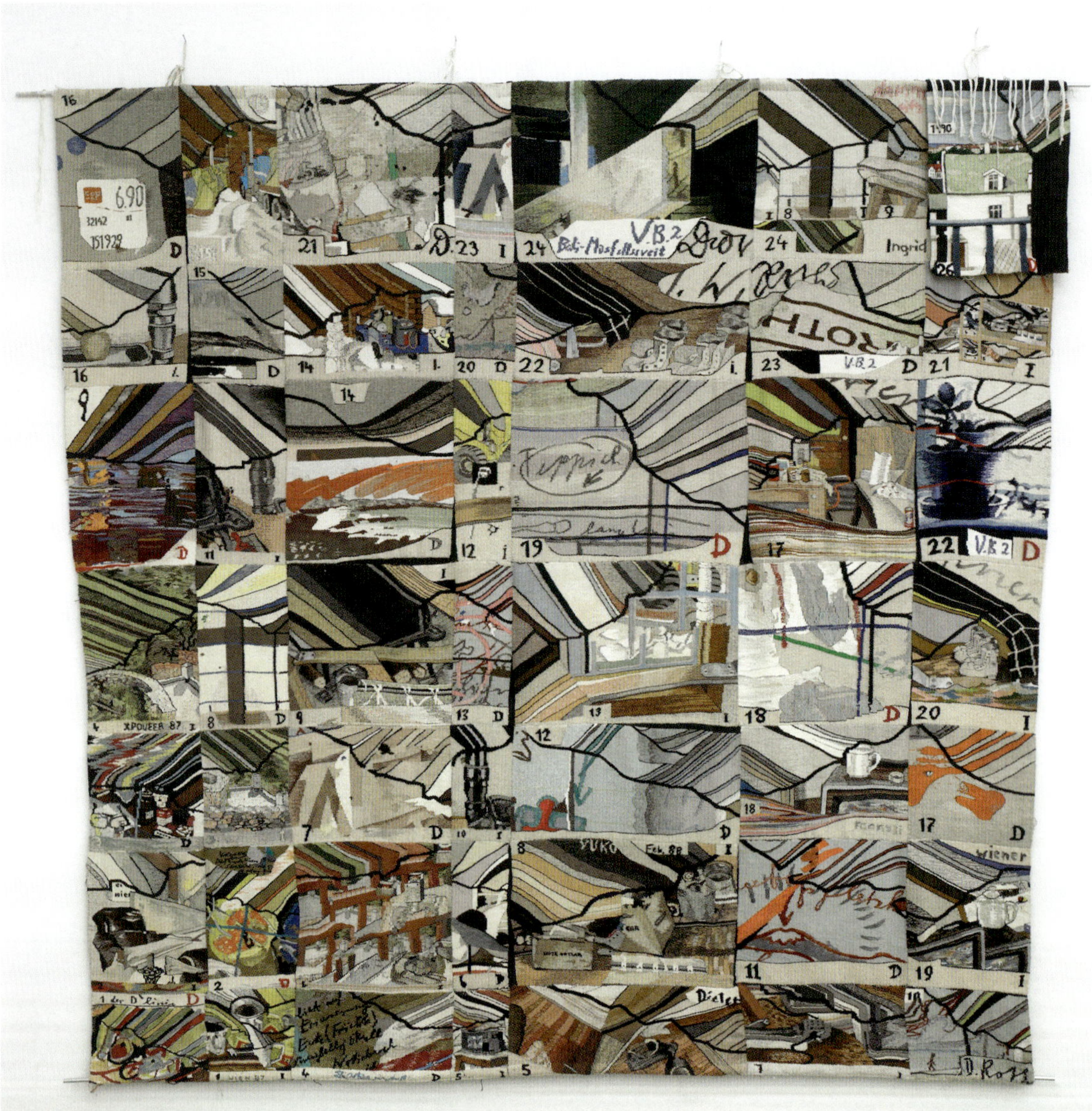

Plate 14. Ingrid Wiener and Dieter Roth, *Teppich Nr. 3. (Korrespondenz Teppich)* (Tapestry no. 3 [Correspondence tapestry]), 1987–1993. Woven wool, 250 × 240 cm (250 × 255 cm with string). © Dieter Roth Estate, Courtesy Hauser & Wirth © Ingrid Wiener, Courtesy of Ingrid Wiener; Aargauer Kunsthaus, Gift of Franz Wassmer; photo: Jörg Müller.

lished the headline: "'We'll Lynch the Boss of the SÖS,'" and the influential tabloid the *Kronen Zeitung* challenged the police to hunt down and punish the students: "Police Sentences for the Porno-Revoluzzer!"[35]

The SÖS had just been inaugurated on May 16, 1968, with the first-ever teach-in at the University of Vienna—a nonviolent protest technique that had been banned in Austria since January 1967. The ban had thus far been obeyed.[36] The SÖS sought to pursue a political platform further left than the VSStÖ (Union of Socialist Students of Austria), which was taken by many students to represent, despite its name, a deep-rooted conservatism and sexism. Women were banned from living in socialist student housing.[37] As Fritz Keller polemically frames it, the VSStÖ published a broadside, *gaudeamus*, with "Bikini-Mädchen" (bikini girls) on the front cover, much in the style of the *Kronen Zeitung*.[38] United or divided, the Left was a minority with very little say at Austrian universities.[39] In 1968, a significant proportion of students voted for the RFS (Students' Freedom Party), the student-run affiliate of the far-right FPÖ (Freedom Party of Austria).[40]

The "tameness" of the student movement, the women's movement, and in turn the Austrian 1968 had much to do with the Second World War and the years of occupation and reconstruction in Austria that followed.[41] Reeducation and denazification had been superficial at best, cynical at worst.[42] Austrian postwar national identity was built in large part on the officially propagated myth that Austria was the "first victim" of National Socialism.[43] The overwhelmingly Catholic-conservative leanings of the general public reflected the national effort to establish a continuity of properly "Austrian" roots, disavowing the annexation of Austria to "Greater Germany" in 1938 and denying what had been in fact a remarkably proactive complicity in Nazism.[44] After 1955, when Austria was declared independent and the occupying forces withdrew, it continued to be the idea of a lost past, concentrated in the memory of the Hapsburg monarchy, that motivated political and cultural policy. The national imagination, like the national budget, was primarily devoted to rebuilding "symbols of an older Austria," such as St. Stephen's Cathedral and the Burgtheater.[45] These paradoxes of national identity belong to what Anthony Bushell calls "polemical Austria."[46] Populist conservative rather than leftist liberal parties seized upon this impotence in Austria in order to hold on to power.

One of the most notorious "academic" figures of the culture of postwar revisionist conservatism was Taras Borodajkewycz, who had been a member of the National Socialist Party and in 1955, the year Austria's sovereign independence was reinstated by the Allies, was given a professorship in economic history at the College for World Trade (today the Vienna University of Economics and Business). Borodajkewycz openly expressed his profascist and anti-Semitic views in his lectures, resulting—a long decade later in March 1965—in a student-led demonstration in protest against his position. The protest turned violent when the RFS intervened in support of Borodajkewycz. Ernst Kirchweger, a former member of the Austrian resistance against Nazism and a concentration camp survivor, was killed.[47] Eventually, in 1971, Borodajkewycz was officially obliged to retire, on full pension.

Following the arrests of the participants in *Kunst und Revolution* on June 12, 1968, the press—goading public opinion—continued to exhort the police to take more extreme action. Calls were made for the students to be thrown out of school and the ringleaders locked up, even expelled from Austria: "At least give them a free ticket to China!"[48] Such demands proved far from innocuous. Jirak and Bauer were "relegated" from their respective universities and forbidden to reenroll in any other Austrian university. They both left Vienna for West Berlin. Subik and Stumpfl were likewise expelled. The RFS helped force the decision, but the members of the VSStÖ had also withdrawn all support, condemning their peers in the SÖS. Having existed for less than two months, the SÖS disbanded within a week of *Kunst und Revolution*.

It quickly became clear in the press coverage, however, that it was the performance not of *Revolution* but of *Kunst* that caused the most outrage. Especially after it was established that Brus, Muehl, and Wiener were not university students, the media turned its attention to them as artists—and in particular to Brus, who was seen, on account of his provocations, to be the most threatening figure. Staged in one of Austria's most venerated institutions, the University of Vienna, such "bad" art undermined a remaining pillar of Austria's much-diminished national pride: the tradition of the arts.

From the start, the media's attack had sought to disparage the artistic dimension of *Kunst und Revolution* by describing it as a "happening." The tendentious term had already been applied in condemnatory press coverage to "*ZOCK*" and "Direct Art" events in which Brus, Muehl, and Wiener had appeared in the previous year.[49] It had been made more mainstream in Austria by the German-language anthology *Happenings. Fluxus. Pop art. Nouveau réalisme. Eine Dokumentation* (1965), which included works by Brus, Muehl, and Nitsch. The art form called the happening was nevertheless an import, as I establish in the introduction, from the US milieu.[50] And the word was used strategically throughout the coming weeks in an anti-contemporary-art campaign that was also anti-American, insofar as happenings were associated with the supposedly detrimental influence in Austria of American art and culture. More loathsome than the student left in a culture as conservative as Vienna was the perceived incursion of participatory, performative, action-based—which is to say, "American"—artistic practice. This condemnatory and often scandalizing association, made by nationalist elements of the press to dismiss an in fact "domestic" artistic tendency, would have an enduring influence on the broader reception—including the art historical reception—of Viennese Actionism, which to this day is typically understood as parasitic of US and West German precedents.

The Crisis of Austrian Impotence

"A hot quarter-hour"—with this pithy turn of phrase, Fritz Keller sums up the whole history of Vienna's 1968.[51] Tellingly, it refers specifically to *Kunst und Revolution*. Keller's suggestive innuendo implies that, for all its supposed steamy intensity, nothing of significance had been brought about by the all-too-brief event. It certainly did not catalyze the sort of participatory revolutionary fervor of the worker and student uprisings taking place at the same time in France.[52] Nor did it, as in West Germany, spawn a movement of students and artists who rallied around antiauthoritarian ideals and such figures as Rudi Dutschke and Dieter Kunzelmann to commit, in theory on a global scale and in solidarity with the Third World, to overturning capitalism and imperialism.[53] This difference was already evidenced in the event's international reception. By Tuesday, June 11, the story of *Kunst und Revolution* had been exported and satirized. The Parisian *Le Monde* reported on the University of Vienna's case of "striptease and revolution," and the Munich *Merkur* headlined "Notdurft gegen Notstand" (Emergency Need [i.e., defecation] versus State of Emergency).[54] In contrast to the real state of emergency in Paris and elsewhere, Austria's incident of "art and revolution" was just a (dirty) joke.

In his eclectic study of art and revolution, Gerald Raunig concludes in a chapter dedicated to *Kunst und Revolution* that the ineffective collision of the activism of the student left with the artistic project of Viennese Actionism resulted in each group losing its already precarious cohesion.[55] Defining *concatenation* as a "political practice of organizing collectivity," Raunig argues that, "in June 1968, the attempt to link artistic Actionism and student activism failed as an unproductive clash, as an antagonism and as a negative form of concatenation." Rather than a coming together of students and artists to form a new and politically effective collectivity, the "negative concatenation" obscures, if not destroys, this possibility, which remains but an "unnamed, covert desideratum."[56] Taking up Raunig's terms, I would insist on the following distinction: *Kunst und Revolution* is the positive production of a "negative concatenation," not simply a failure to bring about a more successful one. Which is to say, *Kunst und Revolution* is not a discrete instance of the failure of actionism and activism, but an incident that explores the very question of "action" that inheres in these two terms. It is an incident of in-action, for it indicates the frustrated conditions of passivity that, since well before the 1950s, had pervaded Austrian cultural and political life.[57] It exhibits an inertia both of political activism and artistic practice that had in fact long been underway.

Kunst und Revolution presents a positive display of the crisis of Austrian impotence—of impotence in art and impotence in politics. And it is precisely because it touched on the national pride of a small country profoundly invested in the grand history of its arts that the incident became such a source of anxious fascination. Not by chance did the police interviews persistently

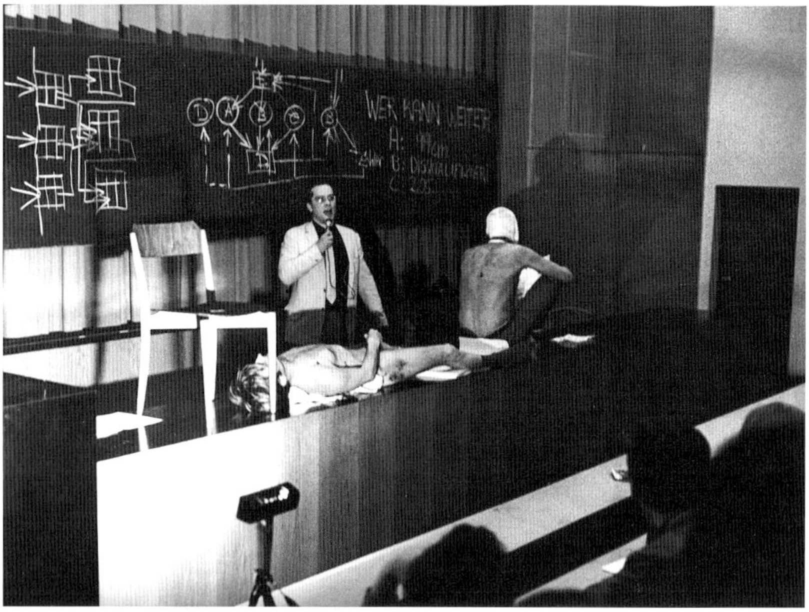

Figure 2.9. Günter Brus with Otmar Bauer, Peter Jirak, Otto Muehl, Herbert Stumpfl, Christof Subik, Peter Weibel, Oswald Wiener, and "Laurids," *Kunst und Revolution* (Art and revolution), 1968. Photograph by Siegfried Klein (Khasaq). © Günter Brus. Courtesy of the BRUSEUM, Universalmuseum Joanneum.

return to the tortured question of whether Brus's masturbation on the lectern actually culminated in an ejaculation (fig. 2.9). Witnesses stated: "Subsequently the accused Brus lay down on the podium desk and tried to masturbate"; "[Brus] masturbated while lying on his back in order to get himself off, however he was not successful"; "Later he masturbated, without results, while four naked men marched in, possibly while someone whistled"; and one answered pointedly, "Whether it came to an ejaculation or not, I did not see."[58]

The sexuality, and above all, the masculinity, of the artists was subjected to bizarre and aggressive public scrutiny. The conclusions of obligatory psychological evaluations were shared with the press: Brus and Wiener were judged to have "psychopathic personalities," with Wiener demonstrating "heightened egotism," and Brus a "conflict-readiness" in the "sexual arena."[59] The evaluations were carried out in part by none other than Heinrich Gross, who despite working at the children's "euthanasia clinic" Am Spiegelgrund in Vienna from 1940 to 1945 remained in official favor.[60] The provocative details of his evaluation contributed to a highly charged atmosphere in which threatening letters were sent and phone calls made to Brus, Muehl, and Wiener—as well as to Anna Brus, Friedl Muehl, and Ingrid Wiener—the violence of which was often sexually loaded and recalled the rhetoric of the Nazi era. Of Brus, one respondent wrote, "This man should have his penis cut off and stuffed in his mouth." Another insisted: "Only a Hitler or a Stalin would be enough for such degenerate creatures. Brus and Muehl would have long been castrated in a concentration camp or Siberia."[61] The *Kronen Zeitung* invited readers to respond to "the happening." One wrote in about the "degeneracy" (*Entartung*) of the event and promised to "stuff the mouths of these public producers of shit with their own product and then have them scream, Dutschke, Heil!"[62] The perverse coupling of the Nazi rhetoric of degeneracy with scenarios that seem to rehearse the spectacularized reception of the very "happening" they attack only underscores the paradoxical efficacy of the incident. The excesses of the mediatization of *Kunst und Revolution* betray themselves as overcompensation for the very impotence it performed.

The Hateful and the Ugly: Politics, Aesthetics, and the Police

When in his first deposition to the police on June 10, 1968, Brus states, "It is my art to produce such incidents (*Es ist meine Kunst, solche Vorfälle zu produzieren*)"—he is at once commenting on and carrying on with the performance.[63] *Kunst und Revolution* is characteristic of Viennese performance art in that it provokes much more than it performs. Or rather, it provokes precisely in relation to its failure to perform and in its failure to conform to expectations about what ought to be taken seriously as action. It reflects on the attrition of space for artistic and political expression and the propagation of policed spaces in Austria in the 1960s. Of this decade, Diedrich Diederichsen has suggested that while the "avant-garde" was not as "politicized" in Austria as it was in West Germany, it was to a disproportionate degree policed.[64] Philip Ursprung goes so far as to argue that the police emerged as the ideal audience for "the Actionists," for it was the police that "really 'saw' and 'reacted' to the transgression."[65]

What interests me is how Viennese Actionism so frequently provoked the attentions of cultural and political authorities, and especially those of the police, because what was going on was so difficult to discern. Which is to say, Viennese performance art is provocative not because it is clearly criminal, but because it operates in a site where the boundaries between aesthetic and moral-political practices become indistinct. It is unclear to the police—as well as to the artists—whether what is happening is properly artistic or political and, furthermore, whether what is happening is a form of active engagement or of passive withdrawal. Without being simply illegal, it intervenes in the gray zone of the law, and therefore of police discretionary powers, where questions of public order and seemliness emerge.

Paradigmatic in this regard is Brus's most iconic, and to all appearances most innocuous, performance: *Wiener Spaziergang* (Viennese walk; 1965, figs. 2.10–2.14 and also fig. 1.18). It was his first performance in a public space.[66] Brus appeared in an ordinary suit, painted white from head to toe with a messy gash of black paint cutting vertically through him. Beginning at Heldenplatz (Heroes' Square), where Hitler had celebrated Austria's annexation in front of jubilant crowds in 1938, Brus traversed the Viennese Hofburg, formerly the imperial palace of the Hapsburgs, where he encountered the police, who promptly stopped him and escorted him to the police station. There appears to have been no compelling reason to arrest the submissive Brus, except for the fact that what he was doing seemed—insofar as he was painted and called

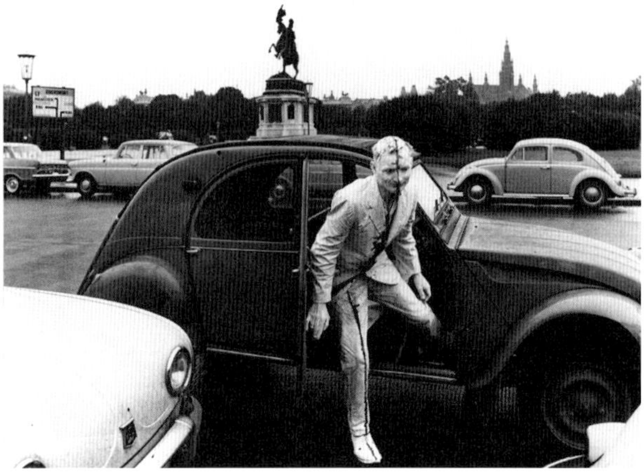

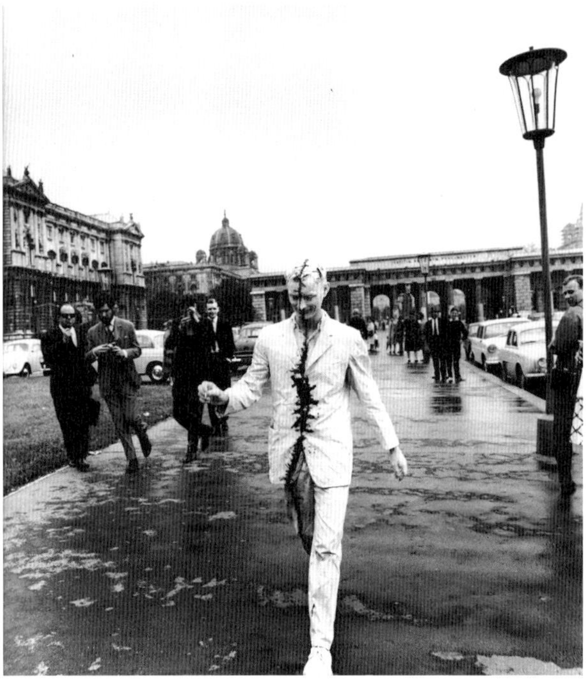

Figures 2.10–2.12. Günter Brus, *Wiener Spaziergang* (Viennese walk), 1965. Photograph by Ludwig Hoffenreich. © Günter Brus. Courtesy of the BRUSEUM, Universalmuseum Joanneum.

himself an artist—to be some kind of "art," which was transgressive only insofar as it was happening in the wrong place. Brus was fined for "causing irritation" and "disturbing the order in a public place," and he was swiftly removed from view in a taxi.[67] His lacerated figure, casually strolling through the heart of the Viennese capital, presents the very divisive yet passive structure that characterizes the political and aesthetic intervention of his performance art.

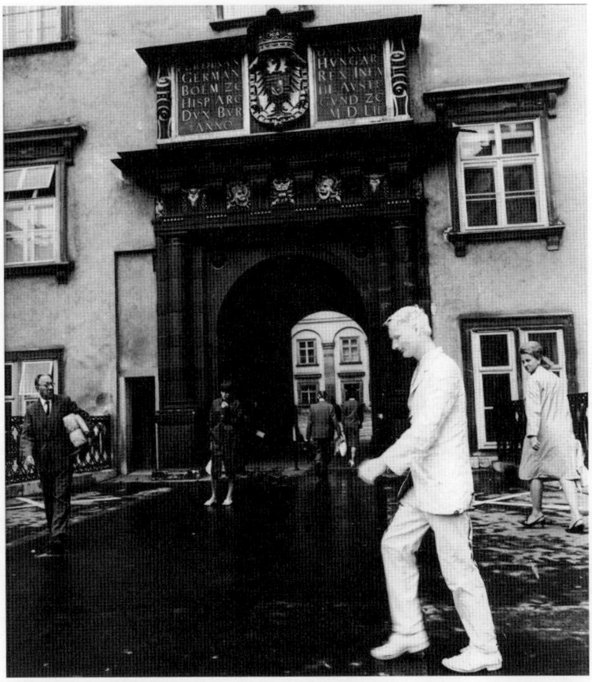

When Brus was formally apprehended by the police, on June 12, 1968, five days after *Kunst und Revolution*, the arrest warrant stated:

> That the so-named is suspected, in the context of an event at the University on June 7, 1968, of defiling and debasing the Austrian national anthem in a malicious manner [*in gehässiger Weise*] in front of an audience of several hundred people insofar as he emptied his bowels while singing the national anthem. Additionally, taking the same opportunity, thus publicly, and in a manner that provoked offense through indecent actions [*unzüchtige Handlungen*], he violated morality and decency insofar as he masturbated for about twenty minutes naked on the podium desk.[68]

The warrant concludes by paraphrasing Brus's own self-incriminating defense regarding the incidental character of his art: "Moreover, the accused Brus stated before the police, it is my art to produce incidents of this kind."[69]

The Austrian Criminal Code states that whoever defiles or debases national symbols, including the federal coat of arms, the national emblem, the flag, and the national anthem "in gehässiger Weise" is punishable by up to a year in prison.[70] Today, the myth persists that at *Kunst und Revolution*, Brus's offense was defecating on the Austrian flag—a fictitious tidbit that falls in line with the spectacularizing rhetoric of the press and art historiographical efforts to distill in a defining image the "indecent actions" of so-called Viennese Actionism.[71] Brus's defilement concerned, however, not the flag, but the Austrian national anthem. In his first deposition, Brus openly admits to singing the first

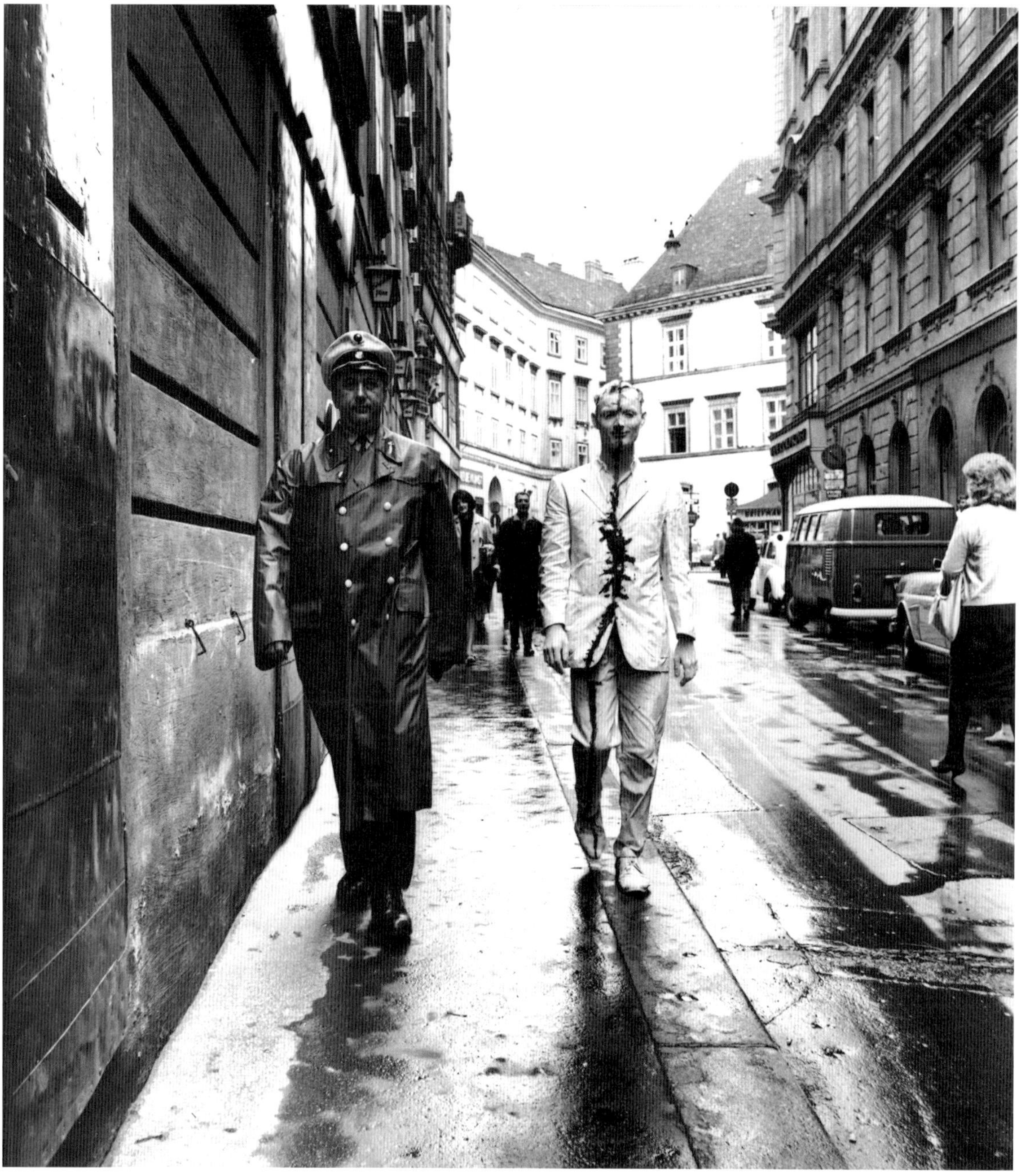

verse of the anthem over and over again, which concludes "much-praised Austria" (*Vielgerühmtes Österreich*).[72] The record states: "I bent forward and shat. I sang the national anthem while doing it."[73] This apparent admission of guilt—of a legal infraction—was seized on by the police, and then the press, and became the linchpin in the case against him.

In style and tone, Brus's deposition is characteristically ironic. It carries

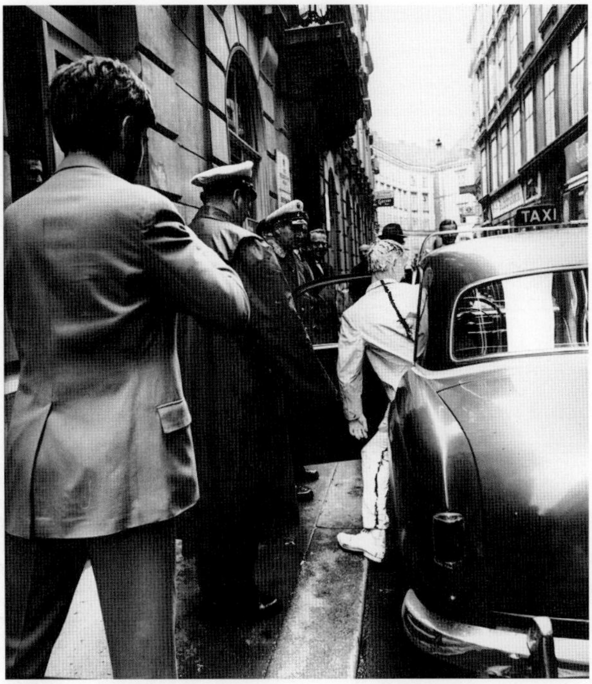

Figures 2.13–2.14. Günter Brus, *Wiener Spaziergang* (Viennese walk), 1965. Photograph by Ludwig Hoffenreich. © Günter Brus. Courtesy of the BRUSEUM, Universalmuseum Joanneum.

on the performance of *Kunst und Revolution* by passively, if not poetically, playing on and within the constraints of the form and the legal-bureaucratic language of the deposition. Without openly defying authority, Brus irritates the police interrogation. He produces an incident by reproducing the very ambivalent sort of performance—ambivalent as to its artistic or political valence—that was, especially for those institutions tasked to preserve public mores, so irritating and agitating about *Kunst und Revolution* in the first place. In his interviews with the police, Brus's narrative begins as follows: "While Peter Weibel gave a talk that I found incomprehensible, I entered the auditorium.... I got undressed as normal, except for my red socks. That I did not take off my socks was a slip [*Fehlleistung*] on my part, which, however, was meaningless."[74] If the purportedly political discourse was incomprehensible, Brus's "slip" is clearly Freudian, a *Fehlleistung* which could be even more literally translated as a failed performance, *Fehl-leistung*. Here, all the questions of the powers and the politics of intentionality, control, capacity, and responsibility coalesce. The efficacy of Brus's performance relies entirely on the earnestness of the bureaucratic line of questioning to which it responds, which seeks to establish facts and meaning where there may well be none and to identify determinate actions where there may be only various tantalizing forms of in-action.

And so the performance carries on: On June 13, Brus was asked to repeat what he had already stated to the police in the initial interrogation on June 10: "I sang the Austrian national anthem in a provocative way in order to express that the appropriate cultural administrations have not done much, especially for the new art."[75] On June 19, asked again to confirm, and account for, why he sang the anthem, Brus repeated, "It is correct that I sang the national anthem in the context of my procedures, because I wanted to indicate that, for a very long time, new Austrian art has been neglected." The police are, of course, uninterested in Brus's statements about "new art" and its neglect. Ostensibly so that they could clarify even more precisely when and for how long he in fact sang the anthem—as if to pinpoint the exact moment at which the "defilement" had occurred—Brus was yet again asked in his deposition on June 19 to reiterate his statement: "I'll give you the timeframe of my entire action again: a long time, up to twenty minutes, of masturbating, defecating, singing of the national anthem, whereby I sang once, in total, the first verse of the national anthem, although I cannot say today whether this also partially occurred during the masturbation. I would like to say once again, that in my opinion I did not sing anymore during the masturbation. During the defecation and the ensuing smearing of my body I sang the first verse of the national anthem continuously."[76] It is unclear whether Brus is answering in earnest, or, to use a fitting colloquialism, "taking the piss."

Brus's interviews and interrogations with the police circle around the question as to whether his behavior could be characterized as *gehässig*—the term that is key to defining the legal consequence of his comportment. The word is related to *hassen*, "to hate." In this sense, it refers to the kind of malicious, hateful antagonism associated with an adversary of the state. It describes an offensiveness that has less to do with the explicit intention to transgress any given law and more to do with the difficult to define behaviors and attitudes that undermine the institutions of law and order by disparaging them. To use a term repeatedly invoked by the authorities, Brus's behavior does not break the law; it "debases" it (*herabwürdigen*). The word *gehässig* thus refers not so much to a clear criminal offense as to a less certain moral-political one, an offense against public morality. Tellingly, it is a word that gives Brus pause. In response to the continued interrogation revolving around the manner in which he sang the national anthem, Brus replied: "I wanted to rouse those present by doing it. I admit that I did it in a hateful way [*in gehässiger Weise*], I would prefer to say in a shocking way, in order to rouse the people and I would like to add, that the word *gehässig* for me is not quite right."[77]

Brus's indecision regarding *gehässig* draws attention to the coincidence of the political and the aesthetic paradigmatic of his work. For another conventional aesthetic term, also derived from *hassen*, may in fact be more fitting, namely, the word *hässlich*, "ugly." In its earliest use in the history of aesthetics, *hässlich* indicates the perversion of classical notions of symmetry, harmony, and balance. It names the opposite of the beautiful and the good. Its appearance was taken to announce something amoral or evil.[78] The *Hässliche* is the mode in which the *Gehässige* makes its demonic appearance. When Brus suggests, but does not offer, a modification of *gehässig* in his deposition, he is perhaps playing on the aesthetic valence of the term. His hesitation indicates the confusion of aesthetic and moral-political spheres that inevitably accompanies its use.[79] Brus's artistic production can be articulated according to this dialectic of the hateful and the ugly, which betrays a structural ambivalence between the policed space of ethical life (*Sittlichkeit*) and the ostensible "aesthetic freedom" of artistic space, an ambivalence concentrated and confounded in the incident *Kunst und Revolution*.

Contrasting what he calls the "Happening Ästhetik" of contemporaneous German and US art with the unbecoming attacks of Viennese Actionism on local "political and cultural power structures," Werner Hofmann draws a distinction between an aesthetically and a politically motivated performance practice precisely by emphasizing the category of hate.[80] Curator and founding director of the Vienna Museum des 20. Jahrhunderts, established in 1962 as Vienna's first museum of modern art and later renamed mumok – Museum moderner Kunst, Hofmann writes that "what the Actionists 'proclaim' is loaded with an acrid hate [*ätzenden Haß*] that cares to know as little about Dada irony and playful alienation as it does about ideological clarity." Hofmann sees little aesthetic or political value in the work of the Viennese Actionists, whom he describes as playing the role of "perpetrators turned victims, who feel like martyrs" and as pursuing "thoroughly fascistic practices of terror."[81] It is their "disdainful hate of culture [*kulturverachtender Haß*]," he concludes, "that differentiates the Viennese scene from other Happenings."[82] These comments from 1983 rehearse an anxiety shared by the media and the police circa 1968 about the regulation and contamination of the aesthetic and moral-political spheres. Yet it is, I would contend, indeed the very ironic play with the ambivalence of these surveilled spheres that constitutes the critical character of Viennese performance art.

Today, in contrast, Viennese Actionism has been reclaimed by a revisionist art history in a shift reflected in its official embrace by Austrian art institutions.[83] According to the general consensus in Austrian scholarship, Viennese Actionism presents Austria's first true "avant-garde," on account of what Hubert Klocker calls its "eminently political act of liberation."[84] The very scenes that had so outraged the public, the press, and the police are celebrated in retrospect for their "radicality."[85] This restitution of Viennese Actionism as Austria's missing avant-garde by means of an inflated idiom of radical activism propels the action paradigm that I address in the introduction. If it is to be oriented in the context of the so-called neo-avant-gardes of the 1960s and 1970s, then it is necessary to frame the discussion, as Mechtild Widrich does, in terms of Viennese performance art's embrace of the historical avant-garde's antiaesthetic program of the ugly.[86]

In contrast with contemporaries who practiced politically motivated *Aktionskunst*, Brus's performances in particular inflect the ambiguity of their political and artistic significance. Joseph Beuys's "social sculpture" advocated for direct democracy; Jon Hendricks and Jean Toche's Guerrilla Art Action Group combined street activism with artistic actionism; and Wolf Vostell understood his "happenings and demonstrations" as the paramount form of *Aktion*.[87] These artists of action sought urgently to reanimate the political dimension of the historical avant-garde in ways that contributed to a broadening of critical artistic practice within art academies, market-driven art institutions, college classrooms, and, above all, out on the street. Brus's work intervenes distinctly less directly in the political sphere, exploring instead the ambiguous moral-political realm of the *Gehässige*, the hateful and the ugly. Brus touches, in this sense, on the tension not so much of art and politics, but of aesthetics and the police.

Intriguingly, it was contemporaries in the United States who recognized the distinctive character of Viennese performance art by situating *Kunst und Revolution* in a long art historical tradition of what can be called the *Gehässige*—art that is politically troubling precisely because it is aesthetically upsetting. An unsigned, undated flyer produced while Brus, Muehl, and Wiener were being held in prison on remand translated into German letters written by Hendricks, Toche, and Al Hansen to the Austrian ambassador in Washington.[88] Hendricks, recalling having met Brus and Muehl in 1966 at the Destruction in Art Symposium in London, describes how both were enthusiastically received by audiences and critics there.[89] He compares their work to that of Grünewald, Bosch, and Goya. Hansen compares them to El Greco and Honoré Daumier, who were incarcerated in part due to their respective subversive approaches to representation. Toche lists newspapers and magazines, as well as "relevant" artists' publications and books in which serious discussions of Viennese performance art had taken place. Invoking an illustrious tradition of aesthetically and politically subversive art, these artists' defense of their Austrian contemporaries suggests the coincidence captured in the term *gehässig* that most unsettles the Viennese establishment: that of the hateful and the ugly.

When Brus speaks in his deposition of the neglect of "new art" in Austria as one of the conditions to which his work responds, he notably avoids the ready-to-hand *avant-garde*. This may well be because the very term that, in the late nineteenth and early twentieth centuries, had been a rallying cry for the artistic exploration of the intersection of aesthetics and politics had in the 1960s increasingly assumed an unambiguously political sense. The action paradigm in performance art exemplifies this tendency. Among Brus's contemporaries, the most widely recognized happenings, demonstrations, actions, exhibitions, and events were hailed as avant-garde insofar as they wore their politics on their sleeves. The art history of so-called neo-avant-gardes in North America and Western Europe after the Second World War has likewise emphasized the recovery of the political dimension of the historical avant-garde, specifically in strategies of institutional critique.[90] Viennese performance art is not easily assimilated to such narratives of the continuity or return of the avant-garde. It stresses, as Brus's work does in particular, a failure to engage in decisive political practice and a failure to locate the missing space in which such political action might positively unfold. Instead, Brus's institutional critique takes shape in a series of ugly incidents, which upset the tacit norms that constitute the sphere of ethical life.

The Domestic *Kunst und Revolution*

To produce incidents considered in one way or another *gehässig* in Vienna in 1968 was to solicit hateful condemnations from the press and risk the excessive attentions of the police. In the period preceding the trial on July 31, 1968, of Brus, Muehl, and Wiener, the press continued to welcome the public to use its pages to issue commentary on the accused artists. Many readers took such opportunities to express incomprehension, hatred, disgust, and even to incite violence. Shocked that "no one jumped up and beat the shit out of these creatures on the spot," a self-identified former military sergeant, for example, wrote in about how he had, "boozed, gambled, chased women, and also incurred debts," but always "with the necessary class."[91] It was in the context of such vitriol, and shortly after Brus underwent his forced psychiatric evaluation, that Anna Brus and Günter Brus invited reporters from the *Wiener Wochenblatt* into their apartment.

On June 22, the couple appeared on the front-page of the paper under the headline, "So lebt der Chef-Nackerte von der Uni" (This is how the nudist-in-chief from the university lives) (fig. 2.15).[92] Posing together apparently naked

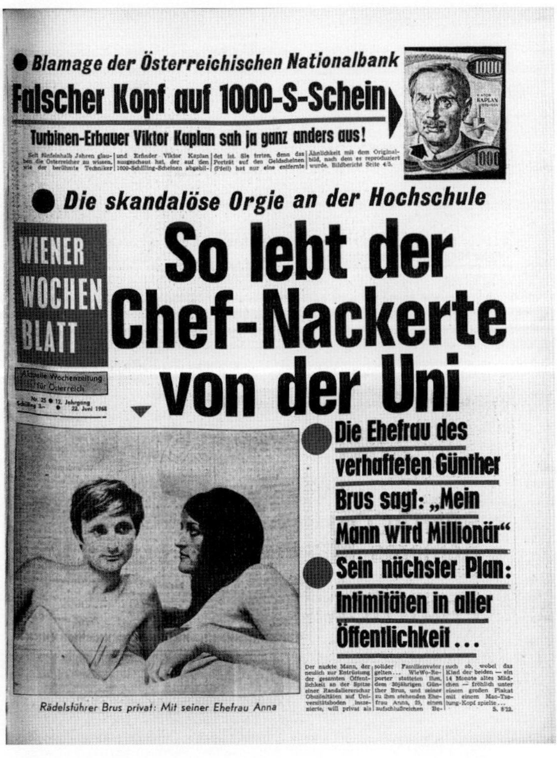

Blamage der Österreichischen Nationalbank

Falscher Kopf auf 1000-S-Schein

Turbinen-Erbauer Viktor Kaplan sah ja ganz anders aus!

Seit fünfeinhalb Jahren glauben die Österreicher zu wissen, wie der berühmte Techniker und Erfinder Viktor Kaplan ausgeschaut hat, der auf den 1000-Schilling-Scheinen abgebildet ist. Sie irrten, denn das Porträt auf den Geldscheinen (Pfeil) hat nur eine entfernte Ähnlichkeit mit dem Originalbild, nach dem es reproduziert wurde. Bildbericht Seite 4/5.

Die skandalöse Orgie an der Hochschule

WIENER WOCHEN BLATT

So lebt der Chef-Nackerte von der Uni

Die Ehefrau des verhafteten Günther Brus sagt: „Mein Mann wird Millionär"

Sein nächster Plan: Intimitäten in aller Öffentlichkeit . . .

Rädelsführer Brus privat: Mit seiner Ehefrau Anna

Der nackte Mann, der neulich zur Entrüstung der gesamten Öffentlichkeit an der Spitze einer Randaliererschar Obszönitäten auf Universitätsboden inszenierte, will privat als solider Familienvater gelten . . . WieWo-Reporter statteten ihm, dem 30jährigen Günther Brus, und seiner zu ihm stehenden Ehefrau Anna, 25, einen aufschlußreichen Besuch ab, wobei das Kind der beiden — ein 14 Monate altes Mädchen — fröhlich unter einem großen Plakat mit einem Mao-Tse-tung-Kopf spielte . . . S. 8/23.

Figure 2.15. Front page of the newspaper *Wiener Wochenblatt*, June 22, 1968. Scanned by the author in the Austrian National Library, Vienna.

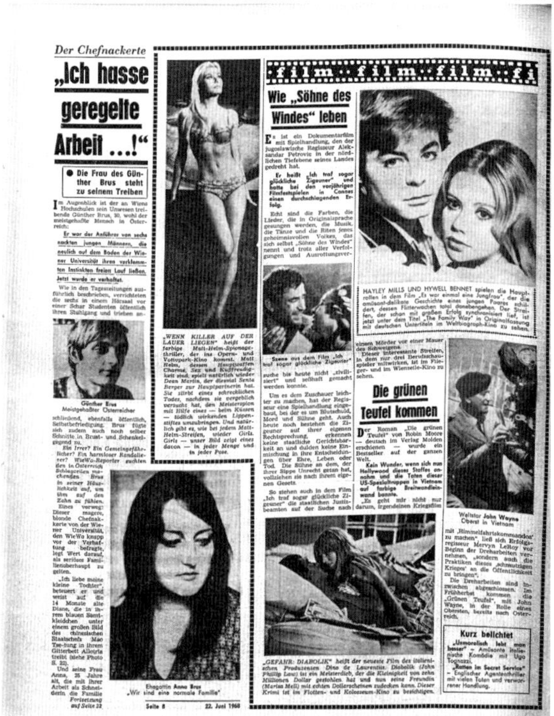

Der Chefnackerte

„Ich hasse geregelte Arbeit ...!“

Die Frau des Günther Brus steht zu seinem Treiben

film · film · film

Wie „Söhne des Windes“ leben

Die grünen Teufel kommen

Kurz belichtet

Seite 8 22. Juni 1968

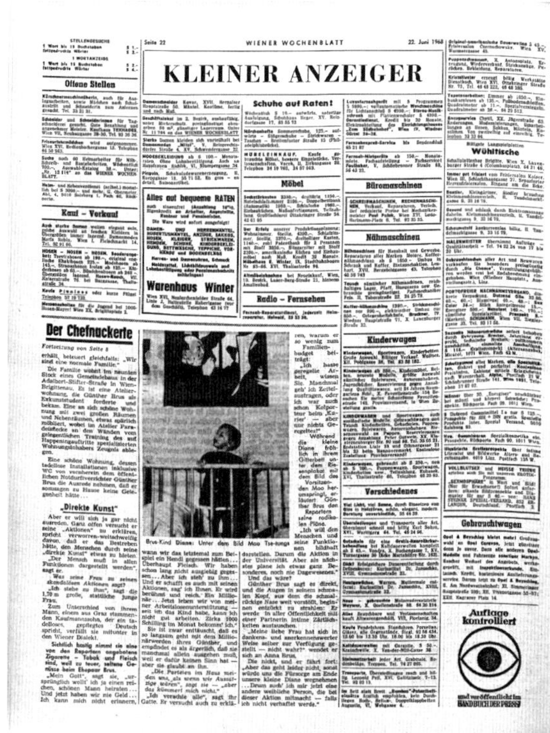

Seite 22 WIENER WOCHENBLATT 22. Juni 1968

KLEINER ANZEIGER

Der Chefnackerte

„Direkte Kunst“

Auflage kontrolliert

Figures 2.16–2.17. Pages 8 and 22 of the newspaper *Wiener Wochenblatt*, June 22, 1968. Scanned by the author in the Austrian National Library, Vienna.

in bed, the Bruses seem somewhat amused. Neither looks directly to camera. The touch of their hands in the foreground sets off the vertical cuts on Günter's chest, which are still visibly raw. Owing to what is called his "Unwesen" ("mischief" or "monstrosity") at the University of Vienna, Günter Brus, the newspaper proclaims in the accompanying article, is probably "the most hated [*meistgehaßte*] human being in Austria." Within the newspaper's pages, alongside advertisements for current cinema with couples shown in postures theirs hardly abides, a portrait photo of Günter, "Meistgehaßter Österreicher" (most hated Austrian) is shown just above one of Anna, "Ehegattin" (the wife), quoted as saying, "We're a normal family" (fig. 2.16). Her look demurs the camera. On the final page, alongside the *Kleiner Anzeiger* (classified ads), their daughter Diana, labeled "Brus-Kind" (Brus-child) appears in her crib "under the picture of Mao Tse-Tung" (fig. 2.17).[93] In their *Wiener Wochenblatt* exposé, the Bruses produce a strangely passive yet acutely critical incident of institutional critique, one that closely parallels *Kunst und Revolution* and that should be read in tandem with it. In this private, domestic space, the Bruses perform a critique not of an Austrian national symbol or official public institution, but of something equally venerated: the Viennese family home.

The reporters observe the following: "It's a beautiful apartment, with two big rooms and adjoining rooms, quite sparsely furnished, while in the atelier tomato-sauce flecks on the walls bear witness to the occasional training of the apartment's occupant for the happening-performances in which he specializes." Anna plays her role as the "loyal wife," saying of Günter: "I stand by him." Far from the figure of the "Uni-Ferkel" (university pig) degraded in the press, Günter, caring father, says: "I love my little daughter." The Bruses respond to the journalists' questions with the same disconcerting combination of earnestness and irreverence with which Günter had responded to the police interrogations. Anna tells them: "At first I wanted to marry a rich, beautiful man. . . . And now I have no money. . . . I can't remember when, for example, we last ate a chicken, or meat. We haven't had a proper meal in a long time. . . . But I stand by him. . . . And he is going to make it with his actions, I'm telling you. He will be famous and rich. A millionaire." Tomato-sauce flecks aside, there is little evidence of Günter Brus's actionism in the apartment, and certainly not of Brus as a man of action. On the contrary, the indolent Brus provocatively explains why they are currently living off Anna's unemployment benefits: "I hate regularized work!" (*Ich hasse geregelte Arbeit!*).

By submitting themselves to the *Wiener Wochenblatt*—and to the very media discourse that was demanding Brus's incarceration, castration, and even death—the Bruses produce, incidentally perhaps, a domestic *Kunst und Revolution* as a continuation of events since June 7 at the university. The profile on the *gehässige* Bruses in their "beautiful" home indeed caused further consternation. The media reception and public response promptly generated the very discourses about marriage, family, the home, and child-rearing, that their comments—recorded in the bedroom and in the kitchen—had so ironically recited. The Bruses received hate mail and death threats at home, with which, after Günter was taken back into prison on remand on June 25, Anna had to deal alone.[94] In the toxic atmosphere, she recalls, her only "shimmer of hope" for getting by came from the support of a woman who had modeled for Oskar Kokoschka and an "old-school communist" who had fought in the resistance to National Socialism.[95]

In the often anonymous personal attacks, the call was repeatedly made for Diana to be taken into institutional care. Anna was a "bad mother"—seen as "failing" to perform her duties to her child even as she was ostracized and isolated. On July 6, Anna appeared without Günter in the pages of the *Wiener Wochenblatt* (fig. 2.18). Her portrait photo from June 22 is reprinted on the cover in reverse with the caption "Bedrohte Anna Brus" (threatened Anna Brus). She features among articles on a supposed diary of Eva Braun, Hitler discovered herding yaks in Tibet, plans for yet another monument to Emperor Franz Joseph, and the booming spa industry in Oberlaa. The address of the Bruses' apartment had been made public in the previous article, and in their neighborhood, a petition was gathering signatures to have Diana taken from the Bruses'

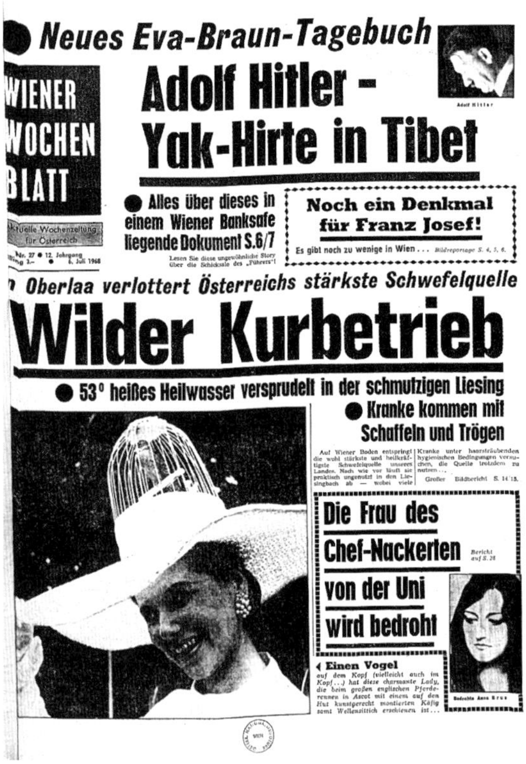
Neues Eva-Braun-Tagebuch
WIENER WOCHENBLATT
Aktuelle Wochenzeitung für Österreich
Adolf Hitler - Yak-Hirte in Tibet
Alles über dieses in einem Wiener Banksafe liegende Dokument S.6/7
Noch ein Denkmal für Franz Josef!
Oberlaa verlottert Österreichs stärkste Schwefelquelle
Wilder Kurbetrieb
53° heißes Heilwasser versprudelt in der schmutzigen Liesing
Kranke kommen mit Schaffeln und Trögen
Die Frau des Chef-Nackerten von der Uni wird bedroht
Einen Vogel

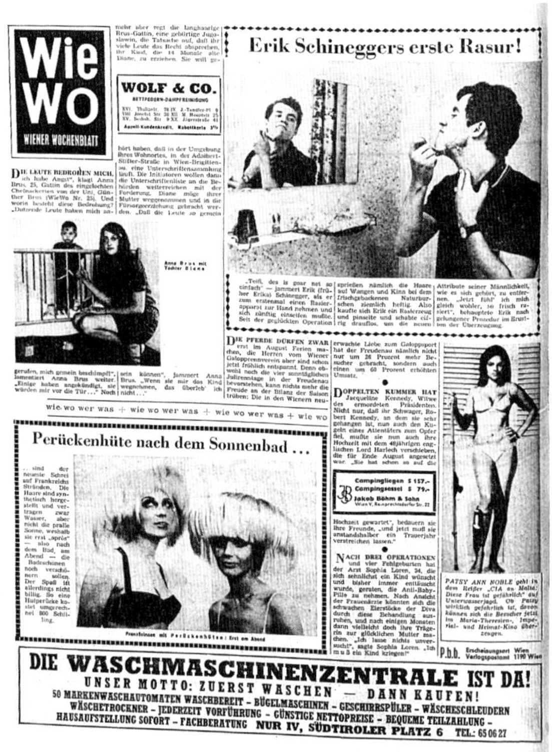
Wie Wo
WIENER WOCHENBLATT
WOLF & CO.
Erik Schineggers erste Rasur!
Perückenhüte nach dem Sonnenbad ...
DIE WASCHMASCHINENZENTRALE IST DA!
UNSER MOTTO: ZUERST WASCHEN — DANN KAUFEN!
NUR IV, SÜDTIROLER PLATZ 6

Figures 2.18–2.19. Front page and page 28 of the newspaper *Wiener Wochenblatt*, July 6, 1968. Scanned by the author in the Austrian National Library, Vienna.

care. Within the pages of the July 6 newspaper, alongside ads for men's razor blades, fashion wigs, and a concert by Patsy Ann Noble, pictured in a bikini, another photograph of Anna appears, this time kneeling beside her daughter's crib, the portrait of Mao cropped from view (fig. 2.19). "I'm afraid," she states.

While Günter was still in prison, a handwritten anonymous letter to "pitiful Anna" arrived, trying to convince her that she did not, and could not, love Günter, who did not and could not love her, and instructing her on how to feed their child properly. Günter, meanwhile, was accused of allowing himself to be supported by Anna, "he was less than a man" and deserved to be beaten, even beaten to death. "A month with Hitler" would be just enough to cure his fear of work wrote one person, who insisted, "In the name of God, I am not a fascist." Brus was encouraged to kill himself in appalling ways in prison. Again and again, the demand was made in hate mail to throw Günter out of Austria: "Such a dirty pig doesn't have the right to be an Austrian!"[96]

Here—around the Bruses' home—Viennese performance art makes contact with the changing political attitudes, and the changing attitudes regarding what counts as political, in the 1960s. Under such mottos as "the private is political," the more subtle structural violence and microaggressions of everyday social relations, above all in ostensibly nonpublic spaces, came into focus as explicitly political concerns. As a consequence, a broader range of practices, including gestures of passivity and withdrawal, began to be recognized as significant forms of political engagement. The Bruses' exposé in the *Wiener Wochenblatt* produced an incident that complements, in the so-called private sphere, the oppressive public context brought into focus by *Kunst und Revolution*. It exhibits the violent domesticity, the hatefulness of intimacy, and the ugliness of affection of the Viennese 1968.

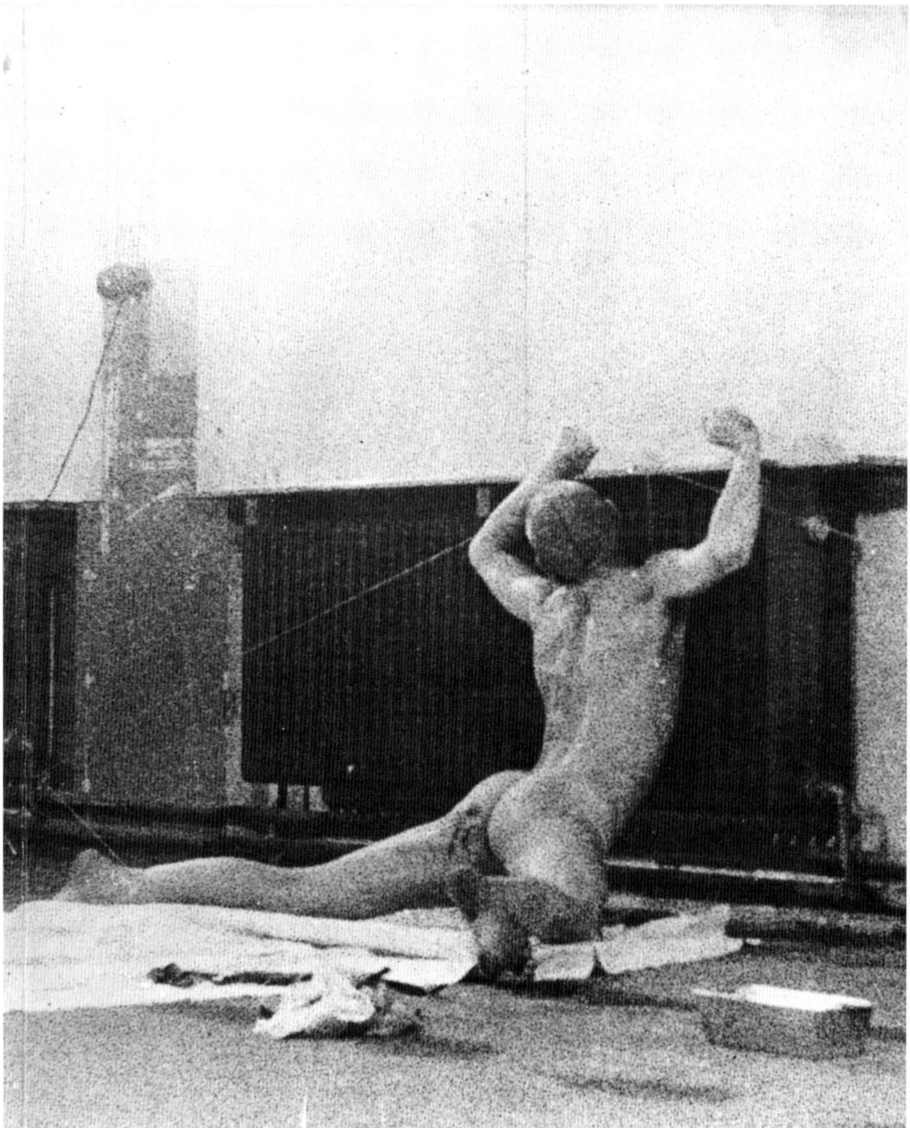
AKTIONSRAUM 1

In-action: Günter Brus's Bad Form

3

Figure 3.1. Günter Brus, *Zerreißprobe* (Stress test), 1970, pictured on the cover of the anthology *Aktionsraum 1, oder, 57 Blindenhunde* (1971, edited by the A1 Informationen Verlagsgesellschaft). Photograph by Klaus Eschen. © Günter Brus. Special Collections, The Sheridan Libraries, Johns Hopkins University; digital image: Digitization Services Unit, Johns Hopkins University.

The iconic photograph of Günter Brus's last performance shows him prostrate and naked from behind, chest propped awkwardly against a radiator, legs spread across a messy cloth with a filthy foot sticking out toward the camera (fig. 3.1). Blood runs from a cut in his shaven head; in the foreground, there appears to be a baking tin. This is *Zerreißprobe* (Stress test), which Brus performed on the evening of June 19, 1970, in the temporary exhibition space for contemporary art in Munich called Aktionsraum 1, with viewers clustered together in the room and seated near him on the floor. Alfred Gulden, an organizer of this action-room, ranks *Zerreißprobe* first on his "hit list" of "actions" presented there, remembering, "Never and nowhere have I experienced an audience as tense, quiet, motionless, even numb, frozen, than in the twenty-five minutes of this action."[1] The photograph of Brus, splayed out from behind, features on the cover of the anthology dedicated to Aktionsraum 1, presented to attest to the exceptionally extreme performance.[2]

Gulden also sought to capture the intensity of *Zerreißprobe* in a "protocol" written "immediately after the action," to articulate what it was about the performance that made the experience of seeing it "like a stab, a shot, no distancing possible, a shock to the core, a primal experience."[3] The vocabulary of his description distills the sense of violence he attributes to the performance:

> Brus kneels, clothed in briefs and women's stockings, on a white cloth. He places a clear plastic triangle on his thigh and cuts along the edge with a razorblade into his flesh. Brus flips the triangle over on his knee and waits until the blood runs down the triangle. Lightning-fast rolling around on the floor. Brus hooks two strings next to the wound in the stocking and pulls it apart. Then he stands up and says in a calm voice: "Can someone give me a glass?" Brus urinates in the glass (the urine is green) and drinks it. He cuts open the stockings and briefs with scissors. He stands naked with his back to the people in front

> of the radiator and slides tensely down the wall, until he kneels. He cuts his bald head with the razorblade and waits until the blood flows from the cut to his buttocks. He ties strings around his ankles and pulls his legs apart with the strings, in the process sliding down the radiator to the floor.[4]

This is about the moment at which the photograph is taken. Gulden's protocol concludes: "He says with a calm voice: 'I would like another glass.' He screams: 'no! no!' Lightning-fast rolling around on the floor. He steps with his feet into small trays (baking trays) full of water, slides out, steps into another. With a calm voice he says: 'can't someone close the window?' but does not wait for a reaction, instead throws himself to the floor, whips the floor with a strap (a leather belt), hits the water, screams, rolls around till exhausted, arches his stomach upwards, touching the floor only with his head and feet. He remains like this. Then goes through the onlookers to the bathroom. End of action."[5] Gulden's protocol merits citing at length not only for its description of the curious sequence of postures Brus performed, but also because it exemplifies a certain way of writing about "action art." The protocol foregrounds Brus's agency over his actions. The staccato use of verbs and omission of periods toward the end of the description generate a sense of acceleration, of increased force and energy leading to a climax and ending with Brus's exhaustion. The emphasis is on Brus's body as the focus of the action: his physical presence, his voice, his shocking movements.

A working assumption in performance art history contends that performance artists put their body into action, perform their body and thereby perform their self.[6] The story of Viennese Actionism is exemplary in this regard. Consider Peter Weibel's 1972 account of *Zerreißprobe*, in which he claims it was "the body of Brus" that was "put to the stress test."[7] Distinguishing "action" from "the theater" and "happening and fluxus," Weibel proposes that it is the use of the raw materiality of the body that allows "action" to "directly affect the vital needs of the population, human reality, politics." "The body," writes Weibel, "is the artistic medium of action."[8] And Viennese Actionism, as he would emphasize a year later, is "the most radical reduction of art to the human body."[9] The fascination with Brus's body in particular, and his performances of so-called "self-injury and self-mutilation," has affected not just "human reality," but also curious mistakings.[10] In the spectacularizing reception of Viennese Actionism, Brus's naked body has even been seen where it is not.[11] Whereas Rosemarie Brucher and Helmut Draxler, in the most attentive readings of Brus's work, see the artist as the ultimate "ascetic," whose excruciating command over his body lends him an almost sacred aura, Weibel has long insisted on his radicality and priority.[12] Brus is the "ultimate founder of body art" for, as Weibel writes, he was "the first to position his body in the center of the action."[13]

This chapter explores assumptions about artistic "action" in the 1960s that motivate these ways of seeing. Doing so requires a shift in focus, from the agential independent body to the body as positioned in space, which discloses an array of relations to other bodies and objects that tend to be overlooked. In the case of *Zerreißprobe*, I am interested in the baking tins, the architect's triangle, and the disconcerting use of strings, as well as Brus's requests for a glass of water and, more perplexingly, to close the window. (The windows, as one can see in figure 3.1, are all in fact already boarded over.) By situating *Zerreißprobe* within the longer arc of Brus's artistic practice in the 1960s, it becomes clear that the performance is a stress test not just of "the body of Brus," but of the spatial dispositive of painting in which that body is articulated. For "the body of Brus" never appears in any straightforward way "in the center of the action." Rather, it occupies—pressed against the wall or supine on the floor, hunched over, turned backward, bound to a chair, leashed upside down from a doorway, or balled up in the corner of a room—disconcerting positions of in-action. Brus's performance art intensively engages painting and its history and performs its immanent critique.

Brus's reception reveals the preponderance of an actionist optic informed by political and aesthetic conventions regarding the agency, composedness, and autonomy of the human body, which are in fact put to the test in his performance art. In contrast with the photo that Gulden chose for the cover of the Aktionsraum 1 anthology, the photo that Brus chose to represent *Zerreißprobe*, in the first Edition Hundertmark box set, foregrounds his analysis of conventions of painting (fig. 3.2).[14] The plastic architect's triangle, baking tin, razor blade, pile of string, and leather strap are all placed near him on the large white cloth on the floor. There are scissors and chalk on the floor in the foreground; farther away, another baking tin. Long strings arc beyond the photograph's frame. Other details also catch the eye: the glint of Brus's wedding ring, the scar on his left chest (from *Kunst und Revolution* two years earlier), and the distinctly "feminine" garter belt and stockings. If, as Weibel has argued, Brus's performance art enacts an "absolute reduction to the body," then this body is curiously prone to exhibiting its situatedness—the ways in which it is bound to other people, times, and spaces.[15] Head inclined, arms tensed, having cut along the triangle into his thigh, Brus is on the verge in figure 3.2—as film footage also shows—of shouting, "Can't someone close the window?" No one responds. "No no no," yelps Brus.[16]

Brus's cryptic remarks invoke the medium that remains a persistent provocation for his performance art—as a site not to be destroyed or overcome, but rather inflected and inhabited. "Window," as Rosalind Krauss has quipped, "is for painting."[17] In distorted form, *Zerreißprobe* recalls the metaphor of painting as a window onto the world, displayed in Albrecht Dürer's famous illustration of the perspectival lattice (fig. 3.3). Yet instead of a reclining supine nude observed by the erect draftsman through a "frame with a grid of strong black thread," Brus's performance is about finding oneself entangled in and between these positions.[18] It is this very dispositive of painting that is put to the "stress test."[19] This is my guiding claim: Brus's performance art is concerned

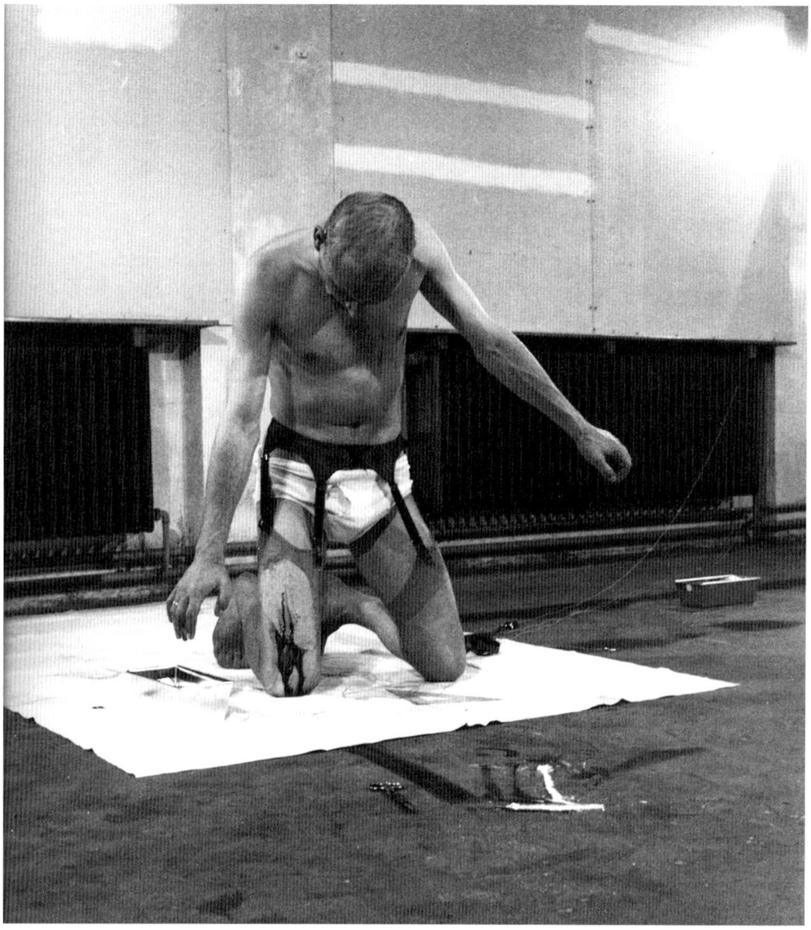

Figure 3.2. Günter Brus, *Zerreißprobe* (Stress test), 1970. Photograph by Klaus Eschen. © Günter Brus. Courtesy of the BRUSEUM, Universalmuseum Joanneum.

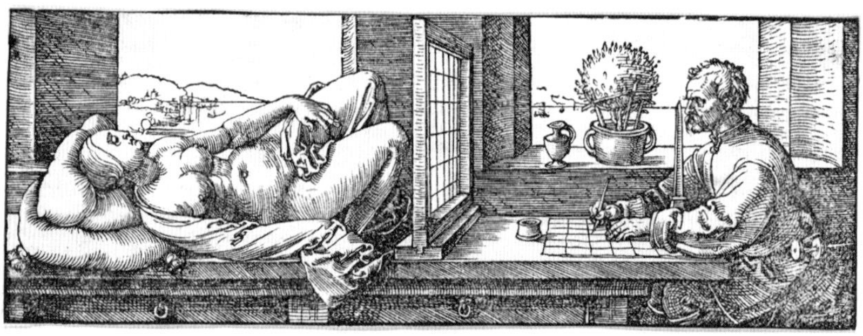

Figure 3.3. Albrecht Dürer, *Draughtsman Making a Perspective Drawing of a Reclining Woman*, c. 1600. Woodcut, 7.7 × 21.4 cm. The Metropolitan Museum, New York.

with the conditions of constraint that belong to the painterly problem of rendering a figure in space. He tests out old conventions of the figure-ground relation, single-point perspective, and emotional detachment rather than trying to escape or destroy them. In so doing, he also tests the tendency throughout the 1960s to celebrate artistic action as a liberation from the constraints of painting, for doing so evades the problem of the figure. Rather than seeking to blur the boundary between art and life, Brus aggravates it—recognizing techniques of painterly figuration as irrevocably ingrained in experience and as the very structures that inform it.

From Painting to Performance: "And to be sure, not in the sense of Pollock"

In the autumn of 1960 in Vienna, Brus, having just turned twenty-two, had little more than a bed and table in the closet-sized space he was living in, formerly a coal merchant's storeroom.[20] While inhabiting the room, he rigged packing paper against the walls and sparse furnishings and proceeded to paint, working on the paper repeatedly in black and brown emulsion. He even stretched his bedsheet: "Even without it I will sleep sweetly," he remarked in his diary that year: "One must live in painting. All around painting" (*Man muß leben in der Malerei. Rundherum Malerei*).[21] This youthfully lighthearted, yet slightly suffocating description of the room-painting in which he lived and slept attests to the spatial confinement as well as the financial poverty and artistic alienation in which Brus found himself at the time. Little of this room-painting remains today. However, Brus recorded in his diary that what he sought to achieve was "a spatial ungraspability—at least not graspable by tradition" (*eine räumliche Unfaßbarkeit—zumindest von der Tradition nicht faßbar*). He wanted to perform "the most complete turning away from the center point in the picture" (*Die vollkommenste Abkehr vom Zentralpunkt im Bild*). Orienting himself self-consciously within the dominant discourse on contemporary abstract painting, Brus emphasized: "And to be sure, not in the sense of Pollock" (*Und zwar nicht im Sinne von Pollock*).[22] A decade later, Brus's *Zerreißprobe* proposed one sense of what painting "not in the sense of Pollock" might look like. Throughout the 1960s, his interest in testing out "spatial ungraspability" in painting would lead him to develop a distinctive kind of performance art.

Brus's oppositional invocation of Pollock indicates a fascinating knot of artistic concerns bound together in ideas about the American painter, especially as these were disseminated from the United States to Europe. Unlike fellow Austrian Markus Prachensky's adulatory action paintings in all-red paint from the late 1950s, or the French painter Georges Mathieu's dramatic *Hommage au Connétable de Bourbon*, a monumental painting performance staged to music and for film cameras in front of a live audience in Vienna in 1959, Brus was interested neither in affirming nor in aggrandizing the possibilities Pollock seemed to offer for action in contemporary art.[23] The "sense" of Pollock that Brus resisted is the very sense that was most often celebrated circa 1960, as I elaborated in the introduction, namely: Pollock the original action painter, asserting his potent physicality across the canvas, which he transformed into an "arena in which to act";[24] Pollock the tragic hero, embodiment of US abstract expressionism and its rhetoric of individuality, masculinity, and freedom; Pollock the inaugurator of action-based practices like the happening, the participatory art form that Allan Kaprow theorized as developing directly out of abstract expressionist action painting.

Brus's distinctive position is particularly clear when compared with the contemporary reception of Pollock in Kaprow's writings. In contrast to Brus's summary negation, Kaprow's adulation of the "legacy" of Pollock, as the introduction shows, is much better known and influential. Taking up Pollock's "futile" yet "heroic stand," Kaprow implores his generation: "Pollock, as I see him, left us at the point where we must become preoccupied with and even dazzled by the space and objects of our everyday life, either our bodies, clothes, rooms, or if need be, the vastness of Forty-Second Street." In the artistic form he invented with the name *happening*, he envisioned how "bold creators" following Pollock's legacy would "show us, as if for the first time, the world we have always had about us, but ignored," making art that would "disclose entirely unheard of happenings and events."[25] Crucially, the trajectory from the "heroic" action painter to the "bold creator" of the happening rests on an epochal art historical claim: Pollock "*destroyed painting*."[26] As Kaprow wrote, "The young artist of today need no longer say 'I am a painter' or 'a poet' or 'a dancer.' He is simply an 'artist.'" The destruction of painting makes space for the unencumbered "artist," who, advancing the project of the historical avant-garde, "discloses" a way out of the restrictive conventions of the medium and onto the "vastness" of the street, where "all of life will be open to him."[27]

In short, Kaprow saw embodied in Pollock a way *out* of painting in a politically consequential transcendence of its traditions. This is a far cry from Brus's experience of the legacy of Pollock across the Atlantic. He was preoccupied, in contrast, by the very uncomfortable positions and discomfiting figures *in* painting that the liberatory sense of Pollock obfuscated. For Brus, in Vienna, painting had by no means been destroyed—and was still urgently relevant for getting situated in everyday life.

Before beginning his room-painting, Brus had ended his studies, traveled to Spain, and gone broke. His degree in graphic design from the Kunstgewerbeschule in Graz had facilitated his enrollment in 1957 at what was then the Akademie für angewandte Kunst in Vienna, where he was, however, discontent both in a class for commercial graphics and in Eduard Bäumer's painting seminar.[28] Increasingly uninterested in commercial art, he also attended classes with Robin Christian Andersen and Herbert Boeckl at the Vienna Akademie der bildenden Künste, but he found the required still-life paintings and paintings based on live models just as unsatisfying. He was far more curious about the contemporary art exhibited at Galerie nächst St. Stephan. In the years 1957 to 1960, Brus would have heard readings and seen visual poetry by members of the Vienna Group (*wiener gruppe*), including Friedrich Achleitner, Konrad Bayer, and Gerhard Rühm, and regularly encountered the unruly gestural abstract paintings of Prachensky and Arnulf Rainer, both of whom he admired, as well as the unusual abstract "Malrezepte" (painting recipes) of Maria Lassnig.[29] But none of these techniques—neither Rainer's distinc-

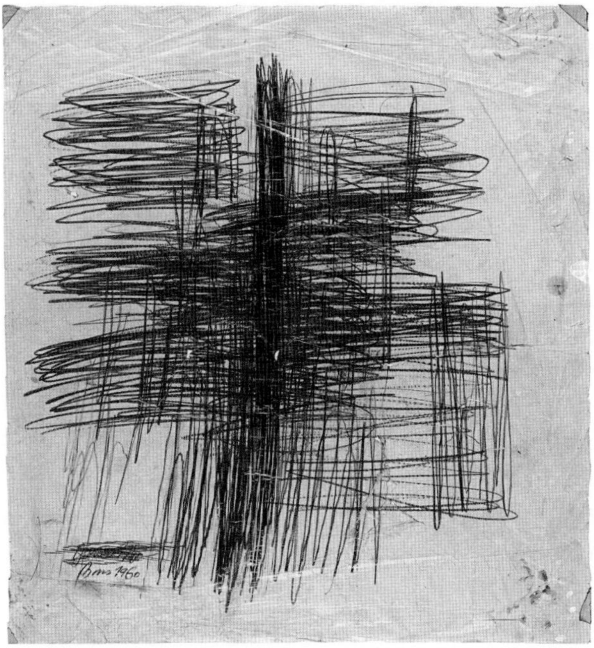

Figure 3.4. Günter Brus, *Ohne Titel (Informel Mallorca)* (Untitled [Mallorca informel]), 1960. Pencil on paper. © Günter Brus. Courtesy of the BRUSEUM, Universalmuseum Joanneum

tive overpainting, nor Prachensky's volatile action painting, nor Lassnig's recipes, and certainly not the performance of concrete poetry—was integrated into the artistic training in the painting departments of the Viennese art academies. Nor, to be sure, were "the 'Act of Painting,' the new space, the personal mark . . . the endless tangle, the great scale, the new materials, etc.," which Kaprow listed in 1958 as "clichés of college art departments" in the United States.[30] In Vienna and New York, art departments could not have been more different.

So when Brus's adventurous Swiss friend from Bäumer's painting seminar, Alfons Schilling, invited him to Mallorca in January 1960, he ended his formal studies and went.[31] The two holed up together making art in an abandoned farmhouse. Of Brus's artistic experiments, a few vigorous drawings in pencil on paper remain (fig. 3.4). The cheap materials attest to his lack of means while the persistent repetition of intersecting vertical and horizontal lines show his fascination with the spatial lattice and often look like overwrought windows. In summer, Brus and Schilling traveled to Madrid to visit the Prado and then parted ways.[32] Brus returned, broke, to his parents' home in Styria, where he could work in his father's store. On a visit to the Venice Biennale—a day away by train—the large size of the abstract paintings of Franz Kline and Philip Guston and the gestural force of Emilio Vedova's *art informel* left an impression on him.[33] After Venice, he made his way back to Vienna, to his little windowless room.

Several rectangles of packing paper extracted from Brus's room-painting of 1960 have survived his harried transformation from art school dropout to "most hated Austrian" in 1968 in the wake of *Kunst und Revolution* (see chapter 2) and ultimately to recipient of the Grand Austrian State Prize, awarded for excellence in art in 1996. In one fragment, an area of tortured overpainting fills the lower-right register, where ugly smudges of black and brown emulsion muddy the ground like fecal smears (plate 9). Above, the white ground is emptier, flecked with reckless unworked spatter, suggesting the strained reach of the artist's hand. Toward the left edge, loose unmixed black paint is brushed in an unsteady vertical band and splashed in an arc of circular droplets that partially land beyond the material support. Near the center, a little lower, a harsh angle painted top to bottom, right to left, demonstrates an emphatic "turning away from the center point in the picture" that Brus described in his diary. This deliberate cornering mark generates, amid the more aleatory and excretory traces around it, a sense of concrete spatial proximity and physical pressure. It is where the ostensibly abstract painting gives way to a figure, yet without any explicit form.

Ironically, this fragment of Brus's room-painting has come to be referred to as an untitled *Aktionsmalerei*, thus an "action painting" very much "in the sense of Pollock" of which Brus was so critical. The designation folds Brus's early work into the familiar US-centric art historical narrative that leads from abstract expressionism and action painting into action-based practices like the happening. When Brus had arrived in Vienna for his studies, contemporary abstract art, and especially American painting, was much discussed at Galerie nächst St. Stephan. Its charismatic curator, Monsignor Otto Mauer, hosted an annual *Kunstgespräch* (discussion of art) in Seckau, a well-attended meeting of contemporary artists, curators, and critics in a former abbey not far from Vienna. In 1958, the discussions were staged in response to the big exhibition *The New American Painting*, which made an extensive European tour, stopping in Switzerland, Italy, Spain, Germany, the Netherlands, Belgium, France, and England—though not Austria, where until 1962, there was no museum dedicated to exhibiting modern and contemporary art.[34]

The impact of *The New American Painting* across Europe was immense. It provided an opportunity for artists and audiences to encounter firsthand a generous selection of work by painters including Willem de Kooning, Sam Francis, Philip Guston, Grace Hartigan, Franz Kline, Robert Motherwell, Barnett Newman, Mark Rothko, Clyfford Still, and, of course, Jackson Pollock. Even on the level of infrastructure, it required significant local adjustments. On the eve of the opening in Madrid, the decision was made to saw open and expand the metal entrance door of the Museo Nacional de Arte Contemporáneo to admit paintings by Hartigan and Pollock.[35] A transformation of space was taking place, especially the space in painting. Reviews in every country reveled in how the works shown in the exhibition established a new "spatial concept," created a "climate of unconstraint," and expressed an "impelling urge toward utter freedom and uninhibited statement." This new American painting was "a kind of painting that seem[ed] to refuse any frame, any imprisonment."[36]

This was also how Arnold Rüdlinger, director of the Kunsthalle Basel, where *The New American Painting* debuted that April, characterized the works exhibited there in the lecture he gave in Seckau that summer, describing Pollock's paintings as "perspective-less monumental pictures."[37] The French art critic Michel Tapié brought slides to the *Kunstgespräch* to show these new paintings in the Austrian countryside, linking in his presentation their "spatial concept" to the eradication of perspectival space and, with it, a repudiation of humanism, asserting, "Man is no longer the center point of the world."[38] Unconstrained by perspective and freed of framing conventions, the new American painting provided the paradigm of contemporary art in existential, political, and artistic terms.[39]

This association of American values of freedom with abstract expressionist action painting was reiterated in exhibitions like *Junge Maler der Gegenwart* (Young painters of the present) at the Vienna Künstlerhaus in the summer of 1959. This exhibition drew special attention to Harold Rosenberg's idea of "action painting," which was presented as the only historically unprecedented painting style worth pursuing.[40] Pollock was proclaimed its master, the paragon of contemporary painters who had, most significantly, "destroyed Picasso's formalism," thus not only breaking beyond the lingering figural aspects of Picasso's late paintings, but also breaking free from a narrative of art history rooted in European traditions.[41]

This effusive view of Pollock's legacy was nowhere more vividly constructed than at the *documenta* 2 of 1959 in Kassel, Germany. Together with Schilling, Brus studied the German-language catalog of the show, which was a touchstone for his early practice.[42] In it, curator Werner Haftmann sums up the exhibition's guiding thesis: "One thing is certain," he claims, "art has become abstract."[43] The curatorial aim of the *documenta* 2 was to establish a continuity from the modernist abstract painting of Kandinsky, Klee, and Mondrian—who feature in the catalog's image-essay as "The Masters of the Art of the Twentieth Century" (*Die Lehrmeister der Kunst des XX. Jahrhunderts*)—to that of three recently deceased painters: Willi Baumeister, the German commercial artist and stage designer who had lived through two world wars and was in fact very much a modernist, and two much younger contemporary painters, the Russian-born Parisian suicide Nicolas de Staël, and Pollock, who died dramatically in an alcohol-fueled car crash in 1956. As Haftmann argues in his catalog essay "Painting After 1945," visual arts at the turn of the twentieth century undertook "the step-by-step eradication and replacement of precisely those pictures of reality that come into the mind through direct reference via the eye, and which were achieved through the classical juxtaposition of human and thing [*Mensch und Ding*]."[44] Haftmann is here describing the eradication of the spatial dispositive of figural painting, which he presents as necessary for attaining the freedom of the spatial concept of abstraction after 1945. In both the exhibition and the catalog, Pollock is presented as the most audacious destroyer of pictures of reality and of the painterly conventions like perspective that framed them.

Sixteen large paintings by Pollock were included in the show, and six were

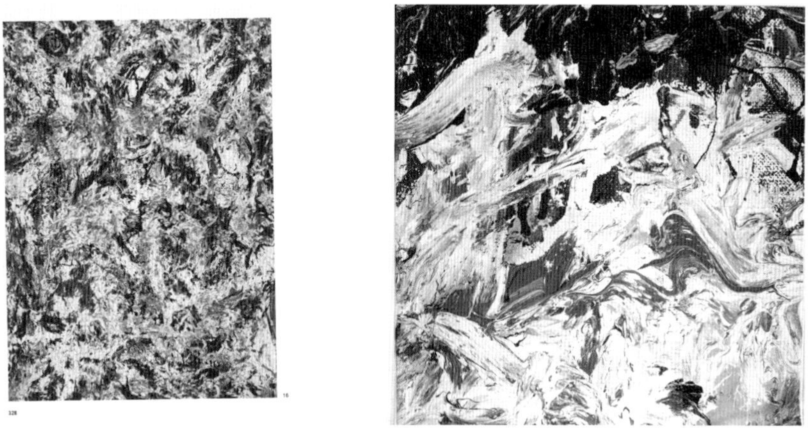

Figure 3.5. Jackson Pollock, *Scent*, 1955, and detail of *Scent*, oil on canvas, 198.2 × 146 cm, pictured in the exhibition catalog *II. Documenta '59: Kunst nach 1945, Malerei, Skulptur, Druckgrafik*, vol. 1 (1959). © 2025 The Pollock-Krasner Foundation / Artists Rights Society (ARS), New York.

selected for reproduction in the catalog. *Number 4* (1949), *Number 32* (1950), and *Scent* (1955), all included, exemplify what Clement Greenberg had recently described as "American type" painting: "a paint-strewn or paint-laden surface as a single synoptic image," the so-called all-over image definitive of the best American abstract expressionism.[45] A close-up color detail of *Scent* shows how Pollock's skein-like traceries of paint and roughly pushed bands of impasto generate this sense of visual undulation and unity (fig. 3.5). In addition to the paintings, the catalog includes Haftmann's translation into German of an excerpt from curator Sam Hunter's essay for the unexpectedly posthumous exhibition *Jackson Pollock* at the Museum of Modern Art in New York in 1956.[46] Hunter's weighty terms are even more so in German. Here are two key phrases from the original text and its translation for the *documenta 2* catalog that give a sense of that "sense" of Pollock that Brus opposed: "An idealist of transcendental powers" (*ein mit transzendenten Kräften ausgestatteter Idealist*), Pollock stands for a new generation of artists as a "revered symbol of their new sense of liberation and hopefulness for the future" (*verehrten Symbol ihres neuen Gefühls für Freiheit und Zukunftshoffnung*). Pollock's paintings are presented as radically breaking with tradition, destroying conventional techniques to pursue what Hunter calls a "centrifugal" approach, without "respecting either the delimiting spatial boundaries of the picture frame or the traditional uses of paint matter" (*ohne Rücksicht auf die Bildgrenzen und die herkömmlichen Malverfahren*).[47] Pollock—transcendent, revered, powerful—breaks beyond the limits of painting; in Kaprow's terms, he destroys them.

This narrative of the transcendence of painting in performance art propels what I call in the introduction the action paradigm, which takes up and extends the "legacy" of Pollock. Ironically, the so-called destruction of painting in fact produces, or rather, reproduces, in the performance artist at its center an altogether classic figure from the tradition of painting. If abstract painting had overcome the "juxtaposition of human and thing," then the legacy of action painting in performance art resurrected an all-too-human figure: the one Kaprow called the "'artist'" who "discloses" reality as the agent of happenings, demonstrations, and actions.[48] In this regard, the tradition of painting had by no means been overcome; on the contrary, it was alive and well, precisely among those who most vociferously pronounced its destruction. What the account of performance art out of action painting unconsciously preserves from the painterly tradition is the medium's problematic implication in the history of the representation, indeed, in the "overrepresentation" of a certain kind of human.[49] Ironically, performance art in this narrative recuperates what abstract painting was supposed to have abandoned once and for all, namely the figure of the ostensibly universal Human of humanism, along with the history of exclusion, obfuscation, and dehumanization that inconspicuously accompanied it. In this regard, the political imaginary of the action paradigm remains beholden to and attests to the ongoing prevalence of a certain reception of the history of painting.

Yet precisely because they were initially formal, Brus's concerns with Pollock's painting perform a critique of this paradigm. Operating between abstraction and figuration, Brus attends to the positions of awkward figures whose bodies and histories never measured up to the upper-case Human of humanism. Brus performs, as discussed in chapter 1, an alternative anthropometry. His art remains skeptical of the contemporary compulsion to eradicate "pictures of reality," whether through abstraction or the blurring of the boundary between art and life. Especially suspicious of the implications of what he called Pollock's "infinite picture" (*unendliches Bild*), which affords that expansive "all-over" aesthetic experience cherished by Greenberg and Kaprow alike, Brus took an intensive approach.[50] To paint "not in the sense of Pollock" involves exploring finitude and constraint. Beginning with his room-painting, Brus's performance art of the 1960s insists upon the difficult task of positioning himself *in* painting—not as an actor in the arena of action painting, but as a figure within the stifling spatial dispositive of "all around painting" (*Rundherum Malerei*). Engaging the history and conventions of painting, Brus's performance art seeks, with consternation and care, to stress and probe its limits from within. This, at least, is what a nearby drawing in his diary labeled "Entwurf für einen labyrinthischen Raum" (Draft for a labyrinthine space; fig. 3.6)—with its trip wires and obstacles scattered about in a room-like enclosure—seems to suggest.

Obstruction: Painting in a Labyrinthine Space, Self-Painting, Self-Dismemberment

Just as he was gaining a foothold in Vienna, Brus was called up in 1961 to complete his mandatory nine-month military service, the experience of which would leave him depressed and unmotivated. Upon completing it in the winter of 1962, rather than return to Vienna, he went back to his parents' home. Meanwhile, his friend Schilling had left Austria for the United States. Before they parted ways, they had seen some of their paintings installed together

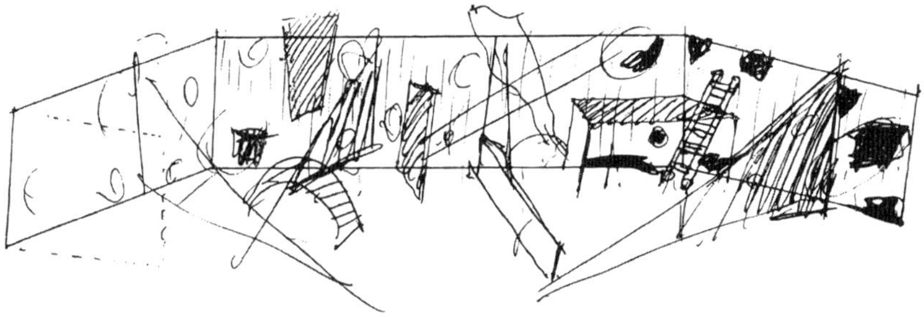

Figure 3.6. Günter Brus, drawing in a lost diary, "Wiener Tagebuch" (1960), pictured in the exhibition catalog *Von der Aktionsmalerei zum Aktionismus, Wien 1960–1965: Günter Brus, Adolf Frohner, Otto Muehl, Hermann Nitsch, Alfons Schilling, Rudolf Schwarzkogler* (1988). © Günter Brus; Scan produced and enhanced by Lael J. Ensor-Bennett, curator, Visual Resources Collection, Johns Hopkins University.

in an exhibition at Galerie Junge Generation in Vienna, and in the summer, while he was serving in the military, two of Brus's paintings had been included in *Who's Who?*, an annual show at the Vienna Secession dedicated to local, often unestablished artists. Most of these wall-covering, black-and-white works in cheap dispersion paint have been lost.[51]

Reviews of the Galerie Junge Generation show, with titles like "Mit Kopf durch die Leinwand" (With head through the canvas), disparaged Brus's and Schilling's work as a bad imitation of the sort of action painting practiced by Mathieu and Pollock and ridiculed them for the way they appeared at the opening "explaining" their art to those present while traipsing excitedly back and forth across the gallery "like a cat on a hot tin roof" and a "Harlem-Globetrotter."[52] These reviewers' critical associations of the artists and their work with US cultural production indicate the perception in Vienna of its local incursions. They also demonstrate the all-too-easy slip of focus in discussions of action painting from the canvas to the painter as locus of the work of art. Evidently, in the gallery setting, Brus failed to effectively demonstrate what it meant to paint "not in the sense of Pollock."

Otto Muehl, in contrast, was utterly compelled by Brus's early work. It inspired his own decisive transition from making junk sculpture to the more painterly exploration of perishable materials that he would call "material action." Muehl encouraged Brus at this pivotal moment in his life, coaxing him from depression back to Vienna and into the artistic project that he had been envisioning before his military service, that draft for "a labyrinthine space" he sketched in 1960.[53] Muehl organized a basement space for Brus to work in, and a five-thousand-schilling grant (about two hundred dollars) from the Institut zur Förderung der Künste alleviated what Brus describes as living at the time "paralyzed by terrible material need" (*gelähmt von schlimmster materieller Not*).[54] In the spring of 1963, he began *Malerei in einem labyrinth-artig verbauten Raum* (Painting in a labyrinth-like obstructed space), rigging ropes along the ceiling from which to suspend swaths of packing paper and molino, a cheap untreated loose-weave cotton fabric much like drop cloth.[55] *Malerei in einem labyrinth-artig verbauten Raum* was a solitary undertaking that few people saw.[56] But it concentrates two key aspects of Brus's earlier room-painting that define his performance art: an understanding of the dispositive of painting as an uncomfortably obstructed and inhabited space and of the artist's body as figured in it, implicated in and made subject to its spatial and material constraints.

There is no photographic documentation of Brus at work in *Malerei in einem labyrinth-artig verbauten Raum*, and like his room-painting, most of it has been lost. Yet the project was a crucial iteration of Brus's painting "not in the sense of Pollock"—and indeed of the kind of performance art he was practicing. In the spring of 1972, he included photographs of three works titled *Malerei in einem labyrinthischen Raum* at the beginning of the first of three issues of his journal *Die Schastrommel: Organ der österreichischen Exilregierung* dedicated to his work, thus consequentially linking these "paintings" to his "actions."[57] In 1984, when he finally gained steady gallery representation with the Viennese gallerist Heike Curtze, he included a "reconstructive sketch" of the project in the first official box set of photographic documents of his performance art, again explicitly connecting *Malerei in einem labyrinth-artig verbauten Raum*, as he had in earlier artist's statements, to the subsequent "actions."[58] In the 1984 sketch, which uses the slightly different title *Malerei in einem labyrinthischen-verspannten Raum* (Painting in a labyrinthine-tensed space), the space itself—more so than the "action" of painting—is shown to be what matters (fig. 3.7). A sense of the basement interior is articulated through an elevated view that aligns the rope rigging and pathways of packing paper with a perspectival

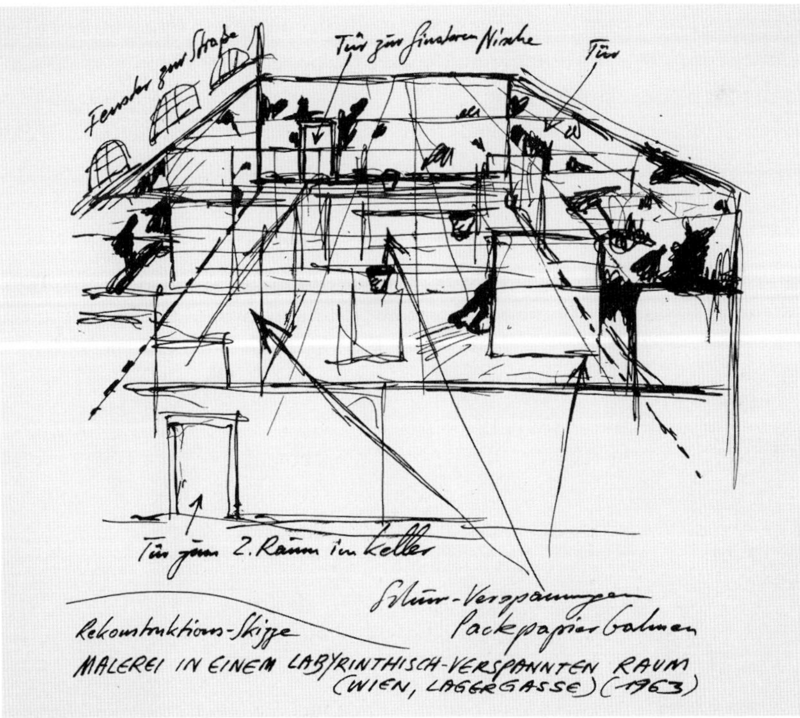

Figure 3.7. Günter Brus, *Malerei in einem labyrinthischen-verspannten Raum* (Painting in a labyrinthine-tensed space), 1984. Ink on paper; printed in the edition *Ana*, edited by Galerie Heike Curtze and Galerie Krinzinger, Vienna. © Günter Brus. Courtesy of the BRUSEUM, Universalmuseum Joanneum.

array. Arrows point into the room, to windows and doors, but also to intersections of the rigging and various obstacles, charting out the topography of the room-painting. Black blots on walls suggest that a more conventional kind of painting is also taking place. Small within the labyrinthine structure, a figure appears, legs kicking out absurdly from behind a panel.

Malerei in einem labyrinth-artig verbauten Raum exemplifies how Brus moves from painting to performance art. But it does not take the destruction of painting as is its premise. Rather, the spatial dispositive of painting is performed through what Brus calls "decomposition." The relationship of figure and ground is thus not at its center, for there is no center here. Nonetheless, the relationship of figure and ground remains utterly and uncomfortably constitutive of the performance. As Brus described his process in an interview from 1974, he began by "strangulating my arms and tying up my legs so that I limited my freedom of movement," intensifying the disorienting spatial constraints of the labyrinth with physical restraint.[59] This practice of obstruction belongs to Brus's formal concern to "avoid an all too quickly solidifying compositional idea."[60] Pursuing neither an abstract "all-over" visual appeal, nor a composition juxtaposing "human and thing," Brus's approach was "to work more or less at the same time on all of the walls as an all-around picture [*Rundumbild*] and to realize through an incessant wandering in the labyrinth a sought-after decomposition [*Dekomposition*]."[61] Significantly, decomposition requires a position. It describes an implication of material and structure—as of body and space, figure and ground—that is also an undoing of these distinctions.

Only two fragments of painted fabric from *Malerei in einem labyrinth-artig verbauten Raum* exist today. The rest literally decomposed. Again broke at the end of 1963, Brus left Vienna in the new year with Anna Steiner. Two years later they would marry and she would take his name. At the time, in St. Moritz, Switzerland, a posh resort town, they boarded for free at a hotel, washing dishes, polishing shoes, and servicing rooms for minimum wage. While Brus was away from Vienna, the basement space where he had left his work was

Figure 3.8. Günter Brus, *Ohne Titel* (Untitled), 1963. Dispersion on drop cloth, 196.53 × 466.09 × 3.49 cm. © Günter Brus; Glenstone Museum; digital image: Courtesy of Hauser & Wirth.

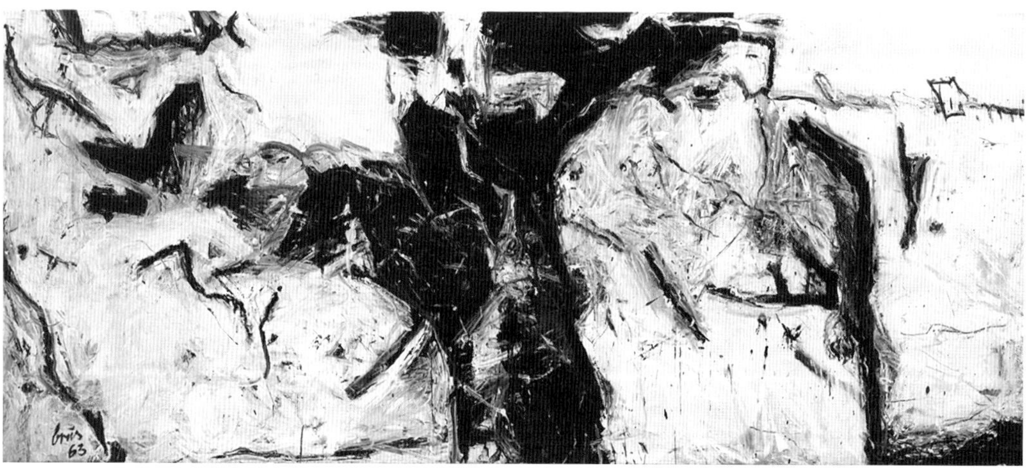

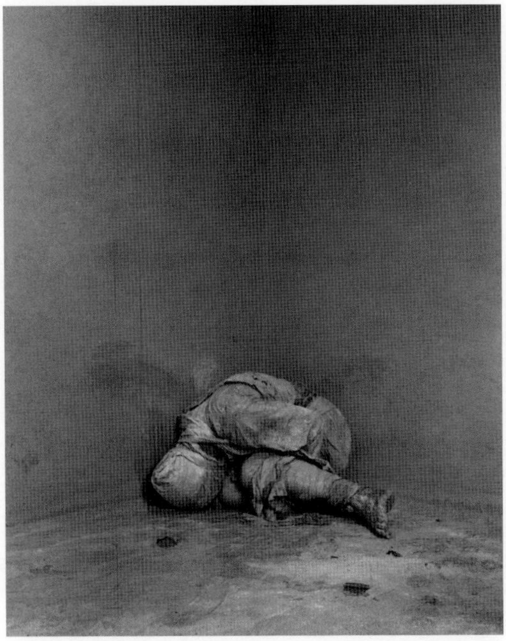
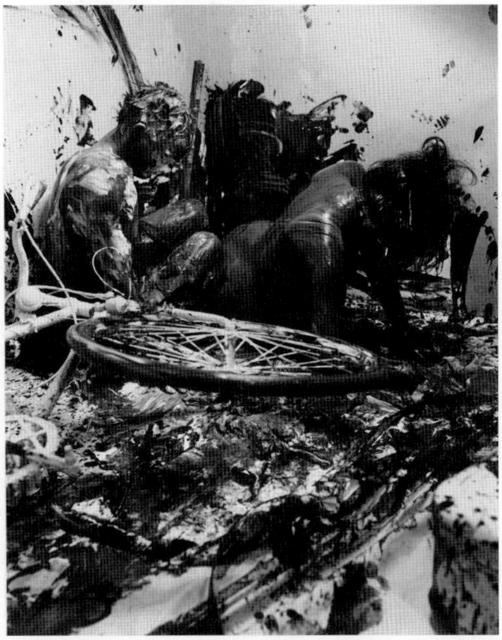

Figures 3.9–3.10. Günter Brus with Anna Brus, *Ana*, 1964. Photograph by Siegfried Klein (Khasaq). © Günter Brus. Courtesy of the BRUSEUM, Universalmuseum Joanneum; Photography of Siegfried Klein courtesy of Julius Hummel.

rented out, and when he returned, the remainders of his labyrinthine painting were heaped in a corner rotting.[62] Of the still-extant pieces he later salvaged, the larger one features a thick black vertical band choking its center (fig. 3.8). Black dispersion paint is pushed inward and outward, toward either edge, while white dispersion is clawed inward again through it. Inclined contours—broken diagonals, zigzags, crushed verticals—map a structurally dense yet apparently vacant pictorial field. The overburdened application of paint indexes an incessant process and converges as a material sludge, coagulating in areas of overpainting around coarse gray sutures. Flicked from a distance, thin spatters of loose black paint also sprinkle the surface. There are justifiable reasons to want to call this a work of action painting in the legacy of Pollock. Yet even considered apart from the labyrinthine space in which it was integrated, and of which it was conceived as a part, this piece of painting discloses the claustrophobic space and impeded body that engendered it. This is in-action painting.

While Brus's room-painting of 1960 and *Malerei in einem labyrinth-artig verbauten Raum* of 1963 already exhibit the preoccupations of his performance art, it was first upon his return to Vienna from St. Moritz in 1964, and again with Muehl's help, that he began to have his work photographed and filmed. Thus the subsequent work can be presented today through those familiar mediating forms that have arguably been the precondition for writing performance art history and out of which the archive of performance art history is made. For this reason, many accounts of Brus's "proper" work—the so-called *Aktionen*—begin with *Ana* (1964; figs. 3.9, 3.10, and see figs 1.31, 1.32, 1.33), which Brus refers to in an early autobiographical entry as a *Selbstbemalung* (self-painting).[63] In Benjamin H. D. Buchloh's formulation, which

I cited in chapter 1, *Ana* "marks his initial step into Actionism." Echoing Weibel's earlier assessments, Buchloh suggests that in and after *Ana*, "Brus shifted the painterly process directly onto the performing body (most often, the artist's own)."[64] This "shift," however, had already been underway—neither in the "radical reduction" of the artistic work to the artist's body nor in the explicit foregrounding of the "performing body," but rather in the decomposition of bodies within the constraints of painting.

Decomposition is painstakingly explored in Brus's performances of *Selbstbemalung*. As in his room-painting and *Malerei in einem labyrinth-artig verbauten Raum*, the technique of *Selbstbemalung* "strangulates" and obstructs limbs and vision, calling attention to confined material and spatial surrounds. Photographs of the earliest performances of *Selbstbemalung* from 1964 show the artist's hand or head painted white, pressed against a white-painted wall, physically and visually bound to it, and juxtaposed to household tools. Between fingers, or in the palm, or affixed next to it on the wall, one can see razor blades, nail scissors, a handsaw, or a serrated kitchen knife (figs. 3.11, 3.12, 3.13). Nails penetrate the wall between the fingers or secure a shirtsleeve to it at the wrist. The hand is not engaged like Pollock's in disseminating paint—or in catching molten lead like Richard Serra four years later, or in dancing and speaking "an uninterpretable language" like Yvonne Rainer. "The hand—particularly the artist's own hand," writes Carrie Lambert-Beatty of Rainer's *Hand Movie* (1966), is "the ideal medium to embody the tendencies Rainer and her generation were most concerned to evacuate from their art: interpretability, personality, transcendence."[65]

If Brus shares these concerns, then he intensifies the critique, performing a complete evacuation of the myth of the "artist's hand," just as of the artist's body. In *Starrkrampf* (Catalepsy; 1965; figs. 3.14, 3.15), the hand is buried under a layer of crumbly white pigment, either flour or laundry powder. It is slowly lifted by someone in an oblique position beyond the camera's frame, by five strings looped around each finger, and then positioned again under bands that restrain it. The artist's hand is not a privileged site of expressivity or identity but is severed from the self, embedded in its material and spatial surrounds. Constrained by defunct perspectival tools and doubly confined by the camera's frame, these performances explore paralysis, positions of being caught, encased, pinned down.

Brus's exclusive use of white and black paint—essential to basic techniques of lending depth, shadow, and compositional line to the picture surface—focus the performance of *Selbstbemalung* as one of positioning figures in a remnant of painting's spatial dispositive. This position, however, is a decomposition. In another *Selbstbemalung*, we see Brus's head, eyes closed and painted over, ears and nose painted over, encrusted with white, lips sealed (figs. 3.16, 3.17). None of this painting is done in an exaggerated or violent way. His orifices are not penetrated, simply painted, and in a manner that foregrounds how the white-painted head and shoulders are pressed up against the white-painted wall and

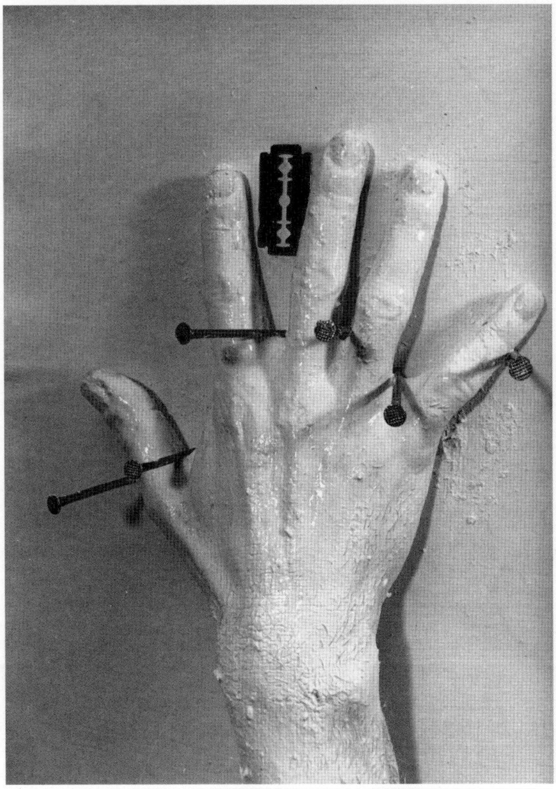

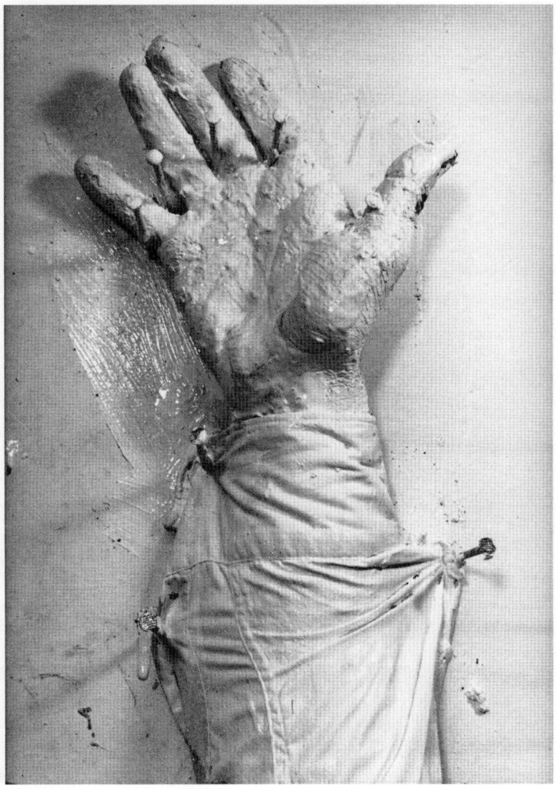

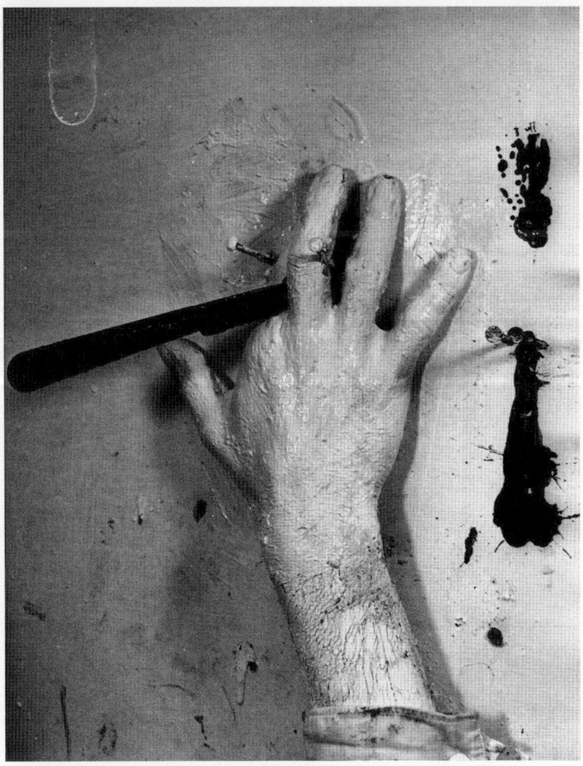

Figures 3.11–3.13. Günter Brus, *Selbstbemalung (Handbemalung)* (Self-painting [Hand-painting]), 1964. Photograph by Ludwig Hoffenreich. © Günter Brus. Courtesy of the BRUSEUM, Universalmuseum Joanneum.

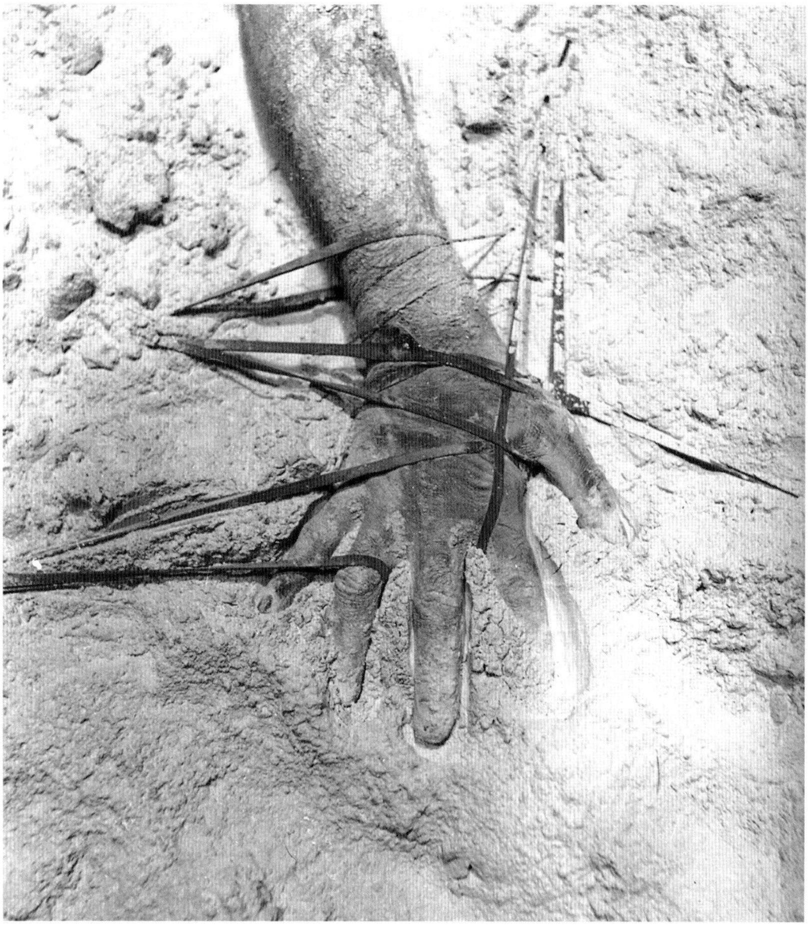

Figures 3.14–3.15. Günter Brus, *Starrkrampf* (Catalepsy), 1965. Photograph by Ludwig Hoffenreich. © Günter Brus. Courtesy of the BRUSEUM, Universalmuseum Joanneum.

thus made proximate to and set in relation with the familiar domestic tools hanging from nails. The tone of Brus's performance art is often muted, like the sound of a nail dropping on a cloth-strewn floor.

When Brus defined *Selbstbemalung* in an artist's statement in 1965, he tellingly described it not as a form of action or actionism, but as "a further development of painting" (*eine Weiterentwicklung der Malerei*). *Selbstbemalung* relocates what Brus refers to as "the pictorial field" (*Bildfläche*) from the canvas of easel painting to "walls, objects, beings [*Lebewesen*], and the human body." This implication of bodies, understood in the broadest sense as architectural supports, objects, and entities, *within* the space in which they are circumscribed is characteristic of Brus's performance art. As he puts it, "Through the involvement of my body as a bearer of expression, the arising result is an occurrence" (*Durch die Einbeziehung meines Körpers als Ausdrucksträger entsteht als Ergebnis ein Geschehen*). The body is "involved." The act of *Ein-beziehung*—literally, "in-relation"—positions the body not as a free expressive agent, but just as a bearer of expression, "strangulated" in the pictorial field. "Everything," Brus emphasizes, "becomes the 'pictorial field.'"[66]

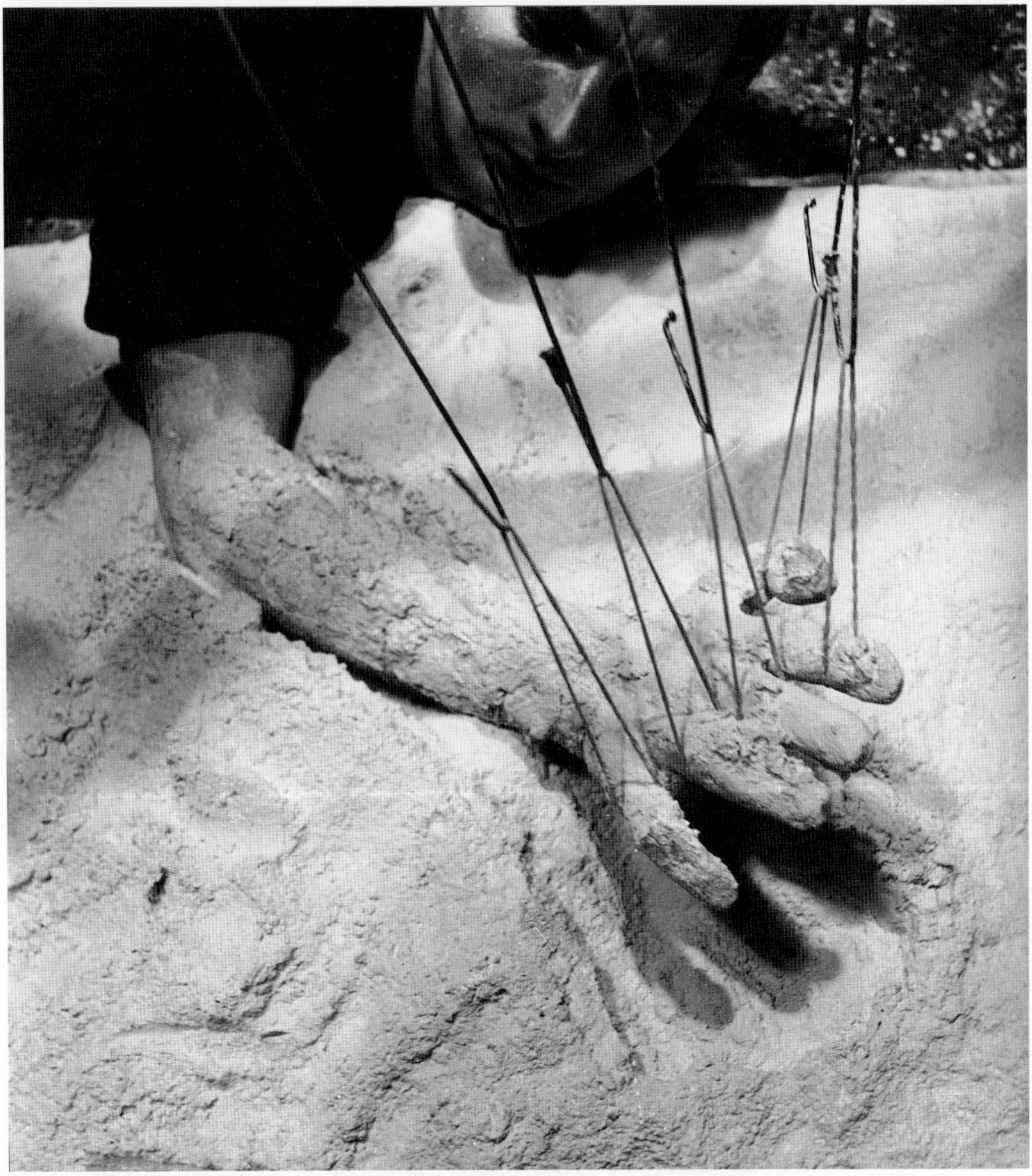

If the term *Selbstbemalung* misleadingly gives the impression that what is being painted is a self-contained and self-composed self, then what is at stake in Brus's practice is better captured in the related term he used at the same time: *Selbstverstümmelung* (self-dismemberment). Brus's performances of *Selbstverstümmelung* make especially clear that the emphasis is not on affirming or constituting a self, but on dissolving it. These self-dismemberments do not presuppose a fully formed self that is then taken apart. On the contrary, the self is from the start obstructed, broken down, cornered, and the performance serves to accentuate this disposition. Not a performance of self-assertion, self-dismemberment renders the body of the artist inexpressive and incoherent.

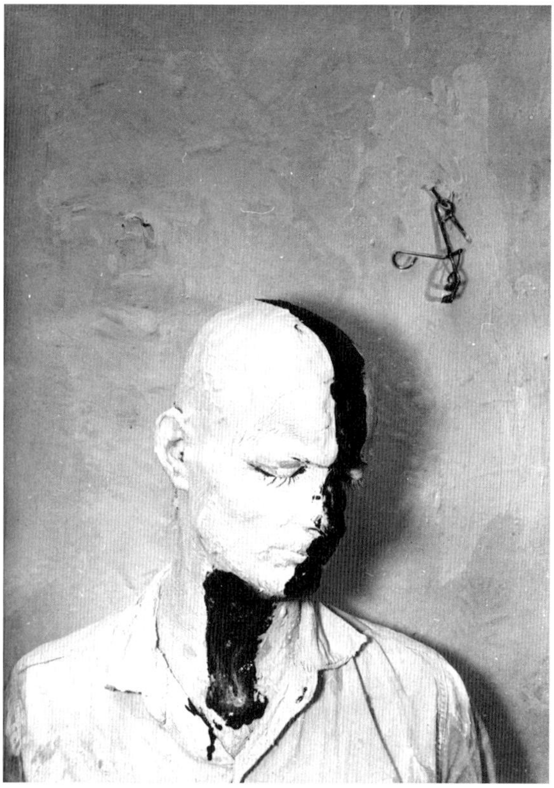

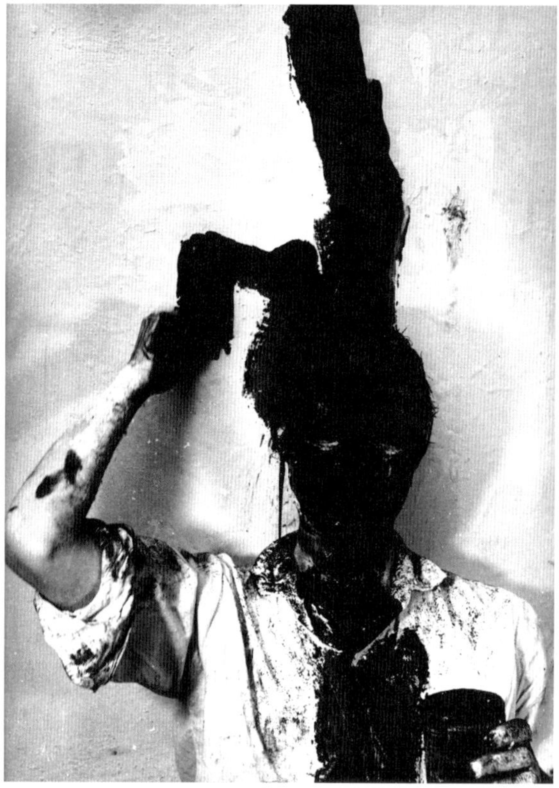

Figures 3.16–3.17. Günter Brus, *Selbstbemalung* (Self-painting), 1964. Photograph by Ludwig Hoffenreich. © Günter Brus. Courtesy of the BRUSEUM, Universalmuseum Joanneum.

Selbstverstümmelung can also be translated as *self-mangling* or *self-garbling*.[67] The decomposition of painting extends to the figure in space. This is just one aspect of so-called Viennese Actionism that Franko B inherited (see figs. I.18, I.19).[68]

Brus's performance art is preoccupied with the irrevocable sense of being "in-relation" in the pictorial field. Far from "the center of the action," the body is figured in its relationships and contingencies. In *Selbstverstümmelung* (1965; fig. 3.18), performed in Muehl's basement atelier, the floor is covered in white paper. Amid an assortment of little utensils from the home—nail scissors, tacks, an eyelash curler, razor blades, and dishes—Brus is prostrate. A prosthetic foot and hand lie nearby, uncanny but also comic doppelgängers of the artist's inert body. Muehl's blurry film footage shows the white-painted Brus begin to cumbersomely move within the space circumscribed by the drop cloth, clutching at metal brackets and getting tangled in messes of cord and wire, materials that appear in so many of his performances as the defunct perspectival array of painting, not opening out onto a world beyond the room, but compressing the space, inducing claustrophobia. Wood panels and a bulky frame lean unsteadily against the wall nearby and provide narrow spaces for this figure to inhabit, to disappear behind. With his typical painterly in-action, Brus drags a paintbrush drenched in black paint up his foot, through his torso, through his face, accentuating his embeddedness in the confining surrounds.

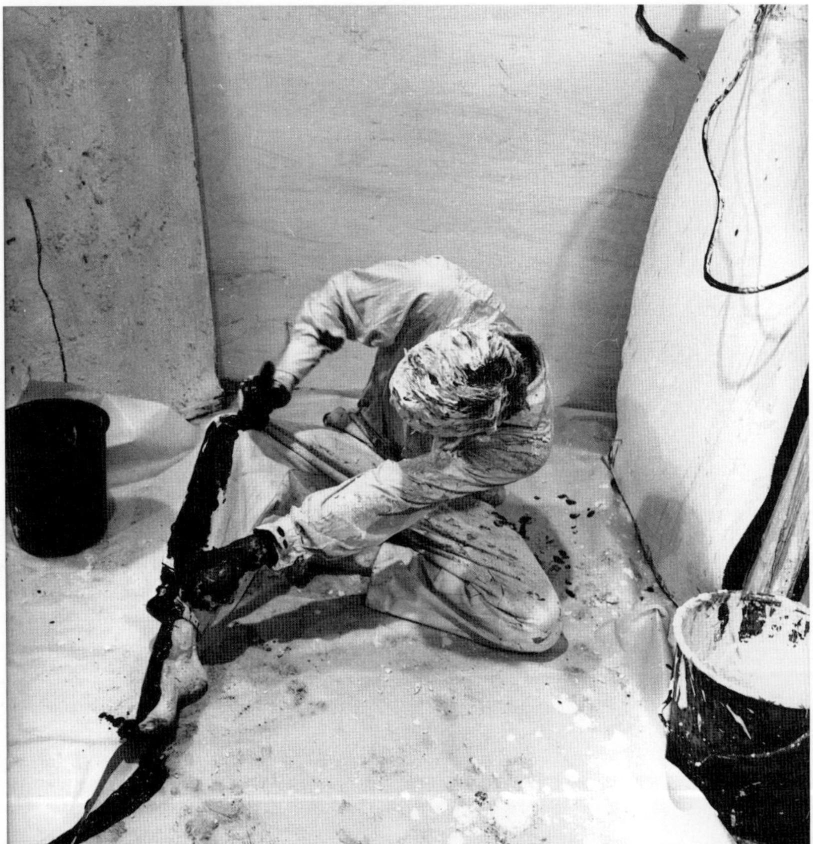

Figure 3.18. Günter Brus, *Selbstverstümmelung* (Self-dismemberment), 1965. Photograph by Ludwig Hoffenreich. © Günter Brus. Courtesy of the BRUSEUM, Universalmuseum Joanneum.

Incidentally yet fittingly, Brus's *Selbstbemalung* and *Selbstverstümmelung* performances often took place in the very same space (Muehl's basement) recycling many of the same objects. In an iteration later that year, Brus tumbles awkwardly on the floor (figs. 3.19, 3.20). His clothes are stripped from his body by various sharp objects lying about. The performance ends with Brus on his back, halfway upside down, pressed against an overturned table, his foot painted against its surface.

In his early writings and titles, Brus developed a remarkable vocabulary that hardly affirms contemporary artistic thinking about "action." He persistently interlinked the development of his performance art *within* painting with the three terms that served as the title of his first solo show in Vienna in 1965: *Malerei-Selbstbemalung-Selbstverstümmelung* (Painting, self-painting, self-dismemberment). Hosted by Galerie Junge Generation in Vienna, *Malerei-Selbstbemalung-Selbstverstümmelung* was provocatively prefaced with a statement by the curator: "We are fully aware of the problematic of such borderline cases in contemporary painting. We think, however, as a matter of principle, that a simple silence about such things is bad."[69] The windowless walls of the

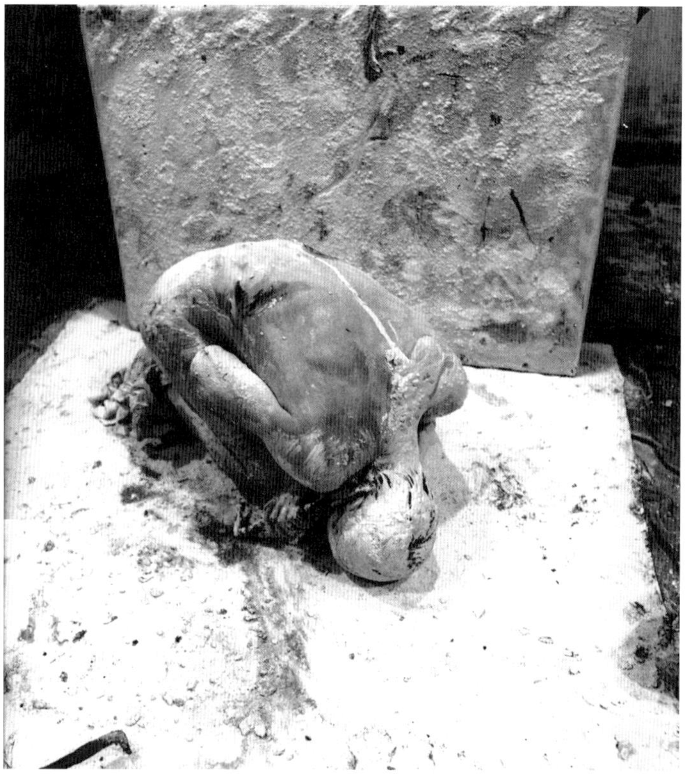

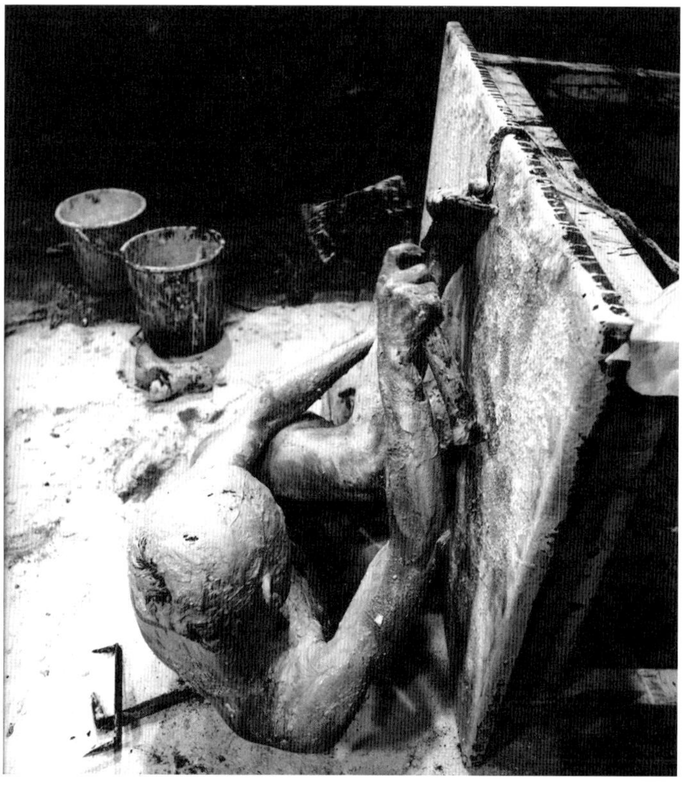

Figures 3.19–3.20. Günter Brus, *Selbstverstümmelung* (Self-dismemberment), 1965. Photograph by Ludwig Hoffenreich. © Günter Brus. Courtesy of the BRUSEUM, Universalmuseum Joanneum.

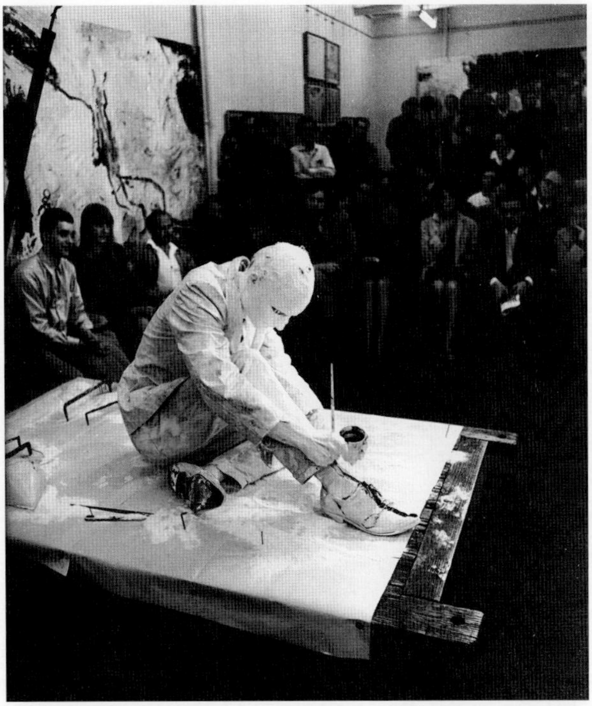

Figure 3.21. Günter Brus, *Malerei-Selbstbemalung-Selbstverstümmelung* (Painting—self-painting—self-dismemberment), 1965. Photograph by Ludwig Hoffenreich. © Günter Brus. Courtesy of the BRUSEUM, Universalmuseum Joanneum.

gallery were covered in remnants of *Malerei in einem labyrinth-artig verbauten Raum*, transforming it into a kind of room-painting.[70] On opening night, Brus involved his body, setting it in relation to the room and the other objects in it.

Reposing supine on a white-painted platform, painted white from head to toe in a suit and shoes, he cannot conceal a grin. He sits up, smears more white paint and crumbly pigment over himself, and draws a messy black line from the toe of his shoe up his leg, torso, and face (fig. 3.21). Rubbing more black pigment into a mess on his stomach, blotting out the line, his reclining body then topples from the wooden platform and hunkers on the floor. The performance *Malerei-Selbstbemalung-Selbstverstümmelung* is composed of gestures of self-effacement and postures prone to collapse. Hardly an expressive subject, the artist is a figure hindered in the space of painting. To the bemusement of the onlookers, the performance ends without the artist even getting up, let alone taking a stand. In an exit as excrescence, Brus squirms from the room on his stomach, a messy trail of paint and debris on the floor all that is left behind (fig. 3.22).

The day before, in protest of Galerie Junge Generation's skeptical framing of his work—including an academic "podium discussion" to address the curator's concerns with his "borderline case"—Brus performed *Wiener Spaziergang* (Viennese walk). Despite the dramatic shift in context, from windowless gallery to Vienna's monumental Heldenplatz (Heroes' Square), Brus's strategies of self-painting and self-dismemberment are strikingly consistent. As I discuss in chapter 2, Brus appeared in Heldenplatz in a white-painted suit and shoes like those he then wore in the gallery the next day, with a gashing

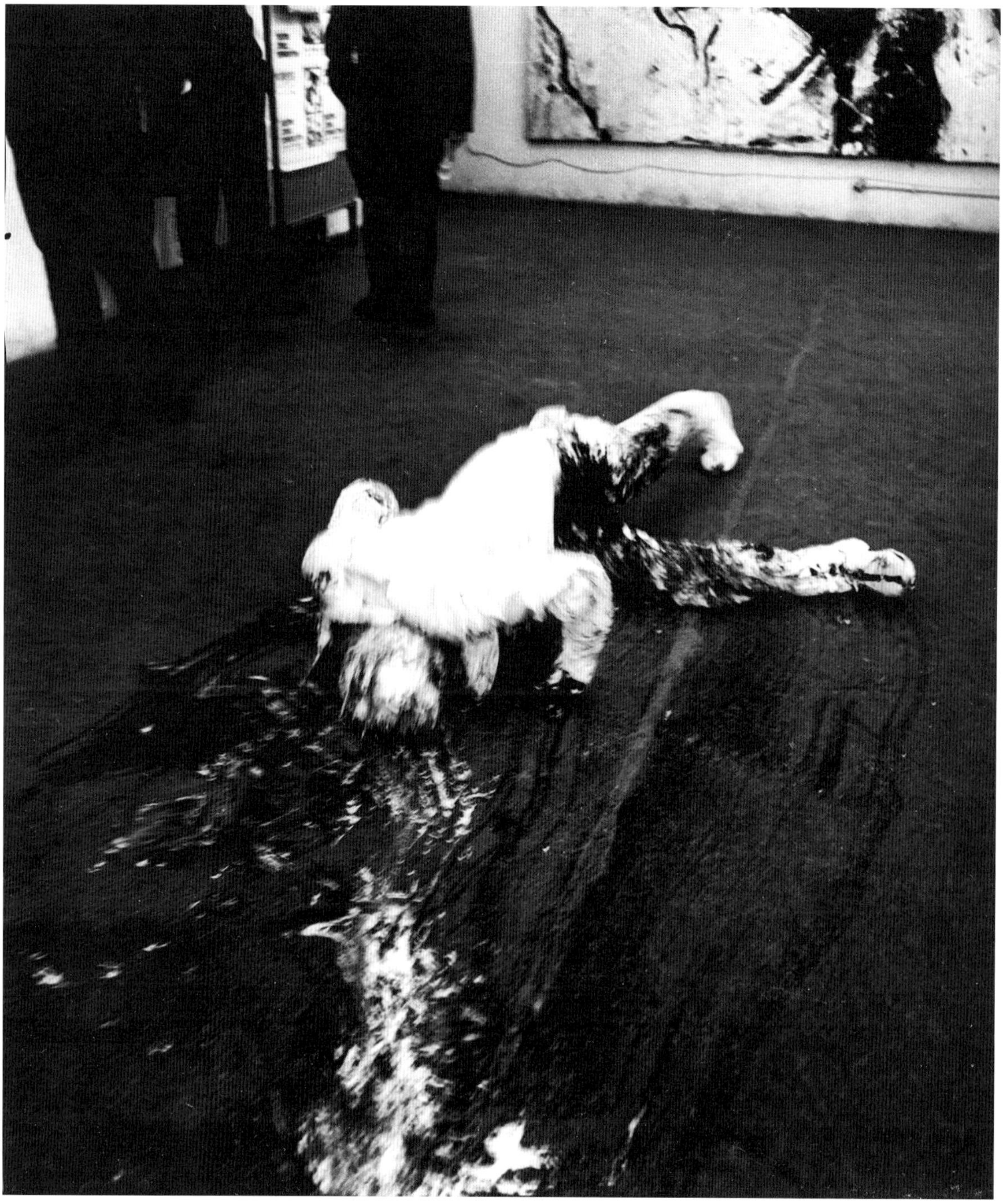

Figure 3.22. Günter Brus, *Malerei-Selbstbemalung-Selbstverstümmelung* (Painting—self-painting—self-dismemberment), 1965. Photograph by Ludwig Hoffenreich. © Günter Brus. Courtesy of the BRUSEUM, Universalmuseum Joanneum.

black line of paint drawn vertically down his body (see figs. 1.18 and 2.10–2.14). He proceeded to stroll through the Vienna Hofburg, epitome of the city's past imperial grandeur and infamous site of Hitler's ecstatically received speech announcing the annexation of Austria to "Greater Germany" in 1938. Brus's unspectacular, yet by no means inconspicuous, performance attracted the attention of the police, who detained and questioned him regarding the motivation of his "actions"—what his peculiar demonstration was intended to mean and at whom it was directed. To be sure, his messy, disheveled figure presented an arresting counterpoint to the erect and forceful figures of verticality in the monumental sculptural program orchestrated around "great men."

Ultimately, however, *Wiener Spaziergang* presented no univocal political aim. It is just, as I suggest in chapter 2, *gehässig*—hateful, ugly. It was thus not so much the artist's actions or body, but *the painting* that was judged to produce a disturbance categorized in police sanctioned terms as "causing irritation" and "disturbing the order in a public place."[71] Like the Galerie Junge Generation curator and Brus's critics, the police were unsettled by the ambiguity of his art. They quickly removed him from view.

Bad Form: Figuration After Formlessness

Rather than as a derivative offshoot of action painting or an extreme example of body art in the action paradigm, Brus's work could better be oriented within what Rosalind Krauss and Yve-Alain Bois describe, with the help of Georges Bataille, as the formless, or *l'informe*. "Nothing in and of itself," they write, "the formless has only an operational existence: it is a performative." Its operation is "to undo form."[72] Spit, intriguingly, is a key example of the formless. Thus, in contrast to abstraction, the formless draws attention to the body in its subjection to processes of expulsion or excretion, which is to say, to what Julia Kristeva calls "abjection."[73]

For Bois and Krauss, the formless stages an explicit counter to formalist art history—and the narratives of verticality, advancement, and purity on which it stands. In working with the notion of the formless, they want to offer an alternative to what they call the dominant modernist "ontology" of art, focalized in the perspective that Greenberg and Michael Fried bring to US abstract expressionism and the "advanced" abstract painting that followed. "Once art was liberated from the constraints of representation," Bois and Krauss write, defining the formalist demand for medium specificity, "it had to justify its existence as the search for its own essence."[74] In a riposte to the formalist pursuit of a purification of this essence, they propose a taxonomy of deviations: Instead of extolling the primacy of visuality, they attend to tactility and base materiality; instead of the instantaneousness of visual apprehension, they consider pulsing durational temporalities; instead of the erect posture of the indifferent viewing subject and the vertical display of the art object, they favor modes of "horizontality." The formless is entropy and waste, enveloping the body of "the perceiver" and retrieving the horizontal "mouth-anus axis."[75] On more than one occasion, they refer to how the formless generates "bad form."[76]

In particular for Krauss, the formless offers a method for rereading Pollock and his legacy, a method for resisting—as Brus too had sought to do—a certain "sense" of Pollock.[77] She seeks to preserve a space for contemporary art against what she considers its foolhardy and suspect aspiration of transcendence. And she wants to delineate a space immured neither in the visual effects of abstraction nor in the hierarchies of formalist discourse. Krauss locates this space in art of the 1960s that registers the horizontality of Pollock's mark making. Her readings of works by Eva Hesse, Robert Morris, Cy Twombly, and Andy Warhol emphasize the low, material, carnal operations they index. She sees these artists as crossing a "formless" rather than a formalist threshold. Thus are Twombly's violent graffiti or Warhol's piss paintings seen to move beyond the operations of such an exemplary abstract expressionist action painting as Pollock's *Number One (Lavender Mist)* (1950). Such works from the 1960s debase what she calls Pollock's "morphology" of painting and "demote the mark from form to *informe*."[78]

Brus's work—from his room-painting to *Zerreißprobe*—would be very much at home in such company.[79] Krauss, however, by approving one premise of the formalism she otherwise contends with, tacitly disqualifies it. For she accepts that, with Pollock, "art was liberated from the constraints of representation."[80] What she thus shares with the formalists is their aversion to figuration. Like them, she rejects the conventional relation of figure and ground that had for so long defined painting and also, by extension, *any* figuration of the human body. "The 'body,'" Krauss remarks impatiently, "is rapidly becoming my phobic object."[81] Within the taxonomy of the formless, therefore, the body is forbidden to appear, except in its traces and excretions. "The disappearance of the first person," she and Bois write, "is the mechanism that triggers formlessness."[82] The formless must be thought in terms of structure not subject. For "everything that resembles something, everything that is gathered under the unity of a concept—that is what the *informe* operation crushes, sets aside with an irreverent wink: nothing but rubbish."[83]

This account of the *informe* paradoxically reproduces and reinforces a myopic take on the history of painting that understands the figure of figuration to represent the figure of the human in general. This generic figure of the human is in fact a very particular one: the able body of a self-contained "first person" oriented in space, upholding a unified form and upright posture. According to this perspective on the history of painting, the subject of figural painting was always also the human subject. This evidently too simple account of the entanglement of the history of painting and the history of subjection is the reason the kind of painting that Bois and Krauss lump together and dismiss under the nomenclature of "European *Informel*" is seen as having "nothing to do" with the formless, because, they write, "it is an art of informing, an art that insists on the emergence of the human figure."[84] The formless, they insist in contrast, "is inimical to this drive toward the transcendental."[85] However, seeking to stall this drive leaves no space for consideration of figurations of a different kind.

The equation of "the human figure" with a "drive toward the transcendental" was anathema to Brus in every way. His performance art operates against the assumption that figuration involves a human form that is integral, upright, righteous, transcendent. At the same time, it operates against the demand, in discourses around abstract art, to eradicate the human figure from painting. Precisely insofar as it maintains, and indeed occupies and explores, "the constraints of representation," Brus's performance art makes space for a consideration of what I propose calling "figuration after formlessness." Figuration after formlessness facilitates attention to figures under constraint—not subject of, but subject to. Preoccupied with gestures and postures associated not with free action, but with base drives and processes, figuration after formlessness makes sensible precarious figures otherwise ignored or overlooked in the humanist history of figurative painting as well as in the posthumanist dismissal of figuration. And there is good reason for this aversion: Aesthetically and morally displeasing, figuration after formlessness exhibits bad form in the full sense of the phrase.

Brus is an exemplar, if one can say this, of bad form. Indeed, bad form would be an apt translation of the untranslatable German term *gehässig* and its oscillation in a zone of indiscretion between the ethical and the aesthetic. Bad form is the position Brus assumes on the cover of *Unter dem Ladentisch* (Under the table; 1969; fig. 3.23, and see fig. 2.8), the first artist's book he made after fleeing to West Berlin following his trial and sentencing for *Kunst und Revolution*. A homemade archive, *Unter dem Ladentisch* collects documents of the media shitstorm the event generated, including press clippings, excerpts from legal proceedings, hate mail, subsequent artist's statements, and photographs of performances. We see Brus naked in profile, hands grasping ankles in a hunched-over squat, scrotum peeking out below thigh, an impish grin on his face. No figure of transcendence, this is rather a posture evocative of immanent need—of *Notdurft*, which colloquially refers to needing to go to the toilet. It thus indicates, not without humor, those abject operations of the body which cannot in good conscience be said to constitute actions. In Brus's performances of bad form, the phallus in its cultural significance is reduced to a mere penis. Erection—of any kind—is ruinously, often hilariously, decomposed, declining. In the performance documents that interpolate *Unter dem Ladentisch*, the flaccid penis of Brus appears dunked in a glass of beer, scrotum buttoned below foreskin in a sweater, and, on the final page, malformed in a lump of unrecognizable flesh.[86] Adding to his assembly of terms for his art, he called this kind of performance *Körperanalyse* (body-analysis).

Brus draws out human figures in positions assumed at moments when they are subject to operations of the formless. He tests out moments of formlessness that already inhere in and deform the human figure understood as fit, proper, and upright—*en forme*. Brus tends to the human figure neither in its independent standing nor in its capacity for action, but rather as inescapably

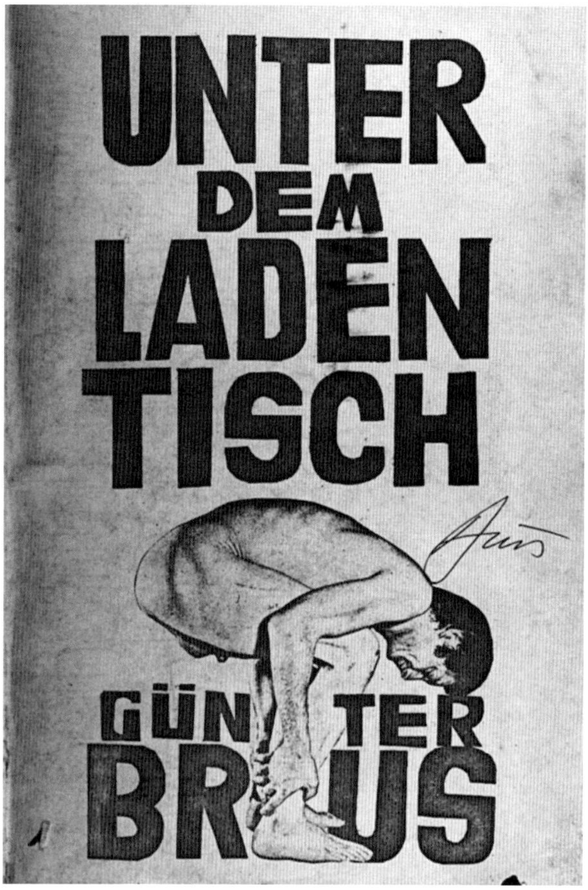

Figure 3.23. Günter Brus, *Unter dem Ladentisch* (Under the table), 1969. Artist's book, cover. © Günter Brus. Courtesy of the BRUSEUM, Universalmuseum Joanneum.

exposed to exigencies that are beyond his and its control. He winks and, squatting down, responds indecorously to Pollock's *Number One (Lavender Mist)* with a "number two"—*großer Notdurft*.

Brus's bad form is what painting not in the sense of Pollock and what performance art not in the sense of "The Legacy of Jackson Pollock" look like. Those performances that he called body-analyses in the late 1960s, which include some of his better-known works, are indeed characterized by the abandonment of paint in favor of found substances, including the body's own excretions. Body-analysis maintains, however, the same attention to formless operations that decompose the "self" in a structure of constraint, where it is exposed in all its ugliness and debasement, its fragmentation and permeability. In his performances in 1969 in exile in West Berlin, rope leashes are tied around his ankles and throat as he reclines awkwardly on a kitchen chair, his legs spread and lifted (fig. 3.24). His body is naked but for a garter belt and stockings split through the crotch, and it is filthy, smeared in excrement, which he also puts in his mouth. The other hand rests on a table, pointing lackadaisically to the camera. On it, his wedding ring shines. This particular photograph, a copy of which is owned by MoMA, New York, is often taken to emblematize Viennese

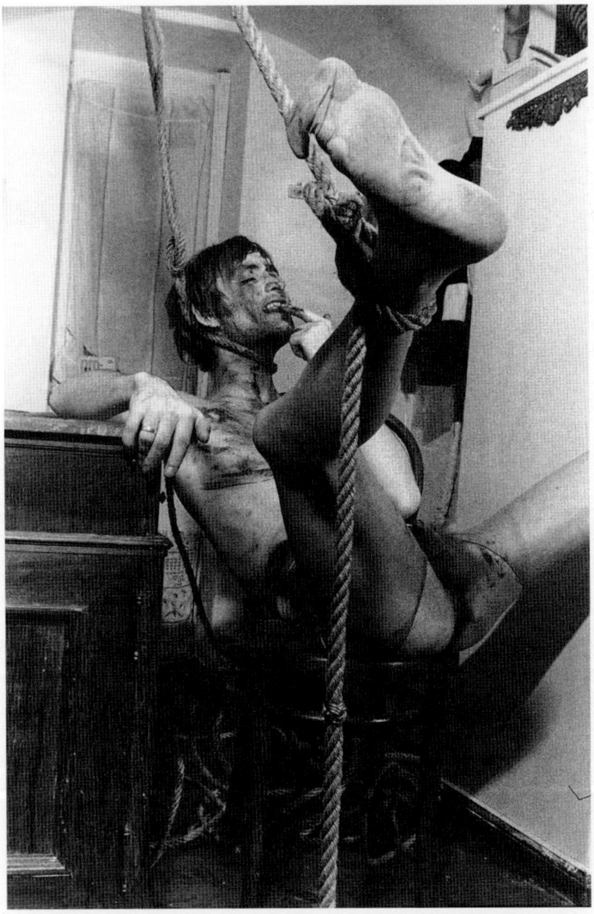

Figure 3.24. Günter Brus, *Körperanalyse* (Body-analysis), 1969. Photograph by Klaus Eschen. © Günter Brus. Courtesy of the BRUSEUM, Universalmuseum Joanneum.

Actionism. It is infamous because of the extreme action it documents: The artist literally eats shit. While this is certainly bad form, I find it more interesting to attend to the way that Brus's disgusting use of excrement belongs—as the photograph also clearly shows—to a broader exploration of a vulnerable and stricken body in a space of constraint. Body-analysis performs figuration after formlessness insofar as it decomposes figure and ground, grappling with the sites at which bodies lose their supposed integrity in abject displays.[87]

Countless drawings in pen from 1966 and 1967 that he called *Aktionskizzen* (action sketches; figs. 3.25, 3.26) show such figures in the most minimal way, bound in arcs of ink to a corner wrought by a simple cornering intersection of lines. Mangled, dismembered figures lie on the floors of cursory rooms, heads in corners, or against walls, threads of rope leashing them to the architecture. Skeletal structures—spine, ribs, femurs—appear to exit the flesh of the human figure, penetrating the walls like a scaffolding. These figures are so ensnared in their proximity, so perplexingly "in-relation" to spatial structures, that their own spatializing axes excise and intersect with those of the room. The "body," in Brus's work, is always subject to such decomposition, to such dislocations

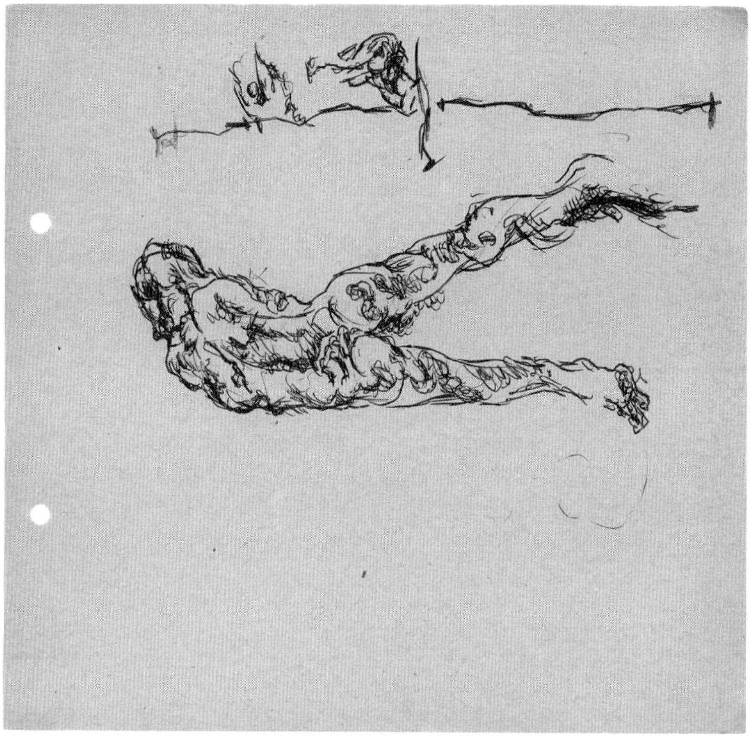

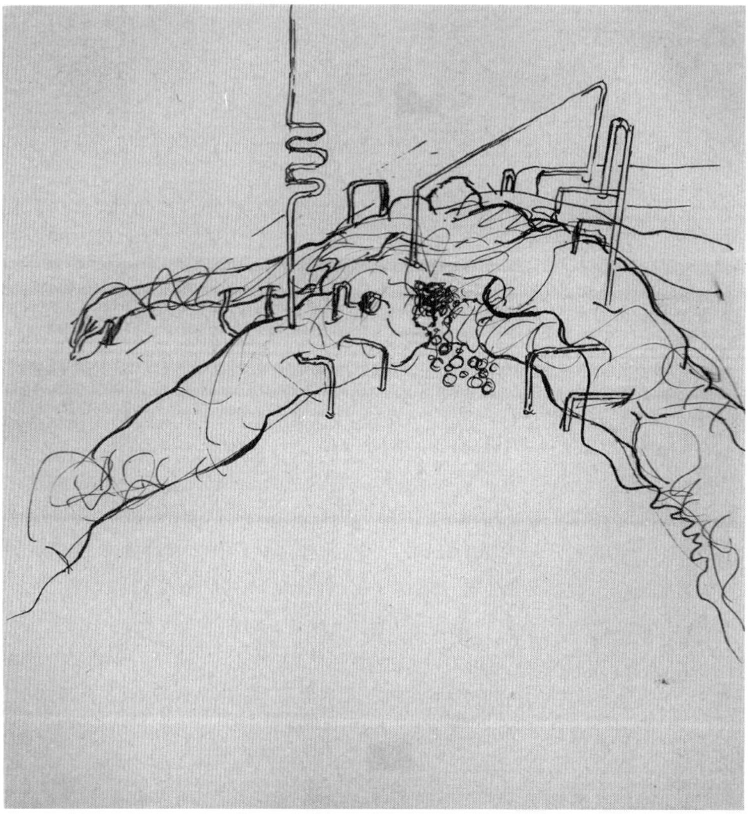

Figures 3.25–3.26. Günter Brus, *Aktionsskizze* (Action sketch), 1966. Pen on paper, 20 × 21 cm (*top*); ink on paper, 19.8 × 20.9 cm (*bottom*). © Günter Brus. Courtesy of the BRUSEUM, Universalmuseum Joanneum.

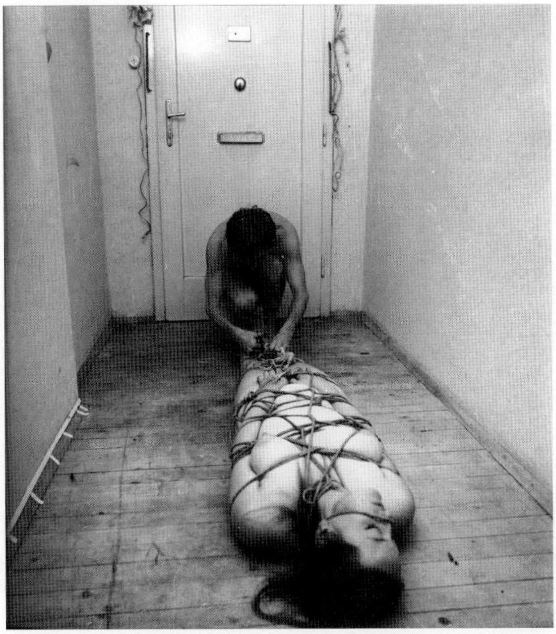

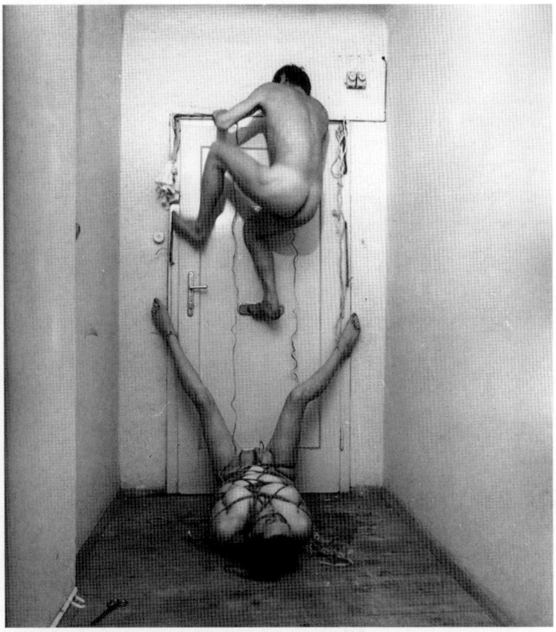

Figures 3.27–3.28. Günter Brus with Anna Brus, *Strangulation*, 1968. Photograph by Ludwig Hoffenreich. © Günter Brus. Courtesy of the BRUSEUM, Universalmuseum Joanneum.

of perspective, and to the positions of delineation and inclination these survey. In bad form, these action sketches present a veritable catalog of in-action.

While his drawings rarely correspond directly to his performances, Brus used the techniques of the draftsman throughout the 1960s as a parallel practice. Bodies like those one sees taking awkward shape in the drawings are tentatively figured in performances like *Strangulation* (1968; figs. 3.27, 3.28), which Günter Brus and Anna Brus performed together in the narrow foyer of their apartment as Günter appealed his sentencing for *Kunst und Revolution*. *Strangulation* articulates the difficult intimacy to which figuration after formlessness gives rise. The space in the foyer is confined, yet familiar. Cleared of furnishings and ornament, a postal slot serves as a reminder of life going on elsewhere. Thick metal brackets of the sort seen in performances of *Selbstbemalung* and *Selbstverstümmelung*, as well as from Brus's drawings, are embedded in the door frame, a supplemental scaffolding of space and objects. Pieces of rope dangle from them. Into this confined space, Günter drags Anna. They are naked. With a large pair of scissors lying on the floor, he partially cuts her legs free. She is inert, heavy, with closed eyes, her arms still bound to her torso haphazardly with thick cloth cord. Reaching the door, Günter squats backward over Anna and lifts her legs to place her ankles in the looped strings bound to the embrasure. He clambers up the door frame, slips his legs into the rope loops rigged from its upper corners, and inverts himself, releasing his torso backward at the knees and falling down, close to her. It is a startling, unsettling picture. With Anna in awkward repose beneath him, both the bottoms of his filthy feet and his soft penis are exposed at the same time. He draws a razor blade, produced from his mouth, down—which is to say, up—his chest, arms

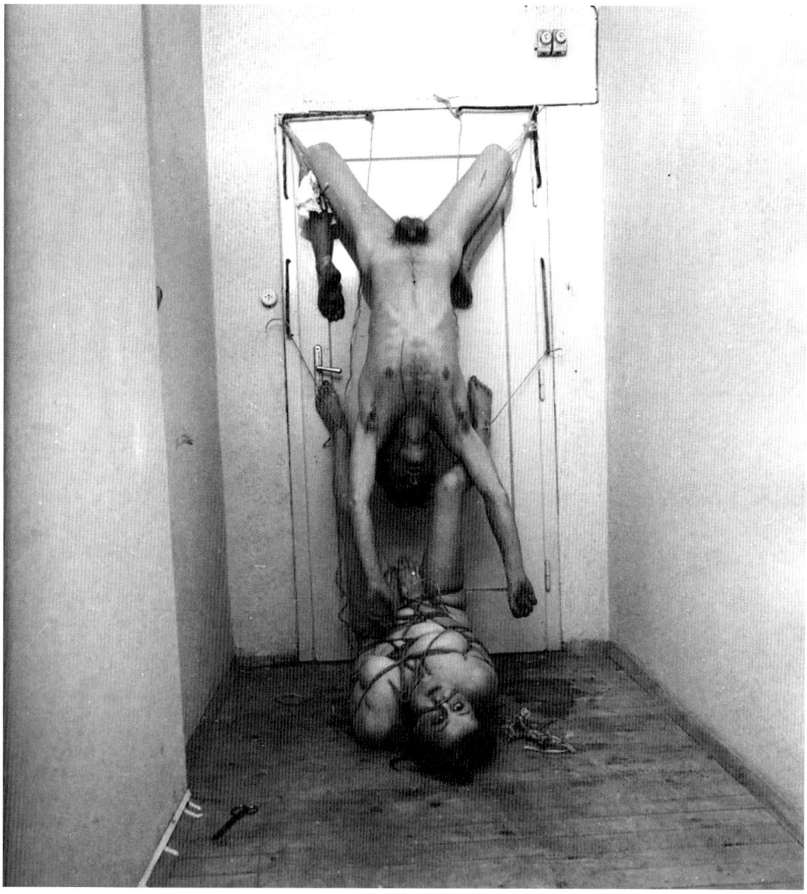

Figures 3.29–3.30. Günter Brus with Anna Brus, *Strangulation*, 1968. Photograph by Ludwig Hoffenreich. © Günter Brus. Courtesy of the BRUSEUM, Universalmuseum Joanneum.

akimbo, then altogether limp (fig. 3.29). As the actionist loses consciousness, Anna turns her face to the camera to ask for help, trying to bring her restrained legs toward Günter in a gesture of support.[88] Günter's right hand brushes her thigh, a touching gesture, at once incidental and intimate. The documentary material breaks off.

In light of Brus's real need for care, photographing and filming of the performance briefly paused. Anna remembers *Strangulation* today as "a horror action." Reflecting on how it made her feel, both then and now, she simply states, "I hate it" (*Ich hasse es*).[89] I have often shared Anna Brus's aversion. At the same time, I remain convinced of the significance of working through the "hard feelings," to draw on Jennifer Doyle's suggestive phrase, to which Viennese performance art, especially that involving Anna Brus and Günter Brus, gives rise.[90] For what Brus's, and especially the Bruses', work invites one to see are the kinds of figures and relations that, on account of their bad form, have largely been omitted in the history of painting and that the postwar consensus in favor of abstraction, which was supposed to criticize the aesthetic and political legacy of figural painting, has arguably only obfuscated.

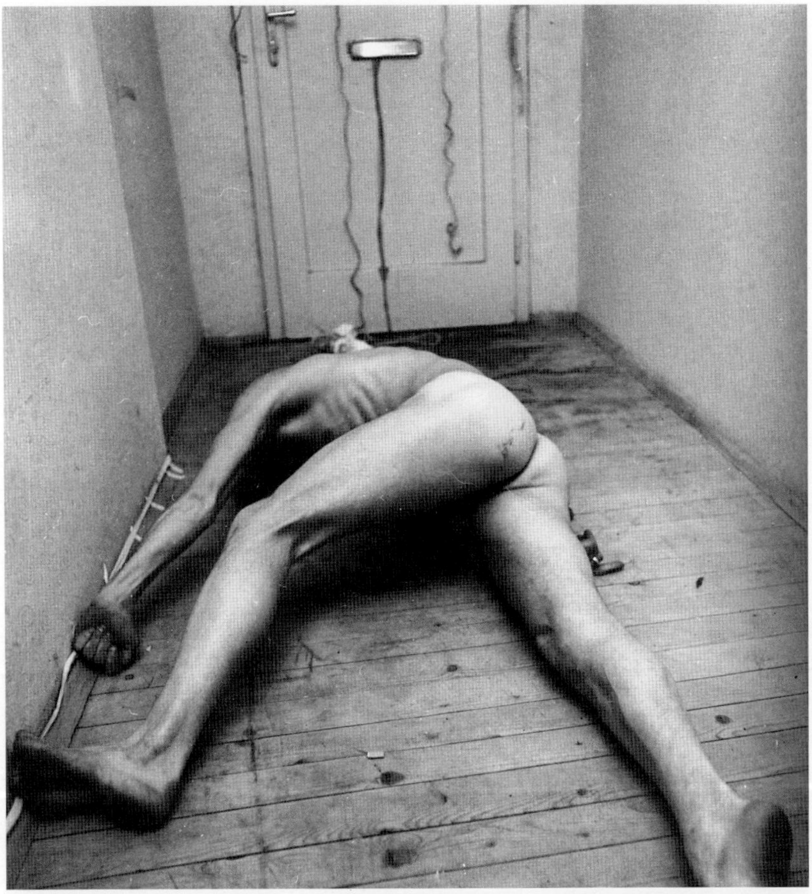

In responding in the early 1980s to the international reception of his work, initiated at the scandalizing *documenta 5* of 1972, Brus considered this: "These terms, 'destruction' and 'self-destruction' are so negatively charged in the art of actionism because the actions were realized by and with living humans." Notably framing his approach to the "human" in terms of contemporary developments in painting, he continues: "Basically, however, these were the same positive achievements for art as, for example, the destruction of the face in Picasso or Soutine or the deformation of bodies in Schiele or De Kooning. One could only speak of an actual destruction if I had exceeded the limits of the humanitarian. This however was never the case, even if recently some busybodies want to stick this on me with malicious insinuations."[91]

Brus is responding once again to the sense of hatefulness his work arouses, and to the kind of inflationary imagination that seems to attend it, as though he had really committed crimes against humanity. Yet he maintains space for the human in his work—just not by the actionist or activist standards of the action paradigm by which so-called Viennese Actionism has been judged. In the 1990s, Brus would distinguish his own position from that of his affiliates with the following critical remark: "Muehl and Nitsch tend towards models with

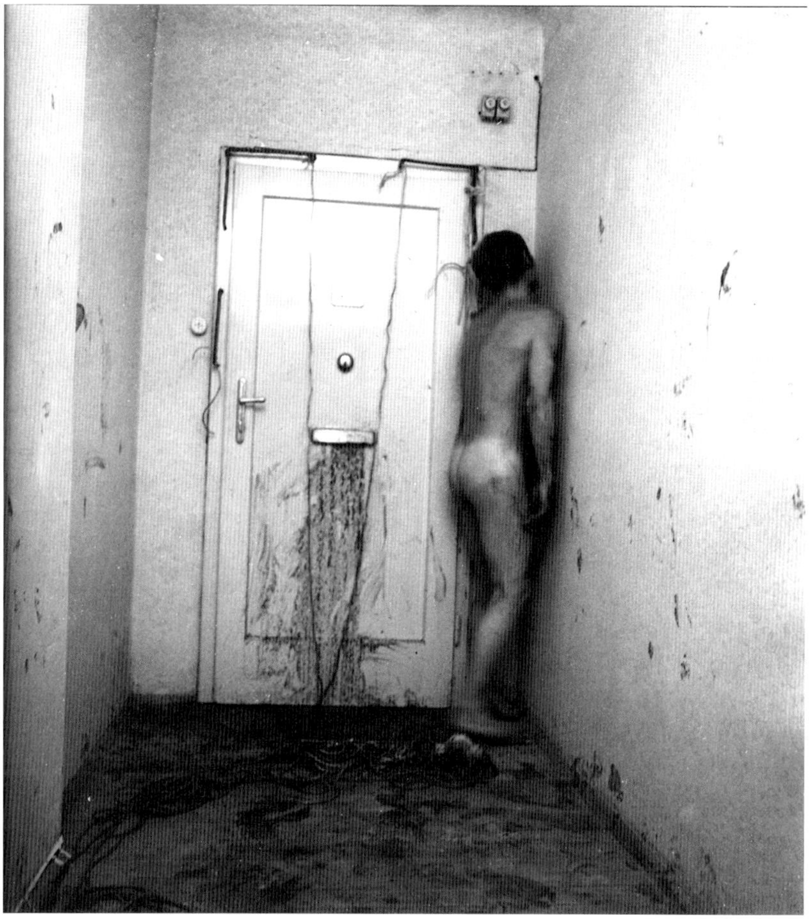

Figure 3.31. Günter Brus with Anna Brus, *Strangulation*, 1968. Photograph by Ludwig Hoffenreich. © Günter Brus. Courtesy of the BRUSEUM, Universalmuseum Joanneum.

incontrovertible claims to truth, to which a certain missionary zeal is added." In contrast, he continues, evoking a Kantian turn of phrase, "I have no worldview [*Ich habe keine Weltanschauung*]. The world looks at me, and I respond to it, with pleasure and with skepticism."[92] To have "no worldview" means to perceive the world, rather than to structure it by viewing it. It is to decline the position of the subject. To have "no worldview" is to be unmoored by, yet attentive to, involvements in other relations. It is a conversion of the perspectival apparatus, in which the artist, who is "in-relation" and responsive, is ensnared—pleasurably, skeptically.

It is with "no worldview" that Brus's performance art develops painting. His bad form is devoted to articulating unseen angles and unsightly aspects that inhere in the historical dispositive of painting, which remains, despite all claims to its destruction and transcendence, a formative architecture of the contemporary political imaginary.[93] Brus's work tests out figurations in relations that good society might prefer not to have to see. This is an involved, trying, tedious, painstaking, and painful process. In *Strangulation*, after Brus came to, the performance recommenced in the empty foyer (figs. 3.30, 3.31).

The ropes that had bound Anna lay unfurled on the floor, damp and messy beneath where Günter had hung. Günter reenters the frame alone, prostrate on the floor, not so much crawling as exerting his body against the floor, moving down the foyer by sheer pressure. When he reaches the door and briefly stands upright, he faces the wall, his body pressed oddly against it, shoulders hunched into it, toes bent back against the wainscoting. Out of fear or repugnance, advocates of formalism and the formless alike summarily dismiss the figuration of this kind of human figure.

Picasso's Impasse

Viennese Actionism has often been dismissed wholesale from the art history of the twentieth century as a bad outcome of action painting. In the most widely circulated account, Benjamin H. D. Buchloh laments, "Clearly, the Viennese Actionists misread Pollock's latent, yet inexorable spectacularization of painting as a celebratory legitimization of art's return to ritual."[94] Yet Brus does not "misread" Pollock; he incisively and carefully refuses what Pollock was taken to stand for. Indeed, when he noted in his diary in 1960 that what he sought to do with painting was "not in the sense of Pollock," Brus may have had another even more imposing figure in contemporary painting in mind—namely, Picasso. And as it happens, at that very moment, those who had once championed Picasso's modernist abstraction now viewed his most recent work with extreme distaste and serious suspicion.

In the catalog of the 1959 *documenta* 2 that was his touchstone to Pollock, Brus encountered some remarkable work by Picasso. Both the exhibition and the catalog documented Picasso's peculiar position in art history. Closer in generation to the deceased trio Kandinsky, Klee, and Mondrian—the exhibition's "masters" of the twentieth century—the very-much-alive Picasso was included as a contemporary artist. In the catalog, his work thus appears in two places: in the introductory image-essay "The Arguments of the Art of the Twentieth Century" (*Die Argumente der Kunst des XX. Jahrhunderts*) and in the main alphabetical section on contemporary artists, incidentally, just before Pollock.[95]

This double placement of Picasso in the past and in the present generates a peculiar schism in Haftmann's narrative celebrating how "art has become abstract."[96] Picasso's *Le violon au café* (1913), a typical example of the dissected planes, truncated typography, and reduced palette of analytic cubism, features as part of the argument for how twentieth-century abstract painting charted the way toward Pollock. Picasso's *Femme en pleurs* (1937) is the final painting included in the catalog's introductory image-essay, construed to visually support this thesis. With a split visage of teeth-chattering, nail-biting despair, *Femme en pleurs* and the year 1937 occupy in the *documenta* 2 narrative an ambiguous artistic and historical threshold, connecting back in time to cubism and the grand narrative of abstraction to which it contributed in the exhibition,

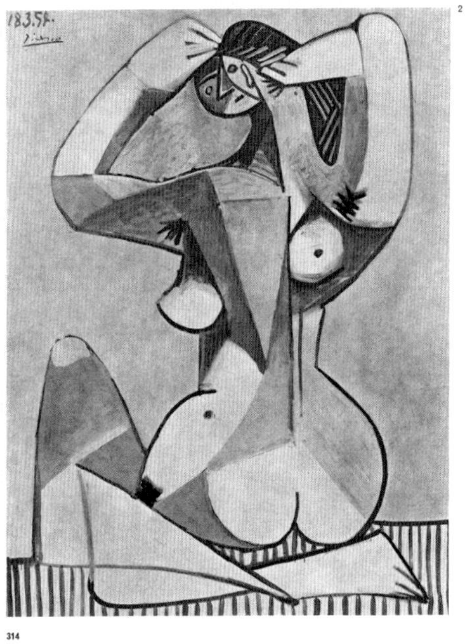

Figure 3.32. Pablo Picasso, *Nu accroupi*, 1954, oil on canvas, 130 × 97 cm, pictured in the exhibition catalog *II. Documenta '59: Kunst nach 1945, Malerei, Skulptur, Druckgrafik*, vol. 1 (1959). © 2025 Estate of Pablo Picasso / Artists Rights Society (ARS), New York.

and gesturing forward to Picasso's work after *Guernica* (1937) and after the Second World War. His paintings from the 1950s, which featured generously in the exhibition of contemporary art and are as generously represented in the catalog's main pages, are conspicuous on account of their commitment to figuration. The corpulent twisting bodies Picasso paints adamantly refuse to remain properly abstract. The emotional distress of *Femme en pleurs* is reconfigured in the stressed physicality of *Nu accroupi* (1954; fig. 3.32), an unwieldy contorted figure whose spine traverses her breasts, extending into a striped textile on which she squats while bending her bulky arms about her tiny face. She appears to be rearranging it.

So behind the veneration of Pollock at *documenta* 2, there loomed the ambiguous figure of Picasso, at once omnipresent and strangely disavowed. This little-discussed art historical circumstance is, in my view, highly significant. While Picasso's achromatic cubist break with his figural rose and blue periods constituted a key moment in the "argument" for abstraction in the twentieth century, he nonetheless turned out not to be the "master" to whom to turn for what Haftmann celebrated as abstract painting after 1945. This artistic and art historical perplexity had been summed up by Greenberg in 1946 in a review critical of Picasso's recent work: "He insists on representation in order to answer our time with an art equally explicit as to the violence and terror, but at the same time the inherent logic of his genius and his period still pushes him toward the abstract." Of this tension between "representation" and "the abstract," Greenberg concludes: "In my opinion it is Picasso's temperamental resistance to the abstract that has landed him in the impasse in which he now finds himself."[97] Juxtaposed to the alluring teleological narrative that culminates in the work of Pollock, Picasso's impasse—his push toward, yet resistance to the abstract—is set in stark relief.

Brus, I think, becomes preoccupied with, or rather occupies, Picasso's impasse. Given his artistic inclinations, Brus would surely have found Picasso's most recent and unashamedly figural paintings arresting among the vast selection of abstract canvases exhibited at *documenta 2*.[98] *Femmes d'Alger I* (1955; plate 10) in particular stands out as the only color reproduction in the catalog of a painting that could be said to make figuration its primary concern. The painting positions four bodies in a room. Two are frontward facing, and one of these balances on one foot holding a pipe while another sits with crossed legs and bent intertwined arms raised up above large breasts and a tiny head. One appears in a knotted supine position in the foreground, feet propped up on a rickety red table. And one more at once recedes into and approaches from the background, also balancing on one foot, with a raised hand and a bent knee, seen, perhaps, from behind. These precariously positioned figures are enclosed and compressed within the proximate space of an interior. Characteristic diagonals from ceiling to wall curtain the upper-right corner of the painting, a citation of the draped interior in Picasso's earlier work *Les demoiselles d'Avignon* (1907), which, among other paintings, including Manet's *Olympia* (1863), recites Vermeer's *The Art of Painting* (1666–1668) in the Kunsthistorisches Museum in Vienna—of which Brus was no doubt aware. Apertures abound: A blackened doorway or window sets the body of the seated nude in relief, while the recumbent figure in the foreground faces her buttocks toward a luminous light blue embrasure. Everywhere such semiobstructed openings appear, the bodies are drained of substantial volume, taking shape as bare contours or simple strokes of paint. The heavy brushwork across the canvas calls attention to tactility and processual proximity but also supplements it with the insides of these evacuated bodies, with the excrements they contain.

Leo Steinberg compellingly describes these figures as performing "devenustation," a term that captures how figuring the human form defaces the beauty both of the body itself (the "Venus") and of the space in which it is positioned.[99] The term rhymes well with *defenestration*, tacitly evoking painting's window by reference to falling from it. Devenustation produces ugly art precisely because it reflects on, and analyzes, old artistic conventions—and reveals how these inform contemporary political-ethical structures. Like the array of terms Brus developed to define his practice—from *Dekomposition* to *Körperanalyse*—devenustation is an operation of the formless missing from Krauss and Bois's writings. It produces bad form in its exploration of how bodies take up and inhere in space, of how figures and ground seep into one another and lose distinction, in a manner explicitly engaged with the history of painting. It is, I am proposing, on account of their bad form that virtually nobody, bar Steinberg, liked Picasso's late paintings—just as few have liked Brus's performance art in the same period. In the work of both artists in the

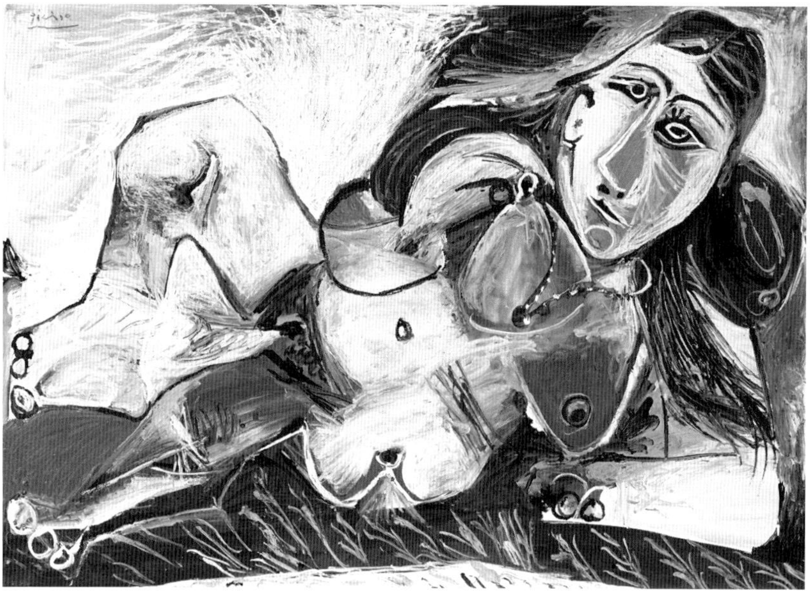

Figure 3.33. Pablo Picasso, *Nude Woman with Necklace*, 1968, oil on canvas, 113.5 × 161.7 cm. Tate Modern, London. © 2025 Estate of Pablo Picasso / Artists Rights Society (ARS), New York; © Succession Picasso/DACS 2020. Photo: Tate.

1960s, the human body is figured not to lend ground relief or as the locus of psychic interiority; rather, it is betrayed by its innards. Such figures are stricken by the processes of embodiment, bearers of expressions and perspectives, as well as organs and bowels.

Instead of fitting Brus into a legacy of Pollock, why not consider him a contemporary of "late" Picasso? For while Picasso's late paintings may not be performance art, I would argue they can most emphatically be taken as body art. In the *Nu accroupi* series he painted throughout the 1960s and works like *Nude Woman with a Necklace* (1968; fig. 3.33), bodies recline and squat, disclosing vulnerable orifices from which fluids gush. Of the less explicitly exposed *Femme nue* (1964), Greenberg could only say that it was "very bad."[100] Of Picasso's late painting in general, he would add: "He has painted a great many bad pictures, and of a more downright badness than before."[101]

Downright bad indeed. For Greenberg, these twisted corporeal topographies affirm the artist's stubborn insistence on figuration. And Bois and Krauss, despite their *informe* leanings, share Greenberg's view that the abstract impulse of Picasso's paintings constitutes their genius. Because Picasso's late paintings not only fail to demonstrate the liberation of art from "the constraints of representation" but also contain these disconcerting figures, they never come up for discussion.[102] Indeed, apart from Steinberg, art historians today will be hard-pressed to find careful readings of Picasso's devenustations. Even T. J. Clark, in his remarkable book *Picasso and Truth*, has virtually nothing to say about Picasso's paintings after *Guernica*, bracketing his study within the pre-impasse period that has long been understood to exemplify Picasso's "good," which is to say, properly abstract paintings.[103] Thus with his late work, hardly and only hatefully received in critical art history, Picasso can be seen as contributing to the performance of bad form. Among a younger generation of Picasso's contemporaries, Brus would not be alone in carrying on this ignominious tradition.

Performed three years before Picasso died and the day before the anniversary of the Bruses' friend Rudolf Schwarzkogler's defenestration, *Zerreißprobe* is, in a certain sense, a culmination of Brus's performance art. Or rather it is just a shift in perspective: After *Zerreißprobe*, Brus devoted himself to graphic work and artist's books, where he continued his investigation of figuration. For testing out the spatial dispositive of painting involves a painstaking rendering of a figure at its most hateful and ugly, but also—and this is the ethical challenge of viewing such work—vulnerable and needy.

In advance of the performance, Brus sketched out the sequence of postures and positions he planned to take up in *Zerreißprobe* in meticulously annotated drawings.[104] Like his 1960 diary sketch "Entwurf für einen labyrinthischen Raum," the first of these is dedicated just to the space of the room, regarded from two perspectives: a bird's-eye view and an angle commensurate with the floor. Carefully drawn and labeled are also the architect's triangle, scissors, chalk, needle and thread, gauze, razor blade, and long loops of string. Instead of the baking tins, a large bowl was intended for water. The white cloth, outlined as a large square, is drawn tight against a line labeled "wall" (*Wand*). Corresponding more or less with Gulden's subsequent protocol of the "action," Brus details each component of the performance in his drawings, including his obstinate evocation of painting: "Can't someone close the window?" (*Kann man nicht das Fenster schliessen?*), which is clearly handwritten in pencil on one of the last pages. The only aspect of the "action" Brus fails to perform would have taken place in the iconic position of collapse against the radiator, legs seen splayed wide from behind (plate 11, and see fig. 3.1). *Ausscheidung*, notes the sketch, "excretion." After all, one has to need to go; one can't just do it—and it turns out that in his last performance, Brus failed to. But this is what figuration after formlessness is all about: It figures the body's in-action.

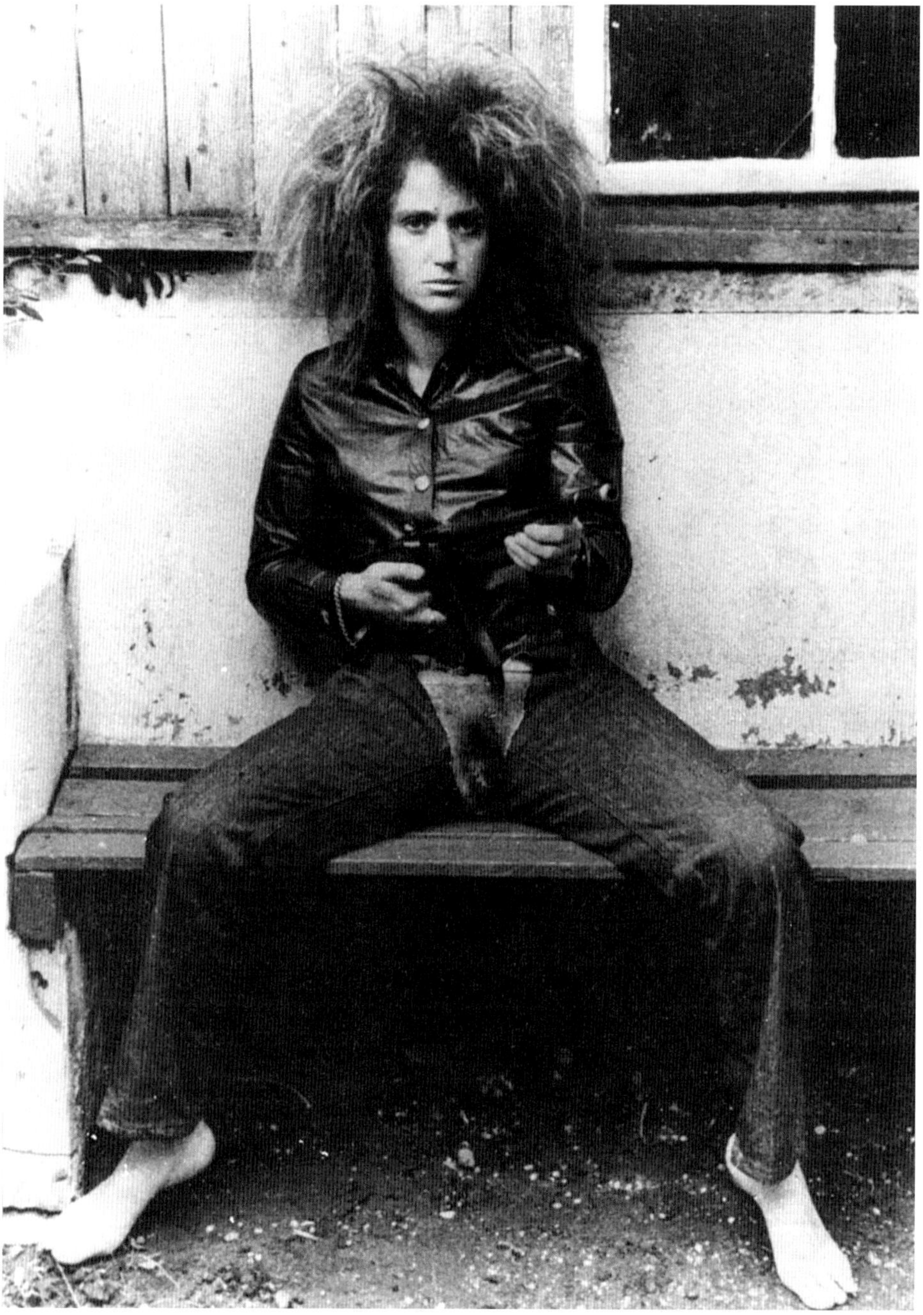

Weaving: Ingrid Wiener's Tapestry Collaborations

4

Figure 4.1. VALIE EXPORT, *Aktionshose: Genitalpanik* (Action pants: Genital panic), 1969. Self-staging. Photograph by Peter Hassmann. © VALIE EXPORT, Bildrecht Wien, 2025.

Consider two self-portraits, two performances of self: the black-and-white photograph *Aktionshose: Genitalpanik* (Action pants: Genital panic; 1969; fig. 4.1) and the colorful life-size tapestry *Großer Teppich* (Large tapestry; 1981–1986; plate 12). These two works present antithetical yet historically intertwined gestures of feminist performance art. In *Aktionshose: Genitalpanik*, VALIE EXPORT confronts the viewer. Holding a machine gun, she manspreads, with the crotch of her pants cut out to expose her genital zone. Her posture and styling simultaneously cite images of Western masculinity and the sexualized feminized bombshell. Appropriating and redressing these patriarchal stereotypes, VALIE EXPORT now wears the (action) pants in a performance calculated to generate not a little "genital panic." This photograph has justly become a poster image of Feminist Actionism. It exhibits, to cite VALIE EXPORT's manifesto from 1980, an "individual actor and creator," asserting herself as "subject of her own history."[1]

Großer Teppich documents a performance of a very different kind. Wiener wove the tapestry in wool on a high-warp loom over the course of five years. At first glance, it presents not herself, but a melancholy-looking man, her artistic collaborator in this painstaking undertaking, Dieter Roth. On closer inspection, his figure unravels in a discontinuous space cluttered with banal objects, pictures, and patterns. The ostensible subject of the tapestry is displaced by other partial, haphazard, fragmentary things. It is as though the extremities of the figure belonged to slightly different versions of itself or were perceived from different positions in continuously changing ways. One trouser leg tangles with color and texture while the other seems to drift away formlessly. Woven into the tapestry is not the image of a self-identical subject, but rather the warp and weft of a relationship. In contrast with VALIE EXPORT's self-assertive exhibitionism, Ingrid Wiener's performance exhibits her self insofar as it slowly reveals an other. It involves the work, the working on, and the working through of the relations that constitute this patient and long-drawn-out process. In 1986, Wiener described this as "weaving on and on" (*immer weiter weben*).[2] Wiener's feminist in-action consists in the performance of these relations of care, in all of their ambivalence.

The juxtaposition of *Aktionshose: Genitalpanik* and *Großer Teppich*, Feminist Actionism and feminist in-action, foregrounds an impasse in feminist artistic practice that is acutely legible in the disparate historiographical and institutional treatment of each artist's work. With good reason, VALIE EXPORT has been at the center of art history's account of performance art and feminist practice. Her explicit, confrontational, and often "hyper-sexualized" work exemplifies the sort of "aggressive self-enactment" of feminist artists that Amelia Jones argues inaugurated performance art in the 1970s.[3] Gabriele Schor has coined the phrase "feminist avant-garde" to capture the defiant, militant comportment of the Feminist Actionist.[4] Conversely, as Mechtild Widrich reminds us, the iconicity of a work like *Aktionshose: Genitalpanik* owes in large measure to feminist art historiography, which has specifically sought out "the aggressive feminist performer, disrupting male hegemony in the most public ways possible."[5] Understandably, Wiener's weaving, which has a more reserved tone and does not take a stand in the public arena, is never included in compendia of Feminist Actionism or in accounts of the feminist avant-garde.

Aktionshose: Genitalpanik is a poster image not only for Feminist Actionism, but also for a similarly titled performance, *Genitalpanik*, which it is often understood to document.[6] The narratives of this performance vary. It would indeed be most accurate to say that the performance is a function of the narratives and images orchestrated around it. In 1970, VALIE EXPORT wrote that the "action" took place in 1968 in a cinema, where she made her way through rows of movie watchers in her modified cowboy suit, compelling "indirect sexual contact with the public."[7] A decade later, she claimed she had been even more direct, wielding a machine gun and antagonizing the audience in a cinema showing pornographic films: "Actual genitalia was available, and they could do anything they wanted to it."[8] By 2007, VALIE EXPORT "revised" her statements in an interview with Widrich: Of course the performance with the gun in the porn cinema never happened.[9] Clearly, what counts is the incendiary effect of the images and narratives generated around the artist's storied performance at the historical moment of its retelling and "documentary" reproduction. In 2005, Marina Abramović had "reperformed" *Genitalpanik* at the Guggenheim, in New York.[10] In 2013, VALIE EXPORT's "action pants" were acquired as the "Original Mustang Jeans of the performance in 1968" by mumok – Museum moderner Kunst in Vienna, where they can be viewed, accompanied by the later photographs *Aktionshose: Genitalpanik*, in a large vertical shadow box frame, a vaunted relic of an action that may or may not have happened.[11]

In contrast, mumok does not hold a single work by Wiener (and certainly none has ever been reperformed). When the Museum of Modern Art, New York, sought to acquire *Großer Teppich* after exhibiting it in an international

Dieter Roth retrospective in 2004, it was "to strengthen the Roth holdings."[12] When *Großer Teppich* was subsequently acquired, along with an array of materials from Wiener's and Roth's correspondence, it was accessioned as a work by Roth, without any mention of Wiener.[13] This is all the more shocking given that Roth—whose work was internationally well known by this time—was most definitely not a weaver. Yet Roth, apparent "subject" of the work, displaced Wiener. Her part in the collaboration, and not only as the weaver of the tapestry, goes unnoticed, along with the artistic and political consequence of her work. That this is easy to mistake is not only because her practice is neither explicitly feminist nor activist, but also because she is engaged in "women's work" and suffers its habitual disregard.

In 1982, two years after VALIE EXPORT published her art historical manifesto of Feminist Actionism promoting "women's self-definition" in artistic practices of self-expression, self-affirmation, and independence, Carol Gilligan opened the field of feminist care ethics in the United States, seeking to shift the optic on how action is appraised in the social sphere.[14] Feminist care ethics can be read as a provocative riposte to the call to action made by the second wave of the 1970s and its artistic counterpart in Feminist Actionism. "Care," writes Gilligan, "is grounded in the assumption that self and other are interdependent, an assumption reflected in a view of action as responsive and, therefore, as arising in relationship rather than the view of action as emanating from within the self."[15] Without direct reference to feminist thought, Wiener's feminist in-action articulates this other "view of action"—but not, it must be emphasized, by affirming or sentimentalizing the promise of mutual relationality. Feminist in-action attests to the incongruities, differences, disappointments, and difficult demands of caring.

The practices of weaving and caring are interwoven. Indeed, the word *web*—from the Germanic *weben*, "to weave"—lends itself as a central metaphor to care ethics.[16] Berenice Fisher and Joan Tronto's oft-cited definition of care, "*a species activity that includes everything that we do to maintain, continue, and repair our 'world' so that we can live in it as well as possible*," emphasizes relationality by way of the metaphor of weaving: "This world includes our bodies, our selves, and our environment, all of which we seek to interweave in a complex, life-sustaining web."[17] Feminist Actionism is the project of self-extrication from this sticky web. Feminist in-action attends to the relations of implication that sustain it. Care ethics, it must be emphasized, is feminist not because it essentializes ostensibly feminine attitudes, but because it recognizes and works through the essential labor of care, which has historically and overwhelmingly been borne by women. Unlike the long-standing association of the emancipated individual with self-righteous autonomy, feminist care ethics insists on the ethical and political primacy of relationality and demands acknowledgment for the self-effacing labor that goes into maintaining such relations. For caring, like weaving, is often written off as "women's work," taken for granted, disregarded, or mistaken for mere passivity. In no small part for this reason, work like Wiener's, which is about weaving and care, has long been overlooked.

Aktionshose: Genitalpanik and *Großer Teppich* reveal an impasse in the history of feminist artistic practice that is relevant well beyond the Austrian context.[18] On the one hand, there is an orientation toward artistic action as political activism. From VALIE EXPORT to Marina Abramović to Pussy Riot, such practices confront viewers by explicitly challenging normative assumptions, inverting habitual categories, and playing with the spectacularization and mediatization of popular culture. These artistic interventions operate by generating powerful affects closely related to political agitation such as panic, shock, excitement, indignation, and rage.[19] On the other hand, there is a less conspicuous current of feminist performance art, the forms and temporality of which seem to be at odds with political activism. The work of Ingrid Wiener, like that of Lea Lublin and Mierle Laderman Ukeles, whom I discuss in the introduction, draws attention to an array of practices that belong to the sphere of care. In stark contrast with Lublin's and Ukeles's everyday actions of child-rearing and cleaning, however, Wiener does so within the artistic tradition of weaving. Her feminist in-action is compelled by deflationary affects or "cares"—concern, patience, empathy, melancholy, longing, affection—that are less powerful and less overtly political than those that drive Feminist Actionism, but arguably more pressing and pervasive. It is to these cares that Wiener's work attends, and invites us to turn our attention. In responding to Wiener's work, my aim is not to make a claim for feminist in-action at the expense of Feminist Actionism. Even if the one demands it and the other demurs, they both deserve consideration for what they together contribute to art and to feminism. In practice, however, Feminist Actionism supplants, rather than supplements, feminist in-action. Feminist art historiography still needs to work through this asymmetry.

Two Artists (Two Feminists) Weaving Gobelins

Feminist Actionism and feminist in-action may be incompatible, but they share an artistic and historical red thread. Looking back to the beginning of her tapestry collaborations, Wiener recalls: "My plan was to make something new out of this old-fashioned art form, with the motto 'anyone can paint' [*malen kann jeder*]. Dieter Roth seemed to me to be the right artist to help realize this plan. For 'two women weaving Gobelins' in 1974 would have been a hopeless undertaking."[20] Ironically, the other woman weaving Gobelins in 1974 was none other than VALIE EXPORT, Wiener's longtime friend. The jagged horizontal red line woven into the bottom left corner of *Großer Teppich*, running under Roth's shoe, indicates the early moment at which she abandoned what was already their second tapestry collaboration with Roth. VALIE EXPORT's departure can be understood as a final disavowal of weaving. Wiener, in contrast, continued to immerse herself intensively in its conventional techniques, transforming an "old-fashioned art form" by exploring its constraints.

When VALIE EXPORT moved to Vienna from Linz in 1960, Wiener, the Vienna local, introduced her to her friends and to the Viennese artistic milieu. The two women met at the Höhere Bundeslehr- und Versuchsanstalt für Textilindustrie, where they studied together from 1960 to 1964 and where each earned a degree in textile design, having chosen to apply themselves to techniques of hand weaving rather than textile printing. While finishing their degrees and shortly after graduating, Wiener and VALIE EXPORT worked together on several tapestries for Friedensreich Hundertwasser, based on his paintings. They made preparatory drawings, their own take on the convention of the "cartoon" used to translate the scale and composition of a painting for a tapestry. Then they wove together on a high-warp loom. The resulting tapestries look just like Hundertwasser's paintings. When exhibited, the tapestries were (and are) attributed, in the traditional manner, as "works" by Hundertwasser, with Wiener and VALIE EXPORT credited for "the weaving."[21] It is certainly at least in part to these hierarchies—of painter and weaver, art and craft, man and woman—that Wiener refers in her remarks cited earlier on the "hopelessness" of two women weaving Gobelins circa 1974. After the Hundertwasser tapestry they wove together in 1966, Wiener and VALIE EXPORT would both, taking very different paths, abandon this collaborative model.

VALIE EXPORT broke not only with her training in textile design but also more emphatically with her past. She branded herself VALIE EXPORT in 1967 in a feminist act of divestment from her family and patriarchal names and a performative critique of prevailing gendered structures of circulation and consumption. Chronologies of VALIE EXPORT's work almost always begin with this act. The tapestries she and Wiener wove for Hundertwasser are understandably excluded from the official corpus of her significant work.[22] As demonstrated in *Aktionshose: Genitalpanik*, throughout the late 1960s and into the 1970s, VALIE EXPORT was focused on the mediation of women's bodies in Western image culture. This preoccupation informs not only her photographic and filmic work but also her well-known performances with Peter Weibel, such as *Tapp- und Tastkino* (Tap and touch cinema; 1968; fig. 4.2). Like the storied *Genitalpanik*, *Tapp- und Tastkino* demands direct contact, reimagining the viewer's encounter with women's bodies in the cinema. Rather than an anonymous, immersive, and primarily visual experience, VALIE EXPORT activates her spectators, inviting them to put their hands into the curtained space of the boxy apparatus she wears over her bare torso. There, for a limited time, they can explore her naked body in an immediate, tactile encounter.[23] As a work of Feminist Actionism, *Tapp- und Tastkino* "deconstruct[s] the cultural coding of women, from art history to mass media."[24] Especially in her collaborations with Weibel, VALIE EXPORT highlights gender binaries and stereotypes, confronting crude oppositions perpetuated in popular culture

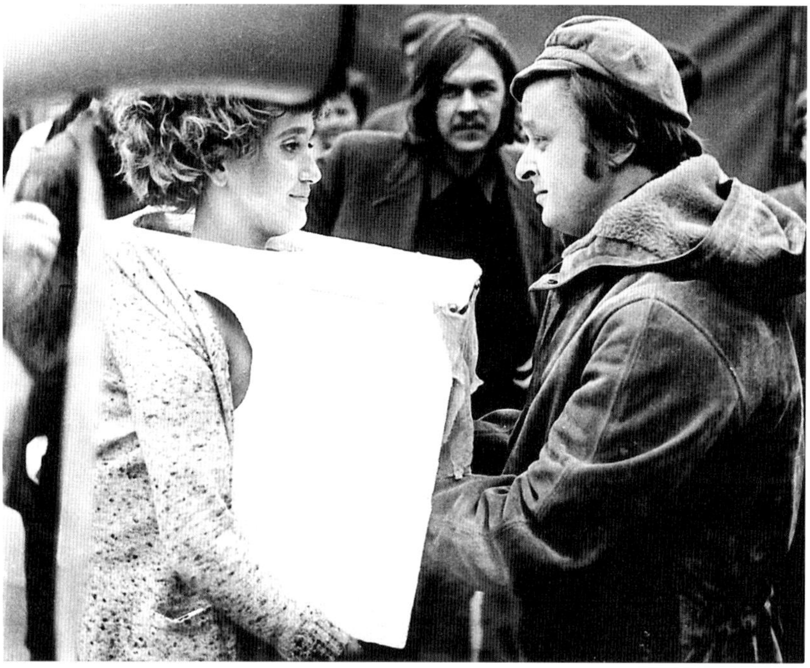

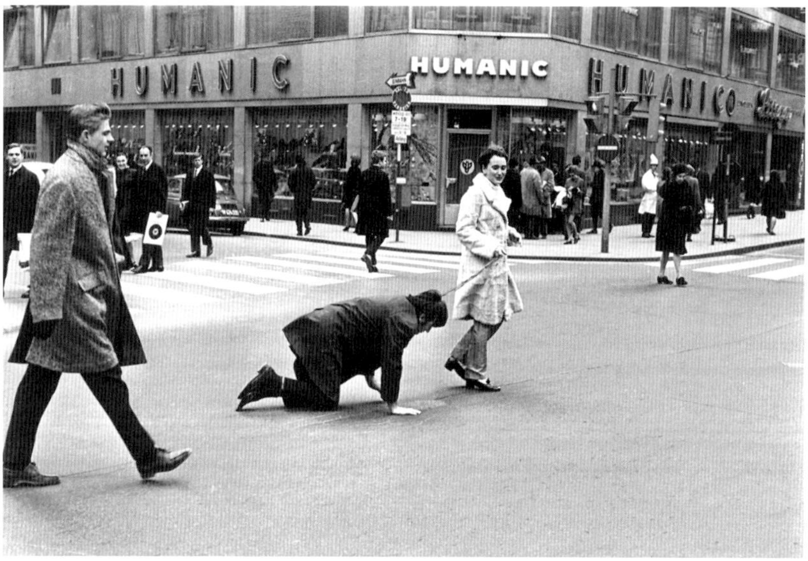

Figure 4.2. VALIE EXPORT with Peter Weibel, *Tapp- und Tastkino* (Tap and touch cinema), 1968. Photograph by Werner Schulz. © VALIE EXPORT, Bildrecht Wien, 2025.

Figure 4.3. VALIE EXPORT with Peter Weibel, *Aus der Mappe der Hundigkeit* (From the portfolio of doggedness), 1968. Photograph by Joseph Tandl. © VALIE EXPORT, Bildrecht Wien, 2025.

and everyday life by crudely inverting them. For *Aus der Mappe der Hundigkeit* (From the portfolio of doggedness; 1968; fig. 4.3), she leads a crawling Weibel through Vienna's seventh district on a leash.[25]

For VALIE EXPORT, her artistic brand-persona was defined on the basis of the public exhibitionism of her 1960s performances. So it is no surprise that in her 1980 manifesto, the array of works she collects under the title of Feminist Actionism, including poetry, painterly and photographic self-portraiture, experimental dance, and live performance, does not include weaving. Nonetheless, it is important to recall that VALIE EXPORT's today well-known Feminist Actionism emerged out of and in protest against her early weaving practice. This is clear in her autobiographical entry in 1970 for *wien: bildkompendium wiener aktionismus und film* (vienna: image compendium of viennese actionism and film), the book she edited with Weibel in which they coined the phrase "Viennese Actionism." There, she includes the Hundertwasser tapestries woven with Wiener and goes on to sketch a Brechtian idea to attempt "a new Gobelin-technique" through the "alienation of material," involving a "woven textile-mirror" and "woven civil rights."[26] However impractical, her ongoing interest in weaving at the time may have motivated her to accept Wiener's invitation in 1974 to revisit the medium for a very different kind of tapestry collaboration.

Before Waltraud Höllinger became VALIE EXPORT, Ingrid Schuppan, with less fanfare, became Ingrid Wiener. In a rare autobiographical note, Wiener refers briefly to her schooling, two years as an office clerk followed by her degree in textile design, and a period from 1958 to 1964 of "intensive preoccupation with experiments of a sexual nature," before concluding, "since 1964 life-partner of Oswald Wiener," as though this had become her ongoing occupation.[27] Significantly, this entry also appears in the *bildkompendium wiener aktionismus*, thus locating Wiener and her various "preoccupations" within Viennese Actionism from the start. While VALIE EXPORT positions herself as a central player in an actionist arena otherwise dominated by men, Wiener dedicates to herself just three short fragmented lines. She does not describe herself as an artist or an actionist. Nonetheless, she was, as she later put it, "weaving on and on." While Oswald was in jail following the *Kunst und Revolution* incident in 1968, Ingrid organized lawyers and witnesses, all the while working on several Gobelins that lent the pair a certain financial stability.[28] It is testament to the consolidation of the action paradigm in performance art history that when mumok finally published what was meant to be the definitive compendium on Viennese Actionism in 2012, Wiener all but disappeared.[29] Never mentioned by name, she surfaces only as "his wife" in a singularly sexist line of Oswald's biography.[30]

What would an art history of Viennese Actionism look like if it responded to her understated position? Wiener rarely put herself in the spotlight. But throughout the 1950s and 1960s, she frequently appeared at the edges of the Viennese art scene. Throughout her adolescence, she had a close friendship with the poet and playwright Konrad Bayer and acted as a seductive "Eve" opposite Bayer's "Dandy" in Ferry Radax's frenetic black-and-white film *Sonne Halt!* (Sun stop!; 1959). Through Bayer, she came to know Oswald Wiener and the other writers and musicians affiliated with the Vienna Group (*wiener gruppe*), named members of which include Bayer, Oswald Wiener, Gerhard Rühm, Friedrich Achleitner, and H. C. Artmann.[31] Ingrid Wiener visited the same locales as these artists and performed in the group's two "literary cabarets" of 1958 and 1959 (figs. 4.4, 4.5).[32] In 1964, Bayer committed suicide, marking the definitive end of the *wiener gruppe*. Not long after, Ingrid took

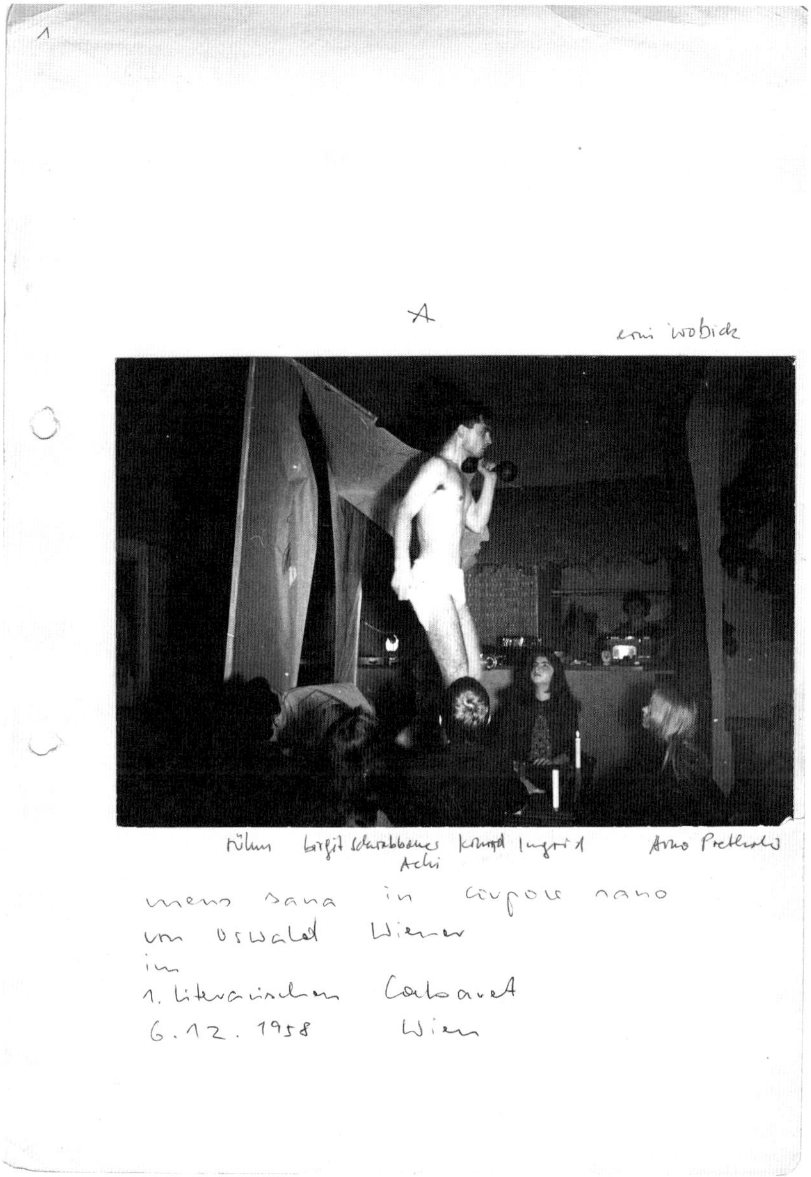

Figure 4.4. Photograph in the archives of Ingrid Wiener showing Oswald Wiener with (*clockwise*) Friedrich Achleitner, Ingrid Wiener, Aino Prethaler, Konrad Bayer, Birgit Schwabbauer, and Gerhard Rühm in *mens sana in corpore sano* in the first literary cabaret of the *wiener gruppe* (Vienna Group) at the artists' association Alte Welt, Vienna, 1958. Photograph by Franz Hubmann. Scanned by the author in the archive of Ingrid Wiener, Kapfenstein.

Oswald's name. Although she does not include it in her autobiographical entry of 1970, she continued to appear as an ambiguous peripheral figure in different groupings of Viennese artists, including as an unnamed sole woman "co-agitator" (*mitagiter*) of Die Zeugen (The Witnesses) and the only woman named in the group Wir nicht (Not us).[33]

Sometimes, in the decade of so-called Viennese Actionism, Wiener and VALIE EXPORT appeared together. At the *ZOCKfest* in Club Grünes Tor in April 1967, they sat next to each other in the front row.[34] Wiener pours a dark liquid on Otto Muehl and the squirming members of his Direct Art Club (fig. 4.6). Hermann Nitsch eviscerates a lamb. In kitten heels and a plaid skirt

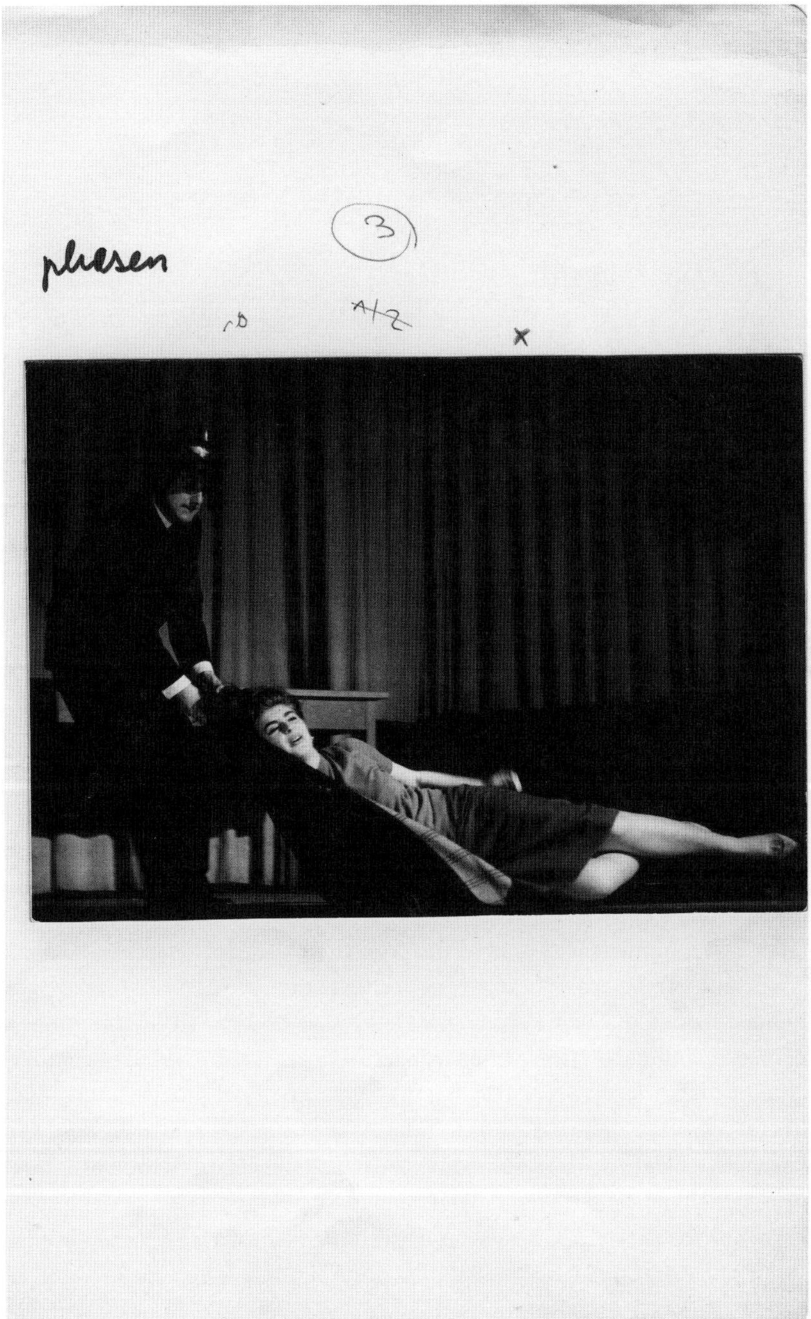

Figure 4.5. Photograph in the archives of Ingrid Wiener showing Ingrid Wiener with Friedrich Achleitner in *phases* in the second literary cabaret of the *wiener gruppe* (Vienna Group) at the Porrhaus, Vienna, 1959. Photograph by Franz Hubmann. Scanned by the author in the archive of Ingrid Wiener, Kapfenstein.

suit, Wiener stands apart from the men's puerile antics even while her smile suggests tolerant amusement. The authorities were less amused; the police put a stop to the event.[35] Following the shutdown, photographs of Wiener populated the press coverage, where she was presented as the victim rather than an agent of the "action." In the *Kurier* daily newspaper, her photograph appeared

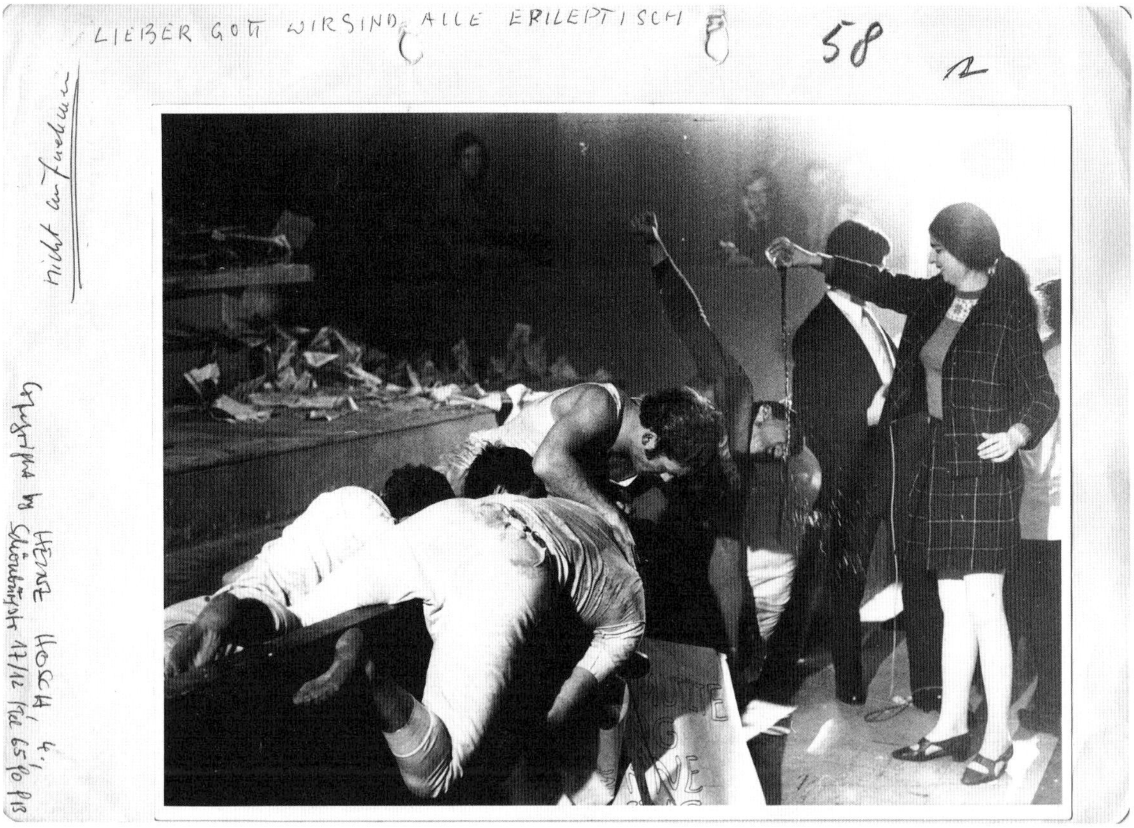

Figure 4.6. Photograph in the archives of Ingrid Wiener showing Ingrid Wiener with Otto Muehl and the Direct Art Group in *ZOCKfest* at Club Grünes Tor, Vienna, 1967. Photograph by Heinz Hosch. Scanned by the author in the archive of Ingrid Wiener, Kapfenstein.

above the byline, "Mädchen vom Knödel befreit" (Girl freed from dumpling). The evening had involved a food fight. In the *Kronen Zeitung* tabloid, she was labeled a "Minimädchen" (minigirl), and pictured in her oft-commented upon "miniskirt" being escorted from the scene by the police.[36] Not "freed" but rather detained that same evening, VALIE EXPORT impassively stares past a helmeted commando from within a police van (fig. 4.7). This kind of confrontation with authority would become the signature of her practice and propel her success as a Feminist Actionist. It was Wiener, though, who in this instance fascinated the press, insofar as she was mistaken for a "girl" in need of saving. Throughout her career, Wiener would inhabit the liminal position of an artist always on the cusp of being seen as just a woman or just a wife.[37]

In *Three Artists (Three Women)* of 1996, Anne Middleton Wagner argues that artists who were also women—Georgia O'Keeffe, Lee Krasner, and Eva Hesse are her case studies—were encumbered throughout modernity not only by the refrain that they were just the wives of their ostensibly more important and significant male counterparts, but also by a modernist expectation, namely, that their art reveal their femininity.[38] To extend Wagner's argument beyond the US context and into the 1970s, the expectations of women artists might be modified as follows: The work of the woman artist should reveal not her femininity but her feminism. And as a rule, that feminism should be

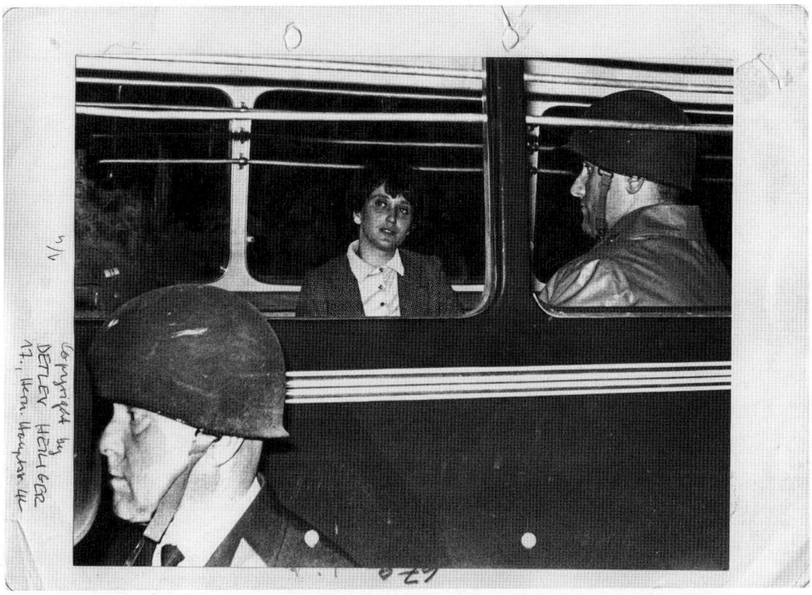

Figure 4.7. Photograph in the archives of Ingrid Wiener showing VALIE EXPORT in a police van after *ZOCKfest* at Club Grünes Tor, Vienna, 1967. Photograph by Detlev Heiliger. Scanned by the author in the archive of Ingrid Wiener, Kapfenstein.

legible as emancipatory Feminist Actionism. From Judy Chicago to Carolee Schneemann, Niki de Saint Phalle to Marina Abramović, women artists gained currency in the 1970s by aligning—and by being taken as aligning—their artistic and feminist pursuits. In 1976, Lucy Lippard called this "body art with a feminist consciousness."[39] By means of their artistic activism, artists who were also women claimed new practices and necessary forms of sensibility that redefined artistic and political space. As a weaver of Gobelins, Wiener would seem to have no place in this history.

Textiling Feminism

Gobelin refers to a French tradition of high-warp loom-based tapestry weaving that was seen as doomed in the 1960s—as utterly un-avant-garde.[40] It was derided as decorative, derivative, a frivolous form of *belle peinture*—associated at once with high art and with kitsch.[41] In response to the formal and historical strictures of weaving, what has come to be called "fiber art" emerged. The year 1962 marks an important confluence in this textile history. On the one hand, celebrations of the three hundredth anniversary of the founding of the Manufacture des Gobelins in Paris took place in exhibitions across Europe, and, on the other, the first Lausanne Tapestry Biennale was staged, a main venue for showcasing international textile and fiber arts for decades to come.[42] There, as Giselle Cotton and Magali Junet put it, "tapestry became fiber art."[43] Insisting on calling her works Gobelins, and persisting in using a high-warp loom to weave, Wiener charted a different course.

If, as Elissa Auther writes, fiber artists "liberated the medium from the loom and thereby released their work from the confines of fiber's historically subordinated position in the art world," then Wiener was interested in testing out the given constraints of the medium.[44] In her comportment *into* weaving and its technical traditions, Wiener shares—perhaps surprisingly—an inclination with Günter Brus, whose dwelling in and on the historical dispositive of figural painting I discuss in chapter 3. Like Brus, Wiener is less interested in enacting her emancipation from the conventions of her medium than in interrogating—and often enough getting caught up in—the rules and restrictions of an "old-fashioned art form." In this resides the interest of her performance art. Under the irreverent motto "anyone can paint," her work also shares with Brus's a commitment to what I have called figuration after formlessness. Without shunning figuration in the name of textile abstraction or textural materiality, Wiener weaves figures that unravel and fray.

In this regard, Wiener's antipainting attitude was the antithesis of the one that informed the fiber art movement. Exponents of fiber art worked explicitly to overcome the historical subordination of weaving to painting by "freeing" soft textile materials. Rejecting everything associated with *belle peinture*, they made "textile sculptures" or "textile objects," eliminating all traces of painting and figuration from weaving.[45] Fiber art celebrated pure materiality and was thus emphatically abstract. It was meant to unambiguously not be "craft," and to resolutely have no use value. In celebrating the purity of the materials and the abstraction of the technique, advocates of fiber art ironically rehearsed the discourse of formalist art history that had emerged a generation earlier in the veneration of abstract painting.[46]

But there were also political stakes. Practiced predominantly by women, fiber art also offered a feminist critique of the art historical and often gendered hierarchy of "fine" and "applied" arts, of art versus craft.[47] In ways that recall the account of the emergence of performance art out of painting, fiber art's emergence from tapestry was presented as a liberation from historical conventions of the materials and techniques of weaving and of the woman artist herself. "It was never a struggle for freedom from the constraints imposed by materials, they were always pliable," writes Irene Waller in her catalog *Textile Objects* from 1977, "but only from the techniques which man had devised to translate the raw materials into a practical object, cloth, and which at one and the same time both inspired and inhibited."[48] Her statement resonates with the logic of Feminist Actionism. Each seeks to find ways to emancipate the artist and her work from the long history of subjugation that bound them.

Weaving Gobelins aligned neither with the Feminist Actionist nor the fiber-focused approach to contemporary art. It was seen as painterly, feminine, pretty. Wiener's tapestry collaborations, however, demonstrate anything but a simple submission to the rules of high-warp weaving. Although they remain committed to a kind of figuration, Wiener's Gobelins are arrestingly ugly—as far from Bauhaus weaver Anni Albers's patterned "pictorial weavings" as they are from French painter Jean Lurçat's monumental "woolen walls."[49] As such, Wiener's tapestry collaborations afford a different view on the entanglement of feminism and textile arts, as well as on the meaning of making art as a woman in the second half of the twentieth century.

In *Fray: Art and Textile Politics* of 2017, Julia Bryan-Wilson recalls that it was the "activism of feminists that brought textiles more prominently into the conversation."[50] Especially in "low craft" projects, she argues, the political possibilities of textile arts were explored by "intertwining activist and artistic purposes."[51] *Fray* is concerned first and foremost with art that is explicitly activist. Bryan-Wilson's titular phrase, "textile politics," offers, however, a dual optic for thinking about the politics of textile art. It means, in the first instance, the use of textiles to "advance political agendas," in short, textile activism.[52] But it also means the textiling of the political: "to textile politics is to *give texture* to politics, to refuse easy binaries, to acknowledge complications."[53] By textiling the historiography of feminist and queer art, by giving political weight to the personal, and by attending to frayed forms of action that do not understand themselves in simple opposition to passivity, Bryan-Wilson brings into view a more diverse archive of artistic and activist projects, from the long-enduring work and restoration of the AIDS Memorial Quilt to the domestic handiwork of the Cockettes. In so doing, she offers a methodology not only for addressing the challenge of writing about an ever-fraying medium but also for attending to the intricacies of the political, especially, I would emphasize, when it comes to relations and practices that can only with difficulty be defined as activist or become rallying points for activism. Wiener's tapestry collaborations contribute to the textiling of this dimension of political life. Her feminist in-action gives rise to an alternative textile politics of care.

Napkin-cum-Gobelin

When she initiated her first major tapestry collaboration in 1974, it is crucial to emphasize that Ingrid Wiener invited not her old friend Waltraud from their hand-weaving classes and projects with Hundertwasser, but the emergent Feminist Actionist by then called VALIE EXPORT. Wiener also invited Dieter Roth, whose equivocal material practices can be aptly described as anti-tapestry. She thus tied into the project two figures whose work at the time was adamantly opposed to the "old-fashioned art form" of weaving and all that it stood for. A friend of Wiener's since his first visit to Vienna in 1966, Roth regularly joined her and her Austrian friends at Café Exil in West Berlin in the early 1970s. In contrast with the long-drawn-out and time-consuming process of weaving a singular tapestry, Roth was interested in speed and quantity, producing innumerable drawings, prints, and editions. The big exhibition of his graphic works, *Graphik und Bücher* (Graphics and books; 1972–1974), had been traveling internationally to some acclaim, lending to his repute as an innovative book artist.[54] His materials are typically cheap, readily available, and often perishable. In his work, processes of visual perception and recognition mirror those of corporeal consumption and excretion. Unpreserved foodstuffs

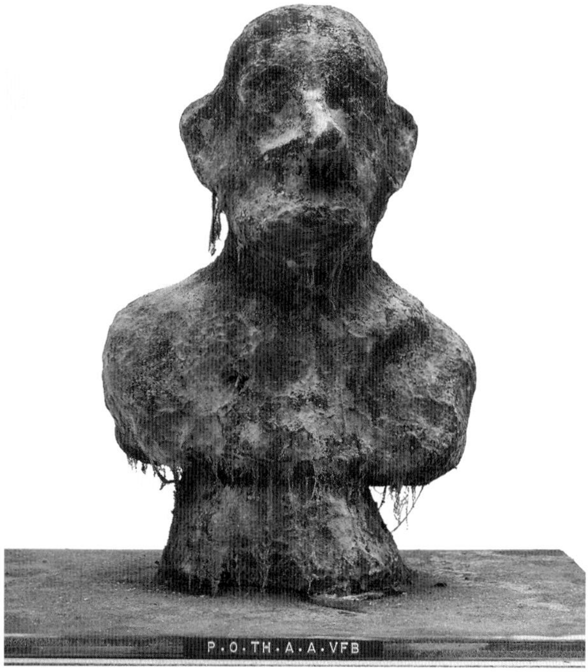

Figure 4.8. Dieter Roth, *P.O.TH.A.A.VFB (Portrait of the Artist as a Vogelfutterbüste)* (birdseed bust), 1968. Bust of molded chocolate and birdseed on wooden board; edition of 30. © Dieter Roth Estate, Courtesy Hauser & Wirth.

often model a form of transient selfhood, vulnerable to time and age, subject to continuing decay.

A characteristic self-portrait to add to those of Ingrid Wiener and VALIE EXPORT introduced above, Roth's *P.O.TH.A.A.VFB* (Portrait of the artist as a *Vogelfutterbüste* [birdseed bust]; 1968; fig. 4.8) is a vanishing edition of thirty molded chocolate busts coated in birdseed and meant, quite literally, for the garden. The self takes form subject to material decomposition, to fraying as it were, or to a slow being-pecked-away-at. His work is about saving the transient in its transience, not raising it up or rescuing it, but just sitting with it for a while. Extraordinarily heterogeneous in his practices, Roth nevertheless may have meant to get out of the tapestry collaboration with Wiener—and certainly to demonstrate his irreverence—when, in reply to her request that he send materials for the project, he mailed her, after considerable delay, a soiled linen dinner napkin from a meal he had just eaten at an Italian restaurant chain in London called Bertorelli's.

Roth's oil-stained napkin, an inexpensive mechanically woven damask fabric, mocks the technically demanding process of hand weaving that Wiener sought to undertake (fig. 4.9).[55] At the same time, it brings weaving into messy abject contact with the body. On it, he scrawled three stocky cats in red pen, sending no accompanying note or letter. His response was hardly the kind of "original work" or template on which a tapestry might conventionally have been based. Yet far from dismissing Roth's seemingly dismissive response,

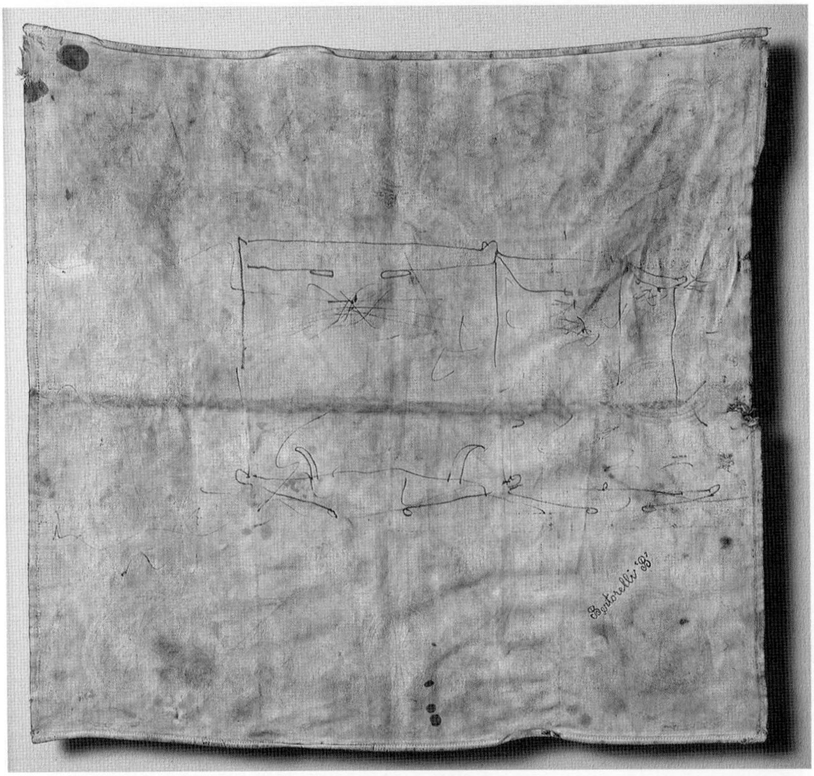

Figure 4.9. Drawing on a dinner napkin by Dieter Roth for *Gobelin (Bertorelli 'B')*, 1974. Felt pen on used linen dinner napkin, 47 × 50 cm. © Dieter Roth Estate, Courtesy Hauser & Wirth © Ingrid Wiener, Courtesy of Ingrid Wiener; Kunsthaus Zürich, 1981.

Wiener and VALIE EXPORT co-responded. In the spirit of Roth's wry humor, they took the ambivalence of the napkin as the impetus for weaving what came to be called *Bertorelli 'B'* (1974–1976; plate 13), a napkin-cum-Gobelin tapestry.

In stark contrast with their previous collaboration on the Hundertwasser tapestries, in *Bertorelli 'B'* Wiener and VALIE EXPORT do away with traditional systems of correspondence: of tapestry to template, weaver to artist. Instead, *Bertorelli 'B'* emphasizes the techniques and materials, as well as the labor and time, of weaving by de-emphasizing the priority and intentionality that might have been accorded Roth's—decidedly unauthoritative—napkin drawing. As the textures of the tapestry show, Wiener and VALIE EXPORT aspired to neither a faithful imitation nor a harmonious marriage of anyone's intentions. Instead, they set about weaving the whole dispositive of their collaboration with Roth and with each other, textiling tensions between action and passivity, chance and intentionality, proximity and distance, communication and miscommunication, art and the everyday.

What to do with the base residues of Roth's food and bodily excretions in a Gobelin? The answer is neither a *belle peinture* nor a woven work of abstraction, but a strikingly ugly tapestry. *Bertorelli 'B'* is not *art informel*, to recall the phrase used to describe gestural abstract paintings popular in Europe at the time. It is rather *informe*—formless, bad form. Wiener and VALIE EXPORT translate stains on the napkin with rotten-orange- and scat-brown-colored weft

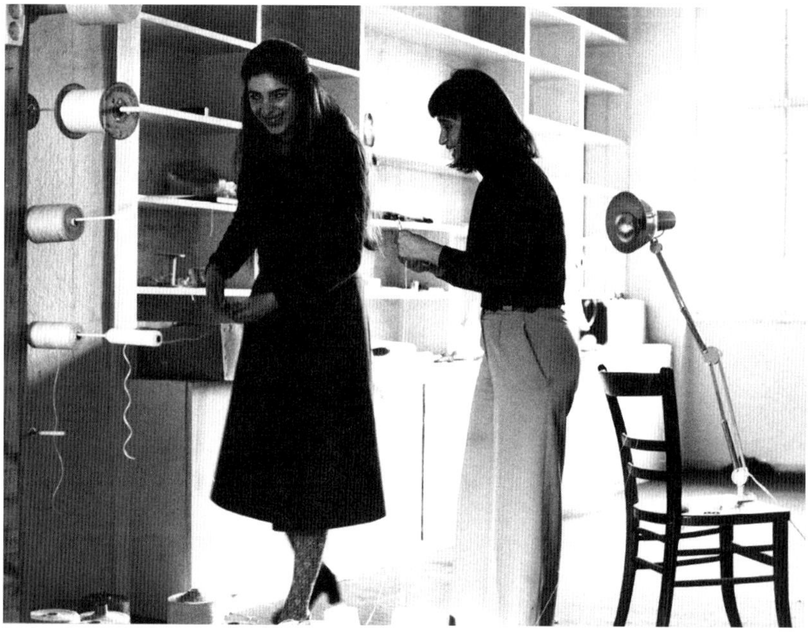

Figures 4.10–4.11. Photographs in the archives of Ingrid Wiener showing Ingrid Wiener and VALIE EXPORT weaving *Bertorelli 'B'*. Photographer unknown. Scanned by the author in the archive of Ingrid Wiener, Kapfenstein.

threads. Muted shades of beige and pink give shape to the underlying damask pattern, yet in contrast with its mechanically produced symmetry, in the weaving of *Bertorelli 'B'* the arabesques and wheels are distorted, their shapes stretched out and fragmented as though by time, their color inconsistent, as though cast in shadow. Loose weft threads peek through the fabric of the tapestry and tangle at its edges. A cluster of warp threads on the right side of the tapestry are omitted from the interlace. *Bertorelli 'B'* makes immanently visible transitions in the weavers' process and their perception of material and light (figs. 4.10, 4.11). Breaks—taken to stand up, alleviate the body, perhaps watch television, or between days, weeks, months—appear as such in abrupt shifts in the color of the weft threads and in disturbances to the interweave. By weaving the contingency of their materials and their selves, Wiener and VALIE EXPORT introduce the duration and endurance of weaving into the tapestry. Instead of erasing relations of media, production, and labor, the tapestry sustains and exhibits them. *Bertorelli 'B'* documents the performance, relations, and practices that brought it into being.

And yet, when the tapestry was acquired in 1981 by the Kunsthaus Zürich, it was attributed solely to Roth. Harald Szeemann, chief curator at the time, marveled in the museum's annual report: "Roth surprised us. With a GOBELIN."[56] If only Szeemann had reflected on this surprise or conveyed it with more generous good humor. He even interviews "the two Viennese women" (*die beiden Wienerinnen*) about the process of working with Roth, quipping in a citation of Friedrich Schiller: "Honor women! They braid and weave / heavenly roses into earthly life." Szeemann, however, honors neither Wiener nor VALIE EXPORT.[57] But he does at the same time acquire Roth's dirty dinner napkin as

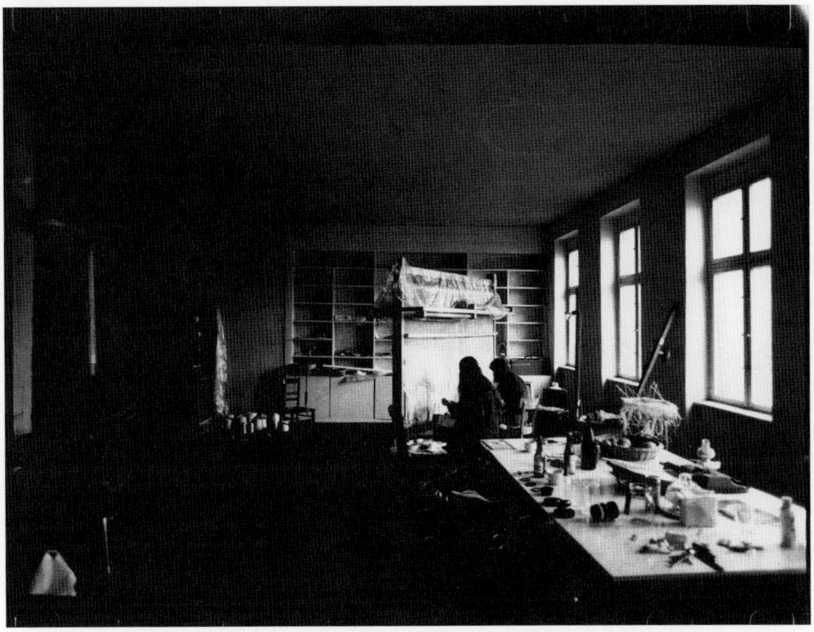

a work in its own right, continuing the tradition of what he calls the Duchampian ready-made's "ennoblement of the banal" (*Veredelung des Banalen*).[58]

Despite his flawed but crucial role in establishing the field of performance art as the curator of *Happening & Fluxus* in 1970 and *documenta 5* in 1972 (detailed in the introduction), Szeemann remains stubbornly unwilling to see that the "surprise" of this Gobelin is that it is not just an art object, but one document in a complex collaborative performance. Even as he treats Roth's napkin drawing as a contribution to avant-garde practice, Szeemann regards the tapestry in the most conventional of senses, separating "the artist" from "the weavers." As perhaps the period's most preeminent art institutional figure in German-speaking space, Szeemann mistakes feminist in-action. It would be understandable if this deeply engrained and institutionally enshrined sexism drove VALIE EXPORT once again, and once and for all, to abandon weaving. But Wiener, arguably driven by it, wove on and on.

Bertorelli 'B' works within and against the conventions of Gobelin tapestry weaving. It registers the anxieties, frustrations, and cares of each of the three collaborators about tapestry as an art form. In turn, it textiles their relationships, even when these are strained or fraying. In contrast with Schiller's celebration of the "heavenly roses" woven into earthly life by women, *Bertorelli 'B'* presents interwoven yet ungraceful components of the world—along with the very cares out of which it was woven. A jagged, vertical teal line, thickest at the center of the upper edge of the tapestry, indicates the division of the loom. Wiener's work took place to its left, and VALIE EXPORT's to its right, in an integrated yet non-subordinating form that leaves space for multiple intentions, techniques, and concerns. In the lower-right corner of the tapestry,

Roth's signature is woven with the year in which the collaboration began, 1974. VALIE EXPORT weaves her own logo-signature in the upper-right corner near the end of the weaving process and, near the center, Berlin 1976, the name of the city in which the weaving took place and the year in which it ended. In the upper-left corner, Wiener weaves her signature in pale red yarn, all in lowercase letters. And at the very top of the tapestry, slipped into a stretch of open warp threads just to the left of the teal diving line, underscored in dark brown yarn and barely visible to the naked eye, Roth's signature appears again in ink on a scrap of paper, accompanied by the dates of the full duration of the collaboration, reaffirming at the very end his contribution to a work into which he may well have initially been duped. A surprise indeed.

Extimate Collaborations

From *Bertorelli 'B'* (1974–1976) through *Großer Teppich* (1981–1986), Wiener's textile politics articulate a feminist practice that refuses to correspond to established understandings of subjectivity, action, and autonomy—neither of artist nor of work. One might be inclined, drawing on the work of Bibiana Obler, to call her tapestry collaborations "intimate collaborations." In a study of artistic projects by artist couples (Wassily Kandinsky and Gabriele Münter and Hans Arp and Sophie Taeuber-Arp are her main examples), Obler locates the intimacy of their collaborations in the privacy and protection of their shared domestic lives at home, where, out of view of the press and their students, colleagues, and friends, they pursued some of their most radical and least-known experiments.[59] With regard to the collaborations of Wiener, Roth and, initially, VALIE EXPORT, I would propose an important distinction. Their "intimate collaborations" were not bound by marriage or life-partnership, often drew in other friends, and traversed an array of different spaces. As such, they exhibit a formal and social promiscuity that is intimate insofar as it is extimate. Their collaborations "refuse simple binaries," to recall Bryan-Wilson, textiling not only the complex implication of private and public, inside and outside, interior and exterior, but also the binary hierarchy of artistic correspondence as such. In the extimate collaborations of Wiener and Roth, their correspondence discloses the ambivalence of care.

I borrow the suggestive term from Lacan, who uses the word *extimité* a single time in his lectures on the ethics of psychoanalysis. Intriguingly, he does so when talking of cave painting and anamorphosis in a reflection on the "impasse," as he refers to it, "between figurative and so-called abstract art." Whether its aim is imitation of the external world or abstraction from it, art betrays what Lacan calls an "extériorité intime," intimate exteriority.[60] This structure, which lacerates the tortured question of representation in art, describes in turn the convoluted constitution of the self. Extimacy refers to an uncanny spatial dispositive in which interiority and exteriority traverse one another: What is most intimate is foreign; what is most strange is intimate.[61]

"Extimacy is not the contrary of intimacy," writes Jacques-Alain Miller. Rather, "Extimacy says that the intimate is Other—like a foreign body, a parasite."[62] Developed at the intersection of the theory of the subject and of art, extimacy describes a decentering relationality to which one is inherently exposed.

Extimacy thus complicates notions of agency and autonomy. For it names a prior disposition of vulnerability from the outside and inclination toward it. I take the term as a way of conceiving the relational model of self that care is devoted to, and that Wiener textiles in her tapestry collaborations. In this regard, extimacy describes the space—the "rich and knotty texture"[63]—with which care concerns itself. Care is not undertaken between self-contained selves, who for their part enter into intimate relations. Care cares about extimate relations. And it is on account of this disconcerting structure that care is so hard to identify, politicize, enact, and represent.

Großer Teppich can be taken as an extimate self-portrait (see plate 12). At first, rather than send Wiener the materials she requested for another collaboration, Roth had suggested an alternative approach: that Wiener and VALIE EXPORT weave an image of themselves as they saw themselves reflected in a mirror placed behind the warp threads. This idea not only displaces the traditional use of a mirror in high-warp weaving to guide the weaver's view of the image taking shape on the smooth face of the tapestry but also upends traditional approaches to subject matter in tapestry. For Wiener, however, Roth's proposal placed "too much emphasis on the weaver and too little on the weaving."[64] This is just one of many gentle rebukes of Roth's naive understanding of the work of weaving that Wiener proceeds to weave into the form and process of their collaboration. Doing away with the mirror, she considered: "Why not just weave what one sees anyhow [*sowieso*] behind the warp threads. But not in a painterly and static reproduction, rather in movement."[65] The weaving would thus not be a painterly imitation, but rather the site of the obstruction of views and a document of the veritable performance of weaving. After VALIE EXPORT's departure from the project, Wiener hoped that Roth would be present, sitting with her behind the loom as her companion and model, a part of what she saw and obscured, *sowieso*, as she wove.

But throughout the early 1980s, Roth was traveling extensively—Paris, Venice, Chicago, Stuttgart, Basel—for big exhibitions and solo shows, all the while working on large-scale projects with his children. In 1982, he represented Switzerland at the Venice Biennale, where his film installation *Tagebuch* (Diary; 1982) was shown, an intimate portrait of his everyday life. The international recognition and exposure drove him into depression.[66] He had no intention of taking part in person in the long-drawn-out process of weaving *Großer Teppich* in situ. Like his napkin, his idea for the reflective sheet had also been a convenient way for him to collaborate in absentia. When Wiener continued to ask him to visit her in West Berlin, he sent instead a life-size poster of a black-and-white image of himself, which Wiener taped to the wall behind her loom.[67] This static image was the anti-image of the intimacy she longed for.

The collaboration stalled. Roth's and Wiener's few brief encounters in Vienna "on long and aggressive evenings" were followed by a long, and perhaps aggressive, pause in their correspondence.[68] Writing to Roth on December 14, 1983, Wiener would express her sense of disappointment and coax him to respond:

> I was really sad in general after I had the feeling that you didn't want to talk to me on the phone. . . . then I was almost determined to simply cut off the tapestry if I didn't have a message from you. Was I really so bad that evening (our last) or were you especially over-sensitive. I only wanted to be nice to your friend because she is after all your friend. . . . Anyways I didn't cut it off and am now really happy. . . . I'd like to know how you're doing. . . . And please write to me about what's going on, otherwise I can't really weave.[69]

Whether cutting the tapestry off the loom, or cutting off the tapestry collaboration with Roth, Wiener articulates her weaving process as contingent on their being in touch, subject to feelings of sadness, badness, and oversensitivity but also, to be sure, moments of happiness and laughter.

In the meantime, VALIE EXPORT also found herself increasingly in the eye of an approving international public. When she initially embarked upon *Großer Teppich* with Wiener, she was already working on several big film projects. *Syntagma* (1983) was devoted to the objectification and animation of women's bodies in film, and *Die Praxis der Liebe* (The practice of love; 1985), a thriller about surveillance, urban violence, and heterosexual affairs, was nominated for the Golden Bear at the Berlin Film Festival in 1985. In the latter, Wiener makes a brief appearance, credited as "barmaid." As Wiener's collaboration with Roth on *Großer Teppich* was faltering, VALIE EXPORT was curating an exhibition in Vienna, *Kunst mit Eigen-Sinn: Aktuelle Kunst von Frauen* (Art with own-sense: Current art by women; 1985).[70] Wiener was not included. None of the women selected wove or practiced textile arts. *Eigen-Sinn* means strong-minded, uncompromising, and determined (*eigensinnig*), but also independent and self-determining (*Eigen-Sinn* translates literally as "own-meaning"). It could be taken, as I suggest in the introduction and chapter 1, as the key term of Feminist Actionism. Through the optic of *Kunst mit Eigen-Sinn*, Wiener does not appear. Her artistic practice and its feminism become legible not in the assertion of her own self, but as a response to, and care for, an other. If she was engaged, like VALIE EXPORT in the same years, in a project on "the practice of love," she was less interested in critiquing what is called love in its prevailing heteronormative forms than in exploring the kind of loving care that could never become the subject of a thriller.

Slowly, with much hesitation and delay, *Großer Teppich* emerged out of Wiener's and Roth's discontented, discoordinated, long-distance correspondence. Its largeness is as much a quality of its scale as a reference to the variety and quantity of materials they exchanged and collected throughout the weaving process, all of which they finally xeroxed and published in 1986 in a limited edition of three big *Kopiebücher* (copybooks).[71] Their letters to each other share updates about family, friends, and health, include discussions of what Wiener should weave next, and are plastered with Polaroids of the everyday things—wine bottles, textiles, floorboards, shoes, a TV, cups in a kitchen, implements for writing, views through windows—that shaped their lives. Through a period in which each artist suffered from loneliness and depression, the tapestry collaboration maintained something of the world that bound them together.

Roth understood Wiener's weaving process in terms of a playful inversion of the perspectival dispositive of painting familiar from Albrecht Dürer's well-known woodblock print (see fig. 3.3). His revised idea for *Großer Teppich* had been for Wiener "to look through the vertically bound warp threads on the loom into the flat knot-space and—like before Dürer's . . . coordinate field of threads—to capture the seen together with the seen, with the guy [*das Gesehene samt dem Gesehenen, dem Kerl*], in two dimensions."[72] Yet *Großer Teppich* presents anything but the seamless time and space of two dimensions. Rather, like works of what I call "bad form" in chapter 3, including Günter Brus's *Zerreißprobe* (Stress test; 1970), it presents an ill-defined figure uncoordinated within a perplexing "field of threads." It performs an extimate entanglement.

Drawing on the banal materials they exchanged in their correspondence, Wiener interwove her everyday life with Roth's—including their differing conceptions of the project. The blocky brown and blue forms that repeat across the tapestry and cut through Roth's shoulders are bits of the table legs at the Wieners' Café Exil in West Berlin. The geometric-floral pattern on the tapestry's left edge is drawn from Roth's carpet in Stuttgart. The little heater in the bottom right, with a waste bin for ashes, is from Wiener's chilly studio, and the distinctive window view, with the bright-blue sky, is what Roth saw from his kitchen in Iceland. The "flat knot-space" and "coordinate field of threads" that belong to the model of painterly figuration Roth cites become in *Großer Teppich* a knotty field of a different kind of co-respondence altogether, one that exhibits the extimacy that inheres in the perspectival paradigm that long modeled how the subject views the external world.

For Wiener, the tapestry collaboration changed her perception: "My way of seeing changed on a number of levels, without becoming rigid. Basically I would have to weave on and on" (*Im Grund müsste ich immer weiter weben*).[73] Her performance of weaving on and on describes the co-responsiveness and interdependence of the multifaceted aspects and relationships that lent texture to *Großer Teppich*. The tapestry is an extimate collaboration insofar as it corresponds not to any one subject, time, or space but rather to the obstacles and contingencies of the environments, responsibilities, and affective dispositions of those involved across five years. Rather than define "her own history," Wiener textiles the history of a relationship including all that is habitually obscured, disparaged, or forgotten—a history of cares.

Correspondence Tapestry

Over the course of more than twenty years, Wiener and Roth collaborated on five tapestries: *Bertorelli 'B'* (1974–1976), *Großer Teppich* (1981–1986), *Korrespondenz Teppich* (Correspondence tapestry; 1987–1993), *Das Schachbrett* (The chessboard; 1992–1997), and an untitled work left unfinished when Roth died in 1998.[74] As Wiener finished weaving *Großer Teppich*, she and Oswald were in the process of a major displacement, resettling from West Berlin to Dawson City, in the Yukon Territory in the northwesternmost corner of Canada. There, they opened the Claims Café, where Wiener cooked Viennese cuisine.[75] Wiener, at this distant frontier of the "New World," and Roth, in the heart of "Old World" Europe in Basel, had never been farther apart. Their next two tapestries, *Korrespondenz Teppich* (plate 14) and *Das Schachbrett* (fig. 4.12), were about keeping in touch. Each was woven over a period of several years on a small portable vertical loom with which Wiener could travel and sit outdoors, and each was completed only long after the weaving was finished, with the publication of another set of thick limited edition *Kopiebücher* that gathered letters, Polaroids, packaging and postage, as well as film stills from their *Videobriefe* (video letters), diary-like testimonials shot on VHS tape. Mailed via the

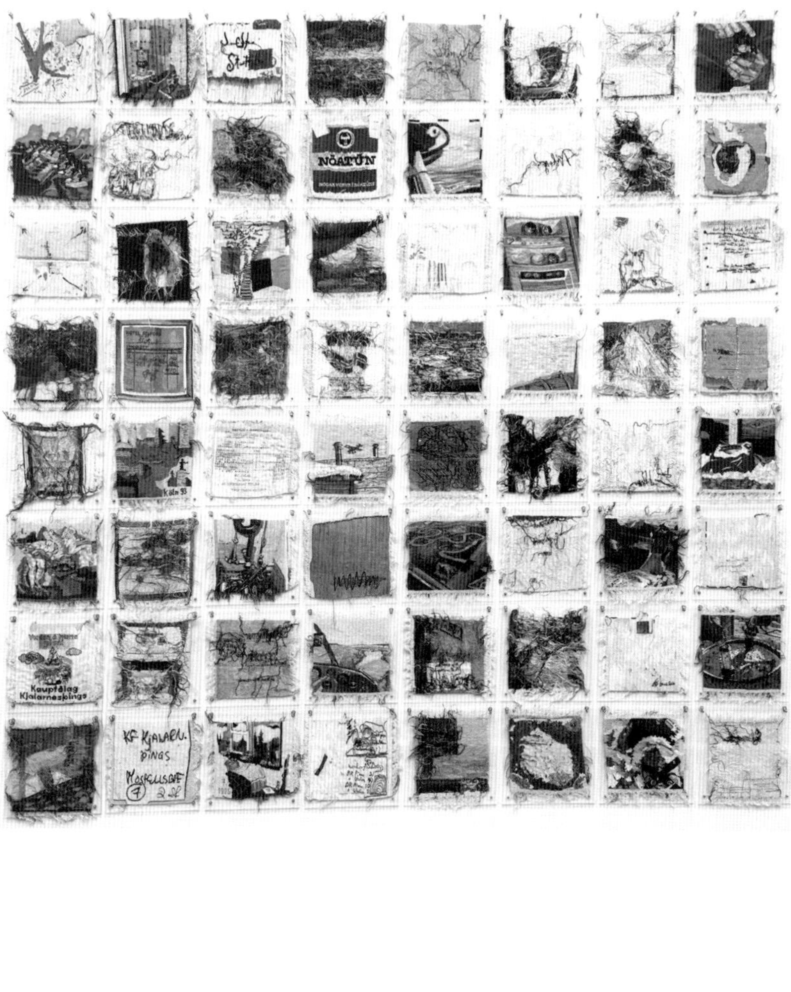

Figure 4.12. Ingrid Wiener and Dieter Roth, *Teppich Nr. 4 (Das Schachbrett)* (Tapestry no. 4 [The chessboard]), 1991–1996. Woven wool, acrylic glass, and steel, 39 × 39 × 0.3 cm (64 parts); when framed: 50 × 50 × 4 cm; whole work: 408 × 408 × 2.5 cm. © Dieter Roth Estate, Courtesy Hauser & Wirth © Ingrid Wiener, Courtesy of Ingrid Wiener; Kunsthaus Zürich, Donated by a private collection, 2012.

post, however, such moving images hardly hastened their exchanges between Canada and Europe.

The continuation of the tapestry collaboration over this great distance makes visible a shift, already underway in *Bertorelli 'B'* and *Großer Teppich*, away from a "subject" of tapestry, in both senses of the word, and toward the complex field of relations that informed the collaboration. While *Bertorelli 'B'* and *Großer Teppich* still retained the minimal structure of an ulterior image even as it frayed—the napkin, the photograph of Roth—the later tapestries shift their attention wholly to a correspondence of the artists' various cares. Accordingly, the later tapestries become even more difficult to look at and take in. While the title of the fourth tapestry, *Das Schachbrett*, at least indicates a certain set of rules by which one might begin to approach its sixty-four reversible square panels, *Korrespondenz Teppich* leaves one without an obvious guiding thread. There is no definite structure, no central figure or given way to move, and there are certainly no coherent points of view. A fiftieth panel folds over backward in the top-right corner of the quilted-together field, obscuring a forty-ninth. There is no strict rule about their arrangement, although each is numbered and attributed with an *I* and a *D*—for Ingrid and Dieter, or perhaps for *ich* and *du* (I and you).[76]

Of the difficulty of surveying *Korrespondenz Teppich*, Wiener wrote to Roth, "I'm very curious—I can't see the tapestry as a whole because the room is too small. Of course I'm also afraid of it [*natürlich fürchte ich mich auch davor*]."[77] Standing before it, one is drawn into the tangle of correspondences that appear as haphazard as the arrangement of the panels, exhibiting relations made by the passage of time, by accident, by chance. Near the middle of the tapestry, a latticed window view onto a cold, snowy winter shares its upper edge with a panel that includes the word *Teppich* in Roth's unmistakable script, with a little arrow pointing into, or just pointing out, the tapestry. To the right, a room takes shape, perhaps a kitchen, with cans of consumables, a roll of paper towel, and something like an orange electrical cord threading its way underneath a door. Above, Roth's name twice—signed and printed, cornered and upside down—and above this, a weaving of the process of weaving *Korrespondenz Teppich*: two panels, "18" and "19," seen through the frame of an axillary crutch. The tapestry makes correspondence its subject, without offering any corresponding subject.

Each woven picture in a panel striates in abstract space, performing what Roth refers to in a letter as the "principle of letting go when tired" (*Bei-Müdigkeit-nachlassen Prinzip*).[78] Wiener formalized this principle of reprieve less by letting go than by tirelessly weaving on (*immer weiter weben*). This formal tension, which archives Wiener's exhausting labor, also captures Roth's and Wiener's clashing moods. Wiener writes to Roth on a melancholy autumn day, "Sometimes it occurs to me that I am already so old, and then I feel really strange [*und dann wird mir ganz komisch*]," encouraging Roth to write to her more quickly and more often.[79] Other letters are more harried: "Dear dieter—

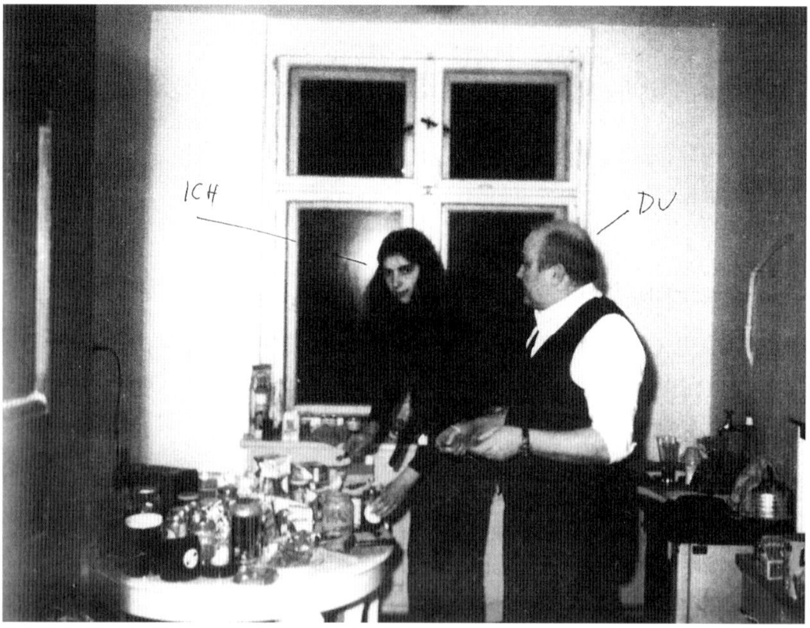

Figure 4.13. Photograph taken in 1974, annotated in 1994, and included with a handwritten letter sent from Ingrid Wiener to Dieter Roth on November 2, 1994, reproduced in Ingrid Wiener and Dieter Roth's artists' book, *Kopiebuch: 4. Roth-Wiener Teppich, 1991–1996* (1997, published by Franz Wassmer). Photograph by Oswald Wiener. © Ingrid Wiener, Courtesy of Ingrid Wiener.

where are you—are you / still in the hospital?" writes Wiener with impatience and worry in January 1988, telling Roth to contact her mother in Vienna given he is, apparently, having trouble reaching her. Her instruction is followed by a plea: "And don't forget your old i. / muddling along penelope-like / till now I've had a good feeling / but really good I only have it first / when from you."[80] She sends along photos of the tapestry in progress. The following month, Roth finally replies, "Mostly I'm lying in bed, with Mr. Depression and Ms. Flu, terrible times," and reassures her about the weaving: "It looks like nothing other than it should look like. Don't worry!" (*Es sieht so aus wies nicht anders aussehn soll. Sei beruhigt!*).[81] *Korrespondence Teppich* is a likeness of their relationship and so cannot look otherwise; it is as inimitable in appearance as their correspondence.

In the text she wrote for the *Kopiebuch*, Wiener describes how the tapestry emerged as "a kind of image-arc of important scraps of life [*Lebensabfällen*] that, woven together, live their own life again."[82] The *I* panels continue Wiener's principle of weaving the everyday, presenting views of landscapes and interiors, always partial, incomplete.[83] The *D* panels draw on diverse flat materials that Roth mailed her—what he called "flat waste" (*flacher Abfall*)—and typically do not look like anything at all. Haphazardly related in the field of the tapestry, these *Abfälle*—scraps, refuse, waste, spoilage—are never far from *Unfälle*, the accidents, mischances, and mishaps of life. In September 1988, Wiener broke her leg while out collecting mushrooms. Adding her injury to his illness, she writes, "It appears that an accident [*Unfall*] is contained in every tapestry," and she goes on to describe the work she has done weaving while otherwise immobilized.[84] For Wiener as for Roth, in *Korrespondenz Teppich*, the transient and the contingent are the very stuff of their correspondence.

Over the years of their long-distance collaboration, there was a risk—perhaps a pleasure—of losing each other, of losing track of who is who and of who is what for whom. In a letter to Roth from 1994, Wiener enclosed a candid photo from 1974, when their correspondence began around *Bertorelli 'B'*. Taken by Oswald, the picture shows Roth and Wiener together in West Berlin (fig. 4.13). "Could it be in the apartment in Kreuzberg I once had?" she asks. Roth gazes at Wiener as she looks to the camera. They are making toast. Wiener has the jam. Between dashes in her letter she remarks fondly and with irony, "Exciting times it seems to me." On the photo, she draws lines to the figure of Roth and writes "DU" (you) and to herself, writing "ICH" (me). "Do you remember?" she asks.[85] Wiener is joking of course. But her letter also registers an amazement that, over twenty years, these two figures are still supposed to correspond to the same "you" and "me."

Korrespondenz Teppich is a work of feminist in-action because it tends to and takes in such "scraps of life," which otherwise just drop out of the picture. These are not rescued to be ennobled as works of art in their own right; they are preserved in all their scrappiness. This archiving of extimacy keeps Wiener and Roth together, despite considerable distances between them in time and space and periods of estrangement and depression. Their tapestry collaboration attends to the affects and cares that exasperate the ideal of seamless correspondence, weaving on and on and working through their relationship without privileging any one position or form of authorship. It shows life lived not as an account of actions and accomplishments, but as incidental correspondences, the tone and significance of which change over time. What I hope to have shown is how performance art history can be a genre of writing that patiently responds to such intractable cares, which might otherwise be forgotten in the name of action.

Acknowledgments

First and foremost, I would like to acknowledge all those whose performances I discuss in this book, some of whom alas have died in the time it has taken me to complete it. I wish Günter Brus could have seen it. I so enjoyed my discussions with him and Anna Brus at their home in Styria, where they welcomed me, at the time a graduate student, with such kindness, and we looked together at old photographs, picture-poems, and the impish early issues of *Schastrommel*. After characteristic reluctance to speak about herself when we first met at the Third Oswald Wiener Symposium in Mürzzuschlag, Ingrid Wiener has shared with me over many years her memories, her archive, her home, her loom, and her love of Austrian cooking. Most recently, I have enjoyed lively correspondence with Hanel Koeck. Early on, Ingrid's weaving changed the way I see; with time I learned from Anna's performances how to look; and Hanel finally showed me what not to overlook. This book shares what I learned from these three women and is dedicated to my intrepid students in Vienna.

At the University of Chicago, Christine Mehring, Ralph Ubl, and Matthew Jesse Jackson were my inspiring advisers, and I remain thankful for their continuing support of my work. Tom Gunning, Wu Hung, Aden Kumler, and David Wellbery modeled ways of thinking that I continue to value. It was in a seminar on European art with Benjamin Buchloh that I first encountered, with some horror, Viennese Actionism as an undergrad at Harvard. The same semester, I walked out of Oliver Simons's screening of Peter Haneke's adaptation of Elfriede Jelinek's *Die Klavierspielerin*. Today I am grateful for those provocations. Reading Walter Benjamin in Holger Brohm's seminars while studying *Kulturwissenschaft* at the Humboldt University of Berlin led me back to art history.

From an early stage, Susan Bielstein showed interest in this book, and her conviction gave me confidence as I saw it through to completion. At the University of Chicago Press, Karen Levine graciously took it on after Susan retired, and I thank her and Victoria Barry for guiding me to production. I am honored to be included in the Abakanowicz Arts and Culture Collection. My thanks to the whole team at the press extend especially to Yves Cao, Katherine Faydash, Jenni Fry, Adrienne Meyers, and Christine Schwab. Production has been generously supported by the Johns Hopkins Department of the History of Art, the Office of the Dean of the Krieger School of Arts and Sciences at Johns Hopkins, the American Council for Learned Societies (ACLS), and the University of Chicago Alumni Publication Grant. Early versions of chapter 2 and chapter 4 appeared as "On Failing to Perform: *Kunst und Revolution*, Vienna 1968" (*October*) and "Feminist In-action: Ingrid Wiener's Tapestry Collaborations" (*FKW//Zeitschrift für Geschlechterforschung und visuelle Kultur*).

This project benefited from several fellowships: the Hervé de la Vauvre Fellowship, with thanks to Françoise Meltzer for the colloquium at the France Chicago Center in Paris; the Fulbright-IFK (Internationales Forschungszentrum Kulturwissenschaften) Fellowship in Vienna, where Helmut Lethen and Ingo Zechner offered an engaging program; a Library Research Grant at the Getty Research Institute; the fellowship of the Berlin Program for Advanced German and European Studies; and a University of Chicago Provost's Dissertation Completion Fellowship. A Getty-ACLS Postdoctoral Fellowship in History of Art supported a year of intense rethinking and revision in Vienna at the height of COVID-19.

As I began research in Austria as a graduate student, Thomas Eder was a generous source of information and support, Eva Badura-Triska shared her expertise, and Peter Weibel met with me and responded to my queries. In the intervening years, many other individuals in Austria, France, Germany, Switzerland, and the United States have supported my research, and I would especially like to thank Roman Grabner, director of the BRUSEUM – Universalmuseum Joanneum in Graz; Claudia Freiberger and Marie-Therese Hochwartner of mumok – Museum moderner Kunst Stiftung Ludwig in Vienna; and the team at the Literaturarchiv of the Austrian National Library in Vienna. In Chicago, Ira Wool and Barbara Mirecki hosted me in their wonderful collection. Most recently, Christa Noel Robbins invited me to the Modern & Contemporary Culture Workshop at the University of Virginia, and I thank her and the participants, especially Paul Dobryden and David Getsy, for their feedback. Since we started grad school together, Jadine Collingwood and Jennifer Sichel have remained respected and dear friends. My thanks to Jadine for comments on the manuscript at a most opportune moment and to Jenn for being my trusted writing and reading companion along the way.

Following my PhD, I was very pleased to join Sebastian Egenhofer's unit for modern and contemporary art at the University of Vienna. My years in Vienna were enriched by conversations with colleagues and friends: Noit Banai, Rosemarie Brucher, Hannah Bruckmüller, Sabeth Buchmann, Máté Csanda, Sandra Eichinger, Lilien Lisbeth Feledy, Anna Frasca-Rath, Fani Gargova, Elisabeth Goldarbeiter-Liskar, Rose-Anne Gush, Sandra Hindriks, Amanda Holmes, Eva Horn, Eva Kernbauer, Stefanie Kitzberger, Marthe Kretzschmar, Alexi Kukuljevic, Sebastian Lederle, Michaela Leutzendorff Pakesch, Magdalena Nieslony, Peter Pakesch, Wolfram Pichler, Stefanie Proksch-Weilguni, Luise Reitstätter, Christian Scherrer, Jordan Troeller, and last but not least

Nora Mészáros, who also provided invaluable research assistance. Organizing the symposium "Untimely Media/Domestic Techniques—The 60s and 70s between New York and Vienna" with Barbara Reisinger was a highlight. In addition to the local participants named above, my thanks to those who traveled to join us for exciting exchanges: Julia Bryan-Wilson, Larne Abse Gogarty, Antje Krause-Wahl, Kevin Lotery, Megan Luke, Christine Mehring, Jennifer Sichel, T'ai Smith, and Mechtild Widrich. In 2022, a Guest Professorship at the Berlin University of the Arts (UdK) afforded great inspiration and transition. My gratitude to the brilliant students I taught there and to Monica Bonvicini, Alexander García Düttmann, Heike-Karin Föll, Thilo Heinzmann, Antonia Kölbl, David Misteli, Stefan Neuner, Barbara Wittmann, and Thomas Zipp.

Since I joined the faculty of History of Art at Johns Hopkins, Rebecca Brown, Stephen Campbell, Lisa DeLeonardis, Marian Feldman, Aaron Hyman, Mia Liu, Mitchell Merback, Ünver Rüstem, Jennifer Stager, Daniel Weiss, and Nino Zchomelidse have given me such a happy and stimulating intellectual home. I am grateful to each of my new colleagues for welcoming me so warmly to Baltimore; to Aaron, Jen, and Rebecca for reading chapters; and to Mitch for teaching the course Vulnerable Images with me, which invigorated my thinking about performance art. It has been a privilege to work with graduate students at JHU, and my special thanks go to Clare Frances Kemmerer, Jason Mientkiewicz, Marco Pomini, and Carter Salis for engaging conversations. Donald Juedes contributed extraordinary support to my research at the Sheridan Library and Winston Tabb Special Collections Research Center; Lael Ensor-Bennett offered expertise with a number of difficult images; and Lauren Crabtree and Viktoria Waith have made everyday life in the department a pleasure. The community of students and faculty associated with the Program for the Study of Women, Gender, and Sexuality has been a most rewarding source of intellectual and social exchange. My thanks in particular to Jennifer Culbert for welcoming me into the fold. And for intellectual comradery and friendship grown in Baltimore, my affectionate thanks to Jo Giardini, Jacob Haubenreich, and Catherine Popovici.

My fondest thanks to Elizabeth Lewis for her encouragement and careful reading, to Peter Robinson for his steadfast optimism, and to my life-partner, Benjamin Lewis Robinson, for all that we share. Finally and most of all, to my parents, Rebecca and Kenneth Schopp, siblings, Charlie and Catherine, and Oma: Thank you for your unwavering love and belief in me.

Notes

All translations from German into English are the author's own unless otherwise noted.

Introduction

1 Arthur Danto, "Danger and Disturbation: The Art of Marina Abramović," in *Marina Abramović: The Artist Is Present*, ed. Klaus Biesenbach (Museum of Modern Art, New York, 2010), 31. An early version of this essay names "Rudolph Schwartzkogler [*sic*]" as "a kind of fool" for dying by way of "self-administered mutilations." Arthur Danto, "Art and Disturbation" (1985), in *The Philosophical Disenfranchisement of Art* (Columbia University Press, 1986), 123.

2 The most important overview of Schwarzkogler's work, published on the occasion of his only comprehensive retrospective, remains Eva Badura-Triska and Hubert Klocker, eds., *Rudolf Schwarzkogler: Leben und Werk* (Ritter Verlag, 1992), partially translated into French and reprinted as *Rudolf Schwarzkogler: Photographies d'actions, Vienne 1965–66* (Centre Pompidou, 1993). In these volumes, Schwarzkogler's death is not mistaken as a performance. The dedicated "internationales Kompetenzzentrum für Wiener Aktionismus" (international center of expertise for Viennese Actionism) at mumok – Museum moderner Kunst Stiftung Ludwig in Vienna published a long-awaited compendium of Viennese Actionism in 2012. See Eva Badura-Triska, Hubert Klocker, and Museum moderner Kunst Stiftung Ludwig, eds., *Wiener Aktionismus: Kunst und Aufbruch im Wien der 1960er-Jahre* (Verlag der Buchhandlung Walther König, 2012); Eva Badura-Triska, Hubert Klocker, and Museum moderner Kunst Stiftung Ludwig, eds., *Vienna Actionism: Art and Upheaval in 1960s' Vienna*, trans. Thomas Morrison, Christina Oberstebrink, Michael Turnbull, and Mark Willard (Verlag der Buchhandlung Walther König, 2012). For an incisive critical review of the latter two volumes, see Mechtild Widrich, "Lights, Camera, Action!," *Art Journal* 71, no. 4 (2012): 122–24. For a good overview in English of the artist's works and writings, see Malcolm Green, ed. and trans., *Brus, Muehl, Nitsch, Schwarzkogler: Writings of the Viennese Actionists* (Atlas, 1999).

3 Philip Ursprung's otherwise excellent introduction to Viennese Actionism takes part in this reception when he writes that "the actions of Günter Brus, Otto Mühl, Hermann Nitsch, and Rudolf Schwarzkogler" perform "shocking quasi-religious rituals of self-castration, rape, and slaughter using excrement, food, blood, and dead animals staged in secluded old coal-cellars and ruined castles." Philip Ursprung, "'Catholic Tastes': Hurting and Healing the Body in Viennese Actionism in the 1960s," in *Performing the Body, Performing the Text*, ed. Amelia Jones and Andrew Stephenson (Routledge, 1999), 138.

4 Günter Brus's performances involving cutting include *Der helle Wahnsinn* (1968), *Kunst und Revolution* (1968), *Strangulation* (1968), *Psychodramolette* (1970), and *Zerreißprobe* (1970).

For an overview of Muehl, see the retrospective exhibition catalog *Otto Muehl: Leben/Kunst/Werk; Aktion Utopie Malerei 1960–2004*, ed. Peter Noever (König, 2003), and the catalog of his complete works, Hubert Klocker, *Otto Muehl: Works 1956–2010* (Schlebrügge, 2019). For an overview of Nitsch, see the catalog inaugurating the founding of his dedicated museum, Museumzentrum Mistelbach, ed., *Hermann Nitsch Museum* (Hatje Cantz, 2007), and the publications dedicated to his "Six Day Play," still hosted after the artist's death by the Nitsch Foundation: Otmar Rychlik, ed., *Hermann Nitsch: Das Sechstagespiel des Orgien Mysterien Theaters 1998* (Hatje Cantz, 2003).

5 On misogyny, see Lea Vergine, *Body Art and Performance: The Body as Language*, trans. Henry Martin (1974; repr., Skira, 2000), 20. On sadism and extreme violence, see Adrian Henri, *Total Art: Environments, Happenings, and Performance* (Praeger Publishers, 1974), 168–69. On fascistic violence, see Werner Hofmann, "Die Wiener Aktionisten," in *Luther und die Folgen für die Kunst*, ed. Werner Hofmann (Prestel Verlag, 1983), 642. On Muehl, Nitsch, and satanic cult, see Gerhard P. Zacharias, *Satanskult und Schwarze Messe: Ein Beitrag zur Phänomenologie der Religion* (Limes Verlag, 1964), 151–63.

6 Carrie Lambert-Beatty, "Against Performance Art: On the Art of Marina Abramović," *Artforum*, May 2010, 210.

7 Danto, "Danger and Disturbation," 31. In his reference to Acconci, Burden, and Abramović, Danto presents an archive of performance art first collected in English-language art criticism in the 1970s and established in formative art histories of performance art, including Kathy O'Dell, *Contract with the Skin: Masochism, Performance Art, and the 1970s* (University of Minnesota Press, 1998), and Frazer Ward, *No Innocent Bystanders: Performance Art and Audience* (Dartmouth College Press, 2012).

8 See Genesis P. Orridge and Peter Christopherson, "COUM TRANSMISSIONS: Annihilating Reality," in *Performance by Artists*, ed. A. A. Bronson and Peggy Gale (Art Metropole, 1979), 65–71; Sven Drühl, "Düstere Legenden: Vom Mythos des Suizids und der Autoamputation in der Aktionskunst," *Kunstforum* 153 (2000): 74–82.

9 On Schwarzkogler's "unfortunate fate," see Sophie Delpeux, "L'imaginaire à l'Action: L'infortune critique de Rudolf Schwarzkogler," *Études Photographiques* 7 (May 2000): 1–9. On the "redemption" and "resurrection" of the artist, see Kristine Stiles, "Notes on Rudolf Schwarzkogler's Images of Healing," *White Walls*, Spring 1990, 11–26. On his "masochistic and ultimately fatal" art, see Günter Berghaus, "Happenings in Europe: Trends, Events, and Leading Figures," in *Happenings and Other Acts*, ed. Mariellen R. Sandford (Routledge, 1995), 368. On his "narcissism and solipsism," see Stuart Morgan, "Schwarzkogler: The Mystery of St. Rudolf," *Art Monthly*, June 1993, 14. On his "productive melancholy," see Peter Gorsen, "Rudolf Schwarzkogler und die Urphantasien der Wiener Aktionskunst," in *Ich bin tausend Ich: Probleme, Zugänge und Konzepte zur Therapie von Psychosen*, ed. Michael Ertl, Brigitta Keintzel, and Rudolf P. Wagner (Facultas, 2002), 366.

10 Elise Archias, *The Concrete Body: Yvonne Rainer, Carolee Schneemann, Vito Acconci* (Yale University Press, 2016); Rebecca Schneider, *The Explicit Body in Performance* (Routledge, 1997); Amelia Jones, *Body Art/Performing the Subject* (University of Minnesota Press, 1998).

11 Günter Brus, "Rudolf Schwarzkogler," *Die Schastrommel: Organ der österreichischen Exilregierung* 3 (1970): unpaginated. See also Stiles, "Notes on Rudolf Schwarzkogler," 12. This performance is *Aktionskonzert für Al Hansen* (1966).

12 Lawrence Alloway, "'Reality': Ideology at D5," *Artforum*, October 1972, 30; Harald Szeemann, with Hanns Sohm, eds., *Happening & Fluxus: Materialien* (Kölnischer Kunstverein, 1970).

13 Reiner Speck, "Kassel sehen und sterben," *Deutsches Ärzteblatt*, August 17, 1972, 2172, newspaper clipping, D5 box 11, *documenta archiv*, Kassel, Germany.

14 Artists were not present on site at *documenta 5* for the entire one hundred days, as one reviewer laments. See Klaus-Dieter Heinrich, "In Kassel endet Kunst oft in der Sackgasse," *Allgäuer Zeitung*, August 23, 1972, unpaginated. Documentation of the reception and preparation for the exhibition, including layout, in D5 boxes 86–88, *documenta archiv*, Kassel, Germany. The catalog for *documenta 5*, a large plastic binder with a cover designed by Ed Ruscha, contains floor plans and brief sketches of each artist's work. See Harald Szeemann, *Documenta 5: Befragung der Realität. Bildwelten heute: Verzeichnis der ausgestellten Werke, der präsentierten Situation, der erwartbaren Ereignisse, ihrer Beschaffenheit, ihrer Hersteller und Besitzer* (Documenta, 1972). On *documenta 5* as a staging ground for performance art history, see Caroline Lillian Schopp, "Active Duty: On the Art of Franz Erhard Walther," *Artforum*, February 2018, 167–74; Dominic Johnson, "Delete the Idea Down: James Lee Byars and the Performance of Abbreviation," *Art Journal* 80, no. 2 (2021): 30–53.

15 This discussion, and documentation of the protests, takes place in the founding issue of the West German journal for art and culture, *interfunktionen*, edited by Friedrich W. Heubach. See "documenta—documentation," special issue, *interfunktionen* 1 (Verlag Heubach, 1968). Maintaining the political impulse of the journal, Benjamin H. D. Buchloh assumed the role of editor in 1974. See Christine Mehring, "Continental Schrift: The Story of *Interfunktionen*," *Artforum*, May 2004, 178–83, 233.

16 On *documenta 4*, see Janni Müller-Hauck, ed., *4. documenta: Internationale Ausstellung*, 3 vols. (Druck + Verlag, 1968). On the prevalence of the happening and fluxus in the international art of the period, see Catherine Spencer, *Beyond the Happening: Performance Art and the Politics of Communication* (Manchester University Press, 2020); Natilee Harren, *Fluxus Forms: Scores, Multiples, and the Eternal Network* (University of Chicago Press, 2020).

17 For this very reason, ironically, many US artists withdrew their work, refusing, as Robert Morris put it, to have it "used to illustrate misguided sociological principles or outmoded art historical categories." Morris was joined by Carl Andre, Donald Judd, Fred Sandback, and Robert Smithson in petitioning *documenta 5*. His letter to Szeemann is housed in D5 box 62, *documenta archiv*, Kassel, and reprinted in François Aubart and Florence Derieux, eds., *Harald Szeemann: Individual Methodology* (JRP Ringier Kunstverlag, 2007), 144.

18 Of the 222 artists included, 17 were women. Szeemann's exchange with Lucy Lippard is exemplary of his sexism. He asked for her help contacting women artists, then did not follow up with them. Lippard's furious letter to Szeemann, beginning, "Who the hell are you calling a whore?" is reprinted in Glenn Phillips, ed., *Harald Szeemann: Museum of Obsessions* (Getty Research Institute, 2018), 365–66. Further criticism in this vein is excerpted in Aubart and Derieux, *Harald Szeemann*, 130–46.

19 On the history of the *documenta* exhibition, see Harald Kimpel, *Documenta: Mythos und Wirklichkeit* (DuMont, 1997); Dieter Westecker, ed., *Documenta-Dokumente: 1955–1968, 4 internationale Ausstellungen moderner Kunst; Texte und Fotografien* (Wenderoth, 1972).

20 Heinrich, "In Kassel endet Kunst oft in der Sackgasse," unpaginated.

21 Exhibition map in Szeemann, *Befragung der Realität*, unpaginated, and reproduced in Aubart and Derieux, *Harald Szeemann*, 108. Szeemann's correspondence with Nitsch, who informs him about the work of Brus and Schwarzkogler, is housed in D5 boxes 55a and 70, *documenta archiv*. Szeemann requests materials by "Franz [*sic*] Schwarzkogler" from Schwarzkogler's partner Edith Adam in a letter dated February 28, 1972, D5 box 54, *documenta archiv*. Muehl was not included.

22 See Hermann Nitsch, *Das Orgien Mysterien Theater: Die Partituren aller aufgeführten Aktionen 1960–1979; Erster Band: 1.–32. Aktion* (Studio Morra, 1979); Hermann Nitsch, *Das Orgien Mysterien Theater: Die Partituren aller aufgeführten Aktionen 1960–1979; Zweiter Band: 33.–65. Aktion* (Studio Morra, 1986).

23 Birgitte Pohl, "Wiener Verstärkung für die 'documenta'—Österreichs Antikünstler emigrieren nach Kassel," *Deutsche Wochenzeitung Hannover*, June 30, 1972, newspaper clipping, D5 box 6, *documenta archiv*. Program for the "documenta filmschau" at the Kino Royal reprinted in Aubart and Derieux, *Harald Szeemann*, 110–13. Also exhibited were original illustrations from Brus's artist's book *Irrwisch* (Imp, 1971).

24 Neither the *documenta archiv* in Kassel nor the Harald Szeemann papers in Los Angeles includes complete documentation of the installation of Schwarzkogler's work. Series IV, Photographs; Series IV.A, Projects: Documenta 5: Questioning reality—Image worlds today (Documenta 5: Befragung der Realität - Bildwelten heute), Harald Szeemann Papers, Getty Research Center.

25 The ordering and numbering of Schwarzkogler's performances was undertaken by his friends after his death. While the catalog for *documenta 5* lists seven actions, more authoritative accounts of Schwarzkogler's work list six, with 5a and 5b closely related. See Badura-Triska and Klocker, *Rudolf Schwarzkogler*, 157–59; Peter Coeln and Marie Röbl, eds., *Rudolf Schwarzkogler: Aktionsfotografie* (WestLicht, Schauplatz für Fotografie, 2012).

26 The exceptions are the documents of *6. Aktion*, two photographs of which can be seen in figure I.6: the second from the left in the upper row, in which Schwarzkogler is wrapped from head to toe in gauze, and the furthest right in the lower row, a dead chicken. Schwarzkogler's hands gut the fish in *2. Aktion*, three photographs of which appear in the bottom row. The remaining photographs in the upper row, from left to right, show Cibulka in *4. Aktion* and then *3. Aktion*.

27 This specific photo, which foregrounds the collaborative aspect of Schwarzkogler's performance art, was also included in the exhibition *Bodyworks*, Museum of Contemporary Art, Chicago, March 8–April 27, 1975.

28 Heinrich, "In Kassel endet Kunst oft in der Sackgasse," unpaginated.

29 Ingobert Jungnitz, "Befragung der Realität? Eine Dokumentation gesellschaftlicher Neurosen," *Petrusblatt*, July 1972, newspaper clipping, D5 box 10, *documenta archiv*, Kassel. Muehl is included in this diagnosis even though his work was not exhibited at *documenta 5*.

30 For a compelling elucidation of how stereotypes of Austrian sexuality took hold, see David S. Luft, *Eros and Inwardness in Vienna: Weininger, Musil, Doderer* (University of Chicago Press, 2003).

31 Harold Rosenberg, "On the Edge: Documenta 5," in *Art on the Edge: Creators and Situations* (Macmillan, 1975), 272, 271, 271. First published as Harold Rosenberg, "Inquiry '72: On the Edge, Documenta 5," *New Yorker*, September 9, 1972. A year later, Rosenberg's statement was echoed in the claim that "the self-castration of Rudolf Schwarzkoggler [*sic*]" was a "shock to morality, not to sensibility." See Paul Stitelman, "Notes on the Absorption of the Avant-Garde into the Culture," *Arts Magazine*, May–June 1973, 56.

32 Hilton Kramer, "Documenta 5: The Bayreuth of the Neo-Dadaist," *New York Times*, July 9, 1972.

33 Lizzie Borden, "Cosmologies," *Artforum*, October 1972, 45.

34 Robert Hughes, "The Decline and Fall of the Avant-Garde," *Time*, December 1972, 111–12.

35 Robert Hughes, "The Decline and Fall of the Avant-Garde," in *Idea Art: A Critical Anthology*, ed. Gregory Battcock (E. P. Dutton & Co., 1973), 184–94. Beyond art history, the "Viennese artist Rudolf Schwarzkogler" is named as an example of the extreme pathology of "mutilation of the skin." Didier Anzieu, *The Skin Ego*, trans. Chris Turner (Yale University Press, 1989), 20.

36 Serge Guilbaut, *How New York Stole the Idea of Modern Art from Europe: Abstract Expressionism, Freedom, and the Cold War* (University of Chicago Press, 1983).

37 Kristine Stiles, "Synopsis of the Destruction in Art Symposium (DIAS) and Its Theoretical Significance," *The Act* (1987), 27.

38 Henry Sayre, *The Object of Performance: The American Avant-Garde Since 1970* (University of Chicago Press, 1989), 2. See the scathing review by Kristine Stiles, "Performance and Its Objects," *Arts Magazine*, November 1990, 35–47. For additional mistakings, see Bronson and Gale, *Performance by Artists* (1974), 69; Thomas McEvilley, "Art After Dark" *Artforum*, Summer 1983, 66; Danto, "Art and Disturbation," 123. For corrections of the mistake following Stiles, see William Martin, "The Death and Times of Rudolf Schwarzkogler," *Art Criticism* 19, no. 2 (2004): 56–65; Susan Jarosi, "The Image of the Artist in Performance Art: The Case of Rudolf Schwarzkogler," *Sztuka i Dokumentacja* 8 (2013): 65–77.

39 This is in stark contrast to German-language art history. In none of their own writings or publications do Brus, Muehl, Nitsch, or their Austrian affiliates make this mistake—but neither do they go to the trouble to redress it. See Peter Weibel and VALIE EXPORT, eds., *wien: bildkompendium wiener aktionismus und film* (Kohlkunstverlag, 1970). At the same time as the Sayre-Stiles exchange, the first major traveling exhibition of Viennese Actionism took place, and the two catalogs offer a valuable though flawed bilingual overview. See Museum Fridericianum Kassel, Kunst Museum Winterthur, and Scottish National Gallery of Art Edinburgh, eds., *Von der Aktionsmalerei zum Aktionismus, Wien 1960–1965/From Action Painting to Actionism, Vienna 1960–1965: Günter Brus, Adolf Frohner, Otto Mühl, Hermann Nitsch, Alfons Schilling, Rudolf Schwarzkogler* (Ritter Verlag, 1988); Hubert Klocker, ed., *Der zertrümmerte Spiegel: Wiener Aktionismus, Wien 1960–1971/The Shattered Mirror: Viennese Actionism, Vienna 1960–1971: Günter Brus, Otto Mühl, Hermann Nitsch, Rudolf Schwarzkogler* (Ritter Verlag, 1989).

40 Jones, *Body Art*, 125. Jones's first reflections on Schwarzkogler are instigated by Stiles's review of Sayre's book. Jones argues that the photographic "documents" of Schwarzkogler's work cannot be taken to show a "truth" not because the artist is not shown dying in them, but because the performance is an "entirely faked ritual castration." Amelia Jones, "'Presence' in Absentia: Experiencing Performance as Documentation," *Art Journal* 56, no. 4 (1997): 15–16. Schwarzkogler is not included in Amelia Jones, "Dis/playing the Phallus: Male Artists Perform Their Masculinities," *Art History* 17, no. 4 (1994): 546–84.

41 Amelia Jones, "Survey," in *The Artist's Body*, ed. Tracey Warr (Phaidon, 2000), 32.

42 Amelia Jones, "Performing the Wounded Body: Pain, Affect and the Radical Relationality of Meaning," *parallax* 15, no. 4 (2009): 47.

43 Jones, "Performing the Wounded Body," 49, 54. Jones maintains this position in Amelia Jones, *In Between Subjects: A Critical Genealogy of Queer Performance* (Routledge, 2021).

44 Jones, "Survey," 32.

45 Jones, "Survey," 32. Jones's incorrect use of the date 1969 has persisted in the reprints of this important book, including the 2006 paperback and the 2012 "abridged, revised and updated" version.

46 The alternative account of Viennese performance art I am proposing resonates with Dominic Johnson's counterhistory, *Unlimited Action: The Performance of Extremity in the 1970s* (Manchester University Press, 2019). While Johnson addresses the paradox of extreme action as that which is "*too much*, as well as *not enough*" (11), I would suggest the case of Schwarzkogler is "too much" on account of being "not enough." Johnson resists "contributing another coinage to a repertoire of unwanted designations" for extreme actions (21); I find it nonetheless necessary to propose the term *in-action* to refer to performances mistaken for "extreme actions."

47 In Schwarzkogler's performance art, the exposed body is not "taken to be an unambiguous (as well as timeless and universal) sign for binary gender." It offers what David Getsy calls "multiplicity." David J. Getsy, "How to Teach Manet's *Olympia* After Transgender Studies," *Art History* 45, no. 2 (2022): 349.

48 Schwarzkogler carefully selected and cropped the photographs of his performances that were printed in his lifetime. See Hubert Klocker, "Das aktionsphotographische Oeuvre: Gestaltung und Organisation," in Badura-Triska and Klocker, *Rudolf Schwarzkogler*, 139–47.

49 Largely overlooked and mistaken in art history, Heinz Cibulka devoted a long poem to his body in performances with Nitsch and Schwarzkogler. Describing himself, intriguingly, as "male body / model / passive actor" (*Männlicher körper / Modell / Passiver akteur*), he reflects: "My body is intentional / knows of no intention / feeds on itself / flows into everything / is the brother of all volcanoes and of all flying seminal bodies." Heinz Cibulka, *Mein körper bei aktionen von Nitsch und Schwarzkogler/Il mio corpo nelle azioni di Nitsch e Schwarzkogler 1965–1975* (Edizioni Morra, 1975), unpaginated.

50 I draw on Jennifer Doyle, *Hold It Against Me: Difficulty and Emotion in Contemporary Art* (Duke University Press, 2013).

51 Stiles, "Notes on Rudolf Schwarzkogler," 12–13. A modified version of this essay appears in Kristine Stiles, *Concerning Consequences: Studies in Art, Destruction, and Trauma* (University of Chicago Press, 2017), 274–83. See also Gerald Schröder, "Schnitt-Techniken. Zur Inszenierung von Schmerz in der Fotografie Rudolf Schwarzkoglers," in *Schmerzensmänner: Trauma und Therapie in der westdeutschen und österreichischen Kunst der 1960er Jahre* (Wilhelm Fink, 2011), 421–53. Schröder reads Schwarzkogler's work, which he insists is "staged photography" of "staged pain," as a confrontation with the violence of Nazism and the Holocaust.

52 Kristine Stiles, "Introduction," *White Walls*, Spring 1990, 9.

53 Stiles, "Notes on Rudolf Schwarzkogler," 13, 15, 23. In 2017 Stiles revised the concluding line of her essay with the following emphasis: "In highly compacted arcane signifiers of regeneration and transformation, Schwarzkogler opposed death with the fragility of mortality, seeking to redefine fragmentation in terms of the contingency of suffering bodies in strange forms of resurrection." Stiles, *Concerning Consequences*, 283.

54 See Franziska Meifert, "Zweimal Geborene: Der 'Wiener Aktionismus' im Spiegel von Mythen, Riten und Geschichten," *Protokolle: Zeitschrift für Literatur und Kunst* 1 (1990): 3–63; Lázsló Földényi, "Purgatory of the Senses: Rudolf Schwarzkogler (1940–1969)," trans. Hans Skirecki, *Parkett* 36 (1993): 137.

55 Kristine Stiles, "Uncorrupted Joy: International Art Actions," in *Out of Actions: Between Performance and the Object, 1949–1979*, ed. Paul Schimmel (Thames and Hudson, 1998), 235.

56 Kristine Stiles, "Performance," in *Critical Terms for Art History*, 2nd ed., ed. Robert S. Nelson and Richard Shiff (University of Chicago Press, 2003), 85. The first edition of 1996 includes no entry on performance.

57 RoseLee Goldberg, *Performance: Live Art 1909 to the Present* (Harry N. Abrams, 1979), 125, reprinted by Abrams as *Performance Art: From Futurism to the Present* in 1988 and twice more as *Performance Art: From Futurism to the Present* (Thames & Hudson, 2001, 2011).

58 Goldberg, *Performance* (1979), 106; Goldberg, *Performance* (1988), 106; Goldberg, *Performance Art* (2011), 165. Given his misspelling of Schwarzkogler's name, it is likely that Danto first encountered it by way of Goldberg's text, which does not include any images of the work.

59 Mechtild Widrich, *Performative Monuments—The Rematerialisation of Public Art* (Manchester University Press, 2014), 53–101; Weibel and VALIE EXPORT, *wien: bildkompendium*. The editors intentionally used lowercase proper nouns. See also Rüdiger Engerth, "Der Wiener

Aktionismus," *Protokolle: Wiener Jahresschrift für Literatur, bildende Kunst und Musik* (1970): 152–69, which makes no reference to Weibel and VALIE EXPORT's book.

60 Weibel himself would subsequently lament how much discussion of the work of individual artists affiliated with Viennese Actionism had suffered from an undifferentiated *Aktionsbegriff* (concept of action). Peter Weibel, "Zur Aktionskunst von Günter Brus," in *Günter Brus: Der Überblick*, ed. Hildegund Amanshauser, Dieter Ronte, and Museum Moderner Kunst Wien (Residenz Verlag, 1986), 37.

61 Günter Brus, "Ausscheidungskämpfe. Das Spiel mit Daten als Wettbewerb," in *Die Schastrommel: Organ der österreichischen Exilregierung* 3 (West Berlin, 1970), unpaginated.

62 Hermann Nitsch, "rudolf schwarzkogler," in Weibel and VALIE EXPORT, *wien: bildkompendium*, 281, 282. See also Hermann Nitsch, "Rudolf Schwarzkogler," *Protokolle: Wiener Jahresschrift für Literatur, bildende Kunst und Musik* 1 (1971): 146–57, in which he never uses the phrase *Wiener Aktionismus*.

63 Heinz Ohff, *Anti-Kunst* (Droste, 1973). The book includes a dedicated section on Joseph Beuys and, in direct reference to *documenta 5*, a section called "Individuelle Mythologie" that considers the work of Nitsch, Muehl, and Schwarzkogler.

64 See A1 Informationen Verlagsgesellschaft, ed., *Aktionsraum 1: Oder 57 Blindenhunde* (A1 Informationen Verlagsgesellschaft, 1971); Szeemann and Sohm, *Happening & Fluxus*; Szeemann, *Befragung der Realität*.

65 On Beuys, see Uwe M. Schneede, ed., *Joseph Beuys, die Aktionen: Kommentiertes Werkverzeichnis mit fotografischen Dokumentationen* (G. Hatje, 1994); Claudia Mesch and Viola Maria Michely, eds., *Joseph Beuys: The Reader* (MIT Press, 2017).

66 On Vostell, see René Block, *Wolf Vostell: Dé-collagen: 1954–69: Plakate, Verwischungen, Objekte, Happening Partituren, Happening Fall Outs, Elektronische Verwischungen, Elektronische Objekte*, Galerie Block Edition 17 (Galerie René Block, 1969); Rolf Wedewer, ed., *Vostell* (Edition Braus, 1992); Caroline Lillian Schopp, "Concrete Violence: Wolf Vostell's Disasters of War," *Oxford Art Journal* 44, no. 2 (2021): 307–30.

67 The stem *akt* does not appear in the *Deutsches Wörterbuch von Jacob Grimm und Wilhelm Grimm*, published 1852–1854. Two stems are imported: the verbal *act*, "to do," with *ācta*, the filing of papers and recording of public events; and the nominal *Acteur*, or "actor," specifically in a theatrical context. See the entry "Aktion" in *Digitales Wörterbuch der deutschen Sprache* (https://www.dwds.de).

68 Edited by Franz Pfemfert, *Die Aktion* was a weekly publication dedicated to revolutionary socialism featuring the writings of Lenin, Rosa Luxemburg, Karl Liebknecht, and Leon Trotsky and the poetry and prose of the contemporary avant-garde. See Lothar Lang and Reinhild Schneider, eds., *Franz Pfemfert und die 'Aktion': Zeitschrift und Verlag 1911–1932* (Staatliches Museum Schloss Burgk, Pirckheimer-Kabinett, 1982).

69 See Frank Böckelmann and Herbert Nagel, eds., *Subversive Aktion: Der Sinn der Organisation ist ihr Scheitern* (Neue Kritik, 2002).

70 Wolf Vostell, *Aktionen: Happenings und Demonstrationen seit 1965* (Rowohlt, 1970); Udo Kultermann, *Leben und Kunst. Zur Funktion von Intermedia* (Verlag Ernst Wasmuth, 1970); Jürgen Schilling, *Aktionskunst: Identität von Kunst und Leben? Eine Dokumentation* (C. J. Bucher, 1978). Additional titles include Heinz Ohff and Wolf Vostell, eds., *Pop und die Folgen: Oder, Die Kunst, Kunst auf der Strasse zu finden* (Droste Verlag, 1968); Wolf Vostell, *Happening & Leben* (Luchterhand Verlag, 1970); Ohff, *Anti-Kunst* (1973).

71 Schilling, *Aktionskunst*, 148–63.

72 Schilling, *Aktionskunst*, 159. Schilling is in fact aware that Schwarzkogler's "auto-amputation" is a myth and contextualizes his negative psychologizing reception in the wake of *documenta*

5, connecting Schwarzkogler's work, as others would go on to do, with the "masochism" of Acconci and Burden.

73 Jürgen Becker and Wolf Vostell, eds., *Happenings. Fluxus. Pop art. Nouveau réalisme. Eine Dokumentation* (Rowohlt, 1965); Allan Kaprow, *Assemblage, Environments & Happenings* (Harry N. Abrams, 1966). Kaprow and Vostell met through Dick Higgins and Alison Knowles, whom Vostell knew from the First Fluxus Festival in Wiesbaden in 1962. In 1963 and 1964, Vostell traveled to New York and met Kaprow. This importation can also be traced in the pages of the Swiss journal for "new art" *artis: Zeitschrift für neue Kunst* in articles by the German art historian Udo Kultermann throughout the mid-1960s. See, e.g., Udo Kultermann, "Happenings Wiege stand in Osaka," *artis: Zeitschrift für neue Kunst* 18 (1966): 26–28.

74 Günter Brus refers to this US and West German cohort as the "Edelhapper" (noble happers). In his review, which comparatively treats Vostell and Becker's documentation with Weibel and VALIE EXPORT's, as well as Kultermann's book, Brus directs much ire against this origin story. Brus, "Ausscheidungskämpfe," unpaginated.

75 Allan Kaprow, "The Legacy of Jackson Pollock," *Artnews* (1958): 26 and 56, italics original.

76 Kaprow, "Legacy," 57.

77 Harold Rosenberg, "The American Action Painters" (1952), in *The Tradition of the New* (Thames and Hudson, 1962), 28. Rosenberg and Kaprow were in dialogue about their shared vocabularies and ideas circa 1968. See Eva Ehninger, "What's Happening? Allan Kaprow and Claes Oldenburg Argue About Art and Life," *Getty Research Journal* 6 (2014): 195–202.

78 Rosenberg, "American Action Painters," 30, 25. Ironically, the transformation of the pictorial field of painting into an arena of action, and of the measure of good art into good politics, is nowhere more literally displayed than at the site of Rosenberg's discontent, in Beuys's "boxing for democracy" performance at *documenta 5*. On the reverberations of Rosenberg's concept of action, see Christa Noel Robbins, *Artist as Author: Action and Intent in Late-Modernist American Painting* (University of Chicago Press, 2021).

79 Jürgen Becker, "Einführung," in Becker and Vostell, *Happenings*, 17.

80 Judith Rodenbeck, *Radical Prototypes: Allan Kaprow and the Invention of the Happening* (MIT Press, 2011), 9.

81 Jones, "The 'Pollockian Performative' and the Revision of the Modernist Subject," in *Body Art*, 53–102.

82 Guilbaut, *How New York Stole*; Caroline A. Jones, *Machine in the Studio: Constructing the Postwar American Artist* (University of Chicago Press, 2006).

83 Jones, *Body Art*, 53, italics original.

84 Kultermann, *Leben und Kunst*, 45, plate 17; Kaprow, *Assemblage, Environments & Happenings*, unpaginated. Pollock in the act of painting is also pictured as the first example of contemporary art in Schilling, *Aktionskunst*, 32.

85 Andrew Perchuk, "Pollock and Postwar Masculinity," in *The Masculine Masquerade: Masculinity and Representation*, ed. Andrew Perchuk and Helaine Posner (MIT Press, 1995), 40, 41, 42.

86 Jones, "Survey," 22. On the inextricability of performance art and feminism, see Jayne Wark, *Radical Gestures: Feminism and Performance Art in North America* (McGill-Queen's University Press, 2006).

87 Hubert Klocker, "Gesture and the Object: Liberation as *Aktion*: A European Component of Performative Art," in Schimmel, *Out of Actions*, 172. In striving to present Viennese Actionism as a positive contribution to the avowedly liberational political activism of the 1960s, Klocker must downplay its most authoritarian moment, Muehl's criminal actions at his Friedrichshof Commune, for which he was convicted in 1991. As this book moves toward

publication, a new museum, the WAM (Wiener Aktionismus Museum), is being accused of similar obfuscation by victims of the Muehl commune. Paula Pfosner, "Museum reißt Wunden der Muehl-Kommune auf," March 13, 2024, https://topos.orf.at/wiener-aktionismus-museum100; Catherine Hickley, "Anger as Vienna's New Actionism Museum Shows Child Abuser's Art," April 29, 2024, https://www.theartnewspaper.com/2024/04/29/anger-as-viennas-new-actionism-museum-shows-child-abusers-art#.

88 Compelling recent accounts include Jones, *In Between Subjects*; Amelia Jones and Erin Silver, eds., *Otherwise: Imagining Queer Feminist Art Histories* (Manchester University Press, 2016).

89 In-action, as that which is mistaken as a form of radical "extremity," would thus be an intriguing complement to what Dominic Johnson calls "the performance of extremity" in the 1970s in *Unlimited Action*.

90 VALIE EXPORT, "Feministischer Aktionismus. Aspekte," in *Frauen in der Kunst*, ed. Gislind Nabakowski, Helke Sander, and Peter Gorsen (Suhrkamp, 1980), 1:139–76. Throughout this text, VALIE EXPORT always uses a capital *F* when writing of Feminist Actionism or Feminist Actionists.

91 VALIE EXPORT, interviewed by Danièle Roussel, in *Wiener Aktionismus und die Österreicher: Gespräche*, ed. Danièle Roussel (Ritter Verlag, 1995), 119–20.

92 VALIE EXPORT, "Aspects of Feminist Actionism," *New German Critique* 47 (1989): 82. For an account of Schneemann's battles with the patriarchy, see Carolee Schneemann, *More Than Meat Joy: Carolee Schneemann—Complete Performance Works & Selected Writings*, ed. Bruce R. McPherson (Documentext, 1979).

93 See VALIE EXPORT, "Feministischer Aktionismus. Aspekte."

94 VALIE EXPORT, "Aspects of Feminist Actionism," 69–92 (all in-text citations in English are from this version). See the two exhibition catalogs *Von der Aktionsmalerei zum Aktionismus* and *Der zertrümmerte Spiegel: Wiener Aktionismus*, which accompanied the 1988–1989 exhibition that traveled between Germany, Scotland, and Austria and do not mention VALIE EXPORT's work.

95 Silvia Eiblmayr, VALIE EXPORT, and Monika Prischl-Maier, eds., *Kunst mit Eigen-Sinn: Aktuelle Kunst von Frauen: Texte und Dokumentation* (Löcker Verlag, 1985).

96 VALIE EXPORT, "Aspects of Feminist Actionism," 71.

97 Most disappointingly, in Schilling's *Aktionskunst* (1978), VALIE EXPORT is tacked onto Viennese Actionism by name, but her work never comes up for discussion. This form of exclusion is repeated in Berghaus, "Happenings in Europe," 362–68.

98 VALIE EXPORT, "vorwort," in Eiblmayr et al., *Kunst mit Eigen-Sinn*, 7–8. The title of the exhibition has been translated into English as "Art with a Sense of One's Own /Art with a Sense of Its Own," echoing the title of Virginia Woolf's book *A Room of One's Own*. See VALIE EXPORT, "The Real and Its Double: The Body," trans. Margret Eifler and Kurt Sager, *Discourse* 11, no. 1 (Fall–Winter 1988–1989): 15.

99 VALIE EXPORT, "Aspects of Feminist Actionism," 85. Feminist Actionism can be situated more broadly in discussions of *Eigensinn* in German-speaking space circa 1980. See Oskar Negt and Alexander Kluge, *Geschichte und Eigensinn: Geschichtliche Organisation der Arbeitsvermögen; Deutschland als Produktionsöffentlichkeit; Gewalt des Zusammenhangs* (Suhrkamp, 1981). Negt and Kluge make no mention of VALIE EXPORT. The catalog *Kunst mit Eigen-Sinn* makes little mention of Negt and Kluge, with the exception of Peter Gorsen, "Feminismus und ästhetische Grenzüberschreitung," 99–111. A recent translation of Negt and Kluge's work proposes "obstinacy" for *Eigensinn*. Alexander Kluge and Oskar Negt, *History and Obstinacy*, ed. Devin Fore, trans. Richard Langston (Zone Books, 2014).

100 VALIE EXPORT, "Aspects of Feminist Actionism," 71.

101 Jones, "Survey," 21–22.

102 Jones makes this claim in *Body Art*, 93–94, and "Survey," 21–22.

103 Jones, "Survey," 21. It is ironic that Jones, who insists on the sincerity of feminist performance art, chooses this photograph of a performance that may or may not have happened and is arguably all the more effective on account of this ambiguity. See my discussion in chapter 4.

104 Jones, "Survey," 21.

105 Schneider, *Explicit Body*, 2.

106 Schneemann states that *Up to and Including Her Limits* was "the direct result of Pollock's physicalized painting process." Schneemann, "Statement for *Texte zur Kunst* (1999)," in *Imaging Her Erotics: Essays, Interviews, Projects* (MIT Press, 2002), 165.

107 VALIE EXPORT, "Aspects of Feminist Actionism," 82. Schneemann reflects fondly on meeting VALIE EXPORT in London in 1970. See Schneemann, *Imaging Her Erotics*, 97.

108 Jones, *Body Art*, 2–3. Jones is writing here specifically of Schneemann's *Interior Scroll* (1975–1976).

109 Schneemann, "Up to and Including Her Limits," in *Imaging Her Erotics*, 165.

110 Jones, *Body Art*, 5.

111 The other important frame for aspects of Viennese Actionism, specifically Nitsch's *Orgien Mysterien Theater*, can be found in the work of Erika Fischer-Lichte, which privileges the category of ritual and has developed out of—and today defines—the field of theater studies in Germany. See Erika Fischer-Lichte, *Theatre, Sacrifice, Ritual. Exploring Forms of Political Theatre* (Routledge, 2005), esp. 210–20; Erika Fischer-Lichte, *The Transformative Power of Performance: A New Aesthetics*, trans. Saskya Iris Jain (Routledge, 2008), esp. 52–59. Fischer-Lichte, in *Theatre, Sacrifice, Ritual*, also mistakes Schwarzkogler's in-action, suggesting he "did violence to his own body, almost sacrificing himself" (210).

112 Archias, *Concrete Body*, 1.

113 "Matter-of-fact" is a phrase Archias uses, sometimes citing Yvonne Rainer in *Concrete Body*, 6, 12. Aiming—polemically and in my view problematically—to get away from what she calls "postmodernism's identity politics," Archias argues that "the concrete body," in its sheer "matter-of-fact" materiality, has the potential to make "a claim to general humanity" (88, 27).

114 Specifically, this can be traced to Kaprow's reception of the pragmatist philosophy of John Dewey. See Chay Allen, "Allan Kaprow's Radical Pedagogy," *Performance Research: A Journal of the Performing Arts* 21, no. 6 (2016): 7–12.

115 Kaprow, "Legacy," 57, italics added.

116 For Schneemann, the hierarchies of art and life were clear. Recalling preparations for the exhibition *Happening & Fluxus* in Cologne in 1970, she writes to Kaprow of the matter of meeting the editor of the catalog to discuss the inclusion of work: "You were all lined up in front of Wolf [Vostell]: 1. Kaprow 2. [Dick] Higgins 3. [Robert] Filliou 4. [Al] Hansen 5. [Hermann] Nitsch 6. [Tomas] Schmidt 7....... Wolf said I still must wait another day." Schneemann, "From an Unsent Letter to Allan Kaprow, 1974," in *More Than Meat Joy*, 195–96.

117 Catherine Spencer, "A Calendar of Happenings: Allan Kaprow, Counter-Chronologies and Cataloguing Performance, c. 1970," *Art History* 39, no. 3 (2016): 593; Rodenbeck, *Radical Prototypes*, 217. See also Stephanie Rosenthal, "Agency for Action," in *Allan Kaprow—Art as Life*, ed. Eva Meyer-Hermann, Andrew Perchuk, and Stephanie Rosenthal (Getty Research Institute, 2008), 67–68, in which Rosenthal describes participating in a "new version" of *Household* in 2006. For the score of *Household*, cited in text between dashes, see Allan Kaprow, "Household," in *Some Recent Happenings* (A Great Bear Pamphlet, 1966), 6–9.

118 Catherine Spencer, "Acts of Displacement: Lea Lublin's *Mon fils*, May '68, and Feminist Psychosocial Revolt," *Oxford Art Journal* 40, no. 1 (2017): 65–83.

119 Spencer, "Lea Lublin's Exercises in Denaturalisation," in *Beyond the Happening*, 181–224.

120 Helen Molesworth, "House Work and Art Work," *October* 92 (2000): 82. See also Sven Lütticken, "General Performance," *e-flux journal* 31 (2012): 1–9; Sven Lütticken, "Acts in the Age of Virtuoso Performance," *Texte zur Kunst* 79 (2010): 124–33.

121 Mierle Laderman Ukeles, "Manifesto for Maintenance Art 1969! Proposal for an Exhibition 'CARE'" (1969), *Journal of Contemporary Painting* 4, no. 2 (2018): 235.

122 See Berenice Fisher and Joan Tronto, "Toward a Feminist Theory of Caring," in *Circles of Care: Work and Identity in Women's Lives*, ed. Emily K. Abel and Margaret K. Nelson (State University of New York Press, 1990), 35–62; Sandra Laugier, "The Ethics of Care as a Politics of the Ordinary," *New Literary History* 46, no. 2 (2015): 217–40.

123 See Adriana Cavarero, *Inclinations: A Critique of Rectitude* (2014), trans. Amanda Minervini and Adam Sitze (Stanford University Press, 2016); Donna J. Haraway, *Staying with the Trouble: Making Kin in the Chthulucene* (Duke University Press, 2016); Maria Puíg de la Bellacasa, *Matters of Care: Speculative Ethics in More Than Human Worlds* (University of Minnesota Press, 2017).

124 See Selma Sevenhuijsen, *Citizenship and the Ethics of Care: Feminist Considerations on Justice, Morality, and Politics* (1996), trans. Liz Savage (Routledge, 1998).

125 Ukeles, "Manifesto for Maintenance Art," 235.

126 See Spencer, *Beyond the Happening*; Lisa Baraitser, *Enduring Time* (Bloomsbury, 2017), 47–68; Camille Morineau and Lucia Pesapane, eds., *Women House* (La Monnaie de Paris and Manuella Editions, 2017); Helen Molesworth, ed., *Work Ethic* (Pennsylvania State University Press, 2003); Thalia Gouma-Peterson and Patricia Townley Mathews, "The Feminist Critique of Art History," *Art Bulletin* 69, no. 3 (1987): 326–57. For a different feminist take on "work," see Julia Bryan-Wilson, *Art Workers: Radical Practice in the Vietnam War Era* (University of California Press, 2011).

127 Dominic Johnson, ed., *The Art of Living: An Oral History of Performance Art* (Palgrave, 2015), 1, 3. See also Jones, *In Between Subjects*.

128 David J. Getsy, *Queer Behavior: Scott Burton and Performance Art* (University of Chicago Press, 2022), 68. See also Getsy's argument about "the double-bind of queer visibility"—the tension between coming out as gay and becoming an object of surveillance and scrutiny—in "The Spectacle of Privacy: Geoffrey Hendricks's *Ring Piece* and the Ambivalence of Queer Visibility," *Art Bulletin* 104, no. 3 (2022): 141.

129 In this sense, Getsy's work provocatively extends Peggy Phelan's important claim about the "power of the unmarked, unspoken, and unseen." See Peggy Phelan, *Unmarked: The Politics of Performance* (Routledge, 1996), 7. Phelan's discussion of performance as "the art form which most fully understands the generative possibilities of disappearance" (27) is often displaced by the impact of her strong claim that performance only exists in the present: "Performance cannot be saved, recorded, documented, or otherwise participate in the circulation of representations *of* representations: once it does so, it becomes something other than performance" (146).

130 "Inoperativity," sometimes translated as "deworking," is drawn from the writings of Giorgio Agamben. See Giorgio Agamben, *The Use of Bodies*, trans. Adam Kotsko (Stanford University Press, 2015).

131 Bonnie Honig, *A Feminist Theory of Refusal* (Harvard University Press, 2021), 14. See also Tina Campt, "Black Visuality and the Practice of Refusal," *Women & Performance: A Journal of Feminist Theory* 29, no. 1 (2019): 79–87.

132 Barbara Gronau and Alice Lagaay, eds., *Performanzen des Nichttuns* (Passagen, 2008); Barbara Gronau and Alice Lagaay, eds., *Ökonomien der Zurückhaltung: Kulturelles Handeln zwischen Askese und Restriktion* (Transcript Verlag, 2010). See also Gronau's work on acts of

"stalling, standing still, and interruption" that blur the boundaries between aesthetic and political practice: Barbara Gronau, "Anhalten, Stillstehen, Unterbrechen. Gegenzeiten in den Darstellenden Künste," in *Künste des Anhaltens: Ästhetische Verfahren des Stillstellens*, ed. Barbara Gronau (Neofelis, 2019), 30–34; Barbara Gronau, "Performing Stasis," trans. Jake Schneider, in *Aesthetics of Standstill*, ed. Reinhold Görling, Barbara Gronau, and Ludger Schwarte (Sternberg Press, 2019), 13–28.

133 Franko B has referred directly to Viennese Actionism in writing on his own work and has been compared frequently to aspects of it. See Sarah Wilson, "Franko B: Haute Surveillance, Haute Couture," in *Franko B: Oh Lover Boy*, ed. Franko B (Black Dog, 2001), unpaginated; Stuart Morgan, "The Illustrated Man: Franko B," in *Franko B*, ed. Lois Kiedan, Stuart Morgan, Nicholas Sinclair, and Franko B (Black Dog, 1998), unpaginated. Morgan situates Franko B "half-way between" Nitsch's participatory *Gesamtkunstwerk* and Schwarzkogler's "solitary and demented" work.

134 Jack Halberstam, *The Queer Art of Failure* (Duke University Press, 2011), 129.

135 Doyle, *Hold It Against Me*, 8.

136 Dominic Johnson connects *I Miss You* to "hardship art" in "The Gold Standard: The Performances of Franko B," in *Live Art in the UK: Contemporary Performances of Precarity*, ed. Maria Chatzichristodoulou (Bloomsbury, 2020), 89–104.

137 Doyle, *Hold It Against Me*, xi.

138 Doyle, *Hold It Against Me*, 76, xiv.

139 In this effort, I am in solidarity with Jennifer Sichel's incisive art history writing in *Criticism Without Authority: Gene Swenson's and Jill Johnston's Queer Practices* (University of Chicago Press, 2025).

140 Aliza Shvarts, "Figuration and Failure, Pedagogy and Performance: Reflections Three Years Later," *Women & Performance: A Journal of Feminist Theory* 21, no. 1 (March 2011): 160.

141 Doyle, *Hold It Against Me*, 28–39. See also Jennifer Doyle, "Blind Spots and Failed Performance: Abortion, Feminism, and Queer Theory," *Qui Parle* 18, no. 1 (Fall–Winter 2009): 25–52.

142 Cited in Carrie Lambert-Beatty, "Make-Believe: Parafiction and Plausibility," *October* (Spring 2009): 69.

143 This is how Shvarts puts it in her reply to the university refusing to call her work fiction. Cited in Lambert-Beatty, "Make-Believe," 70.

144 Doyle, *Hold It Against Me*, 28–39; Doyle, "Blind Spots and Failed Performance," 39–45.

145 Lambert-Beatty, "Make-Believe," 68–69.

146 Lambert-Beatty, "Make-Believe," 66, 67.

147 Lambert-Beaty acknowledges this too in a footnote: "Shvarts's project can't be securely categorized as a hoax—or even a parafiction—since it remains unclear what was or wasn't true about her story. But it partakes of the parafictional, because the question about veracity is fundamental to its structure." Lambert-Beatty, "Make-Believe," 70n56.

148 Lee Edelman, *No Future: Queer Theory and the Death Drive* (Duke University Press, 2004).

149 In critical dialogue with Edelman, Doyle offers the most insightful reading of this ethical (and "legal") dimension of Shvarts's piece. See Doyle, "Blind Spots and Failed Performance."

150 Shvarts, "Figuration and Failure," 161.

151 Despite their more thoroughgoing engagement with Schwarzkogler's work, none of these art historians addresses *Hochzeit*: Stiles, "Notes"; Jarosi, "Image of the Artist"; Gorsen, "Rudolf Schwarzkogler"; Schröder, "Schnitt-Techniken."

152 Stiles, "Uncorrupted Joy," 291; Museum moderner Kunst Stiftung Ludwig and Eva Badura-Triska, eds., *Körper, Psyche und Tabu: Wiener Aktionismus und die frühe Wiener Moderne* (Verlag der Buchhandlung Walther König, 2016), 111. This scene is featured as the exemplary Schwarzkogler performance on the cover of Green, *Brus, Muehl, Nitsch, Schwarzkogler*. In the exhibition *Big Bang: Creation and Destruction in 20th Century Art* at the Centre Pompidou, in Paris, June 15, 2005–April 3, 2006, this very photograph (fig. I.20) is centered as the example of Schwarzkogler's work. Object File, Rudolf Schwarzkogler, Department of Photography, Centre Pompidou.

153 Günter Brus appears often in the wider archive of photographs. Ludwig Hoffenreich, Walter Kindler, and Siegfried Klein (a.k.a. Khasaq) photographed the performance and also appear from time to time in one another's documents, as in plate 4, where Klein appears behind Cibulka and Schwarzkogler in Kindler's photograph. The most substantial documentation of the performance is reproduced in Badura-Triska and Klocker, *Rudolf Schwarzkogler*, 161–85. The editors exclude, however, at their own discretion, further images from the negatives. Photographic negatives for Hoffenreich and Kindler are housed in the mumok – Museum moderner Kunst Stiftung Ludwig. Photographic negatives for Klein, whose estate is held by Galerie Julius Hummel Vienna, are stated by Hummel to have been lost.

154 Getsy, *Queer Behavior*, 15. Anna Brus recalls that after *Hochzeit*, "there was never another action in which a woman would have participated." Anna Brus, interviewed by Andrea Schurian, in *Amor Psyche Aktion – Wien. Das Feminine im Wiener Aktionismus* (DOX Centre for Contemporary Art, Prague, 2012), 287. Following *Hochzeit*, Schwarzkogler collaborated only with Cibulka in the works taken as his own, except in *5. Aktion*, in which his partner was Nitsch. The two dress in drag, paint each other white, and stand together in a narrow box grinning mischievously. Speaking in the documentary *Ana: Ihr Leben mit den Wiener Aktionisten*, Anna Brus reflects on what she calls Schwarzkogler's "bisexuality" (digital film, Neue Galerie Graz, 2022). She relates how she and Günter Brus considered Schwarzkogler "also a bit of a father" to their daughter Diana and speaks with difficult emotion about their abrupt departure from Vienna in February 1969, the last time they saw him before his death that June. When he died, Schwarzkogler had a photograph of his mother and a photograph of Anna Brus in his pocket. Interviews indicating the homophobia he experienced in Vienna are included in Yvonne Ziegler, "Rudolf Schwarzkogler: Darstellungen von Gewalt und Anleitungen zur Heilung in Aktion, Fotografie, Zeichnung und Text," unpublished doctoral dissertation, Albert-Ludwigs-Universität Freiburg, 2004.

155 This commitment to figural composition distinguishes Schwarzkogler's work from formal practices of abstraction in the 1960s. See David J. Getsy, *Abstract Bodies: Sixties Sculpture in the Expanded Field of Gender* (Yale University Press, 2015).

156 On the association of queer life with the death drive, for which reason it is seen as such a threat to the heteronormative reproductive futurism of mainstream culture, see Edelman, *No Future*, esp. ch. 1. The mistaking of Schwarzkogler produces a different but related "elision of archival memory" to the one Dominic Johnson describes in his brilliant essay on artists' suicide and death, "Modern Death: Jack Smith, Fred Herko, and Paul Thek," *Criticism* 56, no. 2 (2014): 230.

157 Marriage is the prime example for J. L. Austin's theory of the performative speech act in *How to Do Things with Words* (Clarendon Press, 1962). For a critical reassessment of the heteronormativity of this example with regard to gender performance, see Judith Butler, *Bodies That Matter: On the Discursive Limits of Sex* (Routledge, 1996), 170–75.

158 On the "unusually harsh" conditions of queer life in Austria in the post–Second World War period, see Matti Bunzl, "Queering Austria for the New Europe," in *Sexuality in Austria* (2009), ed. Günter Bischof, Anton Pelinka, and Dagmar Herzog (Routledge, 2017), 131–44. In comparison with Germany, France, and Great Britain, Bunzl notes that "Austria's social conservativism[,] centrally embodied by the cultural stronghold of the Catholic church" (133), enforced a culture that criminalized everyday queer life until well after the 1970s, indeed, until the turn of the twenty-first century. See also Robert Deam Tobin, "'HOMOSEXUALITY' and the Politics of the Nation in Austria, Hungary, and Austria-Hungary," in *Peripheral Desires: The German Discovery of Sex* (University of Pennsylvania Press, 2015), 111–33.

Chapter 1

1 See Eva Badura-Triska, Hubert Klocker, and Museum moderner Kunst Stiftung Ludwig, eds., *Vienna Actionism: Art and Upheaval in 1960s' Vienna*, trans. Thomas Morrison, Christina Oberstebrink, Michael Turnbull, and Mark Willard (Verlag der Buchhandlung Walther König, 2012). Klocker's earlier volumes highlight the radicality of the artists' work in terms of political protest and "acts of liberation." See Hubert Klocker, ed., *Der zertrümmerte Spiegel: Wiener Aktionismus, Wien 1960–1971/The Shattered Mirror: Viennese Actionism, Vienna 1960–1971: Günter Brus, Otto Mühl, Hermann Nitsch, Rudolf Schwarzkogler* (Ritter, 1989); Hubert Klocker, "Gesture and the Object: Liberation as *Aktion*: A European Component of Performative Art," in *Out of Actions: Between Performance and the Object, 1949–1979*, ed. Paul Schimmel (Thames and Hudson, 1998), 159–96, for "radical protest," 172.

2 In activating the double valence of this term, I draw on Hannah Wilke's "performalist self-portrait" and statement from 1977: *I Object: Memoirs of a Sugar Giver*, an interpretation of Marcel Duchamp's *Étant donnés* photographed by Richard Hamilton. Although she does not discuss this work specifically, see Anna Chave's review of the fraught feminist reception of Wilke's work: "'I Object'—Hannah Wilke's Feminism," *Art in America*, March 2009, 104–8, 159.

3 Anna Brus, interviewed by Colette M. Schmidt, "50 Jahre Kunst und Revolution: Die Aktionistin Anna Brus," *Der Standard*, June 7, 2018, https://www.derstandard.de/consent/tcf/story/2000081105033/uni-ferkelei-1968-die-aktionistin-anna-brus. She expresses a similar sentiment in an earlier interview: Anna Brus, in conversation with Johanna Schwanberg, "Akteurinnen im Aktionismus. Anna Brus und Carola Dertnig im Gespräch mit Johanna Schwanberg," in *Carola Dertnig: Nachbilder einer ungleichzeitigen Gegenwart/Afterimages of a Non-Simultaneous Present* (Skarabaeus, 2006), 49–50.

4 Hanel Koeck cited by Almuth Spiegler in "Namenlosen Nymphen und Unbedankte Helferinnen: Die Frauen neben und hinter den Wiener Aktionisten," in *Amor Psyche Aktion - Wien: Das Feminine im Wiener Aktionismus* (DOX Centre for Contemporary Art, Prague, 2012), 282. This catalog has appeared in translation as *Amor Psyche Action—Vienna: The Feminine in Viennese Actionism*, trans. Jeremy Gaines and Steve Tomlin (DOX Centre for Contemporary Art, Prague, 2012); however, all in-text citations are my own translation, based on the original German.

5 This approach would complement and complicate the feminist and queer perspectives collected in Amelia Jones and Erin Silver, eds., *Otherwise: Imagining Queer Feminist Art Histories* (Manchester University Press, 2016).

6 Lea Vergine, *Il corpo come linguaggio (La "body-art" e storie simili)* (G. Prearo, 1974); Lea Vergine, *Body Art and Performance: The Body as Language*, trans. Henry Martin (Skira, 2000), 22. Vergine was also publishing in English in the 1970s. See Lea Vergine, "Bodylanguage," *Art and Artists*, September 1974, 22–27.

7 Adrian Henri, *Total Art: Environments, Happenings, and Performance* (Praeger Publishers, 1974), 169, 179.

8 Gerhard P. Zacharias, *Satanskult und Schwarze Messe: Ein Beitrag zur Phänomenologie der Religion* (Limes Verlag, 1964). For a more nuanced perspective on Viennese Actionism and rit-

ual, see Franziska Meifert, "Zweimal Geborene. Der 'Wiener Aktionismus' im Spiegel von Mythen, Riten und Gesichten," *Protokolle: Zeitschrift für Literatur und Kunst* 1 (1990): 3–63.

9 See the catalog of the Louvre exhibition celebrating this "cursed" criminal character: Régis Michel, ed., *La peinture comme crime, ou La part maudite de la modernité* (Réunion des Musées Nationaux, 2001), and more recently, the praise of the Viennese Actionists as "fallen angels" in Michel Blancsubé and Lorena Moreno Vera, eds., *Accionismo vienés: La revuelta de los ángeles salidos del limbo*, trans. Víctor Altamirano, Citlali Bernhardt, Haydée Silva, and Carmen Testa Hager (Fundación Jumex, 2016). Both publications orient Viennese Actionism within a longer tradition of "dark arts" traced back to figures like Goya, the French symbolists, and Antonin Artaud.

10 For the term *model*, see Badura-Triska et al., *Vienna Actionism*; Johanna Schwanberg uses the term with critical ambivalence for her short text in that volume: "On the Role of the 'Models' and/or Actors in Vienna Actionism," 122–23. For the vocabulary of "die passiven Aktricen und Akteure," drawn from Hermann Nitsch's writings, see the detailed discussion in Thomas Dreher, *Performance Art nach 1945: Aktionstheater und Intermedia* (Wilhelm Fink, 2001).

11 These exhibitions include, first, most recently, *Ana. Ihr Leben mit den Wiener Aktionisten* (Ana: Her life with the Viennese Actionists), curated by Roman Grabner, BRUSEUM – Universalmuseum Joanneum Graz, March 31–September 24, 2023. The show was organized by galleries dedicated to each of the four main protagonists of Viennese Actionism, each of which included a filmed interview with Anna Brus reflecting on her collaborations with each artist. No catalog was produced for the show. As of the finalization of this book manuscript, plans are in place to make the interviews available as a documentary. Second, *Amor Psyche Aktion – Wien. Das Feminine im Wiener Aktionismus. Sammlung Hummel* (Amor, Psyche, Action—Vienna: The feminine in Viennese Actionism, Hummel Collection), DOX Centre for Contemporary Art, Prague, October 19, 2012–January 28, 2013. The Austrian private art dealer Julius Hummel made the selection of works for the show and edited the exhibition catalog of works from his collection. See *Amor Psyche Aktion*.

12 Pilar Parcerisas, "Körper und Politik," in *Amor Psyche Aktion*, 239, 244.

13 Almuth Spiegler, "Namenlosen Nymphen," 282. Spiegler interviewed Anna Brus and Hanel Koeck for her unpublished *Diplomarbeit*, "Die Rolle der Frau im Wiener Aktionismus," University of Vienna, 2008. In it, she draws the same conclusion.

14 See Harald Szeemann, with Hanns Sohm, eds., *Happening & Fluxus: Materialien* (Kölnischer Kunstverein, 1970); Peter Weibel and VALIE EXPORT, eds., *wien: bildkompendium wiener aktionismus und film* (Kohlkunstverlag, 1970); A1 Informationen Verlagsgesellschaft, ed., *Aktionsraum 1: Oder 57 Blindenhunde* (A1 Informationen Verlagsgesellschaft, 1971); Jürgen Schilling, *Aktionskunst: Identität von Kunst und Leben? Eine Dokumentation* (C. J. Bucher, 1978), 153.

15 Mirella Levi D'Ancona, *The Iconography of the Immaculate Conception in the Middle Ages and Early Renaissance* (Published by the College Art Association of America in conjunction with the Art Bulletin, 1957), 3.

16 These men include Christian d'Orville, Peter Gorsen, Peter Müller-Preuss, and Hans Peter Zimmers, whose atelier was used; Ludi Armbruster, Ludwig Hoffenreich, and Knut Nievers, who photographed; and Peter Kubelka, who filmed. See Hermann Nitsch, *Das Orgien Mysterien Theater. Die Partituren aller aufgeführten Aktionen 1960–1979, 1.–32. Aktion* (Studio Morra, 1979), 1:229–37. Nitsch's wife Beate Nitsch appears in everyday dress at the edges of the action. See also Badura-Triska et al., *Vienna Actionism*, 340.

17 A series of close-ups including this image can be found in Weibel and VALIE EXPORT, *wien:*

bildkompendium, 102–14, specifically 102. The photographs of the performance are disconcertingly intermingled with Nitsch's image research into autopsy.

18 This consenting scenario is both kinky and exhilarating from the perspective of the sex club scene in West Germany. See Peter Gorsen, *Das Prinzip Obszön: Kunst, Pornographie und Gesellschaft* (Rowohlt, 1969); Peter Gorsen, *Sexualästhetik: Zur bürgerlichen Rezeption von Obzönität und Pornographie* (Rowohlt, 1972). Both books orient contemporary art within discourses on sex work, sex clubs, and pornography; the latter ends with an image compendium of *Maria Empfängnis – Aktion mit Hanel Koeck*. See Gorsen, *Sexualästhetik* (1972), 181–87.

19 One image from the scene captured in figure 1.6 is reproduced early on in English-speaking space in Amos Vogel, *Film as a Subversive Art* (Random House, 1974), 289.

20 Amelia Jones, *Body Art/Performing the Subject* (University of Minnesota Press, 1998), 114n37. Jones is looking at a photograph reproduced in Renate Berger, "Pars pro toto: Zum Verhältnis von künstlerischer Freiheit und sexueller Integrität," in *Der Garten der Lüste: Zur Deutung des Erotischen und Sexuellen bei Künstlern und ihren Interpreten*, ed. Renate Berger and Daniela Hammer-Tugendhat (DuMont Buchverlag, 1985), 170. This photograph is from the selection Peter Gorsen makes for *Sexualästhetik* (1972), 185.

21 For a compelling collection of primary documents departing from the rise of antipornography feminism in the 1970s and 1980s, and traversing queer feminist and decolonial ripostes through the 1990s, when Jones was writing, see Drucilla Cornell, ed., *Feminism and Pornography* (Oxford University Press, 2000).

22 See Badura-Triska et al., *Vienna Actionism*, 340. Sometimes, Koeck is ambiguously named, as in Weibel and VALIE EXPORT, *wien: bildkompendium*, where her name appears in the context of the presentation of Muehl's work (281), but she does not receive her own entry in the artists' biographies.

23 Nitsch is unfortunately inconsistent. For the use of the complete title, see Michael Karrer, ed., *Hermann Nitsch: The Gesamtkunstwerk of the Orgien Mysterien Theater* (Verlag der Buchhandlung Walther König, 2015), unpaginated. For its absence, see Nitsch, *Das Orgien Mysterien Theater* (1979), 1:229–37, in which the performance is simply titled *31. Aktion* with "h. koeck" listed as "passiver akteur."

24 D'Ancona, *Iconography of the Immaculate Conception*, 5. On disseminations of this iconography, see Suzanne L. Stratton, *The Immaculate Conception in Spanish Art* (Cambridge University Press, 1994).

25 See Maria Mesner, *Frauensache? Die Auseinandersetzung um den Schwangerschaftsabbruch in Österreich* (Jugend & Volk, 1994); Maria Mesner, *Geburten/Kontrolle – Reproduktionspolitik im 20. Jahrhundert* (Böhlau, 2010).

26 Koeck would complement Rosemarie Brucher's compelling case studies of how Günter Brus and VALIE EXPORT "travesty" sexuality in postwar Austria. See Rosemarie Brucher, "Ästhetische Travestie: Zur Inszenierung des Geschlechts in der österreichischen Aktionskunst der 1960er Jahre," *Journal of Austrian Studies* 46, no. 4 (2014): 41–65.

27 Koeck states of her performance: "Die weibliche Gekreuzigte der *Maria Empfängnis*-Aktion war eine—*meine*—Revolte gegen die Reglementierung der Sexualtriebe durch Verwaltung und Zwangsmoral" (The crucified woman in the *Maria-Empfängnis* action was a—*my*—revolt against the regimentation of sexual drives through administration and compulsory morality). See Hanel Koeck, interviewed by Michel Blancsubé, "Entrevista con Hanel Koeck (2014)," in *Accionismo vienés: La revuelta*, 537, published in Spanish only; the citation in German is from the original interview, italics original, shared with me by Hanel Koeck via email on September 26, 2023.

28 See Peter Gorsen, *Pierre Molinier, lui-même: Essay über den surrealistischen Hermaphro-*

diten (Rogner & Bernhard, 1972); Peter Gorsen, "The Artist's Desiring Gaze on Objects of Fetishism," in *Pierre Molinier: From the Collections of Francesco Conz, Hanel Koeck, and the MRI Foundation* (Winnipeg Art Gallery, 1993), 5–26. Koeck performs with Molinier using his handmade *Godemiché* in the series of "photo-portraits" entitled *Hanel Koeck mit Godemiché* (1970). One of Koeck's earliest works with Molinier, *La poupée* (The doll, 1967), is a photomontage positioning her face, with downturned eyes, as an orifice within an array of splayed legs. See Gerhard Fischer and Peter Gorsen, eds., *Pierre Molinier: Die Fetische der Travestie, fotographischen Arbeiten 1965–1975* (Daedalus, 1989).

29 Historical accounts of Koeck are limited. Despite figuring extensively across both books' pages and being cited in the latter, she is not given a biographical entry in Weibel and VALIE EXPORT's *wien: bildkompendium* and is excluded from the "artist index" of *Amor Psyche Aktion*; Koeck receives a brief entry in the section "Who's Who: Field of Players," in Badura-Triska et al., *Vienna Actionism*, 401. For her own writing, see Hanel Koeck, "Mode und Gesellschaft um 1900: Das Künstlerkleid in Wien," in *Wien 1900 – Kunst und Kultur: Focus der europäischen Moderne*, ed. Christian Brandstätter (Deutscher Taschenbuch Verlag, 2011), 211–25, first published in 1984 in the context of the Venice Biennale. Under discussion in particular is the problem of the corset in the Viennese "artist's dress."

30 See Koeck's interview with Molinier, "Hanel Koeck im Gespräch mit Pierre Molinier, Bordeaux 1970," excerpted and translated from French into German by Werner Rappl in *Pierre Molinier: Die Fetische der Travestie*, 27–31, reprinted in Gerhard Fischer, ed., *Daedalus: Die Erfindung der Gegenwart* (Daedalus, 1990), 332–37.

31 Koeck's written correspondence with the author, August 11, 2023. Molinier also used photographs of Koeck in *Maria Empfängnis – Aktion mit Hanel Koeck* for a series of drawings. See Peter Gorsen, *Der gekreuzigte Eros: Zur Künstler-Metaphysik von Pierre Molinier und Hermann Nitsch*, ed. Wolfgang Koch (Hollitzer Verlag, 2023).

32 Gorsen, *Das Prinzip Obszön*, 104–5. See also Peter Gorsen, *Das Bild Pygmalions: Kunstsoziologische Essays* (Rowohlt, 1969).

33 Gorsen, *Das Prinzip Obszön*, 52.

34 Gorsen, *Sexualästhetik* (1972), 166–87.

35 Peter Gorsen, *Sexualästhetik: Grenzformen der Sinnlichkeit im 20. Jahrhundert* (Rowohlt, 1987), 8. Gorsen completed his PhD in Frankfurt in 1965 with Theodor Adorno and Jürgen Habermas. He describes his research after 1980 as addressing "Kunst und Krankheit" and "Kunst- und Sexualwissenschaft (Geschlechterbeziehungen, [Trans]Gender Studies)" (art and illness, art and sexuality studies, gender relationships, and trans-gender studies). See the contributor biographies in Michael Ertl, Brigitta Keintzel, and Rudolf P. Wagner, eds., *Ich bin tausend Ich: Probleme, Zugänge und Konzepte zur Therapie von Psychosen* (Facultas Verlag, 2002), 372, in which Gorsen publishes an essay on Schwarzkogler.

36 See Gislind Nabakowski, Helke Sander, and Peter Gorsen, eds., *Frauen in der Kunst*, vols. 1 and 2 (Suhrkamp, 1980).

37 Peter Gorsen, "Frauen und Frauenbilder in der Kunstgeschichte," in Nabakowski et al., *Frauen in der Kunst*, 2:17.

38 VALIE EXPORT, "Feministischer Aktionismus. Aspekte," in Nabakowski et al., *Frauen in der Kunst*, 1:139–76. About a decade later, VALIE EXPORT translates her own essay into English: VALIE EXPORT, "Aspects of Feminist Actionism," *New German Critique* 47 (1989): 69–92.

39 VALIE EXPORT, "Aspects of Feminist Actionism," 71, 70, 71.

40 Gorsen was subsequently invited to contribute an essay to VALIE EXPORT's exhibition *Kunst mit Eigen-Sinn: Aktuelle Kunst von Frauen* (Art with own-sense: Current art by women). See Peter Gorsen, "Feminismus und ästhetische Grenzüberschreitung," in *Kunst mit Eigen-Sinn: Aktuelle Kunst von Frauen – Texte und Dokumentation*, ed. Silvia Eiblmayr, VALIE EXPORT, and Monika Prischl-Maier (Löcker Verlag, 1985), 99–109. Koeck appears nowhere in *Kunst mit Eigen-Sinn*.

41 Koeck's comments are from her written correspondence with the author, August 28, 2023, and conversation with the author in Vienna, December 13, 2023, respectively. For Molinier's statement, see Koeck's interview with Molinier (1970) cited in French by Peter Gorsen in "Pierre Molinier, lui-même," 18. Koeck certainly has in mind the "iconographies of misogyny" laid out in Bram Dijkstra, *Idols of Perversity: Fantasies of Feminine Evil in Fin-de-Siècle Culture* (Oxford University Press, 1986).

42 VALIE EXPORT, "Aspects of Feminist Actionism," 71.

43 Lucy Lippard, "The Pains and Pleasures of Rebirth: Women's Body Art," *Art in America*, May–June 1976, 73–81.

44 Max Kozloff, "Pygmalion Reversed," *Artforum*, November 1975, 30–37. This essay reviews several recent exhibitions and catalogs dedicated to performance and body art, including Lea Vergine's book of 1974, cited earlier in this chapter, Harald Szeemann's exhibitions *Happening & Fluxus* (1970) and *documenta 5* (1972), discussed in the introduction, as well as the exhibition *Bodyworks* at the Museum of Contemporary Art, Chicago, which included works by Brus, Nitsch, and Schwarzkogler. See *Bodyworks: March 8 to April 27, 1975, Museum of Contemporary Art, Chicago, Illinois* (Museum of Contemporary Art, 1975). Kozloff is aware of German-language publications including the art and literary journal *interfunktionen*, a main conduit for the juxtaposition of US and European positions in contemporary art. Kozloff also references a recent exhibition in Graz. See Horst Gerhard Haberl, ed., *Kunst als Lebensritual/Art as Living Ritual* (Pool-Steirischer Herbst, 1974), which, ironically, foregrounds the work of American artists including Vito Acconci, Lynda Benglis, Chris Burden, Dennis Oppenheim, and Hannah Wilke, among others, while not including any of the Viennese Actionists.

45 Nitsch cited in Kozloff, "Pygmalion Reversed," 37.

46 Kozloff argues that in the works of Nitsch—and Vito Acconci, Chris Burden, Dan Graham, and Alan Sonfist—the myth of Pygmalion is reversed: Instead of an enlivening of sculpture, "we now have the story of the animate body that doubles back into inanimate art." Kozloff, "Pygmalion Reversed," 37.

47 Lippard, "The Pains and Pleasures of Rebirth," 79.

48 Szeemann and Sohm, *Happening & Fluxus*, unpaginated. Lippard is listed in the bibliography of the catalog. The photograph of *Maria Empfängnis - Aktion mit Hanel Koeck* is mislabeled *7. Abreaktionsspiel*. Lippard had a heated exchange with Szeemann in 1972 regarding his sexism; see the section "Individual Mythology" of the introduction.

49 Lippard, "Pains and Pleasures," 75, 79. Surprisingly, VALIE EXPORT is not mentioned.

50 Lippard, "Pains and Pleasures," 75, 76. While Lippard names the performance *Up to and Including Her Limits*, Schneemann is talking about *Interior Scroll* (1975).

51 Lippard, "Pains and Pleasures," 76, 75.

52 For an early formulation, see Judith Butler, "Performative Acts and Gender Constitution: An Essay in Phenomenology and Feminist Theory," *Theatre Journal* 40, no. 4 (December 1988): 519–31. Butler unfolds this argument in *Gender Trouble: Feminism and the Subversion of Identity* (Routledge, 1990) and *Bodies That Matter: On the Discursive Limits of Sex* (Routledge, 1996).

53 See Nitsch, *Das Orgien Mysterien Theater. Die Partituren*, 1:239–49.

54 The Sommers' film is mistakenly titled "Maria-Conception-Action Hermann Nitsch (Maria-Empfängnis-Aktion Hermann Nitsch)" and briefly summarized as Nitsch's "most controversial creation: the crucifixion of a young woman, the disemboweling of a lamb carcass, and her defilement with it," in Vogel, *Film as Subversive Art*, 288. Gorsen also filmed the performance; his footage is housed at mumok but could not be made available for viewing.

55 Anna Brus, in Schwanberg, "Akteurinnen im Aktionismus," 53, 50.

56 Adriana Cavarero, *Inclinations: A Critique of Rectitude* (2014), trans. Amanda Minervini and Adam Sitze (Stanford University Press, 2016), 86.

57 Cavarero, *Inclinations*, 99.

58 Cavarero, *Inclinations*, 1–2.

59 Erich Félix Mautner, ed., "Beiträge der Wiener Aktionsgruppe (Brus, Mühl, Nitsch, Schwarzkogler)," special issue, *Le Marais—The Marsh, Der Sumpf, La Palude* (1965), unpaginated. *Le Marais* was published in twelve issues from 1965 to 1968 and edited by University of Vienna student Erich Félix Mautner. It covered recent publications in literature, philosophy, and the arts, art exhibitions and concerts, as well as the recent student protests against Taras Borodajkewycz, the professor of economics known, as I discuss in chapter 2, for his affiliation with National Socialism and his ongoing anti-Semitism.

60 Mautner, "Beiträge der Wiener Aktionsgruppe," unpaginated.

61 I discuss this phenomenon at length in the introduction. For an array of examples, see Becker and Vostell, *Happenings*; Badura-Triska et al., *Vienna Actionism*; RoseLee Goldberg, *Performance: Live Art 1909 to the Present* (Harry N. Abrams, 1979).

62 Udo Kultermann, unattributed excerpt from *Speculum Artis* in *Le Marais* (1965).

63 Peter Gorsen, "Wiener Aktionismus: Begriffe und Theorie," in *Kunst in Österreich 1945–1995: Ein Symposion der Hochschule für Angewandte Kunst in Wien im April 1995*, ed. Patrick Werkner (WUV-Universitätsverlag, 1996), 149.

64 These works also feature as "forerunners" in chronologies of *Aktionskunst*. See Schilling, *Aktionskunst*, 40–44.

65 Yves Klein, *Overcoming the Problematics of Art: The Writings of Yves Klein*, trans. Klaus Ottmann (Spring Publications, 2007), 114. See also Jones, *Body Art*, 86–89.

66 Badura-Triska et al., *Vienna Actionism*, 405, translation modified based on the original German biography of Schieb in Eva Badura-Triska, Hubert Klocker, and Museum moderner Kunst Stiftung Ludwig, eds., *Wiener Aktionismus: Kunst und Aufbruch im Wien der 1960er-Jahre* (Verlag der Buchhandlung Walther König, 2012), 406.

67 Anna Brus, interviewed by Andrea Schurian, in *Amor, Psyche, Aktion*, 282.

68 See Weibel and VALIE EXPORT, *wien: bildkompendium*, 85–87 and 248; Gorsen, *Sexualästhetik* (1972), 174–76; Vogel, *Film as Subversive Art*, 252. Amos Vogel misidentifies the images that he is looking at but notes that what he calls an "episode in Otto Muehl's *Sodoma*" is "coauthored by Hanel Koeck." Koeck states her interest in inverting Muehl's "sexist" and "antifeminist" treatment of women. Koeck, interviewed by Blancsubé, "Entrevista," 527, 529.

69 Peter Gorsen, "Scheißkerl: Das Drehbuch zur Aktion und wie es dazu kam (1969)," in *Das Nachleben des Wiener Aktionismus: Interpretationen und Einlassungen seit 1969*, ed. Peter Gorsen (Ritter, 2009), 222–27.

70 See Branden Joseph, *The Roh and the Cooked: Tony Conrad and Beverly Grant in Europe* (August Verlag, 2012), 102–3; Otto Muehl, interviewed by Danièle Roussel, in *Der Wiener Aktionismus und die Österreicher: Gespräche*, ed. Danièle Roussel (Ritter, 1995), 31–43.

71 In 1991, Muehl was sentenced to seven years in prison for statutory rape. For a narrative of life growing up in Muehl's commune and testament to Muehl's and the communards' victims, see Paul-Julien Robert, dir., *Meine keine Familie* (FreibeuterFilm, 2013). Robert's account critically contests the largely sympathetic narratives of Muehl's life and work at the commune given by Otmar Bauer, Muehl's longtime friend and co-communard, Robert Fleck, historian of the "Viennese avant-garde," and Hubert Klocker, former director and chief curator of the Sammlung Friederichshof and the Estate of Otto Muehl. See Otmar Bauer, *1968: Autographische Notizen zu Wiener Aktionismus, Studentenrevolte, Underground,*

Kommune Friedrichshof, Mühl Ottos Sekte (Edition Roesner, 2004); Robert Fleck, *Die Mühl-Kommune: Freie Sexualität und Aktionismus – Geschichte eines Experiments* (König, 2003). Curatorial strategies, especially in Austria, have chosen to completely overlook Muehl's crimes. See Peter Noever, ed., *Otto Muehl: Leben/Kunst/Werk; Aktion Utopie Malerei 1960–2004; MAK, Wien, 3.3.-31.5.2004* (König, 2003); Klaus Albrecht Schröder, ed., *The Beginning: Kunst in Österreich 1945 bis 1980* (Albertina; Hirmer Verlag, 2020), especially Brigitte Borchhardt-Birbaumer's essay, which evasively refers to the commune as "the most radical attempt at a social utopia" that "failed because of its hierarchical power structures" (70).

72 Benjamin H. D. Buchloh, "1962b," in *Art Since 1900: Modernism, Antimodernism, Postmodernism*, ed. Hal Foster, Rosalind Krauss, Yve-Alain Bois, Benjamin H. D. Buchloh, and David Joselit, 3rd ed. (Thames and Hudson, 2016), 538.

73 Ana Steiner was born in the region of Slavonia, formerly Yugoslavia, today Croatia. Her family was dispossessed of its farmland during Tito's partisan uprising and immigrated via Hungary to Austria, where they were interned in Carinthia before settling in Styria. See Anna Brus, interviewed by Schurian, in *Amor Psyche Aktion*, 284–92.

74 Günter Brus, *Das gute alte Wien* (Jung and Jung, 2007), 73, also cited by Johanna Schwanberg, "Die beiden Annas: Zur Magdalena Freys digitaler Bildserie über Anna Brus," in *Magdalena Frey: Arbeiten/Works, 1989–2007* (23project art-gallery, 2007), 25. Günter attributes Anna's perseverance in part to her experience as a "child refugee."

75 In contrast, see Parcerisas, "Körper und Politik," where *Ana* is described with reference to Günter: "His wife Ana is again the passive-female model" (239).

76 I very much mean to distinguish the kind of feminism I am interested in from the corporate genre inaugurated by Sheryl Sandberg, with Nell Scovell, *Lean In: Women, Work, and the Will to Lead* (Knopf, 2013).

77 Lippard, "Pains and Pleasures," 81.

78 See especially Julia Kristeva, "Women's Time" (1979), trans. Alice Jardine and Harry Blake, *Signs* (Autumn 1981): 13–35.

79 Catherine Spencer, "Acts of Displacement: Lea Lublin's *Mon fils*, May '68, and Feminist Psychosocial Revolt," *Oxford Art Journal* 40, no. 1 (2017): 65–83. Spencer proposes that *Mon fils* is a "performance of motherhood" that runs against the grain of those "acts of feminist revolt" dedicated to women's access to birth control and the legalization of abortion. This article is expanded in Spencer, *Beyond the Happening: Performance Art and the Politics of Communication* (Manchester University Press, 2020).

80 Judith Butler, *Notes Toward a Performative Theory of Assembly* (Harvard University Press, 2018). See Butler's response to Cavarero, "Leaning Out, Caught in the Fall: Interdependency and Ethics in Cavarero," in *Toward a Feminist Ethics of Nonviolence: Adriana Cavarero with Judith Butler, Bonnie Honig, and Other Voices*, ed. Timothy J. Huzar and Clare Woodford (Fordham University Press, 2021), 46–62.

81 Cavarero is well aware of this but does so anyway, noting: "Some stereotypes, such as that propagated in the iconology of the Virgin Mary, in fact have a great critical potentiality that risks remaining concealed precisely because they are too exposed." Cavarero, *Inclinations*, 14.

82 See Mark Devenney, "Querying Cavarero's Rectitude," in which he aims to "render inclination improper," and Clare Woodford, "Queer Madonnas: In Love and Friendship," in Huzar and Woodford, *Toward a Feminist Ethics of Nonviolence*, 141–50 and 161–76, respectively.

83 Lee Edelman, *No Future: Queer Theory and the Death Drive* (Duke University Press, 2004).

84 Anna Brus, interviewed by Schurian, *Amor Psyche Aktion*, 286.

85 See Bonnie Honig, *A Feminist Theory of Refusal* (Harvard University Press, 2021), 47. Honig—

like Cavarero and Butler—is involved in a rereading of Hannah Arendt's theory of natality and action. See Hannah Arendt, *The Human Condition* (University of Chicago Press, 1958).

86 See Nitsch, *Das Orgien Mysterien Theater. Die Partituren*, 1:186–89.

87 Lippard, "Pains and Pleasures," 79.

88 This film is part of a trilogy including *Satisfaction* and *Günter Brus bittet um Rühe*, the last performances in which Schwarzkogler appears before his death. Film stills are reproduced in Christa Steinle and Peter Weibel, eds., *BRUSEUM: Ein Museum für Günter Brus* (Hatje Cantz, 2011), 242.

89 Cavarero, *Inclinations*, 131.

Chapter 2

1 Fritz Keller, *Wien, Mai 68: Eine heiße Viertelstunde* (Junius, 1983).

2 On the failures of *Kunst und Revolution*, see Gerald Raunig, *Kunst und Revolution: Künstlerischer Aktivismus im langen 20. Jahrhundert* (Turia + Kant, 2005); Oliver Jahraus, *Die Aktion des Wiener Aktionismus: Subversion der Kultur und Dispositionierung des Bewusstseins* (Wilhelm Fink, 2001); Paulus Ebner and Karl Vocelka, *Die zahme Revolution: '68 und was davon blieb* (Ueberreuter, 1998); Martina Novotny, *Die Revolution frisst ihre Eltern: 1968 in Österreich: Kunst, Revolution und Mythenbildung* (Tectum, 2008).

3 See Peter Weibel and VALIE EXPORT, eds., *wien: bildkompendium wiener aktionismus und film* (Kohlkunst Verlag, 1970).

4 Peter Gorsen, "Der Wiener Aktionismus: Begriffe und Theorie," in *Kunst in Österreich 1945–1995 - Ein Symposion der Hochschule für Angewandte Kunst in Wien*, ed. Patrick Werkner (WUV-Universitätsverlag, 1996), 140–54. For a new generation, the event is paradigmatic of Viennese Actionism. See Roman Grabner, "*so geht's heim zu mutti*—Österreich und 1968," in *1968: Die grosse Unschuld*, ed. Thomas Kellein, with Roman Grabner and Felicitas von Richthofen (DuMont, 2009), 176–211.

5 Günter Brus, "Niederschrift Brus," June 10, 1968. Document housed in the Literaturarchiv der Österreichischen Nationalbibliothek, Vienna, Vorlaß Oswald Wiener, accession no. 232/04, group 1.4.2, box signature W27 5/2. All subsequent references to this accessioned group are abbreviated: LIT: OW, followed by the box signature number.

6 "Tame revolution" translates the title of Ebner's and Vocelka's historical study *Die zahme Revolution*. As Ingrid Bauer notes, almost every phrase used to describe Austria's 1968 is a diminutive: "'Mailüfterl,' 'heiße Viertelstunde,' 'zahme Revolution,' 'Revolution light,' 'Beistrich der Geschichte' oder eben Sonate versus Symphonie." Ingrid Bauer, "Das 68er-Gedächtnis in Österreich, männergeschichtliche Deutungen und Models als ‚Expertinnen' der Emanzipation," *L'homme: Zeitschrift für feministische Geschichtswissenschaft* 20, no. 2 (2009): 131.

7 Peter Jirak, "Protokoll: Über die Einvernahme von Herrn. cand. phil. Peter Jirak vom 10.6.1968 durch Herrn Hofrat Dr. A. Kitzler im Rektorat der Universität Wien," June 10, 1968. LIT: OW W27 5/2.

8 Jirak, "Protokoll," June 10, 1968.

9 Herwig Friesinger, "Niederschrift Herwig Friesinger 10.6.1968," June 10, 1968. LIT: OW W27 5/2.

10 Gerhard Lauenstein, "9.6.1968 - Niederschrift: Gerhard Lauenstein, Portier des Neuen Institutgeb.," June 9, 1968. LIT: OW W27 5/2. Brus cites Lauenstein's statement in his self-published artist's book devoted to the event. Günter Brus, *Patent Merde* (Vienna, February–April 1969), edition of 70, unpaginated.

11 On the relationship of performance art, documentation, and disparate publics, see Mechtild Widrich, *Performative Monuments—The Rematerialisation of Public Art* (Manchester University Press, 2014); Mechtild Widrich, "The Informative Public of Performance: A Study of Viennese Actionism, 1965–1970," *TDR* 57, no. 1 (Spring 2013): 137–51; Philip Auslander, "The Performativity of Performance Documentation," *PAJ* 28, no. 3 (2003): 1–10; Philip Auslander, *Liveness: Performance in a Mediatized Culture* (Routledge, 1999).

12 Friesinger et al., "Gedächtnisprotokoll Wien 7.6.1968," June 7, 1968. LIT: OW W27 5/2. Brus includes excerpts from the *Gedächtnisprotokoll* in his first self-published artist's book made "in memory" of the June 7 event. Günter Brus, *Patent Urinoir – Zur Erinnerung an den 7. Juni 1968* (Vienna, October 1968), edition of 50, unpaginated.

13 Filmmaker Ernst Schmidt Jr. incorporates brief black-and-white footage of *Kunst und Revolution* into an eponymous 16 mm film (1968). He can be seen filming in several of the photographs of the event by Siegfried Klein, a.k.a. Khasaq. Along with stills from Schmidt's film reel, some of Khasaq's photographs are reproduced in Weibel and VALIE EXPORT, *wien: bildkompendium*, 206–15. For mumok's official account of the event, see Kazuo Kandutsch, "The Event *Kunst und Revolution*," in *Vienna Actionism: Art and Upheaval in 1960s' Vienna*, ed. Eva Badura-Triska, Hubert Klocker, and Museum moderner Kunst Stiftung Ludwig (Verlag der Buchhandlung Walther König, 2012), 184–85, which draws different conclusions from my own and does not reference the archives of police depositions or press statements.

14 In particular, *Die Neue Zeitung* ran photographs by Kurt Martinek of previous "Happenings." The one exception was the *Kronen Zeitung*, which published an anonymous photograph taken at the event in its June 9 and June 14 issues, and another on August 1 attributed to "Bartl" and "Hofmeister." Newspaper clippings in LIT: OW W27 5/4.

15 Unless otherwise noted, all ensuing press coverage referenced in text and in the endnotes is found in press clippings in LIT: OW W27 5/4. Brus reproduced much of this coverage in *Patent Urinoir*, as well as in his third and final artist's book dedicated to *Kunst und Revolution*, which he made after going into exile in West Berlin. Günter Brus, *Unter dem Ladentisch* (West Berlin, spring 1969), edition unknown, unpaginated.

16 Regional Court for Criminal Affairs Vienna, "Festnahme auf Grund Haftbefehl," June 13, 1968. LIT: OW W27 5/2.

17 Details of each arrest are recorded in the Department of Public Prosecution, "Anklageschrift," June 25, 1968. Brus reproduces it in full in *Patent Merde* and *Unter dem Ladentisch*; see also LIT: OW W27 5/2. Wiener was initially accused of urging the audience at *Kunst und Revolution* to go defecate in St. Stephen's Cathedral.

18 Department of Public Prosecution, "Anklageschrift," June 25, 1968.

19 See Otmar Bauer, *1968: Autographische Notizen zu Wiener Aktionismus, Studentenrevolte, Underground, Kommune Friedrichshof, Mühl Ottos Sekte* (Edition Roesner, 2004).

20 Department of Public Prosecution, "Anklageschrift," June 25, 1968.

21 Regional High Court, Vienna, "Im Namen der Republik!" February 25, 1969. LIT: OW W27 5/2.

22 Regional High Court, Vienna, "Im Namen der Republik!" February 25, 1969.

23 Oswald Wiener initiated a petition for Günter Brus's amnesty in 1974. Documented in *Der Löwe: Eine kulturphilosophische Zeitschrift* 31, no. 1 (1974): 15–16; original documents held at the Getty Research Center, Otto Muehl Papers, box 34.

24 See Brus, *Patent Urinoir*; *Patent Merde*; *Unter dem Ladentisch*.

25 Brus founded *Die Schastrommel: Organ der österreichischen Exilregierung* in West Berlin in May 1969 together with Otmar Bauer, Hermann Nitsch, Gerhard Rühm, and Oswald Wiener. The title can be translated as "Farting drum: Organ of the Austrian exile government," or, teasing out the misogynist Austrian colloquialism in the first term, "fishwife" or "crone."

Brus continued to edit and publish *Die Schastrommel*, through 1976, producing seventeen small-run editions, many of which feature his prints and unique inserts. In 1974, he changed the name of the journal to *Die Drossel* (The choke).

26 Sections of Oswald Wiener's *Die Verbesserung von Mitteleuropa, Roman* were published in the Austrian literary and arts magazine *Manuskripte*. The first installment, "Die Verbesserung von Mitteleuropa (Beginn), Roman," appeared in issue 13, 1965; the eighth installment, including Wiener's essay on the "Bio-Adapter," appeared in issue 22, 1968; the last installment was in issue 27, 1969. See also Oswald Wiener, *die verbesserung von mitteleuropa, roman*, ed. Thomas Eder (Jung und Jung, 2013); Oswald Wiener, "appendix A: the bio-adapter," trans. Gerrit Jackson with Jakob Schillinger, *October* 170 (Fall 2019): 51–60.

27 Peter Jirak, "9.6.1968 Niederschrift Jirak akad. Maler und cand. phil.," June 9, 1968. LIT: OW W27 5/2.

28 Jirak, "Protokoll," June 10, 1968.

29 Jirak, "Niederschrift," June 9, 1968.

30 Half-page broadside titled "Der SÖS lädt ein: kunst und revolution," reproduced in Brus, *Patent Urinoir*, and Brus, *Unter dem Ladentisch*. See also LIT: OW W27 5/3.

31 Michael Jeannée, interviewed by Danièle Roussel (1993), in *Der Wiener Aktionismus und die Österreicher: Gespräche*, ed. Danièle Roussel (Ritter, 1995), 158.

32 Jeannée's article is reproduced in Brus, *Unter dem Ladentisch*, and Roussel, *Der Wiener Aktionismus*, 155.

33 "Linksextremistischen Studenten verursachten Skandal," *Die Presse*, June 10, 1968; "Eine Geschmacklosigkeit auf akademischem Boden," *Kronen Zeitung*, June 9, 1968; "Skandalszenen an Wiener Universität: Schwerste sexuelle Ausschreitungen des Sozialistischen Studentenbundes," *Südost-Tagespost*, June 9, 1968.

34 "Skandalszenen in der Universität," *Volksblatt*, June 9, 1968. The byline reads: "Bei SÖS-Veranstaltung: Hörsaal wird Schweinestall—‚Höhepunkt' dieses Skandals waren schwerste sexuelle Ausschreitungen."

35 "Nach Orgie in Uni: ‚Wir werden den SOeS-Boß lynchen,'" *Express*, June 10, 1968; "Polizeistrafen für Porno-Revoluzzer!" *Kronen Zeitung*, June 10, 1968.

36 Forum Politische Bildung, ed., "Wendepunkte und Kontinuitäten. Zäsuren der demokratischen Entwicklung in der österreichischen Geschichte," special issue, *Informationen zur Politischen Bildung* (Studienverlag, 1998), 158.

37 Novotny, *Die Revolution frisst ihre Eltern*, 71.

38 Keller, *Wien, Mai 68*, 57.

39 The communist student party, the VdS (Union of Democratic Students), represented less than 1 percent of students in Austria, infrequently appearing on ballots. See Ebner and Vocelka, *Die zahme Revolution*, 59–60. National memory of the period is similarly apolitical. See Bauer, "Das 68er-Gedächtnis in Österreich."

40 See Ebner and Vocelka, *Die zahme Revolution*, 70–71.

41 Ebner and Vocelka, *Die zahme Revolution*. On the women's movement, see Maria Mesner, "Political Culture and the Abortion Conflict: A Comparison of Austria and the United States," in *From World War to Waldheim: Culture and Politics in Austria and the United States*, ed. David F. Good and Ruth Wodak (Berghahn Books, 1999), 187–209; Dagmar Herzog, "Sexuality in Twentieth-Century Austria: An Introduction," in *Sexuality in Austria* (2009), ed. Günter Bischof, Anton Pelinka, and Dagmar Herzog (Routledge, 2017), 7–20.

42 See Dieter Stiefel, *Entnazifizierung in Österreich* (Europaverlag, 1981), esp. 79–124; Sebastian Meissl, Klaus-Dieter Mulley, and Oliver Rathkolb, eds., *Verdrängte Schuld, verfehlte Sühne: Entnazifizierung in Österreich, 1945–1955* (R. Oldenbourg Verlag, 1986).

43 See Anton Pelinka and Erika Weinzierl, *Das Grosse Tabu: Österreichs Umgang mit seiner Vergan-*

genheit (Edition S, Verlag der Österreichischen Staatsdruckerei, 1987); Anton Pelinka, "The Great Austrian Taboo: The Repression of the Civil War," in *Coping with the Past: Germany and Austria After 1945*, ed. Kathy Harms, Lutz-Rainer Reuter, and Volker Dürr (University of Wisconsin Press, 1990), 56–65; Peter Utgaard, *Remembering and Forgetting Nazism: Education, National Identity and the Victim Myth in Postwar Austria* (Berghahn Books, 2003).

44 See Stiefel, *Entnazifizierung in Österreich*; Günter Bischof, "Victims? Perpetrators? 'Punching Bags' of European Historical Memory? The Austrians and Their World War II Legacies," *German Studies Review* 27, no. 1 (February 2004): 17–32.

45 Anthony Bushell, *Austria: 1945–1955: Studies in Political and Cultural Re-Emergence* (University of Wales Press, 1996), 7.

46 Anthony Bushell, *Polemical Austria: The Rhetorics of National Identity—From Empire to the Second Republic* (University of Wales Press, 2013).

47 Heinz Fischer, *Einer im Vordergrund – Taras Borodajkewycz* (Ephelant Verlag, 2015); Keller, *Wien, Mai 68*, 57–66; Ebner and Vocelka, *Die zahme Revolution*, 59–68.

48 Letter submitted to the *Kronen Zeitung*, June 18, 1968.

49 "ZOCK schlägt zu: Ein Wiener Happening mit Polizeieinsatz," *Die Presse*, April 24, 1967, in Weibel and VALIE EXPORT, *wien: bildkompendium*, 164. On *ZOCK*, see Thomas Eder, "Kunst-Revolution-Erkenntnis. Oswald Wiener und ZOCK," in *Schluß mit dem Abendland! der lange Atem der österreichischen Avantgarde*, ed. Thomas Eder and Klaus Kastberger (Paul Zsolnay, 2000), 60–81.

50 Jürgen Becker and Wolf Vostell, eds., *Happenings. Fluxus. Pop art. Nouveau réalisme. Eine Dokumentation* (Rowohlt, 1965); Allan Kaprow, *Assemblage, Environments & Happenings* (Harry N. Abrams, 1966).

51 Keller, *Wien, Mai 68*.

52 See Lily Woodruff, *Disordering the Establishment: Participatory Art and Institutional Critique in France, 1958–1981* (Duke University Press, 2020); Kristin Ross, *May '68 and Its Afterlives* (University of Chicago Press, 2002).

53 See Alfred Schäfer, *1968 – Die Aura des Widerstands* (Schöningh, 2015); Frank Böckelmann and Herbert Nagel, *Subversive Aktion: Der Sinn der Organisation ist ihr Scheitern* (Neue Kritik, 2002); Aribert Reimann, *Dieter Kunzelmann: Avantgardist, Protestler, Radikaler* (Vandenhoeck & Ruprecht, 2009).

54 "Vienne, le strip-tease et la révolution," *Le Monde*, June 11, 1968; "Notdurft gegen Notstand," *Münchner Merkur*, June 11, 1968.

55 Gerald Raunig, *Kunst und Revolution: Künstlerischer Aktivismus im langen 20. Jahrhundert* (Turia + Kant, 2005); citations from Gerald Raunig, *Art and Revolution: Transversal Activism in the Long Twentieth Century*, trans. Aileen Derieg (Semiotext(e), 2007), 187–202.

56 Raunig, *Art and Revolution*, 200.

57 Bushell notes: "There is so often an unmistakable air of regret, of weariness, or even of impotence in Austrian writing regarding the notion of Austria." *Polemical Austria*, 33.

58 See respectively "Walter Pichler Niederschrift," June 12, 1968; "Niederschrift Der Zeuge Erwin Ofner," June 10, 1968; "Niederschrift: Zeuge Dr. Robert Jungt," undated; "Niederschrift: Janz Bruno, Pedell des Neuen Institutsgeb.," June 9, 1968. LIT: OW W27 5/2.

59 Psychiatric evaluations by Heinrich Gross and Rudolf Quatember are cited by the Department of Public Prosecution, "Anklageschrift," June 25, 1968. Brus cites from the evaluations extensively in *Unter dem Ladentisch*.

60 See Wolfgang Neugebauer, "Die Klinik 'Am Spiegelgrund' 1940-1945: Eine 'Kinderfachabteilung' im Rahmen der NS-'Euthanasie,'" *Jahrbuch des Vereins für Geschichte der Stadt Wien* 52 (February 1996): 289–305. For his atrocious work in the service of Nazism at this "clinic,"

Gross evaded trial in the 1950s on account of a technicality, and again in 1980 due to the statute of limitations for manslaughter in Austria. Gross was tried only in 2000, when the case against him was dismissed due to his poor health. See the obituary "Heinrich Gross, 90, Psychiatrist at Nazi Death Clinic in Austria, Is Dead," *New York Times*, December 23, 2005.

61 Brus collects and reprints hate mail in *Patent Urinoir* and *Unter dem Ladentisch*; it is also cited in an unsigned, undated flyer made and circulated by friends while he was in custody in 1968. LIT: OW W27 5/3.

62 Erwin Szele, letter to the *Kronen Zeitung* on the topic, "Das Happening," June 28, 1968. Brus excerpts Szele's letter in *Patent Urinoir*.

63 Brus, "Niederschrift Brus," June 10, 1968. LIT: OW W27 5/2.

64 Diedrich Diederichsen, "Gegen die Wirklichkeit. Der Sprung aus der Geschichte und seine Geschichte," in *Teststrecke Kunst: Wiener Avantgarden nach 1945*, ed. Elisabeth Großegger and Sabine Müller (Sonderzahl, 2012), 301.

65 Philip Ursprung, "'Catholic Tastes': Hurting and Healing the Body in Viennese Actionism in the 1960s," in *Performing the Body, Performing the Text*, ed. Amelia Jones and Andrew Stephenson (Routledge, 1999), 147. See also Hubert Klocker, "Viennese Waltzes: Viennese Actionism and the Law," in *The Trials of Art*, ed. Daniel McClean (Ridinghouse, 2007), 273–88; Peter Weibel, "Verhöhnung von Anstand und Sitte: Der Wiener Aktionismus vor Gericht," *Neues Forum*, January–February 1980, 56–63.

66 On the relation of this action to its "uninformed" and "informative" as well as future publics, see Widrich, *Performative Monuments* and "The Informative Public of Performance."

67 Federal Police Vienna, "Strafverfügung," July 7, 1965, reproduced in Monika Faber, *Günter Brus - Werkumkreisung*, ed. Klaus Albrecht Schröder (Verlag der Buchhandlung Walther König, 2003), 73.

68 Regional Court of Criminal Affairs Vienna, "Haftbefehl Brus," June 12, 1968. LIT: OW W27 5/2.

69 Regional Court of Criminal Affairs Vienna, "Haftbefehl Brus," June 12, 1968.

70 Clause 248 of the Austrian Criminal Code, *Strafgesetzbuch*, https://www.jusline.at/gesetz/stgb/paragraf/248.

71 See the repetition of this myth in Beth Hinderliter, "Citizen Brus Examines His Body: Actionism and Activism in Vienna, 1968," *October* 147, no. 3 (Winter 2014): 84.

72 Like all of Austria's national symbols after the Second World War, the national anthem stood under revision. In 1938, the German National Anthem, which includes the well-known phrase "Deutschland, Deutschland über alles," was adopted. A new Austrian anthem was made official in October 1946. Paula Preradović wrote the lyrics, "Land der Berge, Land am Strome" (Land of mountains, land by the river), which were set to Mozart. In 2011, some lyrics were changed to be more gender inclusive.

73 Brus, "Niederschrift," June 10, 1968.

74 Brus, "Niederschrift," June 10, 1968.

75 Brus, "Niederschrift," June 13, 1968. LIT: OW W27 5/2.

76 Brus, "Niederschrift," June 19, 1968. LIT: OW W27 5/2.

77 Brus, "Niederschrift," June 19, 1968.

78 Karl Rosenkranz, *Aesthetik des Hässlichen* (1853) (F. Frommann, 1968). See also Andrei Pop and Mechtild Widrich, eds., *Ugliness: The Non-Beautiful in Art and Theory* (I. B. Tauris, 2014).

79 Peter Gorsen captures aspects of this dynamic in his discussion of Rosenkranz and "Hässlichkeit" in *Das Prinzip Obszön: Kunst, Pornographie und Gesellschaft* (Rowohlt, 1969), 16–38. The etymological connection I foreground would complement the discussion in Nina

Athanassoglou-Kallmyer, "Ugliness," in *Critical Terms for Art History*, ed. Robert S. Nelson and Richard Shiff, 2nd ed. (University of Chicago Press, 2003), 281–95.

80 Werner Hofmann, "Die Wiener Aktionisten," in *Luther und die Folgen für die Kunst*, ed. Werner Hofmann (Prestel Verlag, 1983), 642.

81 Hofmann, "Die Wiener Aktionisten," 642.

82 Hofmann, "Die Wiener Aktionisten," 644.

83 The "internationales Kompetenzzentrum für Wiener Aktionismus" at mumok was established in 2003; the Nitsch Museum in Mistelbach opened in 2007; the BRUSEUM – Universalmuseum Joanneum, Graz, dedicated to Günter Brus, was founded in 2008 and opened in 2011; the Sammlung Friedrichshof was a stand-alone museum in Zurndorf, on the former grounds of Otto Muehl's commune until the collection was partially sold in 2002 to mumok, and again in 2022 to gallerist Philipp Konzett. Most recently, the WAM (Wiener Aktionismus Museum) opened in Vienna with the purchase and relocation of the remaining collection of Sammlung Friedrichshof. Konzett is managing director, and Eva Badura-Triska, formerly curator of mumok, is chief curator.

84 Hubert Klocker, "Gesture and the Object: Liberation as *Aktion*: A European Component of Performative Art," in *Out of Actions: Between Performance and the Object, 1949–1979*, ed. Paul Schimmel (Cantz, 1998), 172.

85 On Viennese Actionism as "avant-garde," see Badura-Triska et al., *Vienna Actionism*; Klaus Albrecht Schröder, ed., *The Beginning: Kunst in Österreich 1945 bis 1980* (Albertina; Hirmer Verlag, 2020); Klaus Kastberger, "Wien 50/60. Eine Art einzige österreichische Avantgarde," in Eder and Kastberger, *Schluß mit dem Abendland*, 5–26.

86 Mechtild Widrich, "The 'Ugliness' of the Avant-Garde," in Pop and Widrich, *Ugliness*, 69–81.

87 See these positions documented in Becker and Vostell, *Happenings* (1965), as well as Jürgen Schilling, *Aktionskunst: Identität von Kunst und Leben? Eine Dokumentation* (C. J. Bucher, 1978). See also Wolf Vostell, *Aktionen: Happenings und Demonstrationen seit 1965* (Rowohlt, 1970); Jörn Merkert, ed., *ADA: Aktionen der Avantgarde, Berlin, 1973* (Neuer Berliner Kunstverein, 1973).

88 Unsigned, undated flyer, ÖNB-OW-27 5/3. Brus reproduces this flyer in *Patent Urinoir*.

89 On the Destruction in Art Symposium (DIAS), a crucial venue for exchange among contemporary artists concerned with action and art, see Kristine Stiles, "Synopsis of the Destruction in Art Symposium (DIAS) and Its Theoretical Significance," *The Act*, March 1987, 22–31; Justin Hoffmann, *Destruktionskunst: Der Mythos der Zerstörung in der Kunst der frühen sechziger Jahre* (S. Schreiber, 1995), 147–66; Paul McCarthy, *Paul McCarthy's Lowlife Slowlife: Tidebox Tidebook* (CCA Wattis Institute for Contemporary Arts and Hatje Cantz, 2010).

90 See Hal Foster, *The Return of the Real: The Avant-Garde at the End of the Century* (MIT Press, 1996); Benjamin H. D. Buchloh, *Neo-Avantgarde and Culture Industry: Essays on European and American Art from 1955 to 1975* (MIT Press, 2000).

91 E. M. Podrecca, writing in to the *Express*, June 25, 1968.

92 *Wiener Wochenblatt*, June 22, 1968. Subsequent in-text citations in this section are from this source. Brus reproduces the June 22 cover with the image of him and Anna in bed (see figs. 2.1, 2.15) as the first page of *Unter dem Ladentisch*.

93 The picture above Diana's crib is an edition of Otto Muehl's two-color screen print *Kettenraucher Mao* (Chain-smoker Mao, 1967).

94 Hate mail and death threats collected in *Patent Urinoir* and *Unter dem Ladentisch*. In *Patent Urinoir*, Brus appropriates the designation "most-hated Austrian," writing a fictional autobiographical text entitled "Meistgehaßter Österreicher."

95 Anna Brus, interviewed by Danièle Roussel (1993), in *Der Wiener Aktionismus*, 26.

96 Anonymous letters reprinted in Brus, *Unter dem Ladentisch*; Brus, *Patent Urinoir*.

Chapter 3

1 Alfred Gulden, "Aktionsraum 1: Erinnerung in Bewegung," *Merkur: Deutsche Zeitschrift für Europäisches Denken*, April 1995, 300.

2 See A1 Informationen Verlagsgesellschaft, ed., *Aktionsraum 1, oder, 57 Blindenhunde* (A1 Informationen Verlagsgesellschaft, 1970), 144–49. See also Kathy O'Dell, *Contract with the Skin: Masochism, Performance Art, and the 1970s* (University of Minnesota Press, 1998), 7. O'Dell notes that it is the Aktionsraum 1 publication that introduces her to Brus's performance art, which she sees as an anomaly. The proximity Brus establishes with his audience in *Zerreißprobe* disengages from the "distance" and "alienation" essential to what she calls "the contract" established between artist and audience in "masochistic" performances by Vito Acconci, Gina Pane, Marina Abramović and Ulay, and Chris Burden. Brus, in short, breaks the contract.

3 Gulden, "Aktionsraum 1," 301.

4 Eva Madelung, Alfred Gulden, and Peter Nemetscheck, "Aus unseren Protokollen," in A1 Informationen Verlagsgesellschaft, *Aktionsraum 1*, 145, revised and reprinted in Gulden, "Aktionsraum 1," 301.

5 Madelung et al., "Aus unseren Protokollen," 145; Gulden, "Aktionsraum 1," 301.

6 See Amelia Jones, *Body Art/Performing the Subject* (University of Minnesota Press, 1998).

7 Peter Weibel, "Aktion statt Theater," *Neues Forum*, May 1972, 50–51.

8 Weibel, "Aktion statt Theater," 50.

9 Peter Weibel, "Wien, 12. November 1973, Äusserungen auf Tonband," *Der Löwe: Eine kunstphilosophische Zeitschrift* 1, no. 31 (May 1974): 18.

10 Thomas McEvilley "Art in the Dark" *Artforum*, Summer 1983, 66, reprinted in *Austrian Drawings: Günter Brus, Hermann Nitsch, Arnulf Rainer* (Renaissance Society, 1986).

11 One account of *Wiener Spaziergang* (Viennese walk), which I discuss in chapter 2 and later in this chapter, mistakenly states that Brus "paints his body white and walks nude through the center of Vienna." See *Austrian Drawings: Günter Brus, Hermann Nitsch, Arnulf Rainer*, unpaginated.

12 With attention to "self-harm," Helmut Draxler and Rosemarie Brucher have compellingly situated Brus's work within the Christian tradition of asceticism and Western philosophy of the sublime, respectively. Helmut Draxler, "Asket der letzen Tagen," *Kunstforum* 75 (1984): 129–61; Rosemarie Brucher, *Subjektermächtigung und Naturunterwerfung: Künstlerische Selbstverletzung im Zeichen von Kants Ästhetik des Erhabenen* (Transcript Verlag, 2014). In contrast, Brus's work is often referred to as "painting" with blood and excreta. See Monika Wagner, *Das Material der Kunst: Eine Andere Geschichte der Moderne* (Beck, 2001); Uwe Schneede, "Der Körper als Material: Wiener Aktionismus," in *Die Geschichte der Kunst im 20. Jahrhundert: Von den Avantgarden bis zur Gegenwart* (Beck, 2001).

13 Peter Weibel, "Zur Aktionskunst von Günter Brus," in *Günter Brus: Der Überblick*, ed. Hildegund Amanshauser and Dieter Ronte (Residenz Verlag, 1986), 37.

14 Edition Hundertmark, *1. Edition Box* (1970), edition 23 of 25, housed in the Jean Brown papers, 1916–1995 (bulk 1958–1985), Getty Research Institute, Research Library, accession no. 890164, series VI, object no. 1362-156.

15 Peter Weibel, "Zur Aktionskunst von Günter Brus," 44.

16 Werner Schulz's fifteen-minute, twenty-one-second 16 mm color film was not authorized by Brus in 1970 but has been subsequently integrated into the standard presentation of Brus's work. See the DVD box set *Günter Brus: Bodyanalysis: Actions 1964–1970* (Edition Kröthenhayn, 2010). Brus's request to close the window is made at minute 1:27 of Schulz's film.

17 Rosalind Krauss, *Under Blue Cup* (MIT Press, 2011), 106.

18 Albrecht Dürer, *The Painter's Manual: A Manual of Measurement of Lines, Areas, and Solids by Means of Compass and Ruler Assembled by Albrecht Dürer for the Use of All Lovers of Art with Appropriate Illustrations Arranged to be Printed in the Year MDXXV*, trans. Walter L. Strauss (Abaris Books, 1977), 434–35.

19 Gerald Schröder compellingly refers to the moment in Brus's performance when he asks to close the window as a "radikalen Bruch" (radical break) with the artistic illusionism associated with the perspectival space of painting. I see it, in contrast, as an attempt to stress and inhibit the spatial dispositive of perspective. Gerald Schröder, *Schmerzensmänner: Trauma und Therapie in der westdeutschen und österreichischen Kunst der 1960er Jahre* (Wilhelm Fink, 2011), 309.

20 See Dieter Schwarz, "Chronologie," in *Von der Aktionsmalerei zum Aktionismus, Wien 1960–1965: Günter Brus, Adolf Frohner, Otto Muehl, Hermann Nitsch, Alfons Schilling, Rudolf Schwarzkogler*, ed. Museum Fridericianum Kassel, Kunstmuseum Winterthur, and Scottish National Gallery of Modern Art Edinburgh (Ritter Verlag, 1988), 123.

21 Günter Brus, *Wiener Tagebuch* (1960), excerpted in Schwarz, "Chronologie," 126.

22 Brus, *Wiener Tagebuch* (1960), excerpted in Schwarz, "Chronologie," 126–27.

23 The so-called Vienna Group (*wiener gruppe*) parodied Prachensky—his action painting, and his posturing as an action painter—in their second literary cabaret of 1959, of which Brus would at least have heard accounts through the circles around Galerie nächst St. Stephan. See Gerhard Rühm, ed., *Die Wiener Gruppe. Achleitner, Artmann, Bayer, Rühm, Wiener. Texte, Gemeinschaftsarbeiten, Aktionen* (Rowohlt, 1967). Brus derides Mathieu's work as "easy prostitution." Brus, "Berlin, 23. April 1974, Gespräch auf Tonband," *Der Löwe* (May 1974): 13.

24 Harold Rosenberg "The American Action Painters" (1952), in *The Tradition of the New* (Thames and Hudson, 1962), 25.

25 Allan Kaprow, "The Legacy of Jackson Pollock," *Artnews* (1958): 25, 56, 57. See also Judith F. Rodenbeck, *Radical Prototypes: Allan Kaprow and the Invention of Happenings* (MIT Press, 2011).

26 Kaprow, "Legacy," 26, italics original.

27 Kaprow, "Legacy," 56–57. Tracing the happening's artistic roots back to US abstract expressionist action painting and further to dada and surrealism, Kaprow writes that happenings "are a moral act, a human stand of great urgency, whose professional status as art is less a criterion than their certainty as an ultimate existential commitment." Allan Kaprow, "Happenings in the New York Scene" (1961), in *Essays on the Blurring of Art and Life*, ed. Jeff Kelley (University of California Press, 2003), 21.

28 Today, the Akademie für angewandte Kunst is the Universität für angewandte Kunst Vienna.

29 Robert Fleck, *Avantgarde in Wien: Die Geschichte der Galerie nächst St. Stephan, 1954–1982: Kunst und Kunstbetrieb in Österreich* (Die Galerie Löcker, 1982).

30 Kaprow, "Legacy," 26.

31 Schwarz, "Chronologie," 115–17. See also Caroline Lillian Schopp, "Exit Strategy: On Günter Brus and Alfons Schilling," *Artforum*, March 2022, 61–62.

32 Johanna Schwanberg, "Chronologie," in *Günter Brus - Werkumkreisung*, ed. Monika Faber (Verlag der Buchhandlung Walther König, 2003), 20.

33 Schwarz, "Chronologie," 116.

34 See *The New American Painting, as Shown in Eight European Countries, 1958–1959* (Museum of Modern Art, New York, 1959). On Austria's (lack of) institutions representing modern and contemporary art in the period, see Fleck, *Avantgarde in Wien*.

35 *New American Painting*, 9.

36 Reviews collected in *New American Painting*, 7–12. These exemplify Serge Guilbaut's compelling diagnosis of how the veritable ideology of freedom conveyed through US abstract expressionism led to New York's stealing "the idea of Modern art" from Europe. Serge Guilbaut, *How New York Stole the Idea of Modern Art from Europe: Abstract Expressionism, Freedom, and the Cold War* (University of Chicago Press, 1983).

37 Arnold Rüdlinger, cited in Egon Vietta, "Ein europäisches Gespräch über Kunst in der Abtei Seckau in Österreich," in Fleck, *Avantgarde in Wien*, 86.

38 Michel Tapié, cited in Vietta, "Ein europäisches Gespräch," in Fleck, *Avantgarde in Wien*, 88.

39 Significantly, Galerie Würthle in Vienna responded to the *New American Painting* exhibition with a smaller iteration, *Amerikanische Maler der Gegenwart* (American painters of the present), June 19–July 8, 1961. It included Pollock's works *Night Ceremony* (1944), *Cathedral* (1947), and *Number 10* (1949). See *Amerikanische Maler der Gegenwart* (Galerie Würthle, organized by United States Information Agency, 1961). This show also appeared at the American embassy in London as *Vanguard American Painting*, February 28–March 30, 1962, and at the Hessisches Landesmuseum Darmstadt as *Abstrakte Amerikanische Malerei*, April 14–May 13, 1962. A small exhibition catalog was produced for the Darmstadt show in German with black-and-white reproductions, including a very small reproduction of Pollock's *Number 10* (1949).

40 Herbert Read, "Introduction," in *Junge Maler der Gegenwart* (Vienna Künstlerhaus, 1959), 6.

41 Julien Alvard, untitled essay in *Junge Maler der Gegenwart*, 25. The essay is in French: "il [Pollock] en [Guernica/Picasso] a brisé le formalism." This is translated in German as "er [Pollock] hat dessen [Guernica/Picasso] Formgebundenheit zerstört" (83). A black-and-white reproduction of Pollock's *One: Number 31, 1950* is reproduced in the catalog in a pitifully small format—and upside down.

42 Schwarz, "Chronologie," 115–16.

43 Werner Haftmann, "Malerei nach 1945," in *II. Documenta '59: Kunst nach 1945, Malerei, Skulptur, Druckgrafik* (DuMont Schauberg, 1959), 1:17.

44 Haftmann, "Malerei nach 1945," 13.

45 Clement Greenberg "'American Type' Painting (1955)," in *Clement Greenberg: The Collected Essays and Criticism*, ed. John O'Brien (University of Chicago Press, 1993), 3:217.

46 Sam Hunter, "Introduction," in *Jackson Pollock* (Museum of Modern Art, New York, 1956), 5–12, excerpted and translated by Werner Haftmann in *II. Documenta '59*, 326.

47 Hunter, "Introduction," 11, and *II. Documenta '59*, 326.

48 Kaprow, "Legacy," 57. Kaprow's and Vostell's interlinked anthologies foreground this vocabulary. Jürgen Becker and Wolf Vostell, eds., *Happenings. Fluxus. Pop art. Nouveau réalisme. Eine Dokumentation* (Rowohlt, 1965); Allan Kaprow, *Assemblage, Environments & Happenings* (Harry N. Abrams, 1966); Wolf Vostell, *Aktionen: Happenings und Demonstrationen seit 1965* (Rowohlt, 1970). See the section "The Action Paradigm" of the introduction.

49 Sylvia Wynter foregrounds "Man," with a capital *M*, as the figure that overdetermines the "descriptive statement" of the human. Sylvia Wynter, "Unsettling the Coloniality of Being/Power/Truth/Freedom: Towards the Human, After Man, Its Overrepresentation—An Argument," *New Centennial Review* 3, no. 3 (Fall 2003): 257–337.

50 Brus, *Wiener Tagebuch* (1960), excerpted in Schwarz, "Chronologie," 126–27. Brus reflected, "with the infinite picture (as I understand it)," Pollock wanted "the painting as a part of the universe . . . infinitely (*unendlich*)." Brus wanted something else.

51 Of those of Brus's works pictured in historical photographs of these shows, the whereabouts of only two are known today. See Christa Steinle and Peter Weibel, eds., *BRUSEUM: Ein Museum für Günter Brus* (Hatje Cantz, 2011).

52 Alfred Schmeller, "Mit Kopf durch die Leinwand. Zur Ausstellung Brus und Schilling in der 'Jungen Generation' am Börseplatz," *Kurier*, June 6, 1961. Reproduced in Schwarz, "Chronologie," 114.

53 Otto Muehl, "Wien, 12. November 1973, Äusserungen auf Tonband," *Der Löwe* (May 1974): 9.

54 Muehl's acquaintance, the psychoanalyst and gallerist Josef Dvorak, offered Brus the basement of his gallery. Brus's notes on *Malerei in einem labyrinth-artig verbauten Raum* are integrated into his short text "Bemerkungen zu *Ana* (1984)," in the edition of performance documents, *Ana (1964)* published by Galerie Heike Curtze in 1985. Reproduced in Steinle and Weibel, *BRUSEUM*, 110. Malcolm Green translates this text in his *Brus, Muehl, Nitsch, Schwarzkogler: Writings of the Viennese Actionists* (Atlas, 1999), 25–26. I offer my own translation.

55 This is how Brus titles the work in his first artist's statement and autobiography. See Erich Félix Mautner, ed., "Beiträge der Wiener Aktionsgruppe (Brus, Mühl, Nitsch, Schwarzkogler)," special issue, *Le Marais—The Marsh, Der Sumpf, La Palude* (1965), unpaginated.

56 Arnulf Rainer and the curator-priest Monsignor Otto Mauer, who ran Galerie nächst St. Stephan, are the only recorded visitors to the work. See Schwarz, "Chronologie," 261.

57 Günter Brus, ed., *Die Schastrommel: Organ der österreichischen Exilregierung* 8a (June 1972): 4–5. Issue 8a was dedicated to *Aktionen* from 1964 to 1966; 8b to *Aktionen* from 1967 to 1968; and 8c to *Aktionen* from 1969 to 1970.

58 In addition to his artist's statement in the art and literary journal *Le Marais* in 1965, Brus includes *Malerei in einem labyrinth-artig verbauten Raum* in his autobiographical statement for Peter Weibel and VALIE EXPORT, eds., *wien: bildkompendium wiener aktionismus und film* (Kohlkunst Verlag, 1970), 278. In 1970, he adjusted the date from 1962 (as it appeared in *Le Marais*) to 1963 and used the same title, without the hyphen. It is excluded, however, from international anthologies of *Aktionskunst*. See, e.g., Harald Szeemann, with Hanns Sohm, eds., *Happenings & Fluxus* (Kölnischer Kunstverein, 1970), which includes *Ana* as Brus's first work, and Becker and Vostell's *Happenings* (1965), which excludes Brus entirely. In each of these, the work of Nitsch and Muehl is represented. The idea that *Ana* is Brus's first performance is formalized by the BRUSEUM, which places *Ana* at the beginning of Brus's *Aktionen*. See Steinle and Weibel, *BRUSEUM*, 107.

59 Brus, "Gespräch auf Tonband," 11.

60 Brus, "Bemerkungen zu *Ana* (1984)," 110.

61 Brus, "Bemerkungen zu *Ana* (1984)," 110.

62 Schwarz, "Chronologie," 251; Brus, "Bemerkungen zu *Ana* (1984)," 110.

63 Brus's artist's statement in *Le Marais* (1965), unpaginated, reprinted in Weibel and VALIE EXPORT, *wien: bildkompendium*, 278. For another discussion of *Ana*, see chapter 1.

64 Benjamin H. D. Buchloh, "1962b," in *Art Since 1900: Modernism, Antimodernism, Postmodernism*, ed. Hal Foster, Rosalind Krauss, Yve-Alain Bois, Benjamin H. D. Buchloh, and David Joselit, 3rd ed. (Thames and Hudson, 2016), 538.

65 Carrie Lambert-Beatty, *Being Watched: Yvonne Rainer and the 1960s* (MIT Press, 2008), 173.

66 Brus's artist's statement in "Beiträge der Wiener Aktionsgruppe," *Le Marais* (1965), unpaginated.

67 *Selbstverstümmelung* is often translated as "self-mutilation." The verb *verstümmeln* also means "to garble." My translation of "self-dismemberment" resonates with this inexpressive character. Brus would alternately use the words *Selbstverstrickung* (self-entanglement), *Selbstverstümmelung* (self-dismemberment), and *Selbstentleibung* (self-disembodiment) to describe his practice of *Selbstbemalung*.

68 For a discussion of Franko B's work, see the introduction.

69 Curator Otto Staininger's statement preceding "Beiträge der Wiener Aktionsgruppe," *Le Marais* (1965), unpaginated.

70 Of the four large remnants visible in the documentation, the whereabouts of only two are known today. See Harald Krejci, ed., *Günter Brus: Unruhe nach dem Sturm/Unrest After the Storm* (Verlag der Buchhandlung Walther König, 2018).

71 Brus published the "Strafverfügung, July 7, 1965" of the Federal Police of Vienna in *Die Schastrommel* 8a, 44; also reproduced in *Günter Brus - Werkumkreisung*, 73.

72 Yve-Alain Bois and Rosalind Krauss, *Formless—A User's Guide* (Zone Books, 1997), 108.

73 Julia Kristeva, *Powers of Horror: An Essay on Abjection*, trans. Leon Roudiez (Columbia University Press, 1982). Krauss in particular rejects the relationship of the *informe* to the abject, arguing that the former is a "structure," the latter too bound to a "subject." The exhibition, *Formless*, at the Centre Pompidou in Paris, for which Krauss and Bois prepared their "user's guide" is also a riposte to recent exhibitions of "abject art." See Bois and Krauss, *Formless*, 236–52.

74 Bois and Krauss, *Formless*, 25.

75 Bois and Krauss, *Formless*, 18–25.

76 Bois and Krauss, *Formless*, 108.

77 See Rosalind Krauss, *The Optical Unconscious* (MIT Press, 1993).

78 Rosalind Krauss, "The Politics of the Signifier II: A Conversation on the 'Informe' and the Abject," with Yve-Alain Bois, Hal Foster, Benjamin Buchloh, Denis Hollier, and Helen Molesworth, *October* (Winter 1994): 9.

79 Andrew Weiner has compellingly described the "economy of abjection" of Viennese Actionism as "transforming formlessness," which in his reading ceased to be "a pictorial strategy" and rather "became a means to decompose the unities of body, performance, subject, and ultimately socius." Andrew Weiner, "Reevaluating Actionism: Austrian Performance, Then and Now," *PAJ* 37, no. 3 (September 2015): 54. See also Lucy Weir, "Abject Modernism: The Male Body in the Work of Tatsumi Hijikata, Günter Brus and Rudolf Schwarzkogler," *Tate Papers Online* 23 (Spring 2015).

80 Bois and Krauss, *Formless*, 25.

81 Krauss, "Politics of the Signifier," 12. The scare quotes around "body" refer to a discussion of what she calls the "literal" body and the literalization of the body in recent theory, among which Krauss counts Judith Butler as a bad example.

82 Bois and Krauss, *Formless*, 78.

83 Bois and Krauss, *Formless*, 79. This is their way of excluding discussions of abjection from their consideration of the formless, for they (all too quickly) dismiss the abject as a "subject" (material) which has no "structural" (processual) form.

84 Bois and Krauss, *Formless*, 141. Part of what they are responding to is the action paradigm. As Kristine Stiles writes, "performance art reconfigured humanist concerns traditionally associated with figuration and refocused attention to actual bodies." Stiles, "Performance," in *Critical Terms for Art History*, ed. Robert S. Nelson and Richard Shiff, 2nd ed. (University of Chicago Press, 2003), 86. For Brus, however, the body too remains subject to representation.

85 Bois and Krauss, *Formless*, 146.

86 Brus's performances of body-analysis are well before Vito Acconci performs his series of *Openings* (1970) and *Conversions* (1971), which, with Amelia Jones, I see as exhibitionist: Acconci is "eager to expose himself" and "desperate to reclaim his authority and coherence as a male subject of artistic production." Jones, *Body Art*, 104, 109. Brus does not share this desperation.

87 This is what distinguishes Brus's body-analyses from what Willoughby Sharp called "Body Works" in 1970. Willoughby Sharp, "Body Works," *Avalanche* 1 (Fall 1970): 14–17.

88 The performance is filmed by Hans-Christof Stenzel, 16 mm black-and-white, 5:31 minutes, collection of the BRUSEUM – Universalmuseum Joanneum, Graz.

89 Anna Brus, interviewed by Andrea Schurian, in *Amor Psyche Aktion – Wien. Das Feminine im Wiener Aktionismus* (DOX Centre for Contemporary Art, Prague, 2012), 289.

90 Jennifer Doyle, *Hold It Against Me: Difficulty and Emotion in Contemporary Art* (Duke University Press, 2013).

91 Günter Brus, "12 Fragen von Plunkett," in *Günter Brus: Augensternstunden* (Stedelijk Van Abbemuseum, 1984), 18.

92 Günter Brus, interviewed by Danièle Roussel (1993), in *Der Wiener Aktionismus und die Österreicher: Gespräche*, ed. Danièle Roussel (Ritter, 1995), 27.

93 Adriana Cavarero, *Inclinations: A Critique of Rectitude* (2014), trans. Amanda Minervini and Adam Sitze (Stanford University Press, 2016). For a discussion of Cavarero's claims and their intersections with Viennese Actionism more broadly, see chapter 1.

94 Buchloh "1962b," 464.

95 *II. Documenta '59: Kunst nach 1945*.

96 Haftmann, "Malerei nach 1945," 17.

97 Greenberg, "Review of the Exhibition of School of Paris Painters (1946)," in *Clement Greenberg: The Collected Essays and Criticism*, ed. John O'Brien (University of Chicago Press, 1986), 2:89. Six years earlier, Greenberg had celebrated Picasso's cubism, which realized the destruction of "realistic pictorial space," in "Towards a Newer Laocöon (1940)," in *Clement Greenberg: The Collected Essays and Criticism*, ed. John O'Brien (University of Chicago Press, 1986), 1:35.

98 Several other artists concerned with figuration—Francis Bacon, Max Beckmann, Marc Chagall, Max Ernst, Alberto Giacometti, Fernand Léger—were included in the exhibition, with fewer works, and represented in black-and-white only in the catalog. See *II. Documenta '59: Kunst nach 1945*.

99 Leo Steinberg, "The Algerian Women and Picasso at Large," in *Other Criteria: Confrontations with Twentieth-Century Art* (University of Chicago Press, 1972), 153.

100 Clement Greenberg, "Picasso Since 1945 (1966)," in *The Collected Essays and Criticism*, ed. John O'Brien (University of Chicago Press, 1986), 4:238.

101 Clement Greenberg, "Picasso at Seventy-Five," in *Art and Culture: Critical Essays* (Beacon Press, 1961), 60. This very essay gets significantly reworked, ironically replacing this passage with the phrase "no more than nice" in Clement Greenberg, "Picasso at Seventy-Five (1957)," in O'Brien, *The Collected Essays and Criticism*, 4:27–28.

102 Only Picasso's early synthetic cubist works with organic materials like sand are integrated into Krauss and Bois's discussions of Bataille's "scatological dimension." Bois and Krauss, *Formless*, 31.

103 T. J. Clark, *Picasso and Truth: From Cubism to Guernica* (Princeton University Press, 2013). *Guernica* (1937) is the latest painting Clark treats, and he limits his understanding of "history" to 1956—intriguingly, just around the time Brus takes up residence in the old coal cellar in Vienna. The virtue of Clark's book is that it brings the painterly problematic of bodies and space into view with his term *room-space*, adapted from Steinberg's past participle to describe Picasso's painted bodies as "roomed." Steinberg, *Other Criteria*, 153.

104 These drawings are held in a private collection and reproduced in *Günter Brus – Werkumkreisung*, 84–85.

Chapter 4

1 VALIE EXPORT, "Feministischer Aktionismus. Aspekte," in *Frauen in der Kunst*, ed. Gislind Nabakowski, Helke Sander, and Peter Gorsen (Suhrkamp Verlag, 1980), 1:140–41; VALIE

EXPORT, "Aspects of Feminist Actionism," *New German Critique*, no. 47 (1989): 71; all subsequent in-text English language citations from this translation by VALIE EXPORT.

2 Ingrid Wiener, "Großer Teppich (Porträt Dieter Roth), gewebt 1981–1984," in *Kopiebuch*, by Ingrid Wiener and Dieter Roth, 3 vols. (Galerie Marlene Frei, 1986), vol. 1, unpaginated, reprinted in *Man darf auch weben was man nicht sieht: Die Teppiche von Dieter Roth und Ingrid Wiener—You Can Also Weave What You Do Not See: The Tapestries of Dieter Roth and Ingrid Wiener*, ed. Karin Schick, trans. Ann Marie Bohan and Orla Muhlholland (Kerber Verlag, 2007), 38–40. All translations into English of original texts by Wiener and Roth reprinted in Schick's *Man darf auch weben* are modified by the author based on the German-language original; untranslated materials reprinted in *Man darf auch weben* are noted as such in footnotes and translated by the author.

3 Amelia Jones, "Survey," *The Artist's Body*, ed. Tracey Warr (Phaidon, 2000), 21.

4 Gabriele Schor, ed., *Feministische Avantgarde: Kunst der 1970er-Jahre aus der Sammlung Verbund* (Prestel, 2015).

5 Mechtild Widrich, "Location and Dislocation: The Media Performances of VALIE EXPORT," *PAJ: A Journal of Performance and Art* 33, no. 3 (2011): 53. See also Rose-Anne Gush, "Obliteration: What Remains of the Body in the Works of Unica Zürn and VALIE EXPORT," *Performance Research* 23, no. 8 (2018): 38–48; Rose-Anne Gush, "Contradictions in Time," *Third Text* 33, no. 3 (2019): 355–73.

6 Mechtild Widrich details the performativity of both the visual and the narrative revisions of VALIE EXPORT's *Genitalpanik*. See Widrich, "Can Photographs Make It So? Repeated Outbreaks of VALIE EXPORT's Genital Panic Since 1969," in *Perform, Repeat, Record: Live Art in History*, ed. Amelia Jones and Adrian Heathfield (Intellect Books, 2012), 89–104.

7 VALIE EXPORT, "VALIE EXPORT," in *wien: bildkompendium wiener aktionismus und film*, ed. Peter Weibel and VALIE EXPORT (Kohlkunst Verlag, 1970), 290–92.

8 VALIE EXPORT, "Interview with Ruth Askey," *High Performance* 4, no. 1 (1981): 80; English in the original.

9 Widrich, "Can Photographs Make It So?," 92.

10 *Marina Abramović: Seven Easy Pieces*, Solomon R. Guggenheim Museum New York, November 9–15, 2005. See also Widrich, "Can Photographs Make It So?," 98–101.

11 Mumok gives as title and date for this object *Genitalpanik/Hose* (1968–1969). See the collection's object description at https://www.mumok.at/en/online-collection/detail/genital panik-hose-16016.

12 "Inventory List," June 26, 2008, six pages in Museum Collection Files, Dieter Roth, Large Tapestry, 1984–1986, 1902.2008, Department of Painting and Sculpture, The Museum of Modern Art, New York. Patricia Mainardi's reminder from 1973 still rings all too true today: "The great pains taken by art historians to identify all work of male artists, even if only by conjecture, coupled with the intentional omission of the names of those women artists, *even when they signed their work*, makes mockery of all pretentions that male 'scholarship' is anything but a tool of sexist oppression." Patricia Mainardi, "Quilts: The Great American Art," *Feminist Art Journal* (Winter 1973): 18.

13 *2008–2009 Annual Listing: Exhibitions, Publications, Acquisitions, Gifts to the Annual Fund, Membership, Special Projects, Donors to the Collection* (Museum of Modern Art, New York, 2009), 51. Today, *Großer Teppich* is attributed by the museum as a work by both Roth and Wiener.

14 VALIE EXPORT, "Aspects of Feminist Actionism," 75; Carol Gilligan, *In a Different Voice: Psychological Theory and Women's Development* (Harvard University Press, 1982). Gilligan's work on care developed at the intersection of psychology and ethics and has been criticized for what is seen as its gender essentialism. See in particular Selma Sevenhuijsen, *Citizenship and the Ethics of Care: Feminist Considerations on Justice, Morality, and Politics*, trans. Liz Sav-

age (Routledge, 1998). Gilligan later addresses this criticism in "Moral Injury and the Ethic of Care: Reframing the Conversation About Differences," *Journal of Social Philosophy* 45, no. 1 (Spring 2014): 89–106.

15 Carol Gilligan, "Moral Orientation and Moral Development" (1987), in *The Feminist Philosophy Reader*, ed. Alison Bailey and Chris Cuomo (McGraw-Hill, 2008), 471. More recent work on feminist care ethics includes Adriana Cavarero, *Inclinations: A Critique of Rectitude* (2014), trans. Amanda Minervini and Adam Sitze (Stanford University Press, 2016); María Puig de la Bellacasa, *Matters of Care: Speculative Ethics in More Than Human Worlds* (University of Minnesota Press, 2017).

16 Gilligan, "Moral Orientation," 469. See more recently Alona Pardo, "Reweaving the Web of Womanist Ecopolitics," in *RE/SISTERS: A Lens on Gender and Ecology*, ed. Alona Pardo (Prestel and Barbican, 2023), 27–36.

17 Berenice Fisher and Joan Tronto, "Toward a Feminist Theory of Caring," in *Circles of Care: Work and Identity in Women's Lives*, ed. Emily K. Abel and Margaret K. Nelson (State University of New York Press, 1990), 40, italics original.

18 See Helen Molesworth, "House Work and Art Work," *October* 92 (2000): 71–97. While Molesworth does not engage feminist ethics of care, she does unpack practices of care and domestic labor in the work of the four artists who serve as her case studies: Judy Chicago, Mary Kelly, Mierle Laderman Ukeles, and Martha Rosler.

19 See Judith Butler, *Who's Afraid of Gender?* (Farrar, Straus & Giroux, 2024).

20 Ingrid Wiener, "Es war 1966 . . . ," in Schick, *Man darf auch weben*, 22.

21 Wiener and VALIE EXPORT wove three tapestries together based on Hundertwasser paintings: *Verlöschendes Haus* (Extinguishing house; 1965), *Brillen im Hausrock* (Glasses in a smoking jacket; 1965), and *Glasbäume im Kupferwald* (Glass trees in a copper forest; 1966). The last was exhibited in the second International Salon of Pilot Galleries in Lausanne in 1966 and reproduced in black-and-white in the exhibition catalog, where "Höllinger and Schuppan" are credited with the "Tissage." See *Artistes et decouvreurs de notre temps: 2ème Salon International de Galeries pilotes* (Musée Cantonal des Beaux-arts, 1966). *Verlöschendes Haus* and *Brillen im Hausrock* were exhibited in Vienna in Hundertwasser's big solo show in 1978 and reproduced in color in the catalogue, where "Ingrid Schuppan and Waltraude [*sic*] Höllinger" are credited as weavers. See *Hundertwasser: Tapisserien* (Österreichisches Museum für Angewandte Kunst, 1978), 41. These two tapestries are also included and attributed in this way in Andrea Christa Fürst and Wieland Schmied, eds., *Hundertwasser 1928–2000: Werkverzeichnis/Catalogue Raisonné* (Taschen Verlag, 2000), 918–19. *Glasbäume im Kupferwald* is also listed, but not pictured. The current location of none of these tapestries is known, and *Glasbäume im Kupferwald* is presumed lost.

22 See, for example, the presentation of her corpus in the retrospective exhibition catalogs Museum moderner Kunst Stiftung Ludwig, ed., *valie export—Split: Reality* (Springer, 1997); Walter Moser, ed., *valie export* (Prestel, 2023); as well as the chronology on the artist's website (https://www.valieexport.at).

23 VALIE EXPORT's work thus intersects with fiber art's aims to activate tactile experience, what Anni Albers called "tactile sensibility." See Anni Albers, *On Weaving* (1965) (Princeton University Press, 2017), 44–47.

24 VALIE EXPORT, "Aspects of Feminist Actionism," 89; this passage is added to the English translation and does not appear in the original German.

25 Weibel's central if subordinated role in these early performances has steadily been effaced in VALIE EXPORT's careful orchestration of her artistic legacy, an appropriation of historiography that is arguably a part of Feminist Actionism. The exhibition *elles@centrepompidou—Artistes femmes dans les collections du Musée national d'art moderne*, May 27,

2009–February 21, 2011, followed by *Elles: Women Artists from the Centre Pompidou*, Centre Pompidou, Paris, October 11, 2012–January 13, 2013, provoked considerable acrimony on Weibel's part. See his discussion with Alfred Weidinger in Peter Weibel, *Medienrebell – Warnung! Diese Ausstellung kann ihr Leben verändern* (21er Haus, 2015), 192–209.

26 VALIE EXPORT, "VALIE EXPORT," in Weibel and VALIE EXPORT, *wien: bildkompendium*, 290.

27 Ingrid Wiener, "ingrid schuppan," in Weibel and VALIE EXPORT, *wien: bildkompendium*, 285.

28 In a letter written from prison cell E83 to Ingrid Wiener on July 1, 1968, Oswald Wiener cautions her about approaching members of the SÖS and provides a list of friends who might help confirm his innocence at *Kunst und Revolution*. On July 9, 1968, Ingrid replies that she is working with the lawyer and with witnesses to clear his name, having completed a third of the Gobelin. Correspondence housed in the Literaturarchiv der Österreichischen Nationalbibliothek, Vienna, Vorlaß Oswald Wiener, accession no. 232/04, group 2.2, box signature b57.

29 The section "Who's Who? The Field of Players" includes VALIE EXPORT and even Oswald Wiener and Dieter Roth alongside the movement's four main protagonists and their lesser-known assistants and "models" (referring to such figures as "Babsi," Anna Brus, Hanel Koeck, and Ziemi Schieb, as discussed in chapter 1); Ingrid Wiener is unnamed. This is despite her actual presence in the section "Action Chronology, 1960–1975: Brus, Muehl, Nitsch, and Schwarzkogler," at performances including *Aktionskonzert für Al Hansen* (Action concert for Al Hansen, 1966) with all of the Viennese Actionists and, alongside Gerhard Rühm and Anna Brus, at Gunter Brus's *Blumenstück* (Flower piece; 1969) in West Berlin. See Eva Badura-Triska, Hubert Klocker, and Museum moderner Kunst Stiftung Ludwig, eds., *Vienna Actionism: Art and Upheaval in 1960s' Vienna*, trans. Thomas Morrison, Christina Oberstebrink, Michael Turnbull, and Mark Willard (Verlag der Buchhandlung Walther König, 2012), 320, 339.

30 It reads: "Lived in Berlin, 1969–1986, where together with his wife and Michael Würthle he ran the bar/restaurant 'Matala' . . . and, after it was sold, the 'Exil' . . . as well as the 'Ax Bar.'" Badura-Triska et al., *Vienna Actionism*, 408. None of these venues would have been possible without Ingrid Wiener, who not only cooked the food but contributed to the financing. See Carolin Würfel, *Ingrid Wiener und die Kunst der Befreiung: Wien 1968/Berlin 1972* (Hanser, 2019), 115–37. For an overview of Wiener's work, including her drawings and tapestry collaborations, see Schick, *Man darf auch weben*; *Ingrid Wiener: Träume* (Verlag der Buchhandlung Walther König, 2006); Michaela Leutzendorff Pakesch, ed., *Ingrid Wiener: Durch die Kette sehen/Seeing Through the Warp* (Schlebrügge, 2020).

31 See Gerhard Rühm, ed., *Die Wiener Gruppe. Achleitner, Artmann, Bayer, Rühm, Wiener. Texte, Gemeinschaftsarbeiten, Aktionen* (Rowohlt, 1967). Typically, the *wiener gruppe* eschewed standard German capitalization.

32 See the documents and photographs collected in Peter Weibel, ed., *Die Wiener Gruppe: Ein Moment der Moderne 1954–1960: Die visuellen Arbeiten und die Aktionen: Friedrich Achleitner, H. C. Artmann, Konrad Bayer, Gerhard Rühm, Oswald Wiener* (Springer, 1997).

33 On "Die Zeugen," see Weibel and VALIE EXPORT, *wien: bildkompendium*, 127–28, 284. In 1965 this group formally comprised Kurt Kalb, Dominik Steiger, Ingrid Schuppan, and Oswald Wiener, to collectively view "floods, emergencies, catastrophes, accidents, crimes." It went on to include Günter Brus, Friedensreich Hundertwasser, Kurt Kren, Hermann Nitsch, Otto Muehl, and Arnulf Rainer. See also Österreichisches Literaturarchiv (ÖLA) Vorlaß Oswald Wiener: accession no. 232/04, group 1.4.1, box signature w26, where Ingrid Wiener is labeled "mitagiter." On "Wir nicht," see Christian Skrein, *68 – Künstler, Legenden, Fotogra-*

fien (Christian Brandstätter Verlag, 2001), 51–53, 119. This group included Dominik Steiger, Kurt Kalb, Walter Pichler, Christian Ludwig Attersee, Ernst Graf, Ingrid Wiener, and Oswald Wiener. Images of "Ingrid," together with Wir nicht, inspired a feminist riposte in the 1980s by the Austrian group Die Damen (The Ladies). See Brigitte Huck, *Die Damen: Ona B., Evelyne Egerer, Birgit Jürgenssen, Ingeborg Strobl, Lawrence Weiner* (Verlag für Moderne Kunst, 2013), 41–42.

34 This event is well documented in Weibel and VALIE EXPORT, *wien: bildkompendium*, 143–65. See in particular the photographs published under the article "ZOCK schlägt zu: Ein Wiener Happening mit Polizeiansatz," 164. This article is also a newspaper clipping in the archive of Ingrid Wiener. For a detailed account of the practices and politics of *ZOCK*, see Thomas Eder, "Kunst-Revolution-Erkenntnis. Oswald Wiener und ZOCK," in *Schluß mit dem Abendland! Der lange Atem der österreichischen Avantgarde*, ed. Thomas Eder and Klaus Kastberger (Zsolnay, 2000), 60–80.

35 As one newspaper reported in its arts section, "Schließlich sorgten neun Funkstreifen- und Staatspolizeiautos sowie drei Einsatzkommando-Wagen mit Polizeihunden und stahlhelmbewehrten harten Männer dafür, dass das Kunstwerk 'Happening' nicht unvollendet blieb." See *Stern*, May 2–9, 1967. Newspaper clipping in the archive of Ingrid Wiener.

36 See "Die 'Knödelschlacht' rief 200 Polizisten herbei," *Kurier*, July 26, 1967; "Im 'Haus der Begegnung' musste Wiener Polizei Ordnung schaffen," *Kronen Zeitung*, December 4, 1967, 7. Newspaper clippings in the archive of Ingrid Wiener; the former is reprinted in Weibel and VALIE EXPORT, *wien: bildkompendium*, 165.

37 Wiener's archive of her own anonymity is striking. As a model in the late 1960s, her image is used to advertise "hairstyles in the style of the painter Klimt," and she is referred to as one of three unnamed "enchanting ladies" (*bezaubernden Damen*); see *Kurier*, January 25, 1969. In an exposé on Ernst Graf's "person-specific design," she is shown, unnamed, wearing a dress of "leather and chrome" described as "for the wife [*für die Frau*] of the famous Austrian poet Ossi Wiener." See Peter Noever, "Ernst Graf: Die Wiener Underground Society," September 13, 1970. Newspaper clippings in the archive of Ingrid Wiener.

38 Anne Middleton Wagner, *Three Artists (Three Women): Modernism and the Art of Hesse, Krasner, and O'Keeffe* (University of California Press, 1996).

39 Lucy Lippard, "The Pains and Pleasures of Rebirth: Women's Body Art," *Art in America*, May–June 1976, 75.

40 Erika Billeter, "Textile Art and the Avant-Garde," in *Art textile contemporain: Collection de l'Association Pierre Pauli/Contemporary Textile Art: The Collection of the Pierre Pauli Association*, ed. Erika Billeter, André Gavillet, Anic Zanzi, and Pierre Magnenat (Benteli, 2000), 57.

41 See Romy Golan, "L'éternel décoratif: French Art in the 1950s," *Yale French Studies* 98 (January 2000): 98–118; Romy Golan, *Muralnomad: The Paradox of Wall Painting, Europe 1927–1957* (Yale University Press, 2009), esp. 189–214.

42 See in particular the following exhibition catalogs: *Les gobelins (1662–1962): Trois siècles de tapisserie française* (Château de Coppet, 1962); *Charles Le Brun: Premier directeur de la Manufacture Royale des Gobelins; exposition organisée à l'occasion du troisième centenaire de la fondation des gobelins, 6 juin 1962, Musée des Gobelins* (Ministère d'État Affaires Culturelles, 1962); *Les Gobelins, trois siècles de tapisserie, Mobilier national, juin-octobre 1966* (Réunion des Musées Nationaux, 1965).

43 See Giselle Cotton and Magali Junet, eds., *From Tapestry to Fiber Art: The Lausanne Biennials, 1962–1995* (Skira, 2017).

44 Elissa Auther, *String, Felt, Thread: The Hierarchy of Art and Craft in American Art* (University of Minnesota Press, 2010), xxi.

45 The exhibitions *Wall Hangings* (1969), *Textile Objekte* (1975), and *Textile Sculptures* (1977) eventually formalized the current parlance of "fiber art." The important exhibition, *Weich und plastisch*, curated by Erika Billeter in 1979, demonstrates the strong affiliation of fiber art with sculpture in contrast with tapestry's historical affiliation with painting. See Mildred Constantine and Jack Lenor Larsen, *Wall Hangings* (Museum of Modern Art, New York, 1969); Barbara Mundt, *Textile Objekte* (Kunstgewerbemuseum, Berlin, 1975); Irene Waller, *Textile Sculptures* (Taplinger Publishing, 1977); Erika Billeter, *Weich und plastisch: Ausstellung, 16. Nov. 1979–4. Feb. 1980* (Kunsthaus Zürich, 1979). More recently, see Jenelle Porter, ed., *Fiber: Sculpture 1960–Present* (Institute of Contemporary Art, Boston, 2014).

46 Because it shares something with the figural tradition of *belle peinture*, Wiener's work does not appear in those exhibitions that narrate contemporary textile techniques as advancing from Bauhaus weaving. See, e.g., Lynne Cooke, ed., *Woven Histories: Textiles and Modern Abstraction* (University of Chicago Press and National Gallery of Art, Washington, DC, 2024).

47 See Auther, *String, Felt, Thread*; Rozsika Parker and Griselda Pollock, "Crafty Women and the Hierarchy of the Arts," in *Old Mistresses: Women, Art and Ideology* (Pantheon Books, 1981), 50–81. For an alternative view, see T'ai Smith, *Bauhaus Weaving Theory: From Feminine Craft to Mode of Design* (University of Minnesota Press, 2014).

48 Waller, *Textile Sculptures*, 7.

49 See Albers, *On Weaving*, 2; Golan, "L'éternel décoratif," 114–15.

50 Julia Bryan-Wilson, *Fray: Art and Textile Politics* (University of Chicago Press, 2017), 13.

51 Bryan-Wilson, *Fray*, 3.

52 Bryan-Wilson, *Fray*, 7.

53 Bryan-Wilson, *Fray*, 7, italics original.

54 The exhibition catalog for *Graphik und Bücher* is also the twentieth volume of Roth's collected works. See Dieter Roth, *gesammelte werke 20: Bücher und Grafik aus den jahren 1947 bis 1971* (Edition Hansjörg Mayer, 1972).

55 Birgit Schneider looks at the "process of medial transfer" between the napkin and the tapestry, and specifically at the history of mechanically woven damask. See Birgit Schneider, "Textile Codierungen: Mediale Übersetzungen von Material und Struktur bei Elaine Reichek, Patricia Waller und Ingrid Wiener," in *Metatextile: Identity and History of a Contemporary Art Medium*, ed. Tristan Weddigen (Edition Imorde, 2011), 109–20.

56 Harald Szeemann, "Dieter Roth, Gobelin (Bertorelli B), 1974–1976," in *Zürcher Kunstgesellschaft Jahresbericht* (Kunsthaus Zürich, 1981), 92. Today, the tapestry is attributed to Roth and Wiener.

57 Szeemann, "Dieter Roth, Gobelin," 93.

58 Szeemann, "Dieter Roth, Gobelin," 94.

59 Bibiana K. Obler, *Intimate Collaborations: Kandinsky & Münter, Arp & Taeuber* (Yale University Press, 2014).

60 Jacques Lacan, *L'éthique, 1959–60*, Staferla version, http://staferla.free.fr/S7/S7%20L'ETHIQUE.pdf, 98, 99, 98; Jacques Lacan, *The Seminar of Jacques Lacan*, book 7, *The Ethics of Psychoanalysis, 1959–1960*, ed. Jacques-Alain Miller, trans. Denis Porter (Norton & Co., 1992), 139, 141, 139.

61 Mladen Dolar suggests that *extimité* is Lacan's translation of the *Unheimliche* in Freud. See Mladen Dolar, "'I Shall Be with You on Your Wedding-Night': Lacan and the Uncanny," *October* 58 (Autumn 1991): 5–23.

62 Jacques-Alain Miller, "Extimité," in *Lacanian Theory of Discourse: Subject, Structure, and Society*, ed. Mark Bracher, Marshall W. Alcorn, Ronald Corthell, and Françoise Massardier-Kenney (New York University Press, 1994), 76.

63 Fisher and Tronto, "Toward a Feminist Theory of Caring," 40.

64 Ingrid Wiener, "Großer Teppich (Porträt Dieter Roth), gewebt 1981–1984," in Wiener and

Roth, *Kopiebuch* (Galerie Marlene Frei, 1986), vol. 1, unpaginated, reprinted in Schick, *Man darf auch weben*, 38.

65 Wiener, "Großer Teppich," 38.

66 For a discussion of Roth's projects in these years, see the catalog of his first major posthumous retrospective: Theodora Vischer and Bernadette Walter, eds., *Roth Zeit. Eine Dieter Roth Retrospektive* (Lars Müller Publishers, 2003), especially Dirk Dobke and Bernadette Walter's excellent "Chronologie und Werkkommentare," 192–269.

67 For an image of this photograph, which Wiener seems at one point also to have torn up, see Schick, *Man darf auch weben*, 41, and Leutzendorff Pakesch, *Durch die Kette sehen*, 30.

68 Wiener, "Großer Teppich," 38.

69 Handwritten letter, Wiener to Roth, December 14, 1983, reproduced in Wiener and Roth, *Kopiebuch* (1986), vol. 1, unpaginated, reprinted untranslated in Schick, *Man darf auch weben*, 46.

70 Silvia Eiblmayr, VALIE EXPORT, and Monika Prischl-Maier, eds., *Kunst mit Eigen-Sinn: Aktuelle Kunst von Frauen: Texte und Dokumentation* (Löcker Verlag, 1985).

71 The six-page inventory list that accompanied the acquisition of *Großer Teppich* by MoMA, New York, includes the color photographs the artists exchanged as "working-images," Wiener's drawings in felt-tip pen that translate the photographs onto transparent foil which she attached to the loom while weaving, the mixed-media gouache works Thomas Hornemann created for Wiener depicting Roth's clothing, watercolors, pen drawings, adhesive blue film, cardboard rolls from yarn, and numerous shoeboxes full of cast-off yarn and foil clippings, receipts, Polaroids, tea bags, and in one case, one of Roth's shoes. When asked about these materials after the acquisition of *Großer Teppich*, Wiener replied, "We considered as equally important all the various parts of the process which lead to the tapestry (drawings, paintings, photographs, polaroids, letters, suitcases, shoes and various waste products). That is why we named it '*Large* Tapestry.'" Ingrid Wiener to Paulina Pobocha, May 7, 2009, Museum Collection Files, Dieter Roth, Large Tapestry, 1984–1986, 1902.2008, Department of Painting and Sculpture, Museum of Modern Art, New York, original italics.

72 Dieter Roth, untitled handwritten text, in Wiener and Roth, *Kopiebuch* (1986), vol. 1, unpaginated, reprinted untranslated in Schick, *Man darf auch weben*, 58. I have sought to maintain the textual disjuncture of Roth's handwritten text in this translation.

73 Wiener, "Großer Teppich," 39.

74 For an overview of these collaborations, the titles of which have shifted slightly over time and in the course of changing institutional affiliations, see Schick, *Man darf auch weben*.

75 See Michaela Leutzendorff Pakesch, "Singen, weben, kochen, filmen: Das Abendteuer zu sein/Singing, weaving, cooking, filming: The Adventure of Being," in Leutzendorff Pakesch, *Durch die Kette sehen*, 6–17/168–75.

76 The *D* panels are numbered 1 through 26, the *I* panels, 1 through 24. They alternate in a messy sequence somewhat chronologically from the bottom left corner.

77 Typed letter, Wiener to Roth, from Dawson City, February 27, 1989, reproduced in Ingrid Wiener and Dieter Roth, *Kopiebuch: 3. Roth-Wiener Teppich* (Franz Wassmer, 1993), unpaginated, reprinted untranslated in Schick, *Man darf auch weben*, 109.

78 Handwritten and illustrated letter, Roth to Wiener, from Basel, October 24, 1987, reproduced in *Kopiebuch* (1993), reprinted untranslated in Schick, *Man darf auch weben*, 70.

79 Handwritten letter, Wiener to Roth, from Dawson City, undated, reproduced in *Kopiebuch* (1993), reprinted untranslated in Schick, *Man darf auch weben*, 69.

80 Handwritten letter, Wiener to Roth, from Greece, January 11, 1988, reproduced in *Kopiebuch* (1993), reprinted untranslated in Schick, *Man darf auch weben*, 76.

81 Handwritten letter, Roth to Wiener, from Basel, February 21, 1988, reproduced in *Kopiebuch* (1993), reprinted untranslated in Schick, *Man darf auch weben*, 83.

82 Ingrid Wiener, untitled handwritten essay interspersed with photographs, in *Kopiebuch* (1993), reproduced in Schick, *Man darf auch weben*, 64–66.

83 Wiener referred to these as "views" (*Aussichten*). On Wiener's tapestry *windowview* (1985–1987), see Caroline Lillian Schopp, "Das Weben des postmodernen Lebens/The Weaving of Postmodern Life," in Leutzendorff Pakesch, *Durch die Kette sehen*, 38–47/175–80.

84 Typed letter, Wiener to Roth, from Dawson City, October 22, 1988, reproduced in *Kopiebuch* (1993), reprinted untranslated in Schick, *Man darf auch weben*, 99.

85 Handwritten letter, Wiener to Roth, from Krefeld, November 2, 1994, reproduced in Ingrid Wiener and Dieter Roth, *Kopiebuch: 4. Roth-Wiener Teppich, 1991–1996*, 3 vols. (Franz Wassmer, 1997), vol. 2, unpaginated, reprinted untranslated in Schick, *Man darf auch weben*, 178.

Index

Page numbers in italics refer to illustrations.